Elisabeth Kendall is Senior Research Fellow in Arabic and Islamic Studies, Pembroke College, Oxford University. She is the author of *Literature, Journalism and the Avant-Garde: Intersection in Egypt* (Routledge, 2006).

Ewan Stein is Lecturer in International Relations at the School of Social and Political Science at the University of Edinburgh. He is the author of *Representing Israel in Modern Egypt: Ideas, Intellectuals and Foreign Policy from Nasser to Mubarak* (I.B.Tauris, 2012).

TWENTY-FIRST CENTURY JIHAD

Law, Society and Military Action

Edited by

Elisabeth Kendall and Ewan Stein

I.B. TAURIS

LONDON · NEW YORK

New paperback edition published in 2017 by
I.B.Tauris & Co. Ltd
London • New York
www.ibtauris.com

First published in hardback in 2015 by I.B.Tauris & Co. Ltd

ISBN: 978 1 78453 671 8
eISBN: 978 0 85773 717 5
ePDF: 978 0 85772 768 8

A full CIP record for this book is available from the British Library
A full CIP record is available from the Library of Congress

Library of Congress Catalog Card Number: available

Typeset in Goudy Old Style by GS Typesetting Services
Printed and bound by CPI Group (UK) Ltd, Croydon, CR0 4YY

Contents

Part II Jihad in Modern Politics and Society

Part III Representations of Jihad in Modern Culture

About the Contributors

Asma Afsaruddin is Professor of Islamic Studies and Chairperson of the Department of Near Eastern Languages and Cultures at Indiana University, Bloomington. She is the author and/or editor of six books, including *Striving in the Path of God: Jihad and Martyrdom in Islamic Thought* (New York, 2013), *Islam, the State, and Political Authority: Medieval Issues and Modern Concerns* (New York, 2011) and *The First Muslims: History and Memory* (Oxford, 2008). Afsaruddin has won grants from the Harry Frank Guggenheim Foundation and the Mellon Foundation and was named a Carnegie Scholar by the Carnegie Corporation of New York in 2005.

Mansour Alnogaidan is a Saudi writer and reformist who has recanted terrorism. He currently acts as General Manager and Editor-in-Chief of the Mesbar Studies and Research Centre, a cultural think tank based in Dubai that focuses on the study of Islamic movements. In his formative years, he was influenced by a strict Wahhabi group in Buraydah, Saudi Arabia, under which he studied the principles of Islamic law during the 1980s. In 1991, he became involved in terrorist activities with a group of jihadists, for which he was sentenced and served time in prison. His ideological transformation began in the mid-1990s after being introduced to the writings of both classical and contemporary Islamic rationalists. This influenced his own thought, and his subsequent writing became harshly critical of Islamic extremism, leading to him being excluded by his former Wahhabi colleagues. In 2003, he was sentenced to 75 lashes and issued with a fatwa for blasphemy. He now lives in Dubai but remains influential among the rising generation of young Saudis. He has published prolifically, including in the *New York Times*, *Washington Post* and Arabic *Newsweek* magazine.

Mustafa Baig is a Research Fellow working on the Islamic reformulations project at the Institute of Arab and Islamic Studies at the University of Exeter. Between 2011 and 2013, he was Lecturer in Islamic Studies at the University of Manchester, where he also completed his doctorate on 'Islamic Jurisprudence in Non-Muslim Jurisdictions: Classical and Modern Perspectives'. His research investigates how Islamic jurists, who predominantly addressed Muslims living under Muslim rule, discussed the legal and theological implications of Muslims living in non-Muslim lands. As well as examining the classical literature on Muslims in non-Muslim jurisdictions, he also follows contemporary discussions on Muslims in minority contexts and the extent to which they draw on classical discourse.

Roberta Denaro is Lecturer in Arabic Language and Literature at the Department of Asian, African and Mediterranean Studies at University 'L'Orientale' in Naples, Italy. Her main fields of interest are hadith literature, comparative studies on martyrdom and jihad, and fictional and non-fictional medieval Arabic prose. Her publications include *Dal Martire Allo Šahid. Fonti, Problemi e Confronti per una Martirografia Islamica* (*From Martyr to Shahid: Sources, Problems and Comparisons for an Islamic Martyrography*, Rome, 2006) and various articles on early Sunni martyrdom literature. She is also active as a translator and has published well-known classical and contemporary literary works translated into Italian from both Turkish and Arabic.

Reuven Firestone is Professor of Medieval Judaism and Islam at Hebrew Union College in Los Angeles and Senior Fellow at the Center for Religion and Civic Culture at the University of Southern California. His books include *Jihad: The Origin of Holy War in Islam* (New York, 1999), *Holy War in Judaism: The Fall and Rise of a Controversial Idea* (New York, 2012), *Who are the Real Chosen People* (Woodstock, Vermont, 2008), *Journeys in Holy Lands: The Evolution of the Abraham-Ishmael Legends in Islamic Exegesis* (Albany, 1990), *An Introduction to Islam for*

Jews (Philadelphia, 2008) and *Children of Abraham: An Introduction to Judaism for Muslims* (New York, 2001), and nearly 100 articles on the historical and religious relations between Jews, Muslims and Christians and the relationship between their religions and cultures.

Eric Germain is Policy Advisor at the Directorate for Strategic Affairs at the French Ministry of Defence. He is tasked with building up a newly founded programme on religious and ethical issues to explore the challenges facing today's military chaplaincy. After studying at the Paris Institute of Political Studies and the École des Hautes Études en Sciences Sociales (EHESS), he conducted interdisciplinary research on Muslims in minority and diasporic contexts as an associate of the Institute for the Study of Islam and Societies of the Muslim World (IISMM). His publications include *Islam in Inter-War Europe*, co-edited with Nathalie Clayer (London, 2008), *L'Afrique du Sud Musulmane* (*Muslim South Africa*, Paris, 2007) and several articles on religious or ethical issues.

Sheikh Rachid al-Ghannouchi is the co-founder and intellectual leader of the moderate Islamist al-Nahda Party in Tunisia that rose to power following the ousting of President Ben Ali in 2011. Having been imprisoned in Tunisia in the 1980s, he spent 22 years in exile in London to avoid three life sentences, before returning to Tunisia after the 2011 revolution. Ghannouchi is a leading Muslim intellectual whose opinions and analyses hold great sway in Tunisia and beyond. In 2012 he was named as one of *Time* magazine's '100 Most Influential People in the World'. He has written extensively on a range of issues including the relation of Islam to democracy.

Carole Hillenbrand is Professorial Fellow in History at St Andrews University and Professor Emerita at Edinburgh University. She was educated at the Universities of Cambridge, Oxford and Edinburgh and held the post of Professor of Islamic History at Edinburgh University between 2000 and 2008. She has published widely on medieval Islamic history and political thought. Her best-known book is *The Crusades: Islamic Perspectives* (Edinburgh, 1999) for which she was awarded The King Faisal International Prize in Islamic Studies in 2005. This was the first time this prize had been awarded to a non-Muslim. She is a Fellow of the British Academy, a Corresponding Fellow of the Medieval Academy of America, an Honorary Fellow of Somerville College, Oxford and was awarded the Order of the British Empire for Services to Higher Education in 2009. She has held visiting professorships at Dartmouth College and St Louis University in the USA and Groningen University in the Netherlands.

Maria Holt is Reader in Politics at the Department of Politics and International Relations at the University of Westminster in London. Her main research interests are gender and violence in the Arab world, women and Islamic resistance, Palestinian refugee women in Lebanon and the Israeli-Palestinian conflict. She has published extensively on these topics. Her books include *Women and Islamic Resistance in the Arab World*, co-authored with Haifaa Jawad (Boulder, 2013) and *Women and Conflict in the Middle East: Palestinian Refugees and the Response to Violence* (London, 2013).

Russell Hopley is Lecturer in Arabic at Bowdoin College in Maine, USA. He studied at Northwestern and Stanford Universities before joining the Department of Near Eastern Studies at Princeton University, where he studied classical Arabic literature with Andras Hamori and Islamic law with John R. Willis, an expert on the nineteenth-century jihads in West Africa. Hopley has published several articles on Andalusia and medieval North Africa, and is currently preparing a study of the Arabic poetry of Islamic Sicily.

Rana Issa is a Kultrans Fellow at the Institute of Cultural and Oriental Languages and the Center for the New Middle East at the University of Oslo. Previously she held research fellowships at the University of Marburg and the German Oriental Institute in Beirut. She wrote her doctoral dissertation on 'Arabia Minor: Bible Translations into Arabic in Late Ottoman Lebanon'. In addition to her research on the history of religion and early modern Arabic literature and language, she is interested in cultural aspects of globalisation, translation studies, conceptual history and book history. She is the author of *Levantine Chronotopes*, co-edited with Einar Wigan (New York, 2014), as well as articles and book chapters including, most recently, 'Biblical reflections in the Arabic lexicon' and 'Peddling bibles: from lips to cheap copies'.

Sherman Jackson holds the King Faisal Chair in Islamic Thought and Culture and is Professor of Religion and Professor of American Studies and Ethnicity at the University of Southern California. He has authored several books, including *Islamic Law and the State: The Constitutional Jurisprudence of Shihab al-Din al-Qarafi* (Leiden, 1996), *On the Boundaries of Theological Tolerance in Islam: Abu Hamid al-Ghazali's Faysal al-Tafriqa* (Karachi, 2002), *Islam and the Blackamerican: Looking Toward the Third Resurrection* (New York, 2005), *Islam and the Problem of Black Suffering* (New York, 2009) and *Sufism for Non-Sufis?: Ibn Ata' Allah al-Sakandari's Taj al-'Arus* (New York, 2012). He has also authored numerous articles on various aspects of Islamic law, theology, history and Islam and Muslims in modern America.

Na'eem Jeenah is Executive Director of the Afro-Middle East Centre, a research institute based in Johannesburg, South Africa that focuses on the Middle East and Africa. He holds a Masters in Religious Studies from the University of the Witwatersrand, with a dissertation entitled 'The Emergence of Islamic Feminisms in South Africa in the 1990s', and is currently working on his doctorate entitled 'Political Islam in South Africa and its contribution to a discourse of a *fiqh* of minorities'. His publications include *Journey of Discovery: A South African Hajj*, co-authored with Shamima Shaikh (Johannesburg, 2000) and *Pretending Democracy: Israel, an Ethnocratic State* (Johannesburg, 2012). He taught political science at the University of the Witwatersrand, and is a sought-after commentator on issues related to the Middle East, the Muslim world, Islam and South African politics.

Elisabeth Kendall is Senior Research Fellow in Arabic and Islamic Studies at Pembroke College, University of Oxford. Her current research focuses on links between Arabic cultural production and political/militant movements in contemporary Yemen and Egypt. Her publications include *Literature, Journalism and the Avant-Garde: Intersection in Egypt* (London and New York, 2006), *Media Arabic* (Edinburgh and

Washington DC, 2nd ed. 2012) as well as several articles on aspects of modern Arab culture. She studied Arabic, Islamic Studies and Turkish at the Universities of Oxford and Harvard and served as Director of the Centre for the Advanced Study of the Arab World (CASAW) at the University of Edinburgh before returning to Oxford in 2010.

Lt. Gen. Sir Simon Mayall is the British Government's Defence Senior Adviser for the Middle East and the Prime Minister's Special Envoy to Iraq and Kurdistan. Based in the UK Ministry of Defence where he holds the rank of Lieutenant General, his appointment intersects with four government departments. His primary responsibility is the development of sustained, high-level personal relationships across the Middle East, in support of wider British national interests. He has extensive experience in the Middle East, and was formerly Assistant Chief of the Army and Deputy Chief of Defence Staff responsible for operations worldwide. In 2006–7 he was Deputy Commanding General of Multi-National Corps – Iraq (MNC-I). He has written about and lectured widely on the Near and Middle East, past and present, and is the author of *Turkey: Thwarted Ambition* (Washington DC, 2005).

Gavin Picken is Associate Professor at the Department of Arabic and Translation Studies, American University of Sharjah, UAE. Previously he taught at the Universities of London, Cambridge and Edinburgh. His teaching and research interests concern the Islamic tradition in the formative period, including the development and codification of Qur'an and hadith studies, jurisprudence, theology and mysticism as part of the evolution of Islamic intellectual history. He is the author of *Spiritual Purification in Islam: The Life and Works of al-Muhasibi* (London and New York, 2011) and the editor of a four-volume compendium of selected articles entitled *Islamic Law* (London and New York, 2010).

Thomas Riegler is a journalist and independent historian. He studied history and politics at the Universities of Vienna and Edinburgh, and has published on a wide range of topics, including terrorism, film studies and contemporary history. He is the author of *Terrorismus: Akteure, Strukturen, Entwicklungslinien (Terrorism: Actors, Structures, Trends*, Innsbruck, 2009) and *Im Fadenkreuz: Österreich und der Nahostterrorismus*

1973–1985 (In the Crosshairs: Austria and Near Eastern Terrorism 1973–1985, Vienna, 2010).

Ewan Stein is Lecturer in Politics and International Relations at the University of Edinburgh. He studied at the London School of Economics and Georgetown University and held a post-doctoral fellowship at the Centre for the Advanced Study of the Arab World (CASAW) at the University of Edinburgh. His research interests include political Islam, the role of ideas in foreign policy and international relations, state-society relations and the links between social and normative change in Middle Eastern regional politics. He is the author of *Representing Israel in Modern Egypt: Ideas, Intellectuals and Foreign Policy from Nasser to Mubarak* (London, 2012) and has published a range of academic articles and book chapters.

Hossam Tammam (d.2011) was an Egyptian journalist and analyst specialising in Islamist movements. He led the Future Research Studies Unit at Bibliotheca Alexandrina and established islamyun.net, which was until 2010 a division of Islam Online. Tammam's books include *Ma' al-Harakat al-Islamiyya fi al-'Alam (With The World's Islamic Movements*, Cairo, 2009) and *Tahawwulat al-Ikhwan al-Muslimin: Tafakkuk al-Idiyulujiyya wa-Nihayat al-Tanzim (The Transmutations of the Muslim Brotherhood: Disintegration of Ideology and the End of Organization*, Cairo, 2010). Tammam has also written for the Carnegie Endowment for International Peace and for numerous Arabic newspapers.

Sami Zubaida is Emeritus Professor of Politics and Sociology at Birkbeck, University of London. He is also Research Associate of the London Middle East Institute and Professorial Research Associate of the Food Studies Centre, both at the School of Oriental and African Studies, University of London. He has held visiting positions at universities in Cairo, Istanbul, Beirut, Aix-en-Provence, Paris, Berkeley and New York. He has written and lectured widely on themes of religion, culture, law and politics in the Middle East, with particular attention to Egypt, Iran, Iraq and Turkey. His other work is on food history and culture. He is the author of *Islam, the People and the State: Political Ideas and Movements in the Middle East* (London and New York, 3rd ed. 2009), *Law and Power* *in the Islamic World* (London and New York, 2003), *Beyond Islam: A New Understanding of the Middle East* (London and New York, 2011) and co-editor of *A Taste of Thyme: Culinary Cultures of the Middle East* (London and New York, 2nd ed. 2000).

Introduction

Contextualising Twenty-First Century Jihad

Elisabeth Kendall and Ewan Stein

The term 'jihad' has come to be used as a byword for fanaticism and Islam's allegedly implacable hostility towards the West. But, like other religious and political concepts, jihad has multiple resonances and associations, its meaning shifting over time and from place to place. Jihad has referred to movements of internal reform, spiritual struggle and self-defence as much as to 'holy war'. Jihad, moreover, can embody principles and concerns by no means unique to Islam and need not necessarily be confined to promoting or safeguarding the interests of Muslims. Among Muslim intellectuals, as well as others concerned with the Arab and Islamic worlds, the meaning and significance of jihad remain subject to debate and controversy.

This book is particularly timely given the renewal of debates about the future of 'jihadism' in the wake of the so-called 'Arab Spring', generally held to date from the uprising in Tunisia in late 2010. The toppling of authoritarian rulers in Tunisia, Egypt, Yemen and Libya through mass 'people power', in conjunction with the death of Osama bin Laden in May 2011, led many to pronounce the death of al-Qa'ida and the bankruptcy of jihadism as an ideology. With the declaration of an Islamic State in June 2014 by jihadists in Syria and Iraq, however, as well as renewed jihadist activities in Mali, Nigeria, Algeria, Yemen, Sinai and elsewhere, the picture appears less clear-cut. What appeared only recently to be a

1

discredited ideology is now gaining traction once again, particularly as the primary exemplar of 'moderate' political Islam, the Muslim Brotherhood in Egypt, has had its experiment with power cut brutally short.

Yet as the contributions in this book collectively illustrate, jihad as a concept means, and has meant, more than the meaning ascribed to it by self-professed 'jihadists'. The mobilisational capacity of jihad, as an ideology underpinning violence, has been contingent on other factors. While the world certainly has changed in the decade since 9/11, many of the debates and mystifications surrounding the concept of jihad, its centrality and limits, and the duties, obligations and responsibilities it enjoins, have recurred throughout history in a diverse range of contexts. To reveal just a fraction of this extensive resonance, contingency and history are the tasks of this book.

This book offers no definitive argument or specific 'line' on jihad. It looks beyond, yet certainly includes, violent jihad. It aims to present, in as neutral a way as possible, some of the academic, as well as non-academic, perspectives and attitudes concerning both the practice and representation of jihad. In addition to the more familiar modern political angles, this book also touches on far less commonly aired instances of jihad. It embraces issues of law, society, literature, poetry and military action. The book showcases work from renowned academics as well as specialist scholars whose work may not often attract general public interest. The contributions represent snapshots of active and ongoing research projects, rather than attempts to summarise or simplify jihad across the ages. It also provides a selection of 'views from within', including timely contributions from the leader of the Tunisian Islamist al-Nahda Party, who returned from exile to post-revolutionary Tunisia in 2011, the UK Ministry of Defence's Senior Advisor to the Middle East and a convicted terrorist who has subsequently recanted militant jihad.

The chapters approach the topic from a range of historical, political and methodological perspectives, which are by no means all in agreement with one another. Nevertheless, taken as a whole, the book challenges a number of enduring suppositions about jihad that are frequently found in popular, policy and scholarly discourse. These assumptions include the idea that jihad is a timeless 'spirit' that animates Muslims throughout the ages and in all places, as well as the notion that jihad is primarily associated with violence and war or that it is principally oriented toward legitimising or requiring war against non-Muslims. In order to gain a good understanding of twenty-first century jihad it is essential to place the concept of jihad in its historical, cultural and political contexts. This introduction represents a brief preliminary attempt to do this.

It is sometimes simply assumed that 'jihad' represents a kind of secret weapon for Muslim leaders, given its unique capacity to rouse Muslims into action against infidel enemies when deployed effectively. As with many such assumptions about Islam and Muslims in general, this exaggerated stereotype is reinforced by Islamist leaders and intellectuals themselves. Contemporary jihadists, in the wake of the Arab Spring, have celebrated the fact that the removal of despotic regimes will allow the spirit of jihad to course through Muslim populations, enabling them to defeat their external foes and establish Islamic states governed according to Islamic shariah law.[1] This assumption was also manifested in Egypt in November 2012 when Islamist activists called upon the then president Muhammad Mursi to 'open the door of jihad' and allow millions of Egyptians to avenge the Israeli bombardment of Gaza, an undoubtedly greatly exaggerated expectation.

We should take neither Western nor Islamist assertions about the intrinsic power of jihad at face value. Examples of jihad's limitations as an instrument of mobilisation can be found throughout history. Jihad becomes an effective force when combined with other factors. Attempts to rouse the population for jihad against the Crusaders, for example, went unheard until the right kind of military leadership coalesced around Nur al-Din and the religious classes, as Carole Hillenbrand explains in the prologue. In a different context, the Almoravids in Muslim Spain called for jihad primarily to discourage people from going on the pilgrimage to Mecca, which other jurists insisted should take priority. The trouble with pilgrimage, Russell Hopley notes in Chapter 5, was that it provided a reason for Iberian and North African Muslims to leave their troubled homelands for more stable climes in the East. Clearly, many calculated that the call to jihad was something that they would prefer not to answer. Centuries later, in French-occupied Algeria, jurists used this early debate as a way of explaining the apparent reluctance of Algerians to join the jihad of 'Abd al-Qadir. In each of these cases, jihad alone was not enough to mobilise large numbers of Muslims.

If the power of jihad to mobilise Muslims against external aggression is not something that can be taken for granted in 'pre-modern' periods, its efficacy is clearly enhanced when combined with nationalism in the modern era. Calls for jihad tend to be most resonant when they are framed as essential to national self-defence. Thus, the jihads of Hizbullah and Hamas against Israel (see Maria Holt, Chapter 12) or that of the Muslim Brotherhood in the 1940s against British and Zionist colonialism generated widespread popular support. The incorporation of jihad and martyrdom motifs in pre-1948 Palestinian nationalist poetry, which Rana Issa analyses in Chapter 15, provides a good illustration of this association of nationalist symbols with religious ones to stir the masses. It is not without reason that so-called 'global' jihadists seek to link their struggles to national causes such as those of Palestine, Chechnya or Iraq. However, it is worth noting that this imperative of defensive jihad as a 'collective duty' (*fard 'ayn*) would find fertile ground among the societies of almost any modern nation-state faced with external aggression. Therefore it should not be understood so much as a peculiarly Islamic condition but as a facet of modernity in a world of nation-states.

If violent jihad for purposes other than national self-defence has struggled to generate mass support in the modern period, this is not to say that other types of violent jihad have not appealed to significant numbers of people. Jihads of the 'sectarian' type cannot be written off as marginal or inconsequential affairs, as the bloody experiences of Iraq and Syria in recent years have made depressingly clear. As important as it is to recognise the limits and contingency of jihad as a mobilisational tool, a contextual understanding of the circumstances in which jihad does achieve ideological traction for reasons other than national defence is also indispensable.

Since, as Sami Zubaida notes in Chapter 7, 'sectarian divisions in any religion are mostly peaceful', the occurrence of violence, jihadist or otherwise, between sects requires an explanation that moves beyond recognition of religious differences and historical grievances. The situation in Syria and Iraq at the time of writing is coloured by the erosion of state authority; and the increase in sectarianism reflects, at least in part, the efforts of rival groups (including the state) to both create and mobilise constituencies for their own agendas in what remains a highly uncertain new order. The contemporary jihad being waged by Salafi-jihadist groups against Shi'ites and other perceived heretics in Syria and Iraq, loosely branded the Islamic State, should be seen in this light.

Preconceptions about the nature of jihad and its power to mobilise Muslims often lead to the irrational fear that Islamists, if they gain power, will wage war on Western interests and the West itself. It is this 'war against the world' that the contemporary Islamic theologian Yusuf al-Qaradawi sought to discredit in his 2009 tome on jihad, to which two of the chapters in this book are devoted. But although jihad has been used as an ideology of imperial expansion, notably under the Umayyad dynasty (661–750), the dominant trend has been for Islamic states to seek to dampen expansionary jihadist fervour in favour of realpolitik once the limits of imperial power have been reached. The assumption that an Islamic state will adopt an expansionary foreign policy because it is an *Islamic* state is thus deeply problematic.

Imperial contraction has tended to be accompanied by a modification in the focus of jihad. The expansionist jihads in Arabia, led by the followers of Ibn 'Abd al-Wahhab and legitimised with reference to Ibn Taymiyyah's Hanbali ideas, pitted zealous settled religious warriors against surrounding (Muslim) nomadic tribes and ended with the consolidation of state power under the Sauds. Once Saudi hegemony had been achieved in Arabia, the jihad waged by Ikhwan warriors, a kind of tribal militia, against fellow Sunni Muslims became, as Zubaida notes, 'an embarrassment to Ibn Saud, and they had to be subdued'. The Ikhwan were crushed and the idea of jihad reoriented toward self-defence and solidarity with other national struggles, primarily that of Palestine.

The aforementioned transformation of jihad in Saudi Arabia constituted a move away from the expansionist crusade against all infidels (which is how the Wahhabis regarded non-Wahhabi Muslims) toward upholding state security. This mirrored the way in which early rules of jihad had been elaborated in Islamic jurisprudence. During the Abbasid period (750–1258), when legal theories of jihad were formalised, a similar process of state consolidation was underway, which obliged the central state to disallow the pursuit of jihad other than under the command of a legitimate ruler. The ascetic frontier warriors who had helped to expand the Islamic empire under the preceding Umayyad dynasty were reined in. As a result, the classical doctrine of jihad 'never describes *jihad* in reference to martyrdom or with the language of ascetic piety, since doing so would play into the logic of non-state actors'.[2]

Even if we accept that the violent interpretation of jihad in Islamic orthodoxy owes much to the way state power was consolidated in the Umayyad and Abbasid periods, it should be emphasised that the doctrine of jihad may not oblige Islamic states to be warlike toward non-Muslims. As Mustafa Baig shows in Chapter 4, classical jurisprudence on jihad also concerned peaceful Muslim abidance in non-Muslim territory. This is an important reminder about the difficulty of translating terms like 'jihad' and '*Dar al-Harb*' into English. Just as jihad does not necessarily signify violence, neither does *Dar al-Harb* straightforwardly connote the 'Abode of War'. This division of the world into opposing zones of 'war' and 'Islam', moreover, was a later construction without any Qur'anic basis (nor even, as Reuven Firestone notes in Chapter 1, any basis in hadith). While war did indeed constitute a feature of Islamic international relations, it was by no means the sole focus. Peaceful interactions between Muslims and non-Muslims continued throughout history, not least in the realm of trade, and the rules laid out under the rubric of jihad reflect this.

Although it is perilous to stretch historical analogies too far, a similar dynamic may be identified in the modern Arab world where, following the end of struggles against colonialism in the region, regimes focused on state consolidation. Non-state actors that had been central to anti-colonial efforts became threats to regime security and were suppressed. Just as the threat posed to the Saudi regime by the Ikhwan warriors in Arabia emerged in a new form later in the twentieth century, as Mansour Alnogaidan recounts in Chapter 8, so too was the idea of jihad turned against local regimes in places like Egypt, Syria and Algeria. These insurrectionary jihads must, however, like expansionary or imperial jihads, be placed in their proper context.

Calls by Osama bin Laden and others for jihad against the Saudi regime (which relied upon the same understanding of *takfir*, or excommunication, that had underpinned previous Wahhabi jihads in Arabia) have had very little mobilisational traction.[3] Groups like al-Qa'ida are regarded as extremist for a reason: they have a limited appeal among Muslims at large. Non-state actors, in a world of nation-states, have generally struggled to generate mass support for insurrectionary (or 'near enemy') jihads.[4] This is something that was thrown into sharp relief by the Arab uprisings of 2011–13, which generated levels of support that jihadists could only dream of, without any specifically Islamic agenda. A look at the historical trajectory of the Sunni world's most significant Islamist group, the Muslim Brotherhood, provides some clues as to why this might be the case.

For the Brotherhood in its early days, violence and jihad were focused on Zionism and British colonialism as clear aggressors against Muslim territory. But the more insurrectionary stance of Sayyid Qutb (1906–66), who labelled the regime as infidel and thus legitimised jihad against it, did not sit well with the Brotherhood at large. As a broad umbrella organisation the Brotherhood had to appeal to diverse constituencies that sought to improve their lot within the existing systems rather than overthrow them. As such, the Brotherhood has, in the main, strategically avoided calling for jihad against local regimes. As Hossam Tammam points out in Chapter 9, the fact that Sayyid Qutb's ideas remain salient within the Brotherhood, and that the group's non-jihadist stance to date has been based primarily on strategic calculation, means that the Brotherhood may seek to lead insurrectionary jihads in the future. But, if history is anything to go by, it is unlikely that such a strategy, which would probably be fuelled by desperation, would succeed in mobilising large numbers of Egyptian Muslims against the regime.

Jihad has thus never been a straightforward doctrine expressing Islam's enmity toward non-Muslims. One of the results of the early 'domestication' of jihad – through the suppression of groups that spearheaded expansionist or liberation movements – was the emergence of groups using jihad against the local state. However, another by-product of the state's monopolisation of the legal right to declare war may also have been to relegate more ascetic and peaceful interpretations of jihad to the private sphere. By studying early Sufi writings and the *musannafs* of early hadith compilers, contributions to this book by Asma Afsaruddin and Gavin Picken highlight discourses on jihad that retained its more spiritual and ascetic dimensions beyond (although also including) the purely military dimension.

The idea of the so-called 'greater jihad' against the passions of the soul, as well as other formulations that stressed the value of living a productive life and providing for one's family, or the need to speak truth to an oppressive ruler, were preserved in poetry and hadith commentaries but excised from the official orthodoxy that reflected the perspective of the state. Modern scholars, as Picken notes, have also accepted this narrative that the early consensus on jihad defined it overwhelmingly as a doctrine obliging or legitimising violence without necessarily recognising that this consensus reflected the interests and priorities of an imperial and then centralising state. Again, broad parallels might be drawn with the twenty-first century. Violent extremism continues to dominate popular perceptions of jihad, particularly among Western audiences exposed to cultural stereotypes that serve to shape, not merely reflect, public opinion (see Chapter 16 by Thomas Riegler). Yet non-violent interpretations of jihad persist and can be identified in various contemporary initiatives recognised under the descriptors of consumer jihad, cyber jihad or gender jihad, all of which are designed to make religiously motivated points in ways that avoid physical combat.

This Book

This book embraces many, but by no means all, of the conflicting inter-pretations and debates that lie behind the practice and representation of jihad in the twenty-first century. It draws inspiration from and adds to a considerable body of scholarship about jihad that has burgeoned in recent years. Most notable among these works are some that have dealt usefully with the political aspects, including the origins and upshots, of violent jihadism in the modern age,[5] and others that have focused more on religious, jurisprudential or psychological aspects of jihad[6] or jihad's social manifestations or status in postmodernity.[7] Other works have suc-ceeded in casting jihad in a broad historical context[8] or illuminating the range and roots of contemporary ideological positions.[9] The current book augments this body of scholarship by bringing together a broad range of original, and in some cases surprising, perspectives on jihad from schol-ars across numerous disciplines whose views do not always gel with one another. While this book looks beyond violent jihad, it is not designed to 'clean up' the image of Islam by self-consciously revealing a politically correct and peaceful essence at its heart. As we have emphasised, jihad in the twenty-first century cannot be seen in isolation from the 14 cen-turies of competing interpretations of the term that preceded it. This book therefore begins with a lightning journey through those centuries as **Carole Hillenbrand** narrates a brief but invaluable history of jihad over the ages. This overview is followed up in the first section of the book by a more detailed examination of some of the historical antecedents of contemporary jihad.

Part I: Historical Antecedents of Twenty-First Century Jihad

In Chapter 1, **Reuven Firestone** takes us back to the earliest roots of the concept of jihad interpreted as holy war. He challenges current public debates that tend to approach religious war in Islam as having arisen out of a vacuum in response to inherent internal imperatives rather than as part of a broader historical continuum. Firestone places the Qur'an's development of the concept of religiously sanctioned war into a comparative historical context that also traces the development of this concept in the Hebrew Bible. The geneses of these two scriptures are separated by more than 15 centuries and several hundred miles, yet striking parallels in the socio-economic and political contexts from which they emerged encouraged similar early attitudes towards war and relations with those outside their respective religious communities. Both scriptures naturally encouraged – even divinely commanded – the rightful authority to engage in military force in order to achieve religious-political independence. In both scriptures God authorises bloodshed and killing in order to secure proper monotheistic religious practice in an environment that is portrayed as overwhelmingly polytheistic and threatening. Certain critical differences in the larger religious environments, however, including concepts of conversion and religious empire, had a powerful impact on how early notions of war developed within the respective scriptures. The relationship between the process of scriptural canonisation and the historical development of religious-political identity also affected the scriptural articulation of fighting and war. This is particularly notable in relation to the idea of territoriality and political control. One perhaps surprising conclusion is that, unlike the Hebrew Bible, the Qur'an lacks the notion of conquest and control of territory as divine command. Firestone's research also aptly demonstrates how, regardless of what is stated in scripture, political exigency and those who are sufficiently determined can generally find a way to bend interpretation to fit the historical moment.

Even during the earliest centuries of Islam, as a body of hadith literature began to grow alongside the Qur'anic revelations, competing views were emerging over the definition of *al-jihad fi sabil Allah*, literally meaning 'to strive in the path of God'. **Asma Afsaruddin**'s contribution (Chapter 2) stems from the premise that early hadith works often preserve for us shades of meaning attributed to critical terms like 'jihad' that are not replicated in later works. The extant hadith literature from before the compilation of the six great authoritative Sunni hadith collections in the third century of Islam remains, therefore, an invaluable source for recreating some of the earliest discourses on the meanings of jihad, as well as the terms *shahid/shahada* which became linked to it in the sense of martyr/martyrdom. By consulting the early collections of the hadith compilers 'Abd al-Razzaq al-San'ani (d.827) and Ibn Abi Shayba (d.849), Afsaruddin retrieves some of these earliest perspectives that have not been preserved in later works. This research unearths valuable clues to the meanings of terms that lie latent in a body of literature that has been woefully understudied to date. Through critical scrutiny of both the chains of transmission (*isnad*) and the content (*matn*), it is possible to speculate on the specific socio-historical circumstances in which the relevant hadiths were produced. Afsaruddin's close reading of the micro-discourses allows her to plot a shifting semantic trajectory for the terms 'jihad' and 'martyrdom' as different groups of people – jurists, ethicists, pietists – negotiated and contested the various significations of these concepts. Based on the evidence provided by these two works, Afsaruddin argues that the concept of jihad provided a discursive template for pre-modern Muslims (and continues to do so for contemporary Muslims) upon which a number of socio-political concerns could and can be creatively ventilated and configured in varying circumstances.

By contrast, in Chapter 3 **Roberta Denaro** explores the great canonical collections of hadith for definitions and narrations of martyrdom. Denaro shows how the original conceptualisation of the martyr, defined simply as 'he who is killed in the path of God', was developed and shaped in early hadith literature rather than in hagiographic writings as in the case of Christianity. The hadiths on martyrdom are loosely divided into two main categories: classificatory texts which identify types of martyrdom; and more fictional texts describing the deeds of fallen jihadists and their rewards in the afterlife. These hadiths extend well beyond the notion of death in jihad and reveal a much broader range and flexibility of definition than can be found in the Christian tradition. Denaro's research points to the influential role of popular preachers and storytellers in shaping more fantastical hadiths on martyrdom and jihad. At the same time, the normalisation process that followed the Abbasid revolution played a role in curbing overtly political uses of the doctrine of martyrdom. This new post-revolutionary reality, in which death by militant jihad was no longer generally practised, coincided with the conclusion of the compilation of the major Sunni hadith collections. Only small circles of pious scholar-warriors who were settled along the frontiers still pursued lives centred upon asceticism, jihad and martyrdom. Nevertheless, the extent to which martyrdom by militant jihad, an ideology that Denaro argues was relatively marginal by this time, may have provided a model for later, indeed contemporary, doctrine on martyrdom remains open to debate.

The non-military aspects of jihad are also the focus of **Mustafa Baig**'s analysis in Chapter 4 of the *Kitab al-Jihad*, a generic name for the section in classical works of Islamic jurisprudence that is primarily concerned with Muslim armies entering non-Muslim lands and vice versa. Baig argues that a closer examination of the *Kitab al-Jihad* shows that Islamic jurists covered a broad range of subjects other than purely military warfare under the heading of jihad, revealing the *Kitab al-Jihad* as a multi-faceted body of literature within Islamic law. Baig focuses on discussions of the various rules and conventions governing a Muslim's sojourn in a non-Muslim land, ranging from the kind of jurisdiction that should apply to aspects of Muslim behaviour towards non-Muslims. Baig's work completely dispels any lingering misconceptions that only hostile relations can exist between Muslims and non-Muslims. The conclusions drawn from his analysis are of clear contemporary relevance to the vast numbers of Muslims living as minorities in non-Muslim lands today.

The nuances that underlie the term jihad are also brought out in Chapter 5 by **Russell Hopley**, whose research into responses to the

Almoravid intervention in Andalusia in the late eleventh and early twelfth centuries reveals how the concept of jihad is contested and flexed to suit political imperatives. The early twelfth century was a momentous time for Muslims of the western Mediterranean. Considerable territory in Islamic Iberia had fallen prey to Christian re-conquest, and large swathes of land in North Africa were being plundered by the Hilali Bedouin tribes as they embarked on their epic migration westward from Egypt. By analysing letters written by leaders and jurists during these centuries, Hopley exposes the range of arguments offered to support or reject the waging of a militant jihad against the Christian kingdoms of northern Iberia. Through analysis of this set of historical case studies, Hopley demonstrates the prevalence of practical and political concerns in shaping the definition and functions of jihad during a period of turmoil in the Islamic lands of the western Mediterranean.

Another little studied perspective on jihad is that offered by Sufism. This is addressed in Chapter 6 by **Gavin Picken**, who draws a parallel between the Sufi concept of combating the soul and the 'greater' jihad in classical Islam. Picken's work takes as its starting point the dichotomous relationship between the so-called 'greater jihad', which involves disciplining one's lower desires manifested in the soul, and the 'lesser jihad', which refers to physical combat. As the terminology itself implies, militant confrontation was deemed of secondary importance to moral discipline in the pursuit of jihad in the literal sense of 'striving' for God. Picken discusses the controversial nature of this 'greater jihad' and its rejection by many in Islam's mainstream 'orthodoxy' from the late medieval period onwards. Despite its repudiation by the majority, the 'greater jihad' maintained considerable currency amongst certain segments of Muslim society and in particular within the circles of Islam's Sufi mystics. Picken offers arguments and evidence to corroborate Sufi claims regarding the validity of the 'greater jihad'. By surveying both the nascent works of the primary period of Sufism (c.750–950) and the apologetic works written during the so-called 'Period of Consolidation/Systematisation' (c.950–1150), Picken examines the genesis of the Sufi concept of an esoteric form of spiritual combat (al-mujahada). This is a key feature of the quest for purification that can lead to mystical experience, within the broader framework of the 'greater' jihad.

Part II: Jihad in Modern Politics and Society

The chapters in this section focus on more contemporary manifestations of jihad in politics and society. In Chapter 7, **Sami Zubaida** traces the roots and character of 'sectarian jihads' in the Arabian Peninsula and Iraq, highlighting their political and historical contingency. He explores the ways in which the expanding and consolidating Saudi state used the idea of jihad, and the related concept of *takfir* (excommunication), to justify warfare against foes and rivals. In subduing the Bedouin tribes of Arabia, Wahhabis used the notion of *takfir*, as elaborated by the Hanbali jurist Ibn Taymiyyah, to declare them outside of Islam. A similar justification was used to underpin sectarian jihads against Shi'ites. Zubaida also notes the limits of jihad as a strategy. When the Saudi state had reached the limits of its expansion, the jihadist violence of its 'Ikhwan' militia became a nuisance to be suppressed. Both *takfiri* (in other words, intra-Sunni) and anti-Shi'ite sectarian jihads have continued in different forms until the present day. On the other hand, Saddam Hussein's oppression of Iraqi Shi'ites was not justified in sectarian terms until the 1990s and 2003, when 'Saddam turned to tribe and religion to reinforce social control'. Other than that, antipathy toward Shi'ites was rationalised in terms of the latter's perceived sympathies with revolutionary Iran.

Mansour Alnogaidan covers related ground in Chapter 8, which traces the uses of jihad under the Wahhabis in Arabia. Jihad, which previously underpinned Saudi expansion, was no longer appropriate following the consolidation of the state. From this point the concept became 'externalised' in the sense that it came to be associated with combating threats to the Islamic community, such as the Israeli occupation of Palestine and the Soviet invasion of Afghanistan. By the end of the 1970s, and especially the 1990s, however, the Saudi regime lost its monopoly on jihad discourse and practice within its own territory. Although novel, the emergence of Juhayman al-'Utaybi's group in the 1970s drew on memories of the suppressed Ikhwan militia that had spearheaded Saudi expansion in Arabia prior to the 1920s. Externalisation also came back to haunt the Saudis as battle-hardened mujahidin returning from Afghanistan declared the Saudi ruling family itself to be unbelievers and a legitimate target for jihad. Alnogaidan explains how interpretations of jihad were reformulated in the second half of the twentieth century, culminating in a new breed of terrorist jihadism in the 1980s. Based on personal experiences as a jihadist in Saudi Arabia – convicted, imprisoned and reformed – Alnogaidan explores the late-twentieth century phenomenon of hybridised models of jihad arising from the fusion of alleged Wahhabi ideals with new militant objectives. He explains how this trend has been led by 'the new Qa'ida Wahhabists', self-appointed theorists outside the traditional Muslim scholarly elite, and directed principally against the Saudi monarchy and Western targets.

The following two chapters in this section focus on the Muslim Brotherhood in Egypt and elsewhere. Chapter 9 by **Hossam Tammam**, a highly respected analyst of Islamist movements who tragically passed away in November 2011, examines the Brotherhood's engagement with the idea of jihad historically, and particularly in relation to the globalist and insurrectionary interpretations articulated by Sayyid Qutb and jihadist groups from the 1970s. Hossam offers powerful explanations for the Egyptian Muslim Brotherhood's reluctance to pursue a confrontational strategy toward the regime under the banner of jihad, or to implement its more expansive global vision. The Brotherhood's internal organisation and target population hold the key. Tammam's contribution also highlights the need to place the Brotherhood in its national and historical context and draws an interesting parallel between the tension between universalism and pragmatism on the part of the Brotherhood, and the regime's Arab nationalist foreign policy on the other. Each was 'pulled in two directions: internally toward reform and consolidation within the state and externally toward the concept of the *umma*'. Tammam moves beyond Egypt to explore the experience of other Brotherhood branches with anti-regime violence. He finds that the overwhelming pattern has been for the Brotherhood to avoid confrontation and instead cooperate with the state.

In some ways constituting a development of Tammam's ideas, **Ewan Stein**'s Chapter 10 explores the ways in which the Brotherhood in Egypt has engaged with jihad discourse following the revolution of 25 January 2011. Stein also finds that the Brotherhood's approach to jihad has been marked by moderation and an 'orthodox' interpretation of the need for a legitimate state authority to decide on matters pertaining to war and peace. The chapter explores the broader, non-violent, dimensions of the

Brotherhood's jihad, which is conceived primarily as a mechanism for the Islamisation of state and society. It also examines the ways in which the idea of jihad as a collective obligation to defend parts of the *umma* under attack have functioned to reinforce the authority of the state and absorb more radical opposition. This pattern is discernable during the Sadat and Mubarak periods and continued under Muhammad Mursi's presidency, despite widespread accusations that the Brotherhood was pandering to militant jihadism. Stein's chapter concludes by drawing a parallel between the role of the Salafi movement vis-à-vis the Mursi presidency in 2012–13 and that of the Brotherhood vis-à-vis Sadat and Mubarak. A key distinguishing feature of the more recent phase has been that the rejectionists under Mursi were not militant jihadists, but a secular opposition that refused to recognise the legitimacy of the Muslim Brotherhood in power. It was this actor that, unlike the jihadists in previous years, was able to join forces with the army and bring down the Mursi regime.

From Egypt, the home of political Islam and source of many of the ideas and groupings behind twenty-first century jihad, the book moves to a more marginal arena. In Chapter 11, **Na'eem Jeenah** examines how Muslim activists in South Africa came to articulate the idea of jihad within a much broader struggle against apartheid. Jeenah recounts how Muslim opposition to colonialism and apartheid in South Africa began soon after the arrival of the first Muslims in the Cape Colony in the mid-seventeeth century. Various acts of resistance through the centuries highlighted the opposition of the Muslim community to the oppression it faced. From the late 1960s, Muslims began playing a more major role in the struggle against apartheid than their number would suggest. Many Muslims joined the various liberation movements and other socialist or nationalist organisations. From the 1970s, an increasing number of individuals and organisations joined the struggle as Muslims. Anti-apartheid resistance, then, increasingly came to be characterised as a jihad. Jeenah evaluates the arguments put forward to justify this position in comparison with the mainstream Muslim position on jihad. He also shows that a novel conception of martyrdom developed alongside the anti-apartheid struggle's notion of jihad, with South African Muslim activists adopting as their martyrs not only Muslims but also non-Muslims killed in the course of the struggle. This chapter ends by highlighting some of the South African offshoots of the 'anti-apartheid jihad', such as the 'gender jihad'. Jeenah's research underscores the important point that jihad has frequently been meaningful beyond Islam. It has been invoked as a way of combating a common enemy of oppressed Muslims and non-Muslims.

The theme of non-violent jihad is taken up in Chapter 12 by **Maria Holt**, who focuses on contemporary struggles in Lebanon and the Palestinian territories from the perspectives of some of the women who are/were present. Holt establishes that jihad, which 'is often used to refer to the resistance', encompasses a plurality of strategies and activities, including but not limited to violence, in which women play central roles. The chapter makes extensive use of personal testimonies from women of all ages and backgrounds, setting these against theoretical perspectives on women and conflict, Islam and modernity, and Islamist movements in the Middle East. In arguing that Islamic resistance movements have successfully mobilised all segments of society, it shows how the efforts of women have been crucial to the success of these movements. In so doing, it challenges international stereotypes of the embodiment of Islamic resistance as violent, irrational, male and terrorist. By examining some of the factors that contributed to women's modes of participation in conflicts and by investigating how religion, patriarchy, traditional practices and revolutionary forms of activism influenced the choices they made (or were unable to make), this chapter demonstrates not only how women in the Arab world are affected by violent conflict but also how their involvement begins to change the rules that govern their societies. The chapter constitutes a salutary reminder that jihad, contrary to some representations,[10] can constitute an integral part, and driver, of modernity rather than being a vestige of medieval tradition.

In the section's final chapter, Lt. Gen. Sir **Simon Mayall** explores the ideological confusion regarding the concept of jihad in the context of the historical development of Islam and the Islamic world, relating this to recent theatres of war in Afghanistan and particularly in Iraq. Resonating with Zubaida's observations, Mayall's account in Chapter 13 grapples with the idea of jihad as a clash within civilisation, rather than conceptualising it within the 'clash of civilisations'. Mayall draws on personal experience as Deputy Commanding General for the Multi-National Corps – Iraq (MNC-I) in 2006–7. By far the largest numbers of victims of violent Islamist extremism are co-religionists, not Christians,

Jews or Hindus. This violence or the threat of it, based on an ideological justification whereby the 'heretic' is viewed as more dangerous than the 'infidel', has proven intensely damaging to the Islamic world's capacity to meet the modern challenges posed by the tensions between state and nation, state and religion and state and individual. The chapter shows how jihadist philosophy, exemplified in its most extreme form by the Jordanian Abu Mus'ab al-Zarqawi, justified violence against the Coalition Forces, Shi'ites, women, the educated, secular middle classes and conservative Sunni tribal leaders and structures. It also reveals how in its violence, language and constant re-classifying of more and more groups and sectors of society as 'enemies', jihadist philosophy resembles the excesses of Bolshevism and Maoism. It was the desire to create security conditions which would allow the establishment of a coalition of moderates from across all Iraqi society, that would take ownership of and advance a political process, which lay at the heart of the US military 'Surge' in 2007. As one of the key orchestrators of the Surge, Mayall suggests that the Coalition was only able to develop the political, developmental and security strategies to contain the horrific level of violence by attempting to understand the socio-religious complexity in which it was rooted.

Part III: Representations of Jihad in Modern Culture

The final section of this book explores a diverse range of representations of jihad in modern culture. The analysis ranges from examining how actual cultural products like poetry, film and television are themselves used as tools in the representation of jihad, to how specific intellectuals have framed representations of jihad in their work. This section begins with Chapter 14 in which **Elisabeth Kendall** demonstrates how contemporary jihadists in Yemen use poetry to legitimise and authenticate their acts and ideas. Scholars and analysts have tended to skip over contemporary Arabic jihadist poetry in order to focus their analysis on more direct pronouncements, rulings and position statements. Yet poetry has the ability to resonate at a deep emotional level among a broader audience as it plugs naturally into a long tradition of oral transmission, particularly on the Arabian Peninsula. Ideas and imagery infiltrate the psyche and are spread emotively and efficiently through repeated recitation and chanting and through conversion into popular anthems.

This is particularly important in remote regions where access to the internet and print media is difficult and literacy rates are low. Kendall posits that poetry also has the ability to reveal clues about jihadist motivation and cultural concerns that can help to illuminate the contemporary political landscape in which jihad is deployed. The various functions of jihadist poetry are explored not simply as a means of cultural and literary analysis but as a potential means of political analysis with the aim of countering terrorism. In the quest to understand both the hearts and minds of those who actively practise or tacitly support militant jihad in Yemen, interrogation of the poetry that speaks to both must be acknowledged as a rich and critical resource.

Chapter 15 by **Rana Issa** also deals with poetry, but here the focus is on the function of martyrdom poetry and the trope of jihad in the construction of Palestinian identity. Issa focuses on a selection of canonical works by recognised poets prior to the 1948 Arab-Israeli war to show how martyrdom came to play a central role in the formation of a Palestinian mythology, nationalist discourse and political identity. By interrogating the prevailing popularity of the classical '*qasida*' form of poetry, Issa examines the genesis of a Palestinian literary modernism through which a common national perception of colonial reality was shaped. Poetry provided an aesthetic resolution of the encounter, or collision, with the West, underscoring the Palestinian struggle as a battle of ideas and culture as well as one of land ownership and political interests. Heated debates arose over the legitimacy of labelling the Palestinian struggle as jihad. The poetry itself portrayed jihad as inextricably linked to the image of the glorious Arab past that poetry was eagerly constructing. Martyrdom, by contrast, was developed into a distinct poetic genre that worked to construct both Palestine's present and future. The Palestinian struggle turned poetry into a supreme cultural product capable of mythologising a common Arab origin. In this constellation, jihad constitutes one such common mythology within a pan-Arab context, while martyrdom has become the localised sacrifice of a fiercely nationalist Palestinian people.

The emphasis moves from poetry to Western popular culture in Chapter 16, with **Thomas Riegler**'s account of the critical role American movies and television series have played in shaping the perception and understanding of the terrorist threat among Western audiences. The stereotypical images that abound in Western popular culture both reflect and construct the political and social dimensions of popular thought. Terrorist characters are generally portrayed as psychotic types who lack justification for their deeds and are righteously eliminated in the course of action. This is especially true of the depiction of radical Islamist terrorism during and after the Reagan administration's confrontation with Shi'ite extremism in the 1980s. Following the bombing in New York of the World Trade Center in 1993, the jihadist finally displaced the left-wing terrorist as the prevailing 'bad guy'. This shift intensified exponentially after the 9/11 terrorist attacks. Jihadists were portrayed as orchestrating dastardly plots whilst barely articulating their causes, although occasionally a more sceptical perspective featured jihadist groups as mere pawns in the service of foreign interests, ranging from the ruthless capitalism of oilmen to the raw pursuit of political power at any price. Riegler shows how movies and television act as critical barometers for the appearance of new dangers and the adjustments deemed necessary to counter them. These cultural products reflect hegemonic interpretations of the roots of Islamist terrorism and shape popular opinion as to the best ways of dealing with it.

From Hollywood, we jump to Victorian England as **Eric Germain** brings to light a novel twist in the representation of jihad through his exploration of the intellectual work of Gottlieb Wilhelm Leitner. In Chapter 17, Germain claims that the notion of jihad was key in forming the image of Islam in the West in the last decades of the nineteenth century and that Leitner played an important role as an apologist for Islam and the 'true meaning' of jihad. Whilst the European perception of 'Muhammadan holy war' was not wholly negative in the mid-nineteenth century, given the romantic image of figures like Imam Shamil and Emir 'Abd al-Qadir, this began to change in the 1880s. In the UK, both the Christian missionary lobby and imperialist circles capitalised on the emotional impact of the fall of Khartoum in 1885. Public opinion became increasingly concerned that jihad represented a Sword of Damocles hanging over the Empire's head, capable of transforming the most obedient of the British Crown's Muslim subjects into a brutal fanatic. Among the rare voices raised against such stereotypes was that of Leitner, an iconoclastic figure of the British orientalist establishment. After retiring from the British civil service in India, Leitner wrote several articles in defence of 'Muhammadanism', including a particularly influential article on jihad. Published in both English and Arabic, it was quoted in a wide range of publications, including Muslim works, in the late nineteenth century, and it continues to be reprinted today. In this seminal article, Leitner stressed Islam's distinction between the 'greater jihad' – the war against sin – and the 'lesser jihad', the war against aggressors; and emphasised the dissociation of jihad from the Crusades. This should be seen as part of a broader apologist agenda that Leitner brought to public attention at an important point in history as the British Empire under Queen Victoria reached its zenith.

This book finishes with two chapters devoted to looking at the representation of jihad by a highly influential contemporary intellectual, Yusuf al-Qaradawi. Al-Qaradawi (b.1926) is a popular Egyptian theologian, now living in Qatar, whose broadcasts on al-Jazeera, together with the prolific publications of the website IslamOnline that he helped to found, reach tens, possibly hundreds, of millions of Muslims globally. In Chapter 18, **Sherman Jackson** analyses some key aspects of al-Qaradawi's complex and comprehensive 2009 book *The Jurisprudence of Jihad (Fiqh al-Jihad)* which has created waves all over the Islamic world. In it, al-Qaradawi argues that Islam is a religion of peace which, though not pacifist, prefers peaceful coexistence over conflict. Jackson explains how jihad, for al-Qaradawi, is to defend Islam rather than to spread it. Al-Qaradawi places himself alongside modern reformers like Muhammad Abduh, Mahmud Shaltut, Hasan al-Banna and Rashid Rida. He also reclaims more ancient scholars like Ibn Taymiyyah for the 'moderate' Muslim camp. Al-Qaradawi's main concern is to show that it is neither admissible nor obligatory to attack non-Muslims who do not pose a threat to Islam. Jackson examines the ways in which al-Qaradawi debunks the arguments of those who support unprovoked violence against non-Muslims, particularly those who refer to the Qur'an's infamous 'sword verse' (*ayat al-sayf*), erroneously arguing that it abrogates less bellicose Qur'anic injunctions. Jackson's analysis provides crucial insights into a complex and important work that aims to establish the notion of defensive jihad as the definitive, mainstream perspective on jihad among Muslims today.

In Chapter 19, Sheikh **Rachid al-Ghannouchi** also reviews and celebrates the novel elements of Qaradawi's hugely influential work on jihad. The views of al-Ghannouchi regarding this vision of jihad are particularly important as he is himself a leading and sometimes controversial Islamic thinker who was finally able to return to his native Tunisia after the 2011 revolution, having spent over two decades in exile to escape three life sentences. Al-Ghannouchi is the co-founder and intellectual leader of the al-Nahda movement that rose to power following the revolution, and his opinions and analyses hold great sway in Tunisia and beyond. In 2012, he was named as one of *Time* magazine's '100 Most Influential People in the World'. Al-Ghannouchi focuses attention on al-Qaradawi's thinking about the methodology and goals of jihad, the relationship between Islam and non-Muslims and the role of jihad within the global Muslim community today. Al-Ghannouchi argues in favour of al-Qaradawi's moderate conception of jihad, including the importance of civil and spiritual jihads which enjoin charity and public service rather than war. In a move directed against extremist scholars, he agrees with al-Qaradawi's rejection of the principle of abrogation in the Qur'an and, in so doing, removes any justification for offensive jihad. Al-Ghannouchi concludes that al-Qaradawi's study is a valuable and authentic exercise in modern-day *ijtihad* (legal interpretative reasoning) which makes jihad once again a relevant and indispensable resource for the Muslim community, while opening a space for dialogue, tolerance and coexistence.

Notes

1. Daveed Gartenstein-Ross, 'Perceptions of the "Arab Spring" within the Salafi-jihadi movement', *Studies in Conflict and Terrorism* 35/12 (November 2012): 831–48.
2. Paul L. Heck, 'Jihad revisited', *Journal of Religious Ethics* 32/1 (March 2004): 95–128 (110).
3. Thomas Hegghammer, *Jihad in Saudi Arabia: Violence and Pan-Islamism Since 1979* (Cambridge and New York, 2010).
4. Fawaz Gerges, *The Far Enemy: Why Jihad Went Global*, 2nd ed. (Cambridge and New York, 2009).
5. Gilles Kepel, *Jihad: The Trail of Political Islam*, 4th ed. (London, 2006); Jason Burke, *Al-Qaeda: The True Story of Radical Islam*, 2nd ed. (London, 2007); Mohammed M. Hafez, *Suicide Bombers in Iraq: The Strategy and Ideology of Martyrdom* (Washington DC, 2007); Lawrence Wright, *The Looming Tower: Al Qaeda's Road to 9/11* (London and New York, 2007); Gerges, *The*

Far Enemy; Hegghammer, *Jihad in Saudi Arabia*; Assaf Moghadam and Brian Fishman, *Fault Lines in Global Jihad: Organizational, Strategic and Ideological Fissures* (London and New York, 2011); Christina Hellmich, *Al-Qaeda: From Global Network to Local Franchise* (London and New York, 2011).

6. Michael Bonner, *Jihad in Islamic History: Doctrines and Practice* (Princeton, 2006); Natana J. Delong-Bas, *Wahhabi Islam: From Revival and Reform to Global Jihad* (Oxford and New York, 2004); Laurent Murawiec, *The Mind of Jihad* (Cambridge and New York, 2008); Nelly Lahoud, *The Jihadis' Path to Self-Destruction* (New York, 2010); Laurent Bonnefoy, *Salafism in Yemen* (London, 2011); Ghazi bin Muhammad, Ibrahim Kalin and Mohammad Hashim Kamali (eds.), *War and Peace in Islam: The Uses and Abuses of Jihad* (Cambridge, 2013).

7. Faisal Devji, *Landscapes of the Jihad: Militancy, Morality, Modernity* (London, 2005); Quintan Wictorowicz, *Radical Islam Rising: Muslim Extremism in the West* (Lanham, 2005); Gabriele Marranci, *Jihad Beyond Islam* (Oxford and New York, 2006); Bernard Rougier, *Everyday Jihad: The Rise of Militant Islam Among Palestinians in Lebanon* (Cambridge, Mass., 2008).

8. Reuven Firestone, *Jihad: The Origin of Holy War in Islam* (New York, 1999); Richard Bonney, *Jihad: From Qur'an to Bin Laden* (New York, 2004); David Cook, *Understanding Jihad* (London, Berkeley and Los Angeles, 2005); Rudolph Peters, *Jihad in Classical and Modern Islam*, 2nd ed. (Princeton, 2005).

9. Brynjar Lia, *Architect of Global Jihad: The Life of Al Qaeda Strategist Abu Mus'ab al-Suri* (London, 2012); Jarret M. Brachman, *Global Jihadism: Theory and Practice* (London and New York, 2008); Jeevan Deol and Zaheer Kazmi (eds.), *Recontextualising Jihadi Thought* (London, 2012); Joas Wagemakers, *A Quietist Jihadi: The Ideology and Influence of Abu Muhammad al-Maqdisi* (New York, 2012).

10. Benjamin R. Barber, *Jihad Vs. McWorld* (London, 1995).

Bibliography

Barber, Benjamin R., *Jihad Vs. McWorld* (London, 1995).

Bin Muhammad, Ghazi, Kalin, Ibrahim and Kamali, Mohammad Hashim (eds.), *War and Peace in Islam: The Uses and Abuses of Jihad* (Cambridge, 2013).

Bonner, Michael, *Jihad in Islamic History: Doctrines and Practice* (Princeton, 2006).

Bonnefoy, Laurent, *Salafism in Yemen: Transnationalism and Religious Identity* (London, 2011).

Bonney, Richard, *Jihad: From Qur'an to Bin Laden* (New York, 2004).

Brachman, Jarret M., *Global Jihadism: Theory and Practice* (London and New York, 2008).

Burke, Jason, *Al-Qaeda: The True Story of Radical Islam*, 2nd ed. (London, 2007).

Cook, David, *Understanding Jihad* (London, Berkeley and Los Angeles, 2005).

Delong-Bas, Natana J., *Wahhabi Islam: From Revival and Reform to Global Jihad* (Oxford and New York, 2004).

Deol, Jeevan and Kazmi, Zaheer (eds.), *Contextualising Jihadi Thought* (London, 2012).

Devji, Faisal, *Landscapes of the Jihad: Militancy, Morality, Modernity* (London, 2005).

Firestone, Reuven, *Jihad: The Origin of Holy War in Islam* (New York, 1999).

Gartenstein-Ross, Daveed, 'Perceptions of the "Arab Spring" within the Salafi-jihadi movement', *Studies in Conflict and Terrorism* 35/12 (November 2012): 831–48.

Gerges, Fawaz, *The Far Enemy: Why Jihad Went Global*, 2nd ed. (Cambridge and New York, 2009).

Hafez, Mohammed M., *Suicide Bombers in Iraq: The Strategy and Ideology of Martyrdom* (Washington DC, 2007).

Heck, Paul L., 'Jihad revisited', *Journal of Religious Ethics* 32/1 (March 2004): 95–128.

Hegghammer, Thomas, *Jihad in Saudi Arabia: Violence and Pan-Islamism Since 1979* (Cambridge and New York, 2010).

Hellmich, Christina, *Al-Qaeda: From Global Network to Local Franchise* (London and New York, 2011).

Kepel, Gilles, *Jihad: The Trail of Political Islam*, 4th ed. (London, 2006).

Lahoud, Nelly, *The Jihadis' Path to Self-Destruction* (New York, 2010).

Lia, Brynjar, *Architect of Global Jihad: The Life of Al Qaeda Strategist Abu Mus'ab al-Suri* (London, 2012).

Marranci, Gabriele, *Jihad Beyond Islam* (Oxford and New York, 2006).

Moghadam, Assaf and Fishman, Brian, *Fault Lines in Global Jihad: Organizational, Strategic and Ideological Fissures* (London and New York, 2011).

Murawiec, Laurent, *The Mind of Jihad* (Cambridge and New York, 2008).

Peters, Rudolph, *Jihad in Classical and Modern Islam*, 2nd ed. (Princeton, 2005).

Rougier, Bernard, *Everyday Jihad: The Rise of Militant Islam Among Palestinians in Lebanon* (Cambridge, Mass., 2008).

Wagemakers, Joas, *A Quietist Jihadi: The Ideology and Influence of Abu Muhammad al-Maqdisi* (New York, 2012).

Wictorowicz, Quintan, *Radical Islam Rising: Muslim Extremism in the West* (Lanham, 2005).

Wright, Lawrence, *The Looming Tower: Al Qaeda's Road to 9/11* (London and New York, 2007).

Prologue

A Short History of Jihad

Carole Hillenbrand

Even before today, when Islam is hardly ever out of the news, there was a perception amongst non-Muslims, and especially Christians, that Islam is a religion of the sword. The lingering heritage of the Crusades has no doubt contributed to the formation of negative stereotypes and, as was clear after the events of 9/11, the words jihad and crusade are still omnipresent slogans, with deep resonances that are both religious and historical. Indeed, the term jihad is bandied about in the world's non-Muslim media, almost without ever being defined; the same imprecision characterises the use of its derivatives like jihadi, jihadists and mujahidin. But serious debates in academic circles, both Muslim and non-Muslim, have revolved around defining jihad. Is it a constant doctrine, unchanging throughout time and space, enshrined in the Islamic canonical sources, or something altogether more fluid, which has evolved and been adapted to specific historical situations? Predictably, there is a whole spectrum of opinions about this. Similarly, the issue of the two kinds or dimensions of jihad – the greater jihad, which is the struggle for personal spiritual improvement, and the lesser jihad, which is a military struggle against infidels – is open to differing interpretations. Ultimately, the position remains that jihad is a nuanced and complex concept; Islamic history shows this very clearly.[1]

What, then, is the aim of this chapter on jihad in history? Certainly not to present a dry excursus on a dead past, and if readers take away nothing else from what follows, they should at least take away a warning.

Medieval history is much more relevant in the Middle East today than it is in the West. And Islamic law is constantly being finessed by memories of what happened in the distant past. Thus, treatments of jihad anchored only in the present and conceived in political terms are simplistic, two-dimensional and therefore flawed. Far too much of modern discourse in the media is of this type.

This chapter will begin by dealing, though only briefly, with jihad in theory, before moving on to discuss some select examples of how jihad was practised in the past, so as to illustrate the diversity, versatility and durability of this concept. These variations should emphasise the likelihood that today too the practice of jihad, even in a world dominated by globalisation and the internet, is not the same everywhere and cannot be reduced to one simple template.

Jihad in Theory

The Qur'an is a book of spiritual revelation, not a legal treatise presented systematically. Since early times, Qur'anic commentators, in their attempts to understand and explain the meanings and ambiguities of the Holy Book, have linked certain verses to specific events in the Prophet's life. This approach is enlightening in the context of what the Qur'an says about jihad. After all, while proclaiming an eternal message for all people in all times and places, the Qur'an also mirrors the evolution of Muhammad's career. Revelations from God came to him in times of crisis. At the beginning, whilst he was in Mecca, his jihad *fi sabil Allah* (his 'struggle in the path of God') was against the forces of polytheism in the hearts of his fellow Meccans. But already in Mecca his life was in danger. After the *hijra* (emigration) to Medina in 622 physical fighting became a pressing issue. Muhammad was building a new theocratic social order there, based on the principles of Islam, and he had to struggle against enemies both inside and outside the city. Above all, the Meccans wanted him dead and they sent armies to attack him; the new faith had to be defended by force.

Non-Muslims, and especially Christians who have before them the model of Jesus, 'the Prince of Peace', find it difficult to accept the idea of a 'warrior prophet'. Yet the Old Testament, which also forms part of the Christian Bible, contains such famous examples as Moses and Joshua,

Jewish prophets who were sent by God to preach His monotheistic message to unbelieving peoples and who fought to preserve the religion of Abraham and God's people. Muhammad was well aware of this ancient Semitic religious tradition of fighting. But within his own tribal society in Arabia, too, tribal raiding and fighting had been part of the struggle for survival in an extremely harsh physical environment since time immemorial. However, Muslims believe that the difference between the traditional fighting between warring tribes in Arabia and Muhammad's own military struggle is that his striving had a religious dimension. It was in the path of God and it was therefore jihad.

Most references in the Qur'an to jihad ('striving') stress the greater jihad and only a few allude to a military struggle against those who oppose Islam. It should also be noted that Paradise is the reward for all those who believe and perform good deeds, whether or not they die striving in the path of God.

The Qur'an mirrors the vicissitudes experienced by the fledgling Muslim community. At first, God permits the believers to fight in order to defend themselves, but not to initiate military conflict. Later, the tone becomes more aggressive, commanding the faithful to kill idolaters if they do not submit to Islam. It is not surprising that in the polytheistic milieu of seventh-century Arabia the Muslims were soon faced with the need to use force on occasion to defend their fragile little community. If they had not done so, it is doubtful that Islam would have survived at all.

The books of hadith (the sayings of Muhammad) – collected by Sunnis, Shi'ites, Sufis and others – amplify Qur'anic pronouncements about jihad and reveal the clear aim of the early Muslims: to lay down detailed rules for the proper conduct of jihad, especially on subjects such as the treatment of prisoners and the avoidance of killing innocent non-combatants.

According to the medieval Muslim religious scholars who formulated the shariah in the eighth and ninth centuries, the whole world is divided into two camps: the Abode of Islam (*Dar al-Islam*) and the Abode of War (*Dar al-Harb*). The Abode of Islam referred to all lands under Muslim control. The Abode of War comprised all the lands outside the Abode of Islam. Theoretically, jihad against such areas should continue until the whole world belongs to Islam. Only the leader of the community, the imam or caliph, could call for and lead the jihad, which is the collective duty of the whole community. After the ninth century some scholars began to recognise a third status, the Abode of Truce (*Dar al-'Ahd*), meaning territories that had entered into a contract of specified duration with the Muslim community.[2]

Over the centuries the theory of jihad was modified in other ways. Just as the ideal of crusade against the infidel was sullied by the infamous Fourth Crusade in which European Christians fought against eastern Christians in Constantinople in 1204, so too in due course Sunni Muslim lawyers permitted jihad against Shi'ites and other so-called Muslim heretics, as well as against rebels and apostates.

Medieval Jihad in Practice

As might be expected, the history of the Islamic world and its relations with its non-Muslim neighbours was by no means one of continuous jihad as the law books prescribed. There were in fact long periods of peace which allowed social, commercial and cultural contact with the infidel 'Other'. Nevertheless, Islamic history is punctuated by famous jihad campaigns; and the memory of some of them still resonates.

It is convenient to begin with the Arab conquests. The Arab armies, flooding out of their remote desert homeland in large numbers for the first time in their history, had by 732 conquered a vast empire that stretched from Spain to northern India and the borders of China. Much ink has been spilt on the phenomenon of the Muslim conquests and why they happened when they did. Some scholars have tried to prove that these conquests might have happened regardless of the influence of Islam, that they were primarily driven by climatic and socio-economic factors. Others have argued that the instrument of jihad was used to drive forward the recently converted Arabs and to establish Islam as the prevailing faith in the newly conquered lands. After all, such scholars argue, Islam was for the whole world, not just for Arabs.[3]

So what role, if any, did jihad play in this extraordinary phenomenon? The timing of the conquests is extremely telling. They took off in an enormous surge immediately after the death of Muhammad in 632. Although it is unlikely that the rank and file of the Bedouin Arab troops were already imbued with the spirit of jihad, it is probable that the inner circle of devoted followers of the Prophet were so inspired. Success led to success for the Arab armies, and their confidence that God's favour was with them increased exponentially.

On balance it seems hard to deny that the impetus of jihad played a key role in the early Arab military successes and that it gave them an ideological edge over their foes. Without this impetus the achievements of the Muslims would have been ephemeral and localised. Islam, as practised by those who had been privileged to work close to Muhammad, provided the foundation of the embryonic Arab state; it was the jihad of this small elite that fired the early conquests.

The next example comes from two centuries later and a world far removed from Arabia, namely Central Asia. This was a key frontier to defend, for it marked the border between the territory of Islam and that of the nomadic Turks. The Turks had lived in the vast steppes of Central Asia for millennia; in the tenth century they were wedged between the Abode of Islam, with its major cities, Bukhara and Samarkand, and the Chinese, who had built the Great Wall to keep them out. The easternmost Muslim state in the tenth century was ruled by the ethnically Persian Samanid dynasty. By virtue of their geographical position, these staunchly Sunni rulers inherited the crucial role of defenders of the eastern frontier.[4]

Medieval Muslim geographers have left detailed descriptions of this frontier against the infidel Turks. They speak of vast numbers of buildings known as *ribat*s (fortifications).[5] Russian archaeologists have excavated many such monuments. These structures, part military camp, part Sufi cloister, were built to house warriors, known as mujahidin or *ghazi*s, who flocked to this area from all across the Islamic world to wage jihad against the infidels. The modern implications of this practice will not escape even casual observers.

A third example is that of the Ghaznavid Turks who present a rather different example of medieval jihad. With the advent of this aggressive Sunni Muslim state based at Ghazna in southern Afghanistan from 977, the Hindu rulers in north-west India were soon under threat. Northern India proved to be a perfect place in which to conduct raids. Although Muslim warriors found Buddhism rather difficult to categorise, they experienced no such problem with Hinduism. The Hindu idols seemed to them clear evidence of polytheism. Between 999 and 1027 the most famous Ghaznavid ruler, Mahmud, raided northern India 15 times.

These raids were retrospectively designated as jihad campaigns by court historians, but their real motive seems to have been booty. Indeed, Mahmud destroyed what he regarded as idolatrous works of art and in the process acquired vast riches from the Indian princes. Nevertheless, he is celebrated in Muslim legend to this day as a mujahid fighting the infidel.[6]

So much for the evidence from the Muslim East. What of the Muslim West? The eleventh-century Almoravid dynasty was the first of two Berber tribal confederations that took power in North Africa and conquered parts of Muslim Spain.[7] The jihad ideology that motivated the Almoravids is demonstrated in their very name – *al-Murabitun* – literally 'those who live in *ribats*'. Their founder, Ibn Yasin, was a strict Maliki Sunni Muslim and he preached a militant jihad ideology to the veiled Sanhaja Berbers in the High Atlas mountains, founding a *ribat* near the mouth of the Senegal river. Ibn Yasin and his followers overran the regions of the Sahara until his death 'as a martyr' in 1058. He was succeeded as leader by Yusuf ibn Tashufin (1061–1107) who seized substantial parts of North Africa, founded a new capital city, Marrakesh, and invaded Muslim Spain. The Almoravids proclaimed their activities to be jihad, both against the pagans of Africa, and, perhaps more surprisingly, against the Muslims of North Africa and Spain, whose adherence to Islam they viewed as lukewarm and who, they believed, were in need of 're-Islamisation'. Their reforms had a character that might strike us as puritan, with their hatred of all luxuries and of dancing, music and poetry, and their intolerance of other interpretations of Islam. Again, modern parallels spring to mind.

And now to Syria, and the particular case of Sayf al-Dawla, seen by posterity as a jihad martyr. On the Muslim border with Byzantium in what is now eastern Turkey, this very famous Syrian Shi'ite scion of the Hamdanid dynasty (who ruled 944–67) conducted annual campaigns of jihad against the Byzantine Christians.[8] As in Central Asia, Muslim warriors for the faith on the Byzantine border were housed in *ribat*s, supported by charitable donations. Sayf al-Dawla (the 'Sword of the State'), as his name denotes, fought in a spirit of jihad more than 40 battles against the Byzantines across the border from his little state centred at Aleppo. Bedridden from 962, he would be carried into battle on a litter, and when he died, he was buried like a true martyr (*shahid*);

a brick laden with dust from one of his campaigns was put under his cheek in his mausoleum. Poets[9] and preachers praised his jihad and the inspiring example of Sayf al-Dawla was not forgotten when the Muslims of Syria and Palestine were facing the Crusaders.[10]

The somewhat parallel cases of the early Muslim Kharijites and the much later so-called 'Assassins' highlight what might be termed, somewhat anachronistically perhaps, 'medieval terrorism'; but whereas there is evidence that the Kharijites saw themselves as fighting jihad, the Arabic or Persian sources rarely mention the term jihad in connection with the 'Assassins'.

Within 30 years of Muhammad's death in 632, the young Muslim community saw the appearance of a marginal breakaway group known as the Kharijites (the 'Dissenters'). Their name came from the Arabic verb *kharaja* meaning 'to go out' or, by extension, 'to rebel'. The Kharijites were implacable foes of any Muslim government other than their own. Theirs was the 'saved community'.[11] They believed in the theocratic slogan: 'Rule belongs to God alone.' They adopted a strict view of Islam, based on the belief that the most *virtuous* person in the community should lead it, not necessarily someone from the Prophet's own family or someone elected by the whole community. The Kharijites went further than that, saying that anyone who did not share their beliefs was *not* a Muslim and should be killed. One section of them believed that the killing of non-Kharijite women and children – i.e. non-combatants – was also permissible. The site of the true faith (*Dar al-Hijra*) – the Abode of Emigration – was their army camp, and the rest of the world was the Abode of Polytheism.

This fierce, uncompromising sectarian group undertook a campaign of murders of leading figures, such as Muhammad's cousin and son-in-law 'Ali, the fourth caliph, and they were persecuted by the early caliphs for some two centuries. The early Kharijites were drawn largely from Arab tribes with a long tradition of reciting poetry. But Kharijite poetry no longer extols tribal virtues; it preaches messages of jihad. These poets praise the courage and piety of their comrades who have fallen in the path of God on the battlefield and they berate themselves for not having died as martyrs too. For Kharijite fighters, death does not bring absolute despair; indeed, it is only the entrance to Paradise, where they will meet again their brothers who have preceded them there. The Kharijite warrior does not wish to die in his bed; he hopes for violent death under the point of the lance. By day, we read in their poetry, the fighters are lions in battle; by night they pray like sobbing women at funerals.[12]

In the last decade of the eleventh century another group of 'extremists' appeared, this time in north-west Iran, namely the breakaway sect known by their Sunni Muslim foes and later, in Syria and Palestine, by their Crusader enemies as the *Hashishiyyun* (the 'hashish eaters', popularly called the Assassins). Hasan-i Sabbah, the Persian founder of this extreme Isma'ili Shi'ite group, normally known in medieval Muslim sources as the Nizaris or the Batinis, taught a form of Islam which he termed 'new preaching' (*da'wa jadida*); this stressed the necessity of a charismatic Imam to interpret true Islamic doctrine for the whole Muslim community.[13] What proved more significant, however, was the programme of politically motivated assassination campaigns that he organised to bring down the rule of the Seljuq Turks in Iran. Indeed, in the space of just under 30 years (1095–1124), the Assassins, under Hasan's orders, carried out a series of around 50 high-profile murders. Their victims were always Sunni government ministers of the Seljuq Turkish state or important military or religious figures. The murders were deliberately conducted in the full glare of publicity, often in the courtyard of the mosque on Fridays. The Assassins worked in pairs, used ritual daggers and were prepared to die if necessary to carry out their task. Contrary to what is often said today, however, the Assassins did not actively seek death – they were not, so to speak, medieval 'suicide bombers'.[14] A number of them are recorded as having escaped after carrying out the murders.[15] But there is no doubt that these high-profile murders gave the Assassins a psychological impact out of all proportion to their numbers.

As for the Nizaris of Syria, whose most famous leader Rashid al-Din Sinan (d.1192) was popularly known as the Old Man of the Mountain (Shaykh al-Jabal), they were held responsible for the killing or wounding of both Crusader and Sunni Muslim leaders. According to a single reference – in a rare but much later Isma'ili work, dated 1324, written by a Syrian Isma'ili called Abu Firas – Rashid al-Din sent out men of jihad (*rijal al-jihad*) on assassination expeditions.[16]

The twelfth to fourteenth centuries saw the coming of the Crusades and the Mongol invasions, and these events triggered a reawakening of jihad. Two key moments in the history of jihad occurred in close succession when the Muslim world was attacked from both west and east, not on its frontiers but in its very heartlands, first by the Crusaders from Christian Europe and then by the pagan Mongol hordes from the very borders of China. In both cases the Muslim world eventually managed to get rid of these two external threats by mounting focused campaigns of jihad.

It is the Crusades that give the clearest demonstration of this process. The First Crusade arrived in Syria in 1098 at a time of extreme Muslim weakness and disunity. Moreover, Muslims in this region had long co-existed with their powerful Christian neighbour, Byzantium. In such an atmosphere, they were simply not ready to wage immediate jihad against the incoming Crusaders.

So the Crusaders easily seized Jerusalem in 1099 and had set up three more Crusader states by 1110. And it took the Muslims well over 50 years to find the right kind of military leadership and the ideological motivation necessary to recover the initiative against the Crusaders and to undertake the re-conquest of long-held Muslim territory. In vain did a Muslim jurist from Damascus called al-Sulami write in his *Book of Jihad* in 1105 that there was still time to remove the Crusaders; his voice went unheard.[17] It was only in the 1150s that the tide began to turn with a remarkable surge of jihad, masterminded by an alliance between the Sunni religious classes in Syria and the Turkish warlord, Nur al-Din (d.1174).[18] His successor in leading the jihad, the more famous Saladin, was able to re-conquer Jerusalem, the third holiest city in Islam after Mecca and Medina. Indeed, Jerusalem provided a unique focus for the jihad of these two great Muslim military leaders, and the medieval Muslim chronicles portray both Nur al-Din and Saladin as figures in whom personal spiritual jihad and public jihad against the infidel were inextricably combined.

During the Crusading period the Muslim leadership in Syria used a wide range of methods to keep the ardour of the faithful for jihad at a high level. This called for careful orchestration on a scale unparalleled in earlier times. Monumental inscriptions on public buildings, for example, harped on jihad themes and were so placed as to be legible.[19] Nur al-Din sponsored jihad books, jihad sermons, collections of jihad hadith,[20] works praising the merits of Jerusalem and rousing jihad poetry.[21] The longer Jerusalem remained in Crusader hands, with its two sacred Islamic monuments, the Dome of the Rock and the Aqsa Mosque, occupied by the infidel, the more the Muslims longed to take the Holy City back. And Saladin's victory over the Crusaders at the Battle of Hattin in 1187 and his triumphal entry into Jerusalem that same year, on the anniversary of the Prophet Muhammad's ascent into heaven from that very city, were the crowning moments of his jihad.

The case of the Mongols is not so clear-cut. The significance of the Mongol invasions for the development of jihad has been somewhat over-looked, for it has been eclipsed by the impact of the Crusades. How-ever, through the writings of the influential Hanbalite Sunni scholar, Ibn Taymiyyah (d.1328), the effect of the devastating Mongol irruption into the heartlands of Islam under Genghis Khan and his successors can be seen as seminal in any overview of medieval jihad.[22] More so than the threat of more crusades from Europe, the Mongol invasions – which destroyed Baghdad and the Abbasid caliphate – dominated the life and thinking of Ibn Taymiyyah. He has constituted a role model for the movement begun by Ibn 'Abd al-Wahhab, as well as for modern Wahhabism, and for many so-called jihadist groups today. In his three, so-called 'anti-Mongol' fatwas,[23] Ibn Taymiyyah records with great ve-hemence the horrors of two Mongol invasions of Syria during 1299 to 1301. At no point does he accept that the Mongols are Muslims, even though the Mongol ruler Ghazan publicly converted to Islam in 1295. He argues that the Mongols do not follow shariah, thus obliging Mus-lims to wage jihad against them. To persuade those Muslims who were hesitant to take up arms against the Mongols, Ibn Taymiyyah likens the Mongols to the Kharijites.[24]

Instead of the overwhelming preoccupation with jihad focused on Jerusalem which characterised Saladin's time, for Ibn Taymiyyah a cen-tury and a half later jihad was aimed at preempting external military aggression against the House of Islam. But he also argued that it was necessary in a much more profound sense to wage the greater jihad and to purge Muslim society of the spiritual defilement caused by contact with non-Muslims, especially Christians and Mongols.[25] That sense of defilement, of religious pollution caused by infidels, is alive and well among many mujahidin today.

These varied but interrelated case studies point to the availability of a historical reservoir upon which modern ideologists of jihad can draw in the twenty-first century.

Jihad in Recent Times

Western imperialism, colonialism and foreign occupation since the nine-teenth century have provoked jihad movements in many parts of the Muslim world. For some, the call for jihad has a specific nationalist focus, such as the ongoing Palestine/Israel problem. Other groups have resorted to terrorist acts across the whole world under the banner of jihad in protest against Western, and especially US, interventionism. Crusade/jihad imagery has often surfaced in the twentieth-century writings of Sayyid Qutb, Abu al-A'la Mawdudi and others. More recently, the self-styled *mujtahid* (interpreter of legal texts), Osama bin Laden, delivered fatwas and referred in his speeches and letters to jihad against Jews and Crusaders. The juxtaposition of crusade/jihad continues apace, as in the hotel bomb blasts in Jakarta in 2009 or the ongoing suicide op-erations against the Iraqi and Afghan regimes that are deemed puppets of the so-called Zionist-Crusader alliance. The theme of Jerusalem is often repeated by spokesmen from jihadi groups and in the rhetoric of some Muslim governments. Khomeini was fully behind the concept of an anti-Zionist jihad to liberate Jerusalem, a theme that recurred in Ah-madinejad's speeches. Saladin's jihad has been viewed as a blueprint for anti-Western struggle, as banknotes, postage stamps, posters and websites attest.[26]

Other medieval jihad motifs also recur. The rhetoric of Osama bin Laden and others was directed against the 'paganism' of the West, re-calling Ibn Taymiyyah's tirades against the Mongols. The 'proto-terrorist' group mentioned earlier, the Kharijites, also figured in bin Laden's manifestos – he cited Kharijite poetry[27] – and, in operations such as 9/11, al-Qa'ida, like the Assassins, adopted the strategy of committing violent murder in high-profile locations to attract maximum publicity.[28] Nowadays, there are thousands of websites about the Assassins. Very few, if any, of those responsible for them have any knowledge of the religious beliefs of this group; instead, they prefer to indulge in the kind of pseudo-mysticism that also surrounds the medieval Knights Templar on the internet. One Assassin website even has a picture of the Assassin leader, Hasan-i Sabbah, placed next to Osama bin Laden. Both men are made to look very much like each other, despite the wide difference in their religious beliefs; bin Laden was a Sunni and Hasan an Isma'ili

Shi'ite.[29] Moreover, unlike the campaigns of bin Laden, the killings carried out by Hasan were aimed at single individuals, whereas those of bin Laden were focused on mass murder.

Al-Qa'ida and the numerous copycat groups that it has spawned across the world deploy a highly simplistic and eclectic interpretation of jihad. They are an elusive formation. Their weapons include terrorism and exemplary violence that resonates around the world. The jihadists' 'martyrdom' is amplified because it is splashed all over the internet. They claim to be waging global jihad against the West. But what is to-day's jihad? The world's Muslim communities hold a broad spectrum of beliefs on this topic. For the vast majority, however, their views are based on a doctrine of jihad that has been laboriously refined by many generations of scholars, Sunni and Shi'ite, modernist and traditional-ist. Can this venerable edifice created by Islamic legal scholarship be overturned by any upstart warlord and terrorist with no recognised re-ligious or legal credentials? It seems so. Research conducted in Wash-ington in the last decade concluded that only 7 per cent of the world's Muslims are 'politically radicalised'.[30] But it is precisely the voices of those radical groups that are the ones that are picked up and spread round the world by the media. How can the indiscriminate slaughter of the innocent on 9/11, 7/7 or the dates of other so-called jihad-motivated attacks, conducted not on the battlefield but in airports, shopping malls or train stations, legitimately be called 'jihad in the path of God'? Yet the French-Algerian 'jihadist' Mohammed Merah, perpetrator of the Toulouse killings in March 2012, publicly declared: 'I fight for Allah.' Likewise, two British Muslims of Nigerian descent proclaimed '*Allahu Akbar*' as they butchered a young British soldier on a London street in May 2013.

We are now used to movements all over the world whose names include the terms jihad or mujahidin – in Indonesia, Mali, Chechnya, Nigeria, Afghanistan, France, the UK, the USA, to name but a few of the countries affected. Clearly, by giving such prominence to the doctrine of jihad, the members of such groups are placing it at the very heart of their activities. And the word has acquired new usages. Proponents of 'consumer jihad' issue fatwas which focus on economic boycotts, as in the example of Danish butter in 2006. The notorious Danish cartoons infamously included a picture of the Prophet Muhammad wearing a turban in the shape of a ticking bomb on which was written the Islamic profession of faith. The news of the cartoons reverberated around the world and reignited old tensions in areas such as Nigeria.

The derivative term 'McJihad' has been coined to denote alliances in recent years between the USA (the home of the McDonald's empire) and oil-rich conservative Muslim states.[31] To this list we may now add 'cyber jihad', which can be waged by hacking into the computers of individual citizens, and indeed those of government departments and agencies, with defensive or hostile intent.

Nowadays, of course, jihad is an overused word; but it can serve as a powerful rallying cry against perceived forces of aggression and interference. And the broad spectrum of meanings accommodated under that convenient umbrella term means that this process will continue and expand. This chapter has shown that it is a serious error to treat jihad simplistically, as a monolithic concept or rigidly defined category of actions. Fighting for widely differing aims and in sharply varied contexts was dressed up retrospectively in jihad rhetoric by medieval Muslim historians. And that same process continues today.

The past is not 'another country' for modern Muslims. And indeed certain aspects of medieval jihad that recur nowadays, sometimes under a slightly different guise, should be emphasised with that in mind. This historical dimension is frequently overlooked in modern discussions of jihad; hence my emphasis on it in this prologue. The model of the military campaigns of the Prophet Muhammad is never forgotten in modern jihad discourse. Of great importance too have been the famous battles of the early Arab conquests, such as Qadisiyya, and Saladin's victories against the Crusaders. The twelfth-century proponents of jihad used the full range of propaganda devices available at the time; their modern descendants of course have a much wider panoply of options – radio, television, newspapers, posters, the internet, social media and so on. But the underlying aim is much the same. Similarly, such medieval manifestations of jihad activity as high-profile killings, the flocking of Muslims from distant lands to the battlefields of jihad, the puritanical attitudes of many mujahidin and even (as practised on occasion by the early Kharijites) the targeting of non-combatants, such as women and children – all these aspects of medieval jihad have their modern counterparts. This is no mere coincidence.

Jihad continues to be a multivalent symbol; indeed, today's jihadis, unlike those in the Middle Ages, have dared to deploy the term *istishhad* (seeking martyrdom) to a context of suicide bombing. But that is quite another matter and it needs to be dealt with by the learned muftis and sheikhs who interpret the precepts of Islamic law and faith for today's Muslims.

Notes

1. See, for example, Albrecht Noth, *Heiliger Krieg und Heiliger Kampf* (Bonn, 1986); Reuven Firestone, *Jihad: The Origin of Holy War in Islam* (New York, 1999); Michael Bonner, *Jihad in Islamic History: Doctrines and Practice* (Princeton, 2006); David Cook, *Understanding Jihad* (Berkeley, 2005); Christopher J. van der Krogt, 'Jihad without apologetics', *Islam and Christian-Muslim Relations* 21/2 (2010): 127–42.

2. See Majid Khadduri, *The Law of War and Peace in Islam* (London, 1940).

3. For an excellent treatment of this much-discussed topic, see Hugh Kennedy, *The Great Arab Conquests: How the Spread of Islam Changed the World We Live In* (London, 2007).

4. See Luke Treadwell, 'The account of the Samanid dynasty in Ibn Zafir al-Azdi's *Akhbar al-duwal al-munqati'a*', *Iran* 43 (2005): 135–71.

5. See Abu Bakr Muhammad ibn Ja'far Narshakhi, *The History of Bukhara*, trans. Richard N. Frye (Cambridge, Mass., 1954), p. 18; Sergei P. Tolstow, *Auf den Spuren der altchoresmischen Kultur*, trans. O Mehlitz (Berlin, 1953), p. 267.

6. Clifford Edmund Bosworth, *The Ghaznavids; Their Empire in Afghanistan and Eastern Iran 994–1040* (Edinburgh, 1963).

7. See Dierk Lange, 'The Almoravid expansion and the downfall of Ghana', *Der Islam* 73 (1996): 122–59; Ronald A. Messier, *Almoravids and the Meanings of Jihad* (Santa Barbara, 2010).

8. Marius Canard, *Histoire de la dynastie des Hamdanides de Jazîra et de Syrie*, Vol. I (Paris, 1953).

9. See Régis Blachère, *Un Poète Arabe du IVe Siècle de l'Hégire (Xe siècle de J.-C)* (Paris, 1935); Régis Blachère, 'La vie et l'oeuvre d'Abû ṭ Ṭayyib al-Mutanabbi', in Régis Blachere, *Analecta* (Damascus, 1975): 401–30; Andras Hamori, *The Composition of Mutanabbī's Panegyrics to Sayf al-Dawla* (Leiden, 1992); Carole Hillenbrand, 'Jihad poetry in the age of the Crusades', in Thomas Madden, James L. Naus and Vincent Ryan (eds.),

Crusades – Medieval Worlds in Conflict. Proceedings of the Crusades conference held at the University of St Louis, 2007 (Aldershot, 2010): 10–12.

10. Abu Tayyib al-Mutanabbi, *Al-Mutanabbi carmina cum commentario Wahidii*, ed. F. Dieterici (Berlin, 1856–61), pp. 481–4.

11. See Nasir ibn Sulayman ibn Sa'id al-Sabi'i, *Al-Khawarij wa'l-Haqiqa al-Gha'iba* (Muscat, 1420/1999); Wilferd Madelung, *Religious Trends in Early Islamic Iran* (Albany, 1988), pp. 54–5. Paul L. Heck, 'Eschatological scripturalism and the end of community: The case of early Kharijism', *Archiv für Religionsgeschichte* 7 (2005): 137–52.

12. See Francesco Gabrieli, 'La poesia harigita nel secolo degli Omayyadi', *Rivista degli studi orientali* 20 (1943): 331–72; id., 'Religious poetry in early Islam', *Arabic Poetry: Theory and Development. Third Giorgio della Vida Conference* (Wiesbaden, 1973), pp. 5–17; Ihsan 'Abbas, *Diwan Shi'r al-Khawarij* (Beirut and Cairo, 1982); Knysh, Alexander, 'Kharijis', 'Kharijite literature', *Encyclopedia of Arabic Literature* (London, 1998), Vol. 2: 436–7.

13. See Madelung, 'Isma'ilism: the old and the new *da'wa*' in *Religious Trends*, pp. 93–105; see also the classic work on this still little-known subject – Marshall G.S. Hodgson, *The Secret Order of Assassins: The Struggle of the Early Nizari Isma'ilis against the Islamic World*' (reprint) (Philadelphia, 2005).

14. See the discussion in Carole Hillenbrand, 'Unholy aspirations: Review of Richard Bonney, *Jihad: From Qur'an to bin Laden*, London, 2004 and Faisal Devji, *Landscapes of the jihad: Militancy, morality, modernity*, London, 2005', *The Times Literary Supplement*, 4 August 2006.

15. Hodgson mentions the widespread story of a mother who grieved when her son had not died in an assassination attack but had come home alive; Hodgson, *The Secret Order of Assassins*, p. 83.

16. For this rare source see S. Guyard, 'Un grand maitre des Assassins au temps de Saladin', *Journal Asiatique*, 7th Series: 9 (1877): 324–489.

17. See Emmanuel Sivan, *L'Islam et la Croisade: Idéologie et Propagande dans les Réactions Musulmanes aux Croisades* (Paris, 1968), pp. 30–2.

18. Ibid., pp. 59–91; Carole Hillenbrand, *The Crusades, Islamic Perspectives* (Edinburgh, 1999), pp. 117–70.

19. Carole Hillenbrand, 'Aspects of *jihad* propaganda: the evidence of 12th century inscriptions', in *Proceedings of the Conference on the History of the Crusades, University of Bir Zeit* (Bir Zeit, 1993): 53–63.

20. The famous Damascene scholar, Ibn 'Asakir, wrote a work entitled *The Forty Hadiths for Inciting Jihad* at the request of his patron Nur al-Din; see Suleiman A. Mourad and James. E. Lindsay, *The Intensification and Reorientation of Sunni Jihad Ideology in the Crusader Period: Ibn 'Asakir of*

Damascus (1105–1176) and His Age, with an Edition and Translation of Ibn 'Asakir's The Forty Hadiths for Inciting Jihad (Leiden and Boston, 2013).

21. Hillenbrand, 'Jihad poetry', pp. 14–17.
22. See Henri Laoust, 'La biographie d'Ibn Taimiya d'après Ibn Kathir', *Bulletin d' études orientales* 9 (1942): 115–62.
23. Denise Aigle, 'The Mongol invasions of Bilad al-Sham by Ghazan Khan and Ibn Taymiyah's three "anti-Mongol" fatwas', *Mamluk Studies Review* 11/2 (2007): 89–120.
24. Aigle, p. 103.
25. A. Morabia, 'Ibn Taymiyya, dernier grand théoricien du jihad mediéval', *Bulletin d' études orientales* 30/2 (1978): 85–99.
26. See Carole Hillenbrand, *The Crusades. Islamic Perspectives* (Edinburgh, 1999), pp. 594–600; Carole Hillenbrand, 'The legacy of the Crusades', in T. Madden (ed.), *Crusades: The Illustrated History* (London, 2004): 208–9; Anne-Marie Eddé, *Saladin* (Paris, 2008), pp. 576–9.
27. For example, in one of his speeches Osama bin Laden quoted a rousing jihad poem by the seventh-century poet, al-Tirrima al-Ta'i.
28. *Jay Nelson's Weird Load Article Archive*, 'Curse of the assassins: Part 1, the prototype of terror', n.d. (http://archives.weirdload.com/hasan.html, last accessed 27 December 2013); J. Mackinlay, 'Tackling bin Laden: lessons from history', *The Observer*, 28 October 2001.
29. *Jay Nelson's Weird Load Article Archive*, 'Curse of the assassins'.
30. John L. Esposito and Dalia Mogahed, *Who Speaks for Islam? What a Billion Muslims Think* (New York, 2007).
31. Timothy Mitchell, 'Islam in the U.S. global order', *Social Text* 73 (Winter 2003): 1–18 (3).

Bibliography

'Abbas, Ihsan, *Diwan Shi'r al-Khawarij* (Beirut and Cairo, 1982).

Aigle, Denise, 'The Mongol invasions of Bilad al-Sham by Ghazan Khan and Ibn Taymiyah's three "anti Mongol" fatwas', *Mamluk Studies Review* 11/2 (2007): 89–120.

Blachère, Régis, *Un Poète Arabe du IVe Siècle de l'Hégire (Xe siècle de J.-C)* (Paris, 1935).

———, 'La vie et l'oeuvre d'Abû ṭ Ṭayyib al-Mutanabbi', in Régis Blachere, *Analecta* (Damascus, 1975): 401–30.

Bonner, Michael, *Jihad in Islamic History: Doctrines and Practice* (Princeton, 2006).

Bosworth, Clifford Edmund, *The Ghaznavids; Their Empire in Afghanistan and Eastern Iran 994–1040* (Edinburgh, 1963).

Canard, Marius, *Histoire de la Dynastie des Hamdanides de Jazîra et de Syrie*, Vol. 1 (Paris, 1953).

Cook, David, *Understanding Jihad* (London, Berkeley and Los Angeles, 2005).

Eddé, Anne-Marie, *Saladin* (Paris, 2008).

Esposito, John L. and Mogahed, Dalia, *Who Speaks for Islam? What a Billion Muslims Think* (New York, 2007).

Firestone, Reuven, *Jihad: The Origin of Holy War in Islam* (New York, 1999).

Gabrieli, Francesco, 'La poesia harigita nel secolo degli Omayyadi', *Rivista Degli Studi Orientali* 20 (1943): 331–72.

———, 'Religious poetry in early Islam', *Arabic Poetry: Theory and Development. Third Giorgio della Vida Conference* (Wiesbaden, 1973): 5–17.

Guyard, S., 'Un grand maitre des Assassins au temps de Saladin', *Journal Asiatique* 7th Series: 9 (1877): 324–489.

Hamori, Andras, *The Composition of Mutanabbī's Panegyrics to Sayf al-Dawla* (Leiden, 1992).

Heck, Paul L., 'Eschatological scripturalism and the end of community: The case of early Kharijism', *Archiv für Religionsgeschichte* 7 (2005): 137–52.

Hillenbrand, Carole, 'Aspects of *jihad* propaganda: the evidence of 12th century inscriptions', in *Proceedings of the Conference on the History of the Crusades, University of Bir Zeit* (Bir Zeit, 1993): 53–63.

———, *The Crusades, Islamic Perspectives* (Edinburgh, 1999).

———, 'The legacy of the Crusades', in T. Madden (ed.), *Crusades: The Illustrated History* (London, 2004): 202–11.

———, 'Unholy aspirations: Review of Richard Bonney, *Jihad: From Qur'an to bin Laden*, London, 2004 and Faisal Devji, *Landscapes of the jihad: Militancy, morality, modernity*, London, 2005', *The Times Literary Supplement*, 4 August 2006.

———, 'Jihad poetry in the age of the Crusades', in Thomas Madden, James L. Naus and Vincent Ryan (eds.), *Crusades – Medieval Worlds in Conflict. Proceedings of the Crusades conference held at the University of St Louis, 2007* (Aldershot, 2010): 9–23.

Hodgson, Marshall G.S., *The Secret Order of Assassins: The Struggle of the Early Nizari Isma'ilis against the Islamic World* (reprint) (Philadelphia, 2005).

Jay Nelson's Weird Load Article Archive, 'Curse of the assassins: Part 1, the prototype of terror', n.d. (http://archives.weirdload.com/hasan.html, last accessed 27 December 2013).

Kennedy, Hugh, *The Great Arab Conquests: How the Spread of Islam Changed the World We Live In* (London, 2007).

Khadduri, Majid, *The Law of War and Peace in Islam* (London, 1940).

Knysh, Alexander, 'Kharijis', 'Kharijite literature', *Encyclopedia of Arabic Literature* (London, 1998), Vol. 2: 436–7.

van der Krogt, Christopher J., 'Jihad without apologetics', *Islam and Christian-Muslim Relations* 21/2 (2010): 127–42.

Lange, Dierk, 'The Almoravid expansion and the downfall of Ghana', *Der Islam* 73 (1996): 122–59.

Laoust, Henri, 'La biographie d'Ibn Taimiya d'après Ibn Kathir', *Bulletin d' 'etudes orientales* 9 (1942): 115–62.

Mackinlay, J., 'Tackling bin Laden: lessons from history', *The Observer*, 28 October 2001.

Madelung, Wilferd, *Religious Trends in Early Islamic Iran* (Albany, 1988).

Messier, Ronald A., *Almoravids and the Meanings of Jihad* (Santa Barbara, 2010).

Mitchell, Timothy, 'McJihad: Islam in the U.S. global order', *Social Text* 73 (Winter 2002): 1–18.

Morabia, A., 'Ibn Taymiyya, dernier grand théoricien du jihad mediéval', *Bulletin d' études orientales* 30/2 (1978): 85–99.

Mourad, Suleiman A. and Lindsay, James. E., *The Intensification and Reorientation of Sunni Jihad Ideology in the Crusader Period: Ibn 'Asakir of Damascus (1105–1176) and His Age, with an Edition and Translation of Ibn 'Asakir's The Forty Hadiths for Inciting Jihad* (Leiden and Boston, 2013).

al-Mutanabbi, Abu Tayyib, *Al-Mutanabbi carmina cum commentario Wahidii*, ed. F. Dieterici (Berlin, 1856–61).

Narshakhi, Abu Bakr Muhammad ibn Ja'far, *The History of Bukhara*, trans. Richard N. Frye (Cambridge, Mass., 1954).

Noth, Albrecht, *Heiliger Krieg und Heiliger Kampf* (Bonn, 1986).

al-Sabi'i, Nasir ibn Sulayman ibn Sa'id, *Al-Khawarij wa'l-haqiqa al-gha'iba* (Muscat, 1420/1999).

Sivan, Emmanuel, *L'Islam et la Croisade: Idéologie et Propagande dans les Réactions Musulmanes aux Croisades* (Paris, 1968).

Tolstow, Sergei P., *Auf den Spuren der altchoresmischen Kultur*, trans. O Mehlitz (Berlin, 1953).

Treadwell, Luke, 'The account of the Samanid dynasty in Ibn Zafir al-Azdi's *Akhbar al-duwal al munqati'a*', *Iran* 43 (2005): 135–71.

Part I

Historical Antecedents of Contemporary Jihad

1

Divine Authority and Territorial Entitlement in the Hebrew Bible and the Qur'an

Reuven Firestone

Current public debates about jihad tend to examine religious war in Islam as a virtually *sui generis* phenomenon, and inquiries into religiously sanctioned war in Islam tend to investigate Islam independently of any larger context. But religions always exist within historical contexts, and religious responses to historical exigency can be compared and yield surprisingly fresh and interesting results. This chapter compares and contextualises the formation of biblical religion and Qur'anic religion to posit how and why the scriptural stratum for both is so similar on war and relations with the other. It then isolates the variables that caused the major difference in religious doctrinal expectations between Judaism and Islam regarding territorial control. Both Judaism and Islam recognise a divine right to be in political control of territory, and both accept the legality and even the responsibility of engaging in military force in order to achieve that control. Both base their positions on the authority of scripture, which in both Bible and Qur'an authorises bloodshed in order to secure proper monotheistic religious practice within a polytheistic environment that is believed to be threatening and improper. Both scriptures also provide significant detail regarding military tactics as well as the treatment of peoples holding other religious beliefs within the areas under divinely authorised control. The result is a scriptural stratum in both Judaism and Islam that reveals a remarkably similar phenomenology of war and relations with peoples outside the community.

This chapter argues that the similarity results from the related political, social and economic conditions in the local context under which the two religions emerged into history, even though their geneses are separated by more than 15 centuries and several hundred miles. While the local contexts exhibit important parallels and initially produced similar behaviours, both behaviours and expectations changed significantly after the initial stages of community emergence. The topic of concern for this chapter is territoriality. Whereas one religious community remained focused on a very limited area of political control, the other developed a position that assumed no geographical limit to political control. The divergence appears to reflect differences in two general areas: first, the relative success of the movements within the local context; and second, the impact of the larger religious and political environments outside of the local contexts. The initial similarities elicited similar behavioural and doctrinal responses, while the environmental differences that were later encountered caused the two communities to develop different paradigms of political expectation with regard to the control of territory.

This observation is of interest because it shows that the major differences in religious doctrine do not reflect essential differences in religion at the scriptural level. They reflect, rather, the differences in the way that religion has responded to the circumstances of history. One perhaps surprising conclusion is that, unlike the Hebrew Bible, the Qur'an lacks the notion of conquest and control of territory as divine command.

The Torah and the Qur'an

The Torah and the Qur'an are understood in their respective religious systems to represent the literal word of God. The Torah, which literally means 'instruction' in Hebrew, is the common religious term for the first five books of the Hebrew Bible (Genesis, Exodus, Leviticus, Numbers and Deuteronomy) that are understood in Jewish tradition to have been given fully and directly by God through the prophet Moses in one great public revelation at Mt. Sinai. While the other 19 books that make up the remainder of the Hebrew Bible have different levels of importance in the development of biblical and post-biblical Jewish legal and ethical tradition, the Torah represents the absolute core for Jewish legislation in all spheres of human activity. The Qur'an, likewise, represents the record of divine instruction given not in one public experience, as at Mt. Sinai, but rather serially throughout the course of the approximately 23-year prophetic career of Muhammad. Both represent the core of divine authority as a record of God's personal communication. Even when other factors become sources or motivations for the development or even genesis of religious law and tradition, such as custom or local tradition, historical exigencies, influence from other cultures and peoples or internal politics and social movements, the authority for religion resides in God, and the most obvious and acknowledged repository of divinely authoritative information is scripture. It is therefore appropriate to examine the Torah and the Qur'an as the authoritative foundation for the development of religious law and tradition, and the worldviews that these reflect and perpetuate.

While scripture represents the timeless and unlimited universal wisdom of God, it is contextualised in the particulars of 'scripted' – meaning written or recorded – revelation. The very nature of scripture reduces revelation to a finite record bound to the narrow particulars of era, culture, physical setting and language. It is limited further by its contextualisation within the limiting particularity of language in general. That is, words are finite vessels of meaning. In scripture, words are the containers holding specific messages of the divine. They are the remaining evidence of communication by a transcendent power no longer immediately accessible. In fixed form, words are the inert record of the unfathomable will of God, reduced to a static form in orthographic signs that are forbidden from being altered or replaced. While the will and wisdom of God is by definition eternal and unlimited, once recorded it becomes limited by the confining attributes of scripture described above.

On the other hand, the supple nature of language is such that words, phrases and idioms always have a range of meanings, and those meanings evolve and are adjusted by changes in culture, technology and social systems, among other factors. These same cultural and technological changes influence the worldviews of the believers who read and respond to their scripture. New ways of reading and understanding the meaning of scripture therefore emerge in every generation based on the changes and evolution in language and in the human condition in general (which are of course closely related). Evolving ways of reading are then reflected in the derivative literatures and behaviours recorded by communities of believers. This record is 'interpretation' in its widest sense, and many genres and schools of interpretation have evolved within both Judaism and Islam, not only within the specific discourse of official scriptural interpretation in these religions (*midrash, perush, ta'wil, tafsir*) but in law, ethics, theology, cosmology, metaphysics and ritual practice, among other fields. It is the combination of the fixed wording of the scriptural core and the constantly changing and evolving process of interpretation that makes for the development of religion.

With that in mind, our first task in understanding the divine right of a religious authority or community to exercise political control over territory in these religions is to understand the most basic, contextual messages regarding this issue as conveyed in scripture. 'Contextual', in this sense, means getting as close as possible to the meaning of scripture in its un-interpreted, original context of articulation. It must be acknowledged that from the scholarly perspective this is an impossible task. We do not have all the necessary tools to understand the full contextual meaning of scripture because we cannot reconstruct the exact meanings of the ancient words in which it was conveyed, the historical contexts of its revelation, or even the absolute veracity of the text itself. While religious authorities sometimes claim to have resolved these problems, the literatures of religious tradition prove the opposite by their intense examination of the structure of scriptural discourse and the meanings of scriptural language, and by their obvious disagreements about virtually any issue that is discussed.

War and Territorial Control in the Hebrew Bible

The Torah is the core of the Hebrew Bible from the perspective of all forms of Judaism. Many modern studies have examined the notion of war in the Hebrew Bible, with special emphasis on the Book of Deuteronomy and the Deuteronomic material found in other biblical books because of their late redaction according to most biblical scholarship, and their well-developed notions of war. Fighting between polities, usually defined as tribal (kinship) groups, was a well-attested activity in the ancient Near

East, and the Israelites, like all the communities among whom they lived, are depicted in both biblical and extra-biblical texts as engaging in wars. Wars – or what might be more accurately called battles – in the ancient Near East were typically sanctioned by divine powers. Just as God or 'the God of Israel' provided authority, moral and material support, and is even depicted as fighting on behalf of the Israelites,[1] other gods are depicted as doing virtually the same on behalf of their own peoples.[2]

The Torah is contextualised in the experience of the Sinaitic revelation that occurred, according to the Bible, prior to the biblical conquest of Canaan and the transition of that land to the control of Israel. But according to current biblical scholarship, the Torah record of the Sinaitic revelation is not a pre-conquest source as it indicates itself to be, but rather a document that assumed its present form after the Israelites were in control of the territory that would be called the Land of Israel. The Book of Deuteronomy, for example, often makes oblique reference to Jerusalem without mentioning its name because it was not supposed to have been conquered yet. It is referred to as 'the site where the Lord your God will choose to establish His name', language that carefully articulates a political reality which existed many centuries after the period of revelation.[3]

The Torah is thus made up of layers of text that reflect different historical periods, which in turn reflect different political realities within the tribes and communities that were unified under the name of Israel. The centrality of the Torah did not render the remaining books irrelevant. In fact, other biblical books often work out notions, authorised and centralised by their appearance in the Torah, through narrative and by strengthening, interpreting and sometimes adjusting what is considered to be their general thrust or value.[4] What follows, therefore, is supported by citation from both the most important texts of the Torah and the biblical books lying outside that central core.

Territorial Boundaries in the Hebrew Bible

The first issue that must be examined in this discussion is political context. The Israelite people emerge into history in a place and time in which empires had little immediate impact on the political relations of local peoples.[5] This period is characterised in the scholarly literature as the 'crisis' of the Late Bronze Age (Late Bronze II) during which previously established imperial control of the northern Levant collapsed. This resulted in the fragmentation of Canaan into relatively weak, regionally defined units, which allowed for the gradual emergence of a community that called itself 'Israel' in the early Iron Age (late thirteenth and twelfth centuries BCE – Iron I).[6] The contraction of empire enabled rival tribes and tribal confederations to compete for control of economic and military resources on a largely even playing field. Fighting was a natural and expected part of political and communal life in the region, and coalitions of tribal communities regularly engaged in defence or initiated conflict in order to protect or expand access to trade and natural and human resources.

Religion reflected kinship and tribe during this period. Tribal communities had their own tribal gods, and religion was similar to ethnicity – something one was born into rather than something one joined.[7] Fighting between tribes, therefore, also meant fighting between discrete religious communities, and victory for the tribe was also the victory of the tribal god.[8] One religious/tribal group that emerged into history during this period established a federated tribal kingdom that became associated with the name 'Israel'.[9] What is particularly unique about this kingdom is that it developed a complex literature and record of its history and rule which survived it. That literature became the sacred text of a people which, after losing its political independence, came to be defined (not necessarily by itself) as a religion. The Hebrew Bible is this literature and record, and it contains information about the territorial boundaries of the land that Israel claimed to have controlled under the God that brought it victory.

God is the creator of the universe (Genesis 1) and is therefore its sovereign and owner. This is articulated clearly in Psalm 24:1: 'The earth is the Lord's and all that it holds, the world and its inhabitants.'[10] There is no direct relationship, however, between the universal nature of God's sovereignty and the limited nature of the political sovereignty of God's special people (Israel). In all cases, the latter is severely limited. Nevertheless, the Bible is not consistent in its delineation of official boundaries of the 'Land of Israel', meaning the territories that God authorised the Israelites to control. Moshe Weinfeld describes two different, idealised views that emerged out of earlier biblical sources.[11] The earliest depicts the smallest area, using the idiom 'from Dan until Be'er-Sheva', meaning near today's northern border between the modern states of Israel and Lebanon and southward to the current city of Beersheba.[12] National (or ethnic/tribal) borders are fluid and shift with time and fluctuations in power, and this was certainly the case with ancient Israel. However, the following two 'maps' represent idealised delineations that do not seem to have conformed with the reality of political power. The first of these is associated with the cult centre in Shiloh before the tenth century BCE and expands the territory northward to today's Hama (biblical Levo-Hamath) on the Orontes River and then moves east of Damascus. These borders are articulated most distinctly in Numbers 34:3–12.[13] The second is the latest delineation of the First Temple Period, which Weinfeld associates with the revival and national expansion in the days of Hezekiah (reigned c.715–687 BCE) or Josiah (reigned c.641–609 BCE) and represented by a revisionist programme referred to in biblical scholarship as the Deuteronomist School.[14] In this depiction, found in part in Genesis 15:18–21 and Exodus 23:31, the borders are expanded as far as to include a portion of the Euphrates River from just north of Carchemish (around today's Turkish town of Birecik), southward along the Euphrates to today's Al-Raqqah.

According to Weinfeld, these territorial demarcations represent back projections that reflect idealised stages in the history of Israelite settlement, for which there is no corroborative information to support actual political/military control. The different territorial maps reflect different units of power that were dominant in different periods of First Temple Israelite history. The competing maps, representing different communities, suggest (along with other data) that the Bible we have today was finalised long after the end of any fighting that would have been necessary in order to establish control of territory. The purpose of each map was to provide divine authority for what already was a fait accompli.

The three biblical maps described here suggest an expansion of territory that probably occurred as a result of demographic expansion, but it is unlikely that the borders of the latter maps represent real political power over the territories demarcated. In any case, Israelite political power weakened and shrank, most drastically as a result of the destruction of the First Jerusalem Temple by the Babylonian Empire in 586 BCE and the exile of many Israelites to Babylon. Some 70 years later, a portion of the Babylonian exiles returned and began to rebuild the Jerusalem Temple with those who had remained in the land. This marks the beginning of the Second Temple Period, during which the territory under Israelite control was smaller than the smallest of the earlier maps. The borders of this territory are not outlined in the Bible, which by this time had reached a certain level of fixity, but are referred to in the post-biblical tradition literature of the Talmud, which contains material as early as the third or second century BCE but did not become canonical until around the time of the Arab conquests of the seventh century.

The Talmud does not refer to the borders of the Land of Israel using political terms because of the complete loss of political power over those lands. It refers, rather, to a consecration of territory when idolatry was eliminated and life was regulated according to the laws of God and the Torah. The earlier and larger biblical maps discussed above are conflated into a single map associated with the great conquest by the Israelites under Joshua. Joshua's conquest is referred to as the 'first consecration' of the land. This consecration was not permanent, however; it ended with the destruction of the First Temple. The smaller area of control during the Second Temple period re-settled by the returning exiles from Babylon represented to the Talmudic sages a 'second consecration', and this consecration remained forever.[15]

The maps provided by Jewish scripture and tradition differ in territorial reach and reflect different periods and different factions within the Israelite community. They have in common a clear and distinct limitation in territory. There is no expectation that the Israelites would become a world empire or that their political, military or even religious control would extend beyond the borders delineated and limited in the sacred text of scripture. This endures even in the face of empires such as Babylon that credited its reach, at least in part, to the strength of its national god, Marduk.

Conquest as Divine Command

The Torah contains numerous passages that legitimate the conquest of Canaan by God's command, and the narratives contained in the biblical Book of Joshua describe a successful military campaign by a united community of Israel responding to God's command to fight. An alternative account is provided in the Book of Judges, in which Israel takes possession of Canaan through gradual settlement that was fragmented, difficult and fraught with setbacks.[16] Over the past century, biblical scholarship in combination with archaeological evidence and developing methodologies in the study of history and society has produced a number of theories to account for the appearance of Israel in the Land of Canaan. These may be broken down into the following categories: conquest of Canaan or peaceful infiltration from without; social revolution from within Canaanite society or a change in internal economics within it; or an ethnogenesis out of a 'mixed multitude' of loosely organised indigenous and non-indigenous tribal and kin-based groups and refugee individuals that congregated in the marginal hill-country to emerge as Israel in the Iron I highlands of Canaan.[17] Of all the theories presented, the one that is *least* likely from the standpoint of biblical scholarship and archaeological evidence is the theory of unified military conquest as presented in Joshua and authorised by a range of Torah verses.[18] Nevertheless, whether or not a historical Israelite conquest of Canaan actually occurred, the Hebrew Bible clearly includes the divinely authorised – even *commanded* – conquest of Canaan as a primary theme, and it is this fact that must be addressed when considering the Jewish view of divine authority and territorial entitlement. It is not the only account of the conquest of Canaan, however, and in that fact lies the possibility of a range of interpretive strategies – even from within the religious tradition – that can be anchored in authoritative biblical texts.

Extent of Rule

We have noted, following Weinfeld, that the greatest extent of rule as depicted in the Bible did not extend beyond the third map cited above and it is virtually certain, in any case, that these borders were idealistic and theoretical only. Moreover, there seems to be little or no evidence for a universal political or religious vision for Israel. Occasional verses can be interpreted in a more universal way, but they are exceptional; for example, Abraham and his descendants are expected to become a great nation (*goy gadol* – Gen. 12:1ff.) that will rule multiple peoples ('Let peoples serve you and nations bow to you' – Gen. 27:29). Another places Jerusalem at the religious centre of the ecumene (*oikoumene*):

> The peoples shall gaze on it with joy, and the many nations shall go and shall say: 'Come, let us go up to the Mount of the Lord, to the House of the God of Jacob; that He may instruct us in His ways, and that we may walk in His paths, for instruction shall come forth from Zion, and the word of the Lord from Jerusalem.'[19]

If these verses articulate a view of imperial conquest, which is hardly arguable, it would represent a minor view, as the overwhelming message embedded in the Hebrew Bible argues for and justifies the domination of a rather small and discrete geographical area, persistently characterised more as a safe haven, a shelter protected against the temptations of idolatry and the predations of neighbouring peoples rather than as a platform for extended or universal conquest.

War and Territorial Control in the Qur'an

Although not yet as thoroughly examined by modern scholarship as the Bible, a number of studies on war in Islam discuss the Qur'an. These have demonstrated without doubt that whatever might be the operative term for fighting ('*qital*' or 'jihad', for example), the obligation laid upon Muhammad's followers to fight 'in the path of God' (meaning on behalf of God's religion or community) is an oft-repeated message of the Qur'an.[20] Fighting between tribal (kinship) groups was a well-attested activity in pre-Islamic Arabia, and communities had their own patron deities that served as sources for tribal cohesion.[21] Although the evidence is not as overwhelming as in the case of the ancient Near East, sources from pre-Islamic Arabia and later sources treating the period describe offerings of thanksgiving and vows associated with war or protection from war to gods.[22] The early Muslims, like all the Arabian communities among whom they lived, were involved in raids and battles against groups defined as 'other' – usually via kinship distinctions, particularly during the early period after fighting became an option for the community. And like their polytheist Arabian brethren, they appealed to God for help in war and conflict. Like the Hebrew Bible, the Qur'an assures the believers of reward and military success,[23] requires material support of the war effort (Q. 57:10) and assistance referred to as a loan that will be repaid in great abundance[24] and even advises certain military formations.[25] Great reward in this world and the next is assured to those engaging in fighting.[26] As in the Torah, a variety of purposes for fighting are also spelled out in the Qur'an, as well as rules for the treatment of prisoners in various categories.[27]

Unlike the Torah, however, the Qur'an does not offer clear guidance regarding the conquest of territory. On the one hand, the Qur'an is quite clear that 'the dominion of the heavens and the earth and all between them belongs to God',[28] but it does not follow this assertion with what could be considered to be the logical next step: that of authorising military conquest by the Messenger of God. In fact, the Qur'an has little to say about territory in general. This is especially the case in those verses, such as Qur'an 54:1ff., that seem to convey an eschatological sense of an impending 'end time', where physical place is unimportant as a stage for worldly human affairs.[29] According to Angelika Neuwirth, in the earliest period when the revelations conveyed a sense of approaching apocalypse, a concept of territory had virtually no importance.[30] In relation to this early perspective but perhaps somewhat later, the Qur'an articulates the notion that the deserted territories of extinct peoples are signs of divine destruction in recompense for those peoples' theological and ethical failures. According to this historical topos, ubiquitous in the Qur'an, all peoples that ignore or abandon the divine message urged upon them by God's prophets are inevitably destroyed, leaving the possibility of salvation open for those communities that hold proper beliefs and engage in proper behaviours.[31]

Concurrently with the articulation of this view, the Qur'an begins to identify Mecca as a locus of salvation, presenting it as a calque on the sacred biblical sites of the holy land and making it a 'second Jerusalem'. The early Medinan period represents a period of exile from the holy Mecca, but by the end of Muhammad's life Mecca and the region at large acquire biblical associations – for example, through Abraham's personal association with the raising up of the Ka'ba and the blessings of Mecca[32] – which carry salvific as well as historical significance. When the sacred precinct of Mecca and its environs in the Hijaz come under the control of the new community of believers, 'a divinely blessed topography of the new religion' is brought under Muslim control.[33] The parallel with the Bible becomes complete with the divinely guided conquest of the Hijaz under the guidance of God's (warrior-)prophet, an event that parallels and perfects the incomplete conquest of the Land of Canaan by Joshua, the warrior-successor of the biblical prophet Moses.

Two likely historical parallels may be added to the parallel literary topos noticed by Neuwirth. The first is the socio-political and religious environments out of which the Israelite and Islamic expressions of monotheism emerged. In neither the time of the emergence of Israel nor the emergence of Islam was any imperial power able to exert or monopolise control over the local communities and the peoples of the immediate area. We have noted how, in the biblical context, the collapse of earlier empires left the area called Canaan outside the political control of any powerful entity that could prevent the emergence of a new independent community in the Israelites. In the region of west-central Arabia called the Hijaz, likewise, no imperial power had been able to monopolise control over local communities during the period leading up to the emergence of Islam. This was not the case in northern Arabia, where large areas bordering Byzantium in the west and Persia in the east were under the influence and often political control of the two great empires; nor in South Arabia, which was under the influence and occasional control of Axum/Abyssinia.[34]

One could apply to the Arabian context much of the same language that was used to describe the environment out of which Israelite religion had emerged a millennium and a half earlier. The lack of an overarching unifying power enabled evenly matched rival communities – meaning tribes and tribal confederations – to compete for economic and military resources. Socio-political organisation in the region was based upon units and relationships of kinship and tribe. Fighting was a natural and expected part of political and communal life in the region, and coalitions of tribal communities regularly engaged in offensive or defensive conflict in order to protect or expand access to trade and natural and human resources. The lack of imperial power allowed central Arabia a degree of political fragmentation into relatively weak, regionally defined kinship units that could not prevent the emergence of a new community that would define itself as a community (*umma*) of 'believers'.

The second parallel is found in the religious environment of the Hijaz, which according to Islamic sources was overwhelmingly polytheistic prior to the emergence of Islam. Here the parallel seems less comprehensive and the extent of polytheism in pre-Islamic Arabia at the dawn of Islam less certain.[35] Religion perhaps had less daily impact on the lives of Arabs in the sixth and seventh centuries than those of Israelites of the seventh and eighth centuries BCE; but, as in the earlier case, it was organised, at least in part, around kinship and tribe. This is not as obvious nor as total in seventh-century Arabia as in the ancient Near Eastern environment. We know through the work of Michael Lecker, for example, that units of pagan tribes could include Jews and vice versa,[36] so the correlation between kinship and religion was not as absolute as seems to have been the case in ancient Canaan. Nevertheless, some tribes seem to have had their own tribal gods, referred to by Robert Hoyland as 'patron deities'.[37] Fighting between tribes, therefore, could also mean fighting between religious communities and/or their tribal gods, and victories would be considered victories of patron deities as well as of their peoples.[38]

While we know that Jewish and Christian communities lived in the Hijaz, and there is evidence of other possible independent pre-Islamic expressions of monotheism,[39] the impression the sources give is that the overwhelming majority of the population of central and west-central Arabia was polytheist. To Montgomery Watt, pre-Islamic Arabs were not particularly interested in religion of any kind.[40] According to classical Islamic sources (including the Qur'an), they were hopelessly and deeply mired in the muck of idolatry and its associated immorality. Like Israel more than a millennium before, the early emerging community of Arabian believers therefore would have considered themselves to have been opposed from all sides, feeling themselves isolated and beleaguered in a sea of non-believers. This was certainly the case in Mecca, according to the classical Islamic sources, but there remained the expectation, at least, that the situation would change when the believers moved to Medina where they anticipated being recognised by fellow-believers in the form of the Medinan Jews. They were, of course, severely disappointed. Like adherents of new religious movements throughout time and place, the early Muslims were opposed by the establishment religions of their day – not only did the Arabian polytheists reject them, but so did the Jews (and Christians). Jews and Christians could no more accept the prophethood of Muhammad than Muslims today could accept the prophethood of Baha'ullah, the post-Muhammad prophet of the Baha'i faith.

The Qur'an expresses bitterness and disappointment that the Prophet was not acknowledged as such by the Jews as well as the polytheists.[41] The community felt under pressure from all sides, and this feeling finds a parallel in Israel's sense of itself as embattled, expressed in the Hebrew Bible. With this observation we move from noting phenomenological parallels between emerging Israelite monotheism and emerging Islamic monotheism to treating some of the important distinctions.

Religious Conversion

Perhaps the most significant distinction between the nascent monotheisms of Israel and Islam is the phenomenon of conversion, which was virtually non-existent in the biblical environment but quite at the centre of relations between early Muslims and other Arabians. Conversion is unknown in the Hebrew Bible, a fact which conveys the essential lack of distinction common in the region between religion and tribe. The Hebrew Bible recognises that Egyptians or Edomites could be absorbed into the Israelite community after three generations of living among them (Deut. 23:8–9), presumably because by that time they would have assimilated the language, culture and religious mores of the Israelite community. The Book of Ruth seems to convey a similar world-view when it narrates the story of a Moabite woman who chooses to leave her tribal culture and religion after the death of her husband in order to follow the culture and religion of her Israelite mother-in-law. Moabite and Hebrew languages were dialects of one another, and the economic bases of both communities seem to have been virtually identical. But each community was distinct in terms of tribal kinship and the identity of its god, and that was enough. The radical nature of Ruth's extraordinary dedication to her mother-in-law is the exception that proves the rule of tribal religion's ethnic distinction. These cases reflect the pre-Hellenistic phenomenon of Near Eastern tribal religion. It was no easier to change one's religion (meaning, in essence, loyalty to one's tribal god) than to change one's ethnic identity.

In such an environment it would be virtually impossible to engage in proselytising. Only conquest or the imposition of forced acculturation, something akin to what we call 'cultural imperialism', might cause an absolute change in religious loyalty. Such a notion seems to have been virtually inconceivable to the Israelites, except in some far-off vision of an ideal future in which God would bring about the necessary changes himself (Micah 4:1–3 and Isaiah 2:2–4). There is no command or expectation for the community of Israel to engage in such a programme itself. Territorial control was solely for the purpose of establishing a monotheistic religio-cultural 'safe haven' where the Israelites could practise their unique religious civilisation, sheltered from the universal pull of idolatry.

By the seventh century, however, religious conversion was a commonplace; not only conversion from one religion to another but also from one form or sectarian notion of religion to another. Certainly among Christians, but also to a significant extent among Jews, religious identity did not necessarily conform to ethnic or tribal identity. Most of the names associated with the Jews of seventh-century Arabia, for example, were not biblical or rabbinic but Arabian, thus suggesting that by that time the old one-to-one association of religion with ethnic culture or tribe had declined to the point where Arabs could remain ethnically Arab and religiously Jewish.[42] The direct correspondence of tribe to religion in the Mediterranean seems to have declined and eventually ended with the destruction and absorption of tribal religions under the Greeks and Romans. Conversion was an obvious reality by the time that an entire pagan empire of many different peoples and religions had converted to Christianity under the Byzantines. There was no reason to assume that something similar could not occur within Arabia. One must keep in mind that early Islam made the claim to be a trans-kinship-based tribe of religious believers. As Qur'an 9:11 says: 'If they repent, establish prayer and give alms, they are your brothers in religion.' When Islam became successful within the peninsula, it was not long before a universal aspiration parallel to that of Christianity was bound to arise.

When Islam emerged into history it may have appeared to its adherents as a distinct Arabian form of monotheism revealed in order to provide a more perfect and indigenous alternative to the flawed, foreign forms of monotheism imported to Arabia by Christians and Jews. Thus God repeatedly informs the Qur'anic audience of an authentic, indigenous Arabian monotheism. *This* revelation is an *Arabic* Qur'an.[43] But by the end of Muhammad's life, according to the traditional sources, invitations to conversion were sent out to the leaders of the major empires, suggesting that, even if such letters are not authentic, the notion of Islam being a universal religion certainly emerged fairly early on.[44] Majid Khadduri notes the personal character of Islamic law as it was first formulated under a caliphal empire that was assumed to become truly universal. All Muslims lived according to obligations and privileges that had no territorial restriction. Only after it became clear that the great expansion of the empire could not be sustained were jurists forced to consider formulations of law that included territorial limitation: 'The overriding principle of coexistence [with stable non-Muslim polities] compelled Islam to accept territorial limitations, although many a jurist continued to view them as irrelevant.'[45]

Territorial Boundaries in the Qur'an

I have already noted the parallel between the Hebrew Bible and Qur'an in the notion of sacred place and divine authority for its ownership. In both scriptures God is the creator, sovereign and owner of the world. Moreover, God can grant authority and divine blessing to whomever he wishes. In the Hebrew Bible, God gives a specific land to a people that will respond to His authority.[46] In the Qur'an, the idiom is constructed around the notion of favoured human communities whose righteousness merits inheriting or taking the place of previous communities that failed to live up to the divine will. One repeated articulation in the Qur'an is 'God will make you successors on earth'.[47]

Notice the precise territorial association in the biblical notion and the lack of specific territory associated in the Qur'anic notion. The Bible notes very carefully, even if not consistently, the territorial boundaries within which the chosen community wields authority. The Qur'an does not. Even in the case of the parallel notion of sacred or inviolate territory in the Sacred Mosque (in Mecca),[48] the Qur'an never delineates actual boundaries. Even the word 'Hijaz', for example, which has become the defining term for the core Islamic heartland and holy land, is never found in the Qur'an.[49]

Another important parallel between the Bible and Qur'an, but with its own crucial distinction, is that both scriptures note the establishment of a divinely authorised community, membership of which is based on religio-ethnic kinship. It is important to note that the recognition by scripture of this notion demonstrates that such a community had come into existence prior to the canonization of scripture. The crucial distinction is again territorial. In the Hebrew Bible, that community is recognised as a polity defined as the people (or nation) of Israel[50] established on the Land of Israel.[51] In the Qur'an the community is not quite a polity, as it is a religious kinship designed to transcend the divisiveness of genealogical kinship, but it is not defined territorially. The reason for this distinction may lie in the chronology by which scriptural text became fixed and canonical. In the case of the Hebrew Bible, final canonization occurred after the establishment (and subsequent loss) of territorial control, subsequent to the long process of formation and territorial negotiation that accompanies the establishment of any territorial polity. In the case of the Qur'an, canonization occurred in the middle of formation, when borders were fluid and the territory under influence or control was expanding.

The lack of consciousness of territorial boundaries in the Qur'an may also reflect the likelihood that the community, which certainly existed, was still in the process of formation and self-definition. Because the canonization of scripture occurred so early in the process of community formation, scripture could not establish a clear structure for the community. Scholars have long noted the lack of Qur'anic interest in political systems, an aspect that is quite different from the Hebrew Bible which invests significant effort in describing systems of governance.

It is clear from the above that, unlike the Hebrew Bible, the Qur'an expresses virtually no concern for specific territorial boundaries. It does express the need, in parallel with the Hebrew Bible, for the chosen community to be in military and/or political control of the political centre and sacred sites, but the notion of a specific land promised to a chosen people would be difficult to construct out of the Qur'an. And although it clearly designates the 'Sacred Mosque', Mecca and the Ka'ba as sacred territory, this seems to have developed late within the Qur'an and possibly as a basis for the claim for authenticity of a religion independent of the religions of the Bible (Judaism and Christianity)[52] rather than as something that required a priori political control. The need for political control of defined territories is a second step, and that step is taken in later Islamic juridical literature. The well-known division of the world into the spheres or abodes of Islam and war (or Islam, war and peace) is not Qur'anic, nor is it even found in the hadith.[53]

Conquest as Divine Command

The Qur'an itself does not contain a clear concept of conquest. It does contain frequent reference to campaigns during the Medinan period to bring tribal entities under the control or influence of the early Muslim community, but not in order to conquer and control land. As Chase Robinson describes them, '[t]he political context of this campaigning was tribal rather than imperial: Forces were small, marches short and shows of strength more frequent than actual violence'.[54] The operative term for conquest in post-Qur'anic literature, *fath,* carries different meanings in the Qur'an and is glossed by early commentators such as Muqatil ibn Sulayman as 'make a judgement'. Thus Qur'an 48:1, generally translated as '[w]e have granted you a clear victory', is glossed by Sulayman as '[w]e have made a clear judgement for you'.[55] The sense of victory associated with the word may have emerged only later and among Muslim intellectuals after the conquest, when the transfer of control of Mecca to Muhammad was envisioned as a triumphal victory.

God's commands to Muhammad and his followers in the Qur'an tend to be couched in terms of defence.[56] Even those that appear particularly aggressive and that suggest the initiation of hostilities look retaliatory rather than imperialist.[57] They do not convey the sense of a campaign to gain and control land or to establish political control over territories as do biblical parallels. In short, the notion of conquest and control of territory as divine command cannot be supported as the contextual message of the Qur'an. That sense of the Qur'an emerges later among the historians and in the accompanying commentary literature.

Conclusion

This chapter has attempted to demonstrate that the historical context out of which both the new community that became known as Israel and the new community that became known as Muslims emerged was similar enough that the scriptures of both communities (which represent the earliest information we have about their emergence) exhibit similar attitudes toward engaging in war. Both condone and even encourage military confrontation in order to carve out space for the practice of the new religion in a hostile environment. However, whereas the Hebrew

Bible delineates clear boundaries of divinely authorised control that are presented through different and competing territorial maps, the Qur'an has no reference to any boundaries of lands requiring divinely authorised control. This has allowed great leeway in interpretation among Muslims in subsequent generations. The young community of believers found itself gaining control of more and more territory during the period of conquest after the death of Muhammad and the end of revelation. Without delineated boundaries, there was no reason to presume a limit to the areas of potential control. As the Muslim world expanded, it was easy to assume that its victories were by God's design and that the Muslim rulers had the divine right to rule. This was the very conclusion that was . drawn by Christians a few centuries earlier as the pagan nature of the Roman Empire collapsed under the influence of Christianity – that God had confirmed through history the truth of religion and the right of the victors to rule all others.

But history has the annoying tendency to upend grand assumptions, and just as the Christian empires collapsed, so too did the Islamic empires. Justification for religious empire cannot be found contextually in any of the three great monotheistic scriptures. But through the interpretive process, some people manage to discover meaning in scripture that can justify their political desires. A maxim might be coined to summarise this tendency: where there is a strong enough political will, there is always an exegetical way.

Notes

1. See, for example, Exod. 15:1–10; Deut. 20:1.
2. James B. Pritchard, *The Ancient Near East, Volume 1: An Anthology of Texts and Pictures* (Princeton, 1958), pp. 209–10; and *The Ancient Near East, Volume 2: A New Anthology of Texts and Pictures* (Princeton, 1975), p. 168.
3. Deut. 12:5, 11, 21, 14:23, 24, 16:6; 2 Kgs. 22–3; 2 Chr. 34–5.
4. See, for example, Moshe Weinfeld, *The Promise of the Land* (Berkeley and Los Angeles, 1993), who regularly cites biblical material outside of the Torah relating to core Torah texts. On internal biblical exegesis that interprets or adjusts prior material, see Benjamin Sommer, 'Inner-biblical interpretation', in Adele Berlin, Marc Zvi Brettler and Michael A. Fishbane (eds.), *The Jewish Study Bible* (Oxford, 2004): 1829–35.

5. The question of the origin of the people of Israel remains unresolved. For a review of the various theories, see Ann Killebrew, *Biblical Peoples and Ethnicity: An Archaeological Study of Egyptians, Canaanites, Philistines, and Early Israel 1300–1100 BCE* (Atlanta, 2005), pp. 149–96.

6. Ibid., pp. 13–14, 21–92.

7. Exod. 5:1–2, Num. 21:29; 1 Kgs. 11:6–8; 1 Sam. 5:1–7; 2 Kgs. 23:13; Ziony Zevit, *The Religions of Ancient Israel* (London, 2001), pp. 612–3, 642–6; A. D. Nock, *Conversion* (Oxford, 1933).

8. A classic example is the battle described in 2 Kings 3 from the Israelite perspective and on the Mesha Stele from the perspective of the Moabites, each claiming victory for its god.

9. Donald Redford, *Egypt, Canaan, and Israel in Ancient Times* (Princeton, 1992), pp. 257–80.

10. See also Pss. 50:12, 89:12; Exod. 19:5, etc.

11. Weinfeld, *The Promise of the Land*, pp. 52–75. I centre my evidence around the extraordinarily broad and careful work of Weinfeld, whose work provides a convenient structure for the thrust of my argument in this chapter.

12. Judg. 20:1; 1 Sam. 3:20; 2 Sam. 3:10; 17:11, etc. See Weinfeld, *The Promise of the Land*, p. 52 n. 1.

13. Weinfeld, *The Promise of the Land*, pp. 55–64.

14. This is because it is most obviously represented by the Book of Deuteronomy, but Deuteronomist material can be found in other biblical books, most notably Joshua, Judges, 1 and 2 Samuel and 1 and 2 Kings. See D. R. Driver, *The International Critical Commentary, Deuteronomy* (New York, 1903), pp. i–xcv; Martin Noth, *The Deuteronomist History of Israel* (Sheffield, 1981); Frank Cross, *Canaanite Myth and Hebrew Epic* (Cambridge, MA, 1973), pp. 274–89.

15. Babylonian Talmud, Hagigah 3b. See also, Mishnah 'Eduyot 8:6, Babylonian Talmud, Megillah 10a, Yebamot 16a, Makkot 19a.

16. See Jo Ann Hacket, '"There was no king in Israel:" The era of the judges', in M. D. Coogan (ed.), *The Oxford History of the Biblical World* (New York, 2001): 132–64; Redford, *Egypt, Canaan and Israel in Biblical Times*, pp. 263–9.

17. These views are presented and critiqued by Killebrew, *Biblical Peoples and Ethnicity*, pp. 181–5.

18. Ibid., p. 182.

19. Mic. 4:1–3 and Isa. 2:2–4.

20. Much Islamic treatment of war is post-Qur'anic, but law and policy is often traced back to scripture for authority. See Majid Khadduri, *War and Peace*

in the Law of Islam (Baltimore, 1955); 'Abd al-Aziz Sachedina, 'The develop-
ment of *jihad* in Islamic revelation and history', in James Turner Johnson and
John Kelsay (eds.), *Cross, Crescent, and Sword* (New York, 1990): 35–50;
Rudolph Peters, *Jihad in Classical and Modern Islam* (Princeton, 1996); Bassam Tibi, 'War and peace in Islam', in Terry Nardin (ed.), *The Ethics of War
and Peace: Religious and Secular Perspectives* (Princeton, 1996): 128–45;
Harfiyah Abdel Haleem, Oliver Ramsbotham, Saba Risaluddin and Brian
Wicker, *The Crescent and the Cross: Muslim and Christian Approaches to
War and Peace* (New York, 1998); Reuven Firestone, *Jihad: The Origin
of Holy War in Islam* (New York, 1999); David Cook, *Understanding Ji-
had* (London, Berkeley and Los Angeles, 2005); Michael Bonner, *Jihad in
Islamic History* (Princeton, 2006); John Kelsay, *Arguing the Just War in Islam*
(Cambridge, MA, 2007).

21. Robert Hoyland, *Arabia and the Arabs From the Bronze Age to the Coming
of Islam* (London, 2001), pp. 139–45.

22. Muhammad's grandfather 'Abd al-Muttalib is depicted in the most authoritative biography of the Prophet as imploring God or the great local deity
Hubal repeatedly to protect his larger tribe or smaller kinship group from
harm. See A. Guillaume, *The Life of Muhammad: A Translation of Ibn Ishaq's
Sirat Rasul Allah* (Oxford, 1955), pp. 24–8.

23. Q. 2:217–18; 3:139, 146, 173–4; 4:74, 94–6; 5:33–6; 8:38–41, 55–63 (cf.
Deut. 9:1–5; Judg. 20:29; Isa. 42:14–17).

24. Q. 2:245; 57:11, 18, 64:17 (cf. Prov. 19:17).

25. Q. 61:4 (cf. Josh. 6:2–5).

26. Q. 33:27 (cf. Deut. 6:10–11); 59:7–8; 3:157–8, 169–172, 195; 4:74; 47:4–6.

27. Q. 8:67, 70–1; 47:4 (cf. Deut. 20:10–21, 21:10–14); Khalid Blankinship,
The End of the Jihad State (Albany, 1994), pp. 12–13.

28. Q. 5:17. See also 3:89, 23:88, 25:2, 36:83.

29. David Cook, *Studies in Muslim Apocalyptic* (Princeton, 2002); Angelika
Neuwirth, 'Geography', *Encyclopedia of the Qur'an* (Leiden, 2002), Vol. 2:
293–313 (299).

30. Neuwirth, 'Geography'.

31. Q. 7:35–115; 11:25–112; 46:21–7, etc.

32. Q. 2:125–32; 14:37–41.

33. Neuwirth, 'Geography', p. 312.

34. G. W. Bowersock, *Roman Arabia* (Cambridge, MA, 1983); Irfan Shahid,
Rome and the Arabs (Washington DC, 1984); Walter Mueller, 'Survey of
the history of the Arabian Peninsula from the first century A.D. to the rise
of Islam', in *Studies in the History of Arabia*, Vol. 2: 'Pre-Islamic Arabia'

(Riyadh, King Saud University, 1984): 125–31; Hoyland, *Arabia and the Arabs*; Klaus Schippman, *Ancient South Arabia from the Queen of Sheba to the Advent of Islam* (Princeton, 2001).

35. Hoyland and others agree on the thorough polytheism of the region at least prior to the fourth century CE despite occasional Jewish inscriptions (*Arabia and the Arabs*, pp. 139–66). Gerald Hawting is sceptical of the Islamic sources' depiction of pre-Islamic polytheism, including al-Kalbi's *Kitab al-Aṣnām* (*The Idea of Idolatry and the Emergence of Islam*, Cambridge, 1999). Where South Arabia is concerned, Schippman is able, like Hoyland for the whole peninsula, to list many deities that were worshipped, but it remains unclear to what extent Christian and Jewish or indigenous Arabian forms of monotheism became popular. Schippman suggests that new monotheistic ideas and practices may not have penetrated beyond the privileged or upper classes (*Ancient South Arabia*, p. 93). See also Bowersock, *Roman Arabia*; Irfan Shahid, *Rome and the Arabs* and *Byzantium and the Arabs in the Fourth Century* (Washington DC, 1984).

36. Michael Lecker, *Muslims, Jews and Pagans: Studies on Early Islamic Medina* (Leiden, 1995); *Jews and Arabs in Pre- and Early Islamic Arabia* (Aldershot, 1998).

37. Hoyland mentions the god Almaqah of the Sabaeans, Wadd of the Minaeans, 'Amm of the Qatabians and Sayin of the Hadramites (*Arabia and the Arabs*, pp. 140–4). As in the ancient Near East, patron deities existed alongside deities associated with certain functions such as irrigation.

38. I have not found conclusive evidence from inscriptions that mention thanksgiving offerings to patron deities for victories in battle. Compare 'Abd al-Muttalib's willingness to offer his son to fulfil a vow to offer a son to the God of the Ka'ba for protecting him by giving him ten sons (Guillaume, *The Life of Muhammad*, pp. 66–8).

39. Schippman, *Ancient South Arabia*, pp. 63, 93. The counter-prophet Muslim (or Musaylima) may be one example in Muhammad's lifetime; see Guillaume, *The Life of Muhammad*, pp. 377, 636, 649; Ahmad ibn Yahya al-Baladhuri, *The Origins of the Islamic State*, trans. Phillip Hitti (Piscataway, 2002), pp. 132–5. There is also the question of the meaning of the term *hanif* in the Qur'an. See Uri Rubin, 'Hanif', in *Encyclopedia of the Qur'an* (Leiden, 2002), Vol. 2: 402–4. See also Polymnia Athanassiadi and Michael Frede, *Pagan Monotheism in Late Antiquity* (Oxford, 1991).

40. W. Montgomery Watt, *Muhammad at Mecca* (Karachi, 1955), pp. 23–9. See also Helmer Ringgren, *Studies in Arabian Fatalism* (Uppsala, 1955).

41. Q. 2:109; 3:78; 4:46; 5:5, 59, etc.

42. R. Dagorn, *La Geste D'Ismaël d'après l'Onomastique et la Tradition Arabes* (Paris, 1981).

43. Q. 12:2; 20:113; 39:28; 41:3, 42:7; 43:3.

44. Al-Bukhari, *Kitab al-Jihad*, Kazi bilingual ed., Vol. 4, Book 52, nos. 151, 175, 189–91, pp. 147–9; al-Waqidi, *Kitab al-Maghazi* (Beirut, 1979), p. 416.

45. Majid Khadduri, *The Islamic Law of Nations: Shaybani's Siyar* (Baltimore, 1966), p. 20.

46. Lev. 18:24–29; Num. 8:6–10; Deut. 18:9.

47. Q. 7:29; 24:55; cf. 6:133; 11:57. See Reuven Firestone, 'Is there a notion of "divine election" in the Qur'an?', in Gabriel Said Reynolds (ed.), *New Perspectives on the Qur'an: The Qur'an in its Historical Context 2* (London, 2012): 393–410, esp. pp. 402–3.

48. Q. 2:144, 149–50, 191, 196, 217; 5:2; 8:34; 9:7, 19, 28; 17:1; 22:25; 48:25, 27.

49. The root occurs twice (Q. 27:61 and 69:47), but with different meanings.

50. 'Children of Israel' or less common 'the people/nation of Israel' ('*am yisra'el* – Exod. 1:9, 17:8; Josh. 8:33).

51. For the term 'the Land of Israel', see Josh. 11:22; 1 Sam.13:19; 2 Kgs. 5:2, 4; 6:23, etc.

52. Q. 2:142–6.

53. A. Abel, 'Dar al-Ḥarb' in *Encyclopedia of Islam* (Leiden, 1983), Vol. 2: 126, and 'Dar al-Islam', *Encyclopedia of Islam* (Leiden, 1983), Vol. 2: 127–8.

54. Chase Robinson, 'Conquest', in *Encylopedia of the Qur'an* (Leiden, 2001), Vol. 1: 398.

55. Rudi Paret understands the meaning of the word as 'reckoning' and shifting toward the sense of 'success' (Robinson, 'Conquest', p. 399).

56. Some of the classic verses are Q. 2:190–4, 216–18; 8:38–40; 22:39–40.

57. Because of the uncertain editorial history of Qur'an sections treating war, it is not clear whether adjacent verses are necessarily related. Meanings of individual verses or clusters of verses vary in relation to whether they are read in relation to adjacent verses. Aggressive verses that appear retaliatory include Q. 2:191, 8:59–69; 9:1–5 (or 9:1–16, which do not seem to reflect a spirit of conquest), 9:73, 123; 47:4–5.

Bibliography

Abdel Haleem, Harfiyah, Ramsbotham, Oliver, Risaluddin, Saba and Wicker, Brian, *The Crescent and the Cross: Muslim and Christian Approaches to War and Peace* (New York, 1998).

Abel, A., 'Dar al-Ḥarb', *Encyclopaedia of Islam* (Leiden, 1983), Vol. 2: 126.

_____, 'Dar al-Islam', *Encyclopaedia of Islam* (Leiden, 1983), Vol. 2: 127–8.

Athanassiadi, Polymnia and Frede, Michael, *Pagan Monotheism in Late Antiquity* (Oxford, 1991).

al-Baladhuri, Ahmad ibn Yahya, *The Origins of the Islamic State*, trans. Phillip Hitti (Piscataway, 2002).

Blankinship, Khalid, *The End of the Jihad State* (Albany, 1994).

Bonner, Michael, *Jihad in Islamic History* (Princeton, 2006).

Bowersock, G. W., *Roman Arabia* (Cambridge, MA, 1983).

al-Bukhari, *Kitab al-Jihad* (Lahore, 1979).

Cook, David, *Studies in Muslim Apocalyptic* (Princeton, 2002).

_____, *Understanding Jihad* (London, Berkeley and Los Angeles, 2005).

Cross, Frank, *Canaanite Myth and Hebrew Epic* (Cambridge, MA, 1973).

Dagorn, Renee, *La Geste D'Ismaël d'après l'Onomastique et la Tradition Arabes* (Paris, 1981).

Driver, D. R., *The International Critical Commentary, Deuteronomy* (New York, 1903).

Firestone, Reuven, *Jihad: The Origin of Holy War in Islam* (New York, 1999).

_____, 'Is there a notion of "divine election" in the Qur'an?', in Gabriel Said Reynolds (ed.), *New Perspectives on the Qur'an: The Qur'an in its Historical Context 2* (London, 2012): 393–410.

Guillaume, A., *The Life of Muhammad: A Translation of Ibn Ishaq's Sirat Rasul Allah* (Oxford, 1955).

Hacket, Jo Ann, '"There was no king in Israel:" The era of the judges', in M. D. Coogan (ed.), *The Oxford History of the Biblical World* (New York, 2001): 132–64.

Hawting, Gerald, *The Idea of Idolatry and the Emergence of Islam* (Cambridge, 1999).

Hoyland, Robert, *Arabia and the Arabs from the Bronze Age to the Coming of Islam* (London, 2001).

Kelsay, John, *Arguing the Just War in Islam* (Cambridge, MA, 2007).

Khadduri, Majid, *War and Peace in the Law of Islam* (Baltimore, 1955).

_____, *The Islamic Law of Nations: Shaybani's Siyar* (Baltimore, 1966).

Killebrew, Ann, *Biblical Peoples and Ethnicity: An Archaeological Study of Egyptians, Canaanites, Philistines, and Early Israel 1300–1100 BCE* (Atlanta, 2005).

Lecker, Michael, *Muslims, Jews and Pagans: Studies on Early Islamic Medina* (Leiden, 1995).

_____, *Jews and Arabs in Pre- and Early Islamic Arabia* (Aldershot, 1998).

Mueller, Walter, 'Survey of the history of the Arabian Peninsula from the first century A.D. to the rise of Islam', in 'Abd al-Qadir Mahmud 'Abd Allah (ed.), *Studies in the History of Arabia* (Riyadh, 1984), Vol. 2: 'Pre-Islamic Arabia': 125–31.

Neuwirth, Angelika, 'Geography', in *Encyclopedia of the Qur'an* (Leiden, 2002), Vol. 2: 293–313.

Nock, A. D., *Conversion* (Oxford, 1933).

Noth, Martin, *The Deuteronomist History of Israel* (Sheffield, 1981).

Peters, Rudolph, *Jihad in Classical and Modern Islam* (Princeton, 1996).

Pritchard, James B., *The Ancient Near East, Volume 1: An Anthology of Texts and Pictures* (Princeton, 1958).

———, *The Ancient Near East, Volume 2: A New Anthology of Texts and Pictures* (Princeton, 1975).

Redford, Donald, *Egypt, Canaan, and Israel in Ancient Times* (Princeton, 1992).

Ringgren, Helmer, *Studies in Arabian Fatalism* (Uppsala, 1955).

Robinson, Chase, 'Conquest', *Encyclopedia of the Qur'an* (Leiden, 2001), Vol. 1: 397–401.

Rubin, Uri, 'Hanif', *Encyclopedia of the Qur'an* (Leiden, 2002), Vol. 2: 402–4.

Sachedina, 'Abd al-Aziz, 'The development of *jihad* in Islamic revelation and history', in James Turner Johnson and John Kelsay (eds.), *Cross, Crescent, and Sword* (New York, 1990): 35–50.

Schippman, Klaus, *Ancient South Arabia from the Queen of Sheba to the Advent of Islam* (Princeton, 2001).

Shahid, Irfan, *Byzantium and the Arabs in the Fourth Century* (Washington DC, 1984).

———, *Rome and the Arabs* (Washington DC, 1984).

Sommer, Benjamin, 'Inner-biblical interpretation', in Adele Berlin, Marc Zvi Brettler and Michael A. Fishbane (eds.), *The Jewish Study Bible* (Oxford, 2004): 1829–35.

Tibi, Bassam, 'War and peace in Islam', in Terry Nardin (ed.), *The Ethics of War and Peace: Religious and Secular Perspectives* (Princeton, 1996): 128–45.

al-Waqidi, Abu, 'Abd Allah Muhammad ibn 'Umar', *Kitab al-Maghazi* (Beirut, 1979).

Watt, W. Montgomery, *Muhammad at Mecca* (Karachi, 1955).

Weinfeld, Moshe, *The Promise of the Land* (Berkeley and Los Angeles, 1993).

Zevit, Ziony, *The Religions of Ancient Israel* (London, 2001).

2

Early Competing Views on Jihad and Martyrdom

Asma Afsaruddin

Various literary genres from the first three centuries of Islam reveal the diversity of views that existed in this early period concerning the meanings of jihad, the conditions under which fighting (*qital*) as a specific aspect of jihad becomes obligatory and the moral and ethical restrictions placed on how the combative jihad was carried out. These ideas became more streamlined with time, and more circumscribed views of jihad as essentially a military activity become manifest in later works. Among these genres, early hadith works in particular often preserve understandings of jihad as a moral as well as a military undertaking that are sometimes not replicated in later works.

This chapter discusses a number of relevant reports contained in the *musannaf* works of two early hadith compilers: the Yemeni scholar and Qur'an commentator 'Abd al-Razzaq al-San'ani (d.827)[1] and the Iraqi historian and traditionist 'Abd Allah ibn Muhammad ibn Abi Shayba (d.849),[2] culled from the section on jihad in these two works. Many of these reports – that are not recorded in the six great authoritative Sunni hadith collections – allow us to recreate some of the earliest discourses on jihad and to nuance and refine considerably our understanding of the contested inflections of this term, particularly during the Umayyad period.

The *Musannaf* of 'Abd al-Razzaq

The *Kitab al-Jihad* ('Book of Jihad') section of this work preserves a number of reports attributed to prominent figures of the first two centuries of Islam, known for their exemplary personal piety and, frequently, opposition to the Syrian Umayyad rulers. Among such prominent figures are the Hijazi scholars Ibn Jurayj (d. *c*.767), 'Abd Allah ibn 'Umar (d.693), 'Amr ibn Dinar (d.743), and Sufyan al-Thawri (d.778). One such report is transmitted by 'Abd al-Razzaq from Ibn Jurayj, who related that he had once inquired of 'Ata' ibn Abi Rabah if fighting (*al-ghazw*) was obligatory 'with everyone'. To which 'Ata' and 'Amr ibn Dinar (who was also present) are said to have replied: 'We do not know.'[3] This report notably records the equivocation of early pious authorities about fighting in Umayyad armies under leaders popularly perceived as immoral and tyrannical.

The multiple significations of the phrase *fi sabil Allah* frequently conjoined to *al-jihad* is indicated in a noteworthy report recorded in 'Abd al-Razzaq's *Musannaf*, which relates that a number of the Companions were sitting with the Prophet when a man of muscular build – apparently a pagan – from the tribe of Quraysh, came into view. Some of those gathered exclaimed: 'How strong this man looks! If only he would expend his strength in the way of God!' The Prophet asked: 'Do you think only someone who is killed [in battle] is engaged in the way of God?' He continued: 'Whoever goes out in the world seeking licit work to support his family is on the path of God; whoever goes out in the world seeking licit work to support himself is on the path of God. Whoever goes out seeking worldly increase (*al-takathur*) has gone down the path of the devil (*fa-huwa fi sabil al-shaytan*).'[4] This report draws our attention for at least two reasons. Firstly, it contains a clear rebuttal to those who would understand 'striving in the way of God' in primarily military terms. It extols instead the quotidian struggle of the individual to live his or her life 'in the way of God', which infuses even the most mundane of licit activities with moral and spiritual significance and thus defines them as deserving of divine approval. Secondly, the report emphasises the importance of personal intention in determining the moral worth of an individual's act. Correct *niyya*, or intention, determines the moral valence of an act; according to the famous hadith, '[a]ctions are judged by

their intentions'. Since the meritorious nature of an individual's striving
for the sake of God is contingent upon purity of intent, one may understand this report as counselling caution against accepting ostentatious
pietism at face value or assuming that what appears pious to humans –
such as the claim to be waging a true jihad – will be deemed as such by
God, who alone can know the true intention of the individual.

It seems that such expansive views of striving in the path of God were
already at loggerheads with more exclusively belligerent appropriations
of jihad by the Umayyad period. A particularly hawkish figure in the
Umayyad period was the Syrian jurist Makhul al-Dimashqi (d. between
730 and 737),[5] who himself took part in military campaigns. Several
reports attributed to him in the *Musannaf* advocate relentless military
activity as obligatory jihad. One such report is recorded by 'Abd al-
Razzaq from the Syrian scholar Sa'id ibn 'Abd al-'Aziz (d.783)[6] who heard
Makhul relate the following hadith: 'The Messenger of God, peace and
blessings be upon him, said, "If from among the members of a household
no one emerges as a warrior (*ghazin*), nor do they outfit [someone] as
a warrior, or designate someone as such, then God will surely afflict
them with a calamity before death."'[7] Another hadith of similar tenor is
related by Makhul in which he quotes the Prophet as saying: 'Fighting
in the path of God (*al-jihad fi sabil Allah*) is obligatory on you, for it is
a door among the doors of Paradise and God thereby dispels grief and
distress.'[8] Finally, according to a report which 'Abd al-Razzaq heard from
an unidentified man, Makhul is said to have faced the *qibla* and sworn
ten times that '[f]ighting (*al-ghazw*) is obligatory for you'.[9] The stridency
of Makhul's position as conveyed in this report may be interpreted as
paradoxically suggestive of the strength and prevalence of the opposite,
more dovish, camp.

Counter-reports are recorded by 'Abd al-Razzaq which challenge what
clearly appeared to many as an unwarranted glorification of the military
jihad and stress instead the obligatory nature of the usual religious duties,
especially pilgrimage to Mecca. One report narrated by 'Abd al-Razzaq
from Sufyan al-Thawri relates that Abu Hayyan and others had asserted:
'The greater and the lesser pilgrimage are incumbent upon you.'[10] Both
Sufyan al-Thawri and Abu Hayyan al-Taymi (d.762)[11] are early pietist
Kufan authorities; the former is on record as having regarded only the
defensive jihad to be permissible,[12] a stance that could not have been

popular in official Umayyad and certain juridical circles. Interestingly, a harmonising report is attributed to 'Umar ibn al-Khattab who states that three types of travel are incumbent upon the believer – the greater and lesser pilgrimages, and jihad in the path of God.[13]

A report notable for categorically asserting that the fundamental religious obligations are the most important and cannot be displaced by the military jihad is related by 'Abd al-Razzaq on the authority of a certain al-Hawari ibn Ziyad. According to this report, Ibn Ziyad said that once when he was sitting with 'Abd Allah ibn 'Umar, a young man came up to him and asked: 'Why are you not taking part in jihad (*a-la tujahid*)?' Ibn 'Umar did not answer and turned away from him, and then responded: 'Indeed Islam is founded upon four supports – performance of prayer, giving of the required alms – and no distinction is made between the two; fasting during the month of Ramadan; and pilgrimage to the Sanctuary for the one capable of undertaking it. Jihad and voluntary charity are among the good (recommended) actions (*wa-inna al-jihad wa-l-sadaqa min al-'amal al-hasan*)'.[14] A variant report includes Sufyan al-Thawri in the *isnad* (chain of transmission) and is attributed to the Companion Hudhayfa ibn al-Yaman who affirms that Islam is founded on eight parts – the two parts of the *shahada*, prayer, *zakat*, fasting, pilgrimage, the commanding of good and forbidding wrong.[15] The first report attributed to 'Abd Allah ibn 'Umar clearly challenges what is perceived as an excessive valorisation of military activity in the Umayyad environment and reiterates that the traditional religious duties are the most important. The second report, attributed to Hudhayfa, makes no mention of the military jihad and emphasises instead the broad moral imperative of commanding good and preventing wrong – what might be regarded as an iteration of a basic and holistic understanding of jihad.

Battles fought for worldly reasons were dubbed jihad by the Umayyad (and later) rulers to legitimise them in the eyes of the public, a trend which appears to have been challenged by at least some Muslims. Evidence to this end is indicated in 'Abd al-Razzaq's *Musannaf*, which records the displeasure of some pious Muslims at the military adventurism of the worldly Umayyads. One report specifically expresses anxieties about taking part in the military campaigns of these unscrupulous rulers. A certain Abu Hamza al-Dab'i lamented to Ibn 'Abbas: 'We go on campaigns (*naghzu*) with these commanders/rulers (*al-umara'*) but they

[only] fight seeking [the gains of] the world.' Ibn 'Abbas counselled him to fight for 'your portion in the hereafter'.[16]

Pro-Umayyad bias becomes most transparent in those *fada'il al-jihad* reports which vigorously promote the merits of *ribat* or armed vigilance on the frontiers of the Islamic realms against enemy incursions, a practice that began in the post-prophetic period and became common during the Umayyad period. One particularly hyperbolic report is attributed to Salman al-Farisi, who encouraged Shurahbil ibn al-Samat in his vigils by quoting the Prophet thus: '*Ribat* for one day in the path of God is better than fasting and standing in prayer for a month. Whoever dies as a *murabit* in the path of God is protected from the torments of the grave and his good deeds multiply until the Day of Judgement.'[17] Another report purports to convey the following exhortation from 'Umar ibn al-Khattab: '*Ribat* is prescribed for you for it is the best of military activity.'[18]

According to several reports in the *Musannaf*, the naval campaigns of the Umayyads appear to have been distinctly unpopular in pietist circles and invited the same kind of criticism that their ground campaigns did. Thus 'Abd al-Razzaq relates a significant report according to which Ibn Jurayj queried 'Ata' ibn Abi Rabah about campaigning at sea, at which the former expressed his dislike and replied: 'I am fearful [of them] (*akhsha*).'[19] Other pious objectors included Sa'id ibn al-Musayyab and 'Umar ibn al-Khattab, both of whom are quoted as expressing repugnance for naval campaigns.[20]

The *Musannaf* of Ibn Abi Shayba[21]

The *Kitab al-Jihad* section in Ibn Abi Shayba's *Musannaf*, like 'Abd al-Razzaq's work, records a number of prophetic and non-prophetic reports, attesting to competing views regarding which activities undertaken 'in the path of God' are to be considered the most religiously meritorious. In certain reports recorded by Ibn Abi Shayba, a moral equivalence rather than a hierarchy of excellence is established between various pious activities, including the combative jihad. For example, in one hadith, the Prophet states: 'Whoever eats after having fasted or prepares himself to embark upon fighting or to perform the pilgrimage or provides for his offspring among his family, will have the equivalent of the reward of all of them, without their reward being diminished in any way.'[22] Another hadith states that the fighter in the path of God (*al-mujahid fi sabil Allah*) who does not slacken in his zeal is 'like the one who fasts and stands [in prayer]' until he returns.[23] A non-prophetic statement emanating from al-Nu'man ibn Bashir similarly compares the 'warrior in the path of God (*al-ghazi fi sabil Allah*)' to the one 'who fasts during the day and stands [in prayer] at night until the warrior returns'.[24] Worthy of note is that it is the 'warrior in the path of God' who is being compared to the prayerful, abstemious person in these reports, clearly indicating that through the Umayyad period, 'fighting in the path of God' was more commonly considered to be either inferior or at most morally equivalent, rather than superior, to supererogatory prayer and fasting, which constituted the moral yardstick. In the later period, the equation was often made in the reverse, indicating a progressively higher moral valuation of the military jihad in influential circles vis-à-vis more common, voluntary acts of piety.

This process of inversion is already evident in a few reports recorded by Ibn Abi Shayba himself which compare the relative merits of supererogatory fasting and prayer and the combative jihad. One such report is narrated on the authority of Abu Hurayra, who said that a number of unspecified people asked Muhammad about 'an activity that would be the equivalent of jihad in the path of God'. The Prophet replied: 'You will not be able to bear it.' When they protested to the contrary, he said that the equivalent of the fighter in the path of God was the fasting, prayerful individual, who is obedient to the commandments of God and who does not slacken in his zeal for fasting or in spending for charity, until the warrior returns to his family.[25] Such reports are relatively few in Ibn Abi Shayba's *Musannaf* but multiply in the later *fada'il al-jihad* literature, which praise the excellences of fighting.

We also find evidence of growing concern among a section of the population that the Umayyad rulers did not constitute righteous leadership and therefore were not qualified to undertake jihad in the path of God. The prerequisites for a legitimate jihad – just cause, right intent and righteous leadership – could easily be fulfilled during the Prophet's time. Could such a situation, however, be replicated in the post-prophetic period in the absence of a truly righteous leader, the purity of whose motives could not be impugned in any way? The doubts we saw expressed by the pious in 'Abd al-Razzaq's *Musannaf* concerning fighting 'in the way of

God' under the worldly, dissolute, Umayyad rulers indicates that some were indeed concerned that battles in their time were being waged for baser motives and thus not religiously meritorious acts at all. Such 'slackers' and 'doubters' would have to be convinced that the Umayyad rulers were in fact fighting 'in the path of God'. One obvious way to do this was to circulate hadiths and non-prophetic reports exhorting the faithful to rally to the Umayyad side by discounting the importance of the personal probity of the military and political leaders, as we saw earlier in 'Abd al-Razzaq's *Musannaf*. Another was to take hadiths already in existence which refer to specific battles fought under the Prophet and generalise these statements to any military campaign fought under any (at least ostensibly) Muslim leader. The level of exhortation was occasionally ratcheted up to new emotive levels in these reworked hadiths, which suggests some reluctance on the part of the targeted audience to fall in with Umayyad ambitions. These hortatory attempts could be quite transparently blatant, as *isnad* scrutiny reveals. A number of these reports have chains of transmission which, beyond the first-generation Companion, contain the names of distinctive Umayyad and Syrian personalities, some of whom – like the military commander Khalid ibn al-Walid, the first Umayyad caliph Mu'awiya and the Damascene jurist Makhul – were known for their enthusiasm for campaigning against the Byzantines.

An example of such a hortatory hadith with an exclusively Umayyad pedigree after the mention of the Companion from the first generation is as follows: 'Abd Allah ibn Mubarak reporting from al-Awza'i from 'Abd Allah ibn al-Mubarak from Abu Sa'id al-Khudri related that the Prophet said: "Those who press themselves into the first row and do not turn their faces until they are killed are those who are cavorting in the highest pavilions (*al-ghuraf al-'ula*) of paradise. Your Lord laughs [in pleasure] at them. Indeed when your Lord laughs at a people [in pleasure], there is no reckoning for them."[26] Significantly, the *isnad* contains the names of 'Abd Allah ibn al-Mubarak and 'Abd al-Rahman al-Awza'i, two Umayyad scholars who promoted jihad against the Byzantines. The former was a pious 'ascetic' warrior who wrote a well-known work cataloguing the merits of the combative jihad and the latter was the well-known jurist close to ruling Umayyad circles. There are in fact a number of reports in Ibn Abi Shayba's *Musannaf* with this particular *isnad*.

Several laudatory hadiths and reports from non-prophetic Companions and others occur in the *Musannaf* of Ibn Abi Shayba which specifically praises *ribat*, as we also previously observed in 'Abd al-Razzaq's work. Thus, in a hadith emanating from Salman al-Farisi, the Prophet is quoted as saying: '*Ribat* for a day in the path of God is better than fasting for a month and standing up [for prayer during its nights]. Whoever dies as a *murabit* will be spared the punishment of the grave and his virtuous acts will engulf him until the Day of Judgement.'[27] A Companion report from Abu Hurayra which has al-Awza'i's name in the *isnad* says: 'If you carry out *ribat* for three [days], then one may worship as one pleases.'[28] Other hadiths in which the Prophet asserts that the period of fulfilment of *ribat* is 40 days are equipped with preponderantly Syrian-Umayyad *isnad*s. One such *isnad* lists 'Isa ibn Yunus reporting from Mu'awiya ibn Yahya Sadafi from Yahya ibn al-Harith al-Dhimari from Makhul.[29] 'Isa ibn Yunus ibn Abi Ishaq (d. *c*.802), who is a frequent source of pro-*ribat* reports for Ibn Abi Shayba, was originally from Kufa but settled in Syria. He is said to have undertaken the pilgrimage and *ribat* in alternate years and taken up residence at the frontier, where he also died.[30] These laudatory reports indicate how important *ribat* had become in the Umayyad period and that it had become necessary to exhort what appears to be a reluctant populace to undertake this activity through the circulation of appropriate reports.[31]

Other significant reports indicate that *ribat* was particularly arduous and dangerous along the coast; coastal *ribat* is thus portrayed as morally superior to land-based *ribat* in these hortatory reports. 'Isa ibn Yunus is quoted once again, this time relating on the authority of Abu Hurayra, a variant of the report cited above in which the Companion promises rewards in the grave for *ribat* until the Day of Judgement. The difference is that 'Isa now refers specifically to vigilance on the coast.[32] In another report, 'Abd Allah ibn 'Amr ibn al-'As remarked that taking part in sea campaigns was more beloved to him than spending a single coin in the path of God.[33]

An even more explicit report leaves no doubt in the reader's mind that at some point during the Umayyad period naval campaigns began to take precedence over land forays. As a consequence, this preferred military activity of the time is presented as the more religiously meritorious deed in specific reports which continued to be disseminated in the later period. According to the later Kufan scholar Ishaq ibn Mansur al-Saluli (d.819), the earlier Kufan scholar Yahya ibn 'Ibad ibn Shayban (d. c.737) is reported to have remarked: 'The superiority (*fadl*) of the one who fights on sea (*al-ghazi fi al-bahr*) over the one who fights on land is comparable to the superiority of the one who fights on land over the one who sits at home.'[34] Clearly there were Umayyad supporters among Kufan scholars as well; reports advocating the merits of naval campaigns could be usefully disseminated in the 'Abbasid period as well.

Finally, like his predecessor, Ibn Abi Shayba includes a number of significant reports under the rubric of whether or not the combative jihad is to be considered an obligatory religious duty (*wajib*). He includes the report about Makhul who is said to have faced the *qibla* and sworn for ten days that 'fighting [*al-ghazw*] is incumbent upon you'.[35] Sa'id ibn al-Musayyab appeared to have disagreed with this position. Like 'Abd al-Razzaq, Ibn Abi Shayba records the report according to which when Ibn al-Musayyab was once asked whether fighting (*al-ghazw*) was obligatory on all the people (*'ala al-nas ajma'in*), he remained silent (*fa-sakata*).[36] A similar hesitancy to unequivocally endorse fighting as obligatory is apparent in the cases of the Medinan scholars 'Ata' ibn Abi Rabah and 'Amr ibn Dinar, both known for their pious abstemiousness and self-effacing natures. Like 'Abd al-Razzaq, Ibn Abi Shayba records the report in which they are both queried by Ibn al-Mubarak as to whether *al-ghazw* was a required duty, and both replied: 'We do not know.'[37] Once again, Ibn Abi Shayba documents a significant divergence in views between Hijazi scholars and Syrian scholars on the obligation to fight; Hijazi scholars tended to be quite equivocal about, or even against, the notion of fighting as an obligatory duty, while Syrian scholars located closer to the borders with Byzantium tended to endorse fighting as obligatory duty.

*   *   *

To conclude, these two early *musannaf* works preserve a number of highly significant reports containing contested perspectives on jihad that are either completely missing from later works or exist in reworked forms. Both are important as transitional works, which allow us to monitor the crystallisation of the *fada'il al-jihad* genre, the genre that documents the excellences of jihad, in the critical Umayyad period when this literature was taking shape. Through comparison with later hadith works and *siyar* literature – the legal literature that deals with the law of nations – we are able to document more firmly the evolving paranetic and hortatory function of a number of the *fada'il al-jihad* reports recorded in the two *musannaf*s. These reports clearly show that a broad range of views existed in the first two centuries of Islam regarding the repertoire of meanings to be ascribed to jihad and the moral valence of the activities signified by the term.[38] A close reading of such micro-discourses allows us to plot a shifting semantic and functional trajectory for this term and establish its contested dimensions over time – all of which has important repercussions for us today.

Notes

1. For a brief biography of al-San'ani, see Fuat Sezgin, *Geschichte des arabischen Schrifttums* (Leiden, 1967), Vol. 1: 99.
2. See Charles Pellat, 'Ibn Abi Shayba', in P. Bearman, Th. Bianquis, C. E. Bosworth, E. van Donzel and W. P. Heinrichs (eds.), *Encyclopaedia of Islam*, 2nd ed. (Leiden, 1960–2002), Vol. 3: 692.
3. 'Abd al-Razzaq al-San'ani, *Al-Musannaf*, ed. Ayman Nasr al-Din al-Azhari (Beirut: 2000), 5:118.
4. Ibid., 5:272.
5. See Josef van Ess, *Theologie und Gesellschaft im 2. und 3. Jahrhundert Hidschra* (Berlin and New York, 1991), Vol. 1: 111–13.
6. Sa'id ibn 'Abd al-'Aziz was a well-known Syrian scholar of his time, on a par with al-Awza'i according to a number of sources, and although generally regarded as a *thiqa* (reliable source), was said to have mixed up his reports towards the end of his life; see Ibn Hajar, *Tahdhib al-tahdhib*, ed. Khalil Ma'mun Shiha et al. (Beirut, 1996), 2:325–6.
7. 'Abd al-Razzaq, *Al-Musannaf*, 5:118–19, #9338.
8. Ibid., 5:119, #9341.
9. Ibid., 5:119–20, #9344.
10. Ibid., 5:119, #9340.
11. Yahya ibn Sa'id ibn Hayyan Abu Hayyan al-Taymi was a pious Kufan scholar generally regarded as a *thiqa*. Muslim ibn Hajjaj had a very high opinion of him as did Sufyan al-Thawri. He is described as inclined to night vigils and constant prayer; Ibn Hajar, *Tahdhib*, 6:134.
12. Roy Mottahedeh and Ridwan al-Sayyid, 'The idea of the jihad in Islam before the Crusades', in Angeliki E. Laiou and Roy Parviz Mottahedeh (eds.), *The Crusades from the Perspective of Byzantium and the Muslim World* (Washington DC, 2001): 23–30 (26).

13. 'Abd al-Razzaq, *Al-Musannaf*, 5:119, #9339.
14. Ibid., 5:119, #9342.
15. Ibid., 5:119, #9343.
16. Ibid., 5:189, #9673.
17. Ibid., 5:190, #9680. Variants are given in ibid., 5:190–91, #9681, #9682.
18. Ibid., 5:191, #9684.
19. Ibid., 5:192, #9687.
20. See the reports in ibid., 5:192, #9686; #9688; # 9689 and #9690.
21. Ibn Abi Shayba, *Al-Kitab al-Musannaf fi al-Ahadith wa-l-Athar*, ed. Muhammad 'Abd al-Salam al-Shahin (Beirut, 1995). The *Musannaf*, also known as the *Kitab al-Musnad*, was declared to be of 'canonical' status in the Maghrib along with the authoritative hadith compilations of al-Bukhari, Muslim, Malik, Abu Dawud and others.
22. Ibid., 4:236, #19548.
23. Ibid., 4:221, #19419.
24. Ibid., 4:207.
25. Ibid., 4:208, #19307; see also the variant report in ibid., 4:227, #19472.
26. Ibid., 4:213.
27. Ibid., 4:224–5, #19446.
28. Ibid., 4:224, #19445.
29. Ibid., 4:225, #19450.
30. Ibn Hajar, *Tahdhib*, 4:447–9.
31. Ibn Abi Shayba, *Al-Kitab al-Musannaf*, 4:225, #19452.
32. Ibid., 4:224, #19447.
33. Ibid., 4:219, #19397.
34. Ibid., 4:231, #19501.
35. Ibid., 4:237, #19550.
36. Ibid., 4:237, #19551.
37. Ibid., 4:237, #19552.
38. For a fuller study of these two *musannaf*s and other hadith compilations as well as the *fada'il al-jihad* literature, see Asma Afsaruddin, *Striving in the Path of God: Jihad and Martyrdom in Islamic Thought* (Oxford, 2013), especially chapters 5 and 6.

Bibliography

Afsaruddin, Asma, *Striving in the Path of God: Jihad and Martyrdom in Islamic Thought* (Oxford, 2013).

Ibn Abi Shayba, *Al-Kitab al-Musannaf fi al-Ahadith wa-l-Athar*, ed. Muhammad 'Abd al-Salam al-Shahin (Beirut, 1995).

Ibn Hajar, *Tahdhib al-Tahdhib*, ed. Khalil Ma'mun Shiha et al. (Beirut, 1996).

Mottahedeh, Roy and al-Sayyid, Ridwan, 'The idea of the jihad in Islam before the Crusades', in Angeliki E. Laiou and Roy Parviz Mottahedeh (eds.), *The Crusades from the Perspective of Byzantium and the Muslim World* (Washington DC, 2001): 23–30.

Pellat, Charles, 'Ibn Abi Shayba', in P. Bearman, Th. Bianquis, C. E. Bosworth, E. van Donzel and W. P. Heinrichs (eds.), *Encyclopaedia of Islam*, 2nd ed. (Leiden, 1960–2002), Vol. 3: 692.

al-San'ani, 'Abd al-Razzaq, *Al-Musannaf*, ed. Ayman Nasr al-Din al-Azhari (Beirut: 2000).

Sezgin, Fuat, *Geschichte des arabischen Schrifttums* (Leiden, 1967).

Van Ess, Josef, *Theologie und Gesellschaft im 2. und 3. Jahrhundert Hidschra* (Berlin and New York, 1991).

3

Definitions and Narratives of Martyrdom in Sunni Hadith Literature

Roberta Denaro

The aim of this chapter is to offer an overview of some typological features of martyrdom (*shahada*)[1] in Sunni hadith literature, based on the assumption that it was this kind of text – more than the Qur'an itself – that provided categories and definitions of martyrdom as well as contributing to shaping its various representations. In Sunni Islam, religious and historical literature made scarce use of martyrdom as a literary motif. In most sources detailed accounts of martyrs are rare, and often the meagre lists recording the names of those fallen in battle are the only evidence of a Sunni 'martyrology'. Differing from the Shi'ite tradition,[2] Sunni martyrdom narratives never attained the status of an autonomous literary genre, as the Christian *Acta Martyrum* or the Shi'ite *ta'ziye* (a representation commemorating Husayn's sacrifice at Karbala) did. Nor did any martyr ever play a founding role comparable to that of Husayn. It was mainly hadith literature that shaped the category of martyrdom through a complex process leading to a composite definition of *shahid* (martyr), a label that can be applied to a wide range of believers. In fact, it is not restricted to those who died in the course of jihad, as is usually implied, but, indeed, appears to have been polysemic since its original formulation. Such multiple meanings of martyrdom can be traced back to the Qur'anic definition of a martyr. It is widely held that

82

shahid to mean 'martyr' is, in all probability, a post-Qur'anic usage.[3] Forms derived from the root *sh-h-d* do occur many times in the Qur'an, but they are normally related to the meaning of 'witnessing', that is, of being present at an event, rather than to the sense of 'being a martyr'.[4] A clear distinction between *shahid* (pl. *shuhada'*, 'martyr') and *shahid* (pl. *shuhud*, 'witness', in legal contexts) emerges only in post-Qur'anic Arabic, with the meaning 'martyr' only present in a few verses.[5]

Even without using the term *shahid*, however, the Qur'an clearly lays down the basis of a definition of martyrdom through the formula *man qutila fi sabil Allah,* 'he who is killed for the cause of God' (lit. 'on God's path'). The complex and multifaceted nature of the Qur'anic expression *sabil Allah,*[6] which is not entirely reducible to jihad, anticipates to some extent the multiple definitions of *shahada* in the hadith collections.

On the basis of a general survey, hadith materials on martyrdom[7] can be divided roughly into two typologies according to their textual structure and focus. First, there are hadiths that can be designated classificatory texts, with the aim of providing a definition of martyrdom, displaying all the different instances and possibilities (some examples will be given below in the section dealing with Group I). Second, there are hadiths more akin to fictional texts, with narrative developments. These texts almost invariably deal with the deeds of fallen mujahidin and their reward in the afterlife (some examples will be given below in the section which discusses Group II).[8]

Group I. Definitions

From a textual point of view, the hadiths of the first group (Group I) are structured as lists. The language in these hadiths is concise, uses few adjectives and lacks any narrative insertions. They list all the deaths that may rightly be named martyrdom. If we look at their structure and function, they might be defined as paradigmatic, normative texts.

The following hadith, taken from al-Bukhari's *Sahih,* is a perfect example of this kind of text, offering what may be regarded as the standard definition of *shahid*:

> The Prophet said: 'Five are the kinds of martyrs: he who dies of plague (*al-mat'un*), he who dies of an abdominal disease (*al-mabtun*), he who drowns (*al-ghariq*), he who dies under a collapsed building (*sahib al-hadm*), and he who is killed on the path of God (*man qutila fi sabil Allah*).'[9]

Table 1. Comparing definitions of martyrdom

	Death by plague	Death by abdominal disease	Death by drowning	Death under a collapsed building	Death in jihad
BU	adhan, 32	adhan, 32	adhan, 32	adhan, 32	adhan, 32
MU	imara, 164	imara, 164	imara, 164	imara, 164	imara, 164
HAN	II, 441	V, 315	II, 441	—	II, 441
AD	jana'iz, 11	jana'iz, 11	jana'iz, 11	jana'iz, 11	jana'iz, 11
NA	jihad, 48	jihad, 48	jihad, 48	jihad, 48	jihad, 48
IM	jihad, 17	jihad, 17	jihad, 17	—	jihad, 17
DA	jihad, 22	jihad, 22	jihad, 22	—	jihad, 22
TIR	jana'iz, 65	jana'iz, 65	jana'iz, 65	jana'iz, 65	jana'iz, 65

BU = al-Bukhari (d.870), *Sahih* (Leiden, 1862–1868); MU = Muslim (d.875), *Sahih* (Cairo, 1423/2003); HAN = Ahmad ibn Hanbal (d.855), *Musnad* (Riyadh, 1419/1998); AD = Abu Dawud (d.889), *Sunan* (Cairo, 1928); NA = al-Nasa'i (d.915), *Sunan* (Cairo, [s.d.]); IM = Ibn Maja (d.887), *Sunan* (Cairo, 1372/1952); DA = al-Darimi (d.869), *Sunan* (Medina, 1386/1966); TIR = al-Tirmidhi (d.892), *Sunan* (Homs, 1387/1965).

As shown in Table 1, all the major Sunni collections of hadiths[10] contain this 'lowest common denominator' definition of martyrdom.

This broadly agreed-upon definition of *shahid* is nonetheless elaborated differently in some collections, although there is little variation in al-Bukhari. The process of expansion of military martyrdom develops further to include in the category of *man qutila fi sabil Allah* those who are killed while defending their life, property, family or religion (there are many variants: *duna dami-hi/mali-hi/ahli-hi/dini-hi*).[11] The notion of *shahid* is made to include many violent and untimely deaths, such as those caused by falling from a mount[12] or burning in a fire.[13] In addition, an increasing number of deaths caused by illness, such as pleurisy (*dhat al-janbi*),[14] come to be classified as martyrdom.[15] Within this, the definition of martyrdom that we can consider one of the most interesting – and perhaps least investigated – is that which also assigns the status of *shahid* to women who die in childbirth:

> The Prophet said: '[. . .] he who is killed on God's path is a martyr, he who dies of plague is a martyr, he who dies of a colic is a martyr, and the woman who dies in childbirth (*tamut bi-jum'in*), is a martyr.'[16]

This extended definition of martyrdom is not, however, unanimously shared, as Table 2 shows:

Table 2. Comparing definitions: '... *and the Woman Who Dies in Childbirth is a Martyr*'

BU	—
MU	—
HAN	V, 315
AD	*jana'iz*, 11
NA	*jana'iz*, 14; *jihad*, 36, 48
IM	*jihad*, 17
DA	*jihad*, 22
TIR	—

We can venture a few considerations on the way this female martyrdom was dealt with in hadith collections. The key concept seems to lie in the connection between martyrdom and the belly, as all the hadiths mention death by belly diseases as a cause of martyrdom, and a further concise and powerful definition of martyrdom clearly states that '*al-batn shahada*' (lit.: 'the belly is martyrdom').[17] To some extent, the inclusion of death in childbirth could thus be regarded as a development of the idea that every death caused by abdominal diseases is a form of martyrdom. In his commentary on Malik's *Muwatta*,[18] al-Zurqani, after explaining that the noun '*mabtun*' indicates whoever dies from an illness of his belly (such as diarrhoea, dropsy, colic), explains that the expression '*tamut bi-jum'in*' is used for a woman dying while a fully developed foetus is still in her womb, and that the same expression may also indicate a woman who dies a virgin. Lexically, such different meanings are made to derive from the idea of dying with something contained in the woman, not separate from her, whether it be a burden in her womb or her maidenhood.[19]

If this analogical explanation provides a good starting point, it remains true, nevertheless, that this category of martyrdom – extremely peculiar in that it involves women, and more strikingly, is closely linked to their sexuality – raises some interesting interpretative issues. This hadith is not included in all collections. Its absence in al-Bukhari and Muslim is noteworthy if we consider the canonical role attributed to their collections.[20] It is present, however, in an early hadith transmitted by Ibn al-Mubarak,[21] and it seems to fulfil a role similar to that of other hadiths in that it broadens and redefines the concept of martyrdom in a non-martial context, leading to the creation of a typology of female martyrdom. It is striking that, at least from a theoretical point of view, death in a physical condition of extreme defilement may entirely invert the pure/impure polarity and may make a woman giving birth comparable to a warrior fallen in jihad, whose blood cleanses all sins and is not washed away from the corpse.[22]

A final example of the way in which the definition of *shahada* was enlarged and expanded in prophetic traditions is found in the following hadith: 'He who dies by illness dies as a martyr.'[23] Or, in the following hadith from Ibn Maja's collection:

> The Prophet said: 'Whoever asks in all sincerity for martyrdom on the battlefield, God will place him in the house of martyrs, even if he dies in his bed.'[24]

Finally it is worth noting a famous apocryphal hadith that celebrates chaste and hopeless love, through which we enter the theme of the *shuhada' al-hubb* (martyrs of love) destined to play an important role in later literary production. It declares: 'Whoever loves, remains chaste and dies keeping his love secret, is a martyr.'[25]

In conclusion, at least from a typological point of view, this progressive widening and reshaping of the definition of martyrdom legitimises, from a relatively early period, the classification of many different types of death as martyrdom. If, on one level, the category itself may seem to lose consistency, on another it potentially provides consolation for the grief of many believers. It is significant, however, that apart from the literary tradition that developed around the martyrs of love, no other category of martyrs became the object of literary narrative, except, of course, for the martyrs fallen in jihad.

Group II. Narrations

Even in the context of an enlarged definition of martyrdom, the connection between martyrdom and jihad remains clear and strong. There is no doubt about the fact that dying on the battlefield (which is the prevailing meaning of the Qur'anic *fi sabil Allah* among interpreters) is the main way to attain the status of martyr and is highly praised in many hadiths.

Unlike the type of hadiths examined so far, texts belonging to the second group exhibit, in their form and style, characteristics that may lead us to consider them narrative texts in the fullest sense.[26] They feature dialogues, dreams or visions announcing martyrdom,[27] lively depictions of *huris* (virgins of Paradise) awaiting the martyrs[28] and detailed descriptions of Paradise. These stories might be defined as exemplary, exhortatory texts that situate the category of martyrdom in jihad within a narrative framework. Their aim is to demonstrate its desirability, and to emphasise the special status of martyrs among other believers. This status is, in all probability, a very early feature in eschatological imagery, partly shaped by the political and military circumstances of the first century of Islam.[29] A good example of this emphasis can be found in a text present in many collections, here quoted from al-Bukhari:

> The Prophet said: 'Nobody who enters Paradise would like to come back to this world, even if he could enjoy everything that is in it, except whoever died as a martyr, for he wishes to return to the world in order to be martyred ten times more because of the blessings he knows martyrdom entails.'[30]

Another typical feature of these texts is the wealth of detail describing the life of martyrs in Paradise. Martyrs fallen in jihad seem to be a category worthy of a special ranking in the afterlife. They are, for example, exempted from permanence in the *Barzakh* (the intermediate stage before resurrection).[31] In fact, martyrs represent an exception in many respects. They are not subject to the delay between death and the Day of Judgement, their bodies are preserved intact after death[32] and, according to one of the earliest manuals on jihad, their souls even receive beautiful new bodies.[33] According to a well-known hadith (here quoted from Ibn Hanbal), they are provisionally placed inside green birds:

> The Prophet said: 'When your brothers were killed in [the battle of] Uhud, God placed their souls inside green birds. They go to drink at the streams of Paradise, eat its fruits, and take shelter by golden lamp-holders in the shade of the Throne. When they have tasted the sweetness of their food and have seen the beauty of their fate, they say: "Ah, if only our brothers knew what God gave us and where we are, they would not renounce jihad and would not recoil from war."'[34]

Some of these texts that contain elements closer to fiction shape their plot with a clear eschatological emphasis, in the same way as in the *sira-maghazi* literature (historical texts recording the Prophet's biography and military campaigns). The pre-Islamic literary genre of *Ayyam al-'Arab* ([Battle] Days of the Arabs) is rewritten. Historical facts about the *umma* are set in a meta-historical framework: the battlefield becomes a theatre of martyrdom, where people fight for spiritual defeat or salvation, and *ajr* (monetary reward) becomes the term for the heavenly reward of the martyr.[35] The characters are deeply conscious of the real sense of their fighting, and of their dying, not for victory or booty, but for salvation and divine reward:

> On the day of [the battle of] Uhud a man asked the Prophet: 'If I am killed, where do you think I will go?' 'Paradise' he answered. So he threw away the dates he was eating and fought until he was killed.[36]

From this brief overview we can draw some provisional conclusions. First, an extreme flexibility from a typological point of view is clear from the manifold definitions of *shahada*, including not only the fallen mujahidin but even those who died from illness or in their own beds sincerely desiring martyrdom. Second, only in relation to fallen mujahidin does hadith literature turn from mere definition towards more complex narrative and hortatory texts, displaying some recurrent features. These include the emphasis on death in jihad as the most desirable death, the almost unrestrained enrichment and expansion of narratives concerning the heavenly fate reserved for martyrs[37] and, from a theological-political perspective, the emergence of a meta-historical framework in the rewriting of the (military) history of the first community of believers as salvation history. The battlefield turns into a sacred place, a threshold between this world and the hereafter, easily crossed by martyrs.

If, from a typological point of view, we can observe how the representations of martyrdom in hadith literature are characterised by a substantial continuity through the centuries, from a historical point of view the function of such representations is variable.

There is little doubt, for example, that the process of normalisation that followed the Abbasid revolution must have played a certain role in curbing the political uses of the doctrine of martyrdom.[38] The image of Abbasid caliphs as mujahidin was increasingly emphasised by religious and political propaganda even if along the frontiers the military expansion lost its momentum. At that stage, which also concluded the formative period of the Sunni collections, death in jihad was a kind of martyrdom highly praised (especially among some pious circles of scholar-warriors).[39] However, we can assume that it was a less frequent experience than in the previous century. On the internal front, the Abbasids needed to keep their distance from the Shi'ite movement which brought them to power in 749. In building the religious and ideological foundations of their legitimacy they attempted to bypass Ali (and Husayn's martyrdom at Karbala). Through a process which can be regarded as simultaneously opposing and imitating the Shi'ite biographical pattern of the ideal imam (often a martyr),[40] their propaganda posthumously bestowed the aura of martyrdom upon Abu Hashim, founder of the dynasty.[41]

Thus, typologies and representations of martyrdom were adapted from time to time to particular political and religious circumstances which must be investigated in their specific contexts. The extent to which the imagery specific to military martyrdom, periodically revitalised, may have provided a model at various times and places in Islamic history, and to which some of the current Sunni views on martyrdom can be read in continuity with their foundational texts, remains in question.

Notes

1. For a general survey see Etan Kohlberg, 'Shahid', in P. Bearman, Th. Bianquis, C. E. Bosworth, E. van Donzel and W. P. Heinrichs (eds.), *Encyclopaedia of Islam*, 2nd ed. (Leiden, 1960–2002), Vol. 9: 203–7; Etan Kohlberg, 'Medieval Muslim views on martyrdom', *Mededelingen der Koninklijke Nederlandse Akademie van Wetenschappen* 60 (1997): 281–307; and David Cook, *Martyrdom in Islam* (Cambridge, 2007).

2. It is not possible to give a full bibliography on the subject here. I will confine myself to mentioning the study of Mahmud Ayoub, *Redemptive Suffering in Islam: A Study of the Devotional Aspects of 'Ashura' in Twelver Shi'ism* (The Hague, 1978), and Friederike Pannewick, 'Passion and rebellion: Shi'ite visions of redemptive martyrdom', in Friederike Pannewick (ed.), *Martyrdom in Literature: Visions of Death and Meaningful Suffering in Europe and the Middle East from Antiquity to Modernity* (Wiesbaden, 2004): 47–62.

3. See Ignaz Goldziher, 'Influences chrétiennes dans la littérature religieuse de l'Islam', *Revue de l'histoire des religions* 18 (1888): 186–7; Jan Arent Wensinck, *The Oriental Doctrine of the Martyrs* (Amsterdam, 1921), pp. 155–6; Paul Peeters, 'Les traductions orientales du mot martyr', *Analecta Bollandiana* 39 (1921): 50–64; Wim Raven, 'Martyrs', in *Encyclopaedia of the Qur'an* (Leiden-Boston, 2003), Vol. 3: 281–7; and Cook, *Martyrdom in Islam*, pp. 16–21.

4. See Hanna E. Kassis, 'Shahid', in Hanna E. Kassis, *A Concordance of the Qur'an* (Berkeley, 1983); Martin R. Zammit, 'ŠHD', in Martin R. Zammit, *A Comparative Lexical Study of Qur'anic Arabic* (Leiden, Boston and Köln, 2002): 245; and Arthur Jeffery, 'Shuhada', in Arthur Jeffery, *The Foreign Vocabulary of the Qur'an* (Baroda, 1938): 187.

5. For instance, Qur'anic exegetes (and many translators) read *shuhada'* as 'martyrs' in at least three cases (Q. 3:140; 4:69; 39:69). See Roberta Denaro, *Dal Martire Allo Šahid: Fonti, Problemi e Confronti per Una Martirografia Islamica* (Roma, 2006), pp. 65–81; see also Cook, *Martyrdom in Islam*, pp. 12–21.

6. See C. E. Bosworth, 'Sabil', in P. Bearman, Th. Bianquis, C. E. Bosworth, E. van Donzel and W. P. Heinrichs (eds.), *Encyclopaedia of Islam* (Leiden, 1995), Vol. 8: 679; and Dmitry V. Frolov, 'Path or way', in *Encyclopaedia of the Qur'an* (Leiden and Boston, 2004), Vol. 4: 28–33.

7. For the full reference see the entry for 'Shahid', in Arent Jan Wensinck, *Concordance et Indices de la Tradition Musulmane* (Leiden, 1955), Vol. 3: 198–202.

8. The only exceptions seem to be some hadiths reporting narrations aimed at dissuading people from abandoning a place stricken by plague. See the entry for 'Ta'un' in Wensinck, *Concordance et Indices*, Vol. 4: 3–4; and Jacqueline Sublet, 'La peste prise aux rêts de la jurisprudence: le traité de Ibn Ḥağar al-'Asqalānī sur la peste', *Studia Islamica* 33 (1971): 141–9.

9. BU, *adhan*, 32.

10. The hadiths examined here are taken from the Sunni hadith canon (*al-kutub al-sitta*) which, apart from the perennial core represented by the *Sahihayn*, may include a variable number of collections, depending on geographical and chronological factors.

11. See, for example AD, *sunan*, 29; IM, *hudud*, 21. Cf. Gautier H. A. Juynboll, *Encyclopedia of Canonical Hadith* (Leiden and Boston, 2007), pp. 230, 583 and 637.

12. See, for example HAN, II, 441.

13. DA, *jana'iz*, 11; NA, *jana'iz*, 14; IM, *jihad*, 17.

14. Lit. 'something that has to do with the side', the expression refers to pleurisy or an ulcer that occurs in a man's side. See Edward W. Lane, 'Janb', in Edward W. Lane, *An Arabic-English Lexicon* (London and Edinburgh, 1865).

15. See, for example, DA, *jana'iz*, 11; NA, *jana'iz*, 14; HAN, IV, 157; IM, *jihad*, 17.

16. HAN, V, 315.

17. HAN, V, 315.

18. Muhammad al-Zurqani, *Sharh 'ala Muwatta' al-Imam Malik* (Cairo, n.d.), Vol. 2: 72.

19. Cf. Lane, 'Jum', *'Arabic-English Lexicon'*. Interestingly, aborted foetuses, like martyrs, are awarded a place in Paradise immediately after death; cf. Jane I. Smith and Yvonne Y. Haddad, *The Islamic Understanding of Death and Resurrection* (Albany, 1981), pp. 172–3.

20. On the formation of the Sunni canon and especially on the preeminence achieved by al-Bukhari and Muslim, see Jonathan Brown, *The Canonization of al-Bukhari and Muslim: The Formation and Function of the Sunni Hadith Canon* (Leiden and Boston, 2007).

21. Ibn al-Mubarak (d.797), *Kitab al-Jihad* (Tunis, 1972), n. 68.

22. Cf. Leor Halevi, *Muhammad's Grave: Death Rites and the Making of Islamic Society* (New York, 2007), esp. chapter 2.

23. IM, *jana'iz*, 62.

24. IM, *jihad*, 15. The same hadith is reported also in AD, *jihad*, 40; DA, *jihad*, 16; TIR, *fada'il jihad*, 19; NA, *jihad*, 36, etc. On this tradition see Juynboll, *Encyclopedia of Canonical Hadith*, p. 13.

25. Ibn Dawud, *Kitab al-Zahra* (Chicago, 1932), p. 66. On the subject see Cook, *Martyrdom in Islam*, pp. 98–104; Lois Giffen, *Theory of Profane Love among the Arabs: The Development of a Genre* (New York, 1971), esp. pp. 99–115; Renate Jacobi, 'The 'Udhra: love and death in the Umayyad period', in Pannewick (ed.), *Martyrdom in Literature*, pp. 137–47; and in the same volume Stefan Leder's article on 'The 'Udhri narrative in Arabic literature', pp. 163–88.

26. Cf. Sahair El Calamawy, 'Narrative elements in the Hadith literature', in A. F. L. Beeston, T. M. Johnstone, R. B. Serjeant and G. R. Smith (eds.), *The Cambridge History of Arabic Literature. Arabic Literature to the End of the Umayyad Period* (Cambridge, London and New York, 1983): 308–16. On the theoretical premises for the analysis of fictionality in hadith literature cf. Sebastian Günther, 'Fictional narration and imagination within an authoritative framework: Towards a new understanding of hadith', in

Stefan Leder (ed.), *Story-telling in the Framework of non-fictional Arabic Literature* (Wiesbaden, 1998): 433–71.

27. Cf. Cook, *Martyrdom in Islam*, pp. 119–21.

28. See, for example HAN, II, 297, 427, and IM, *jihad*, 16. For an analysis of traditions featuring *huris* who appear to warriors fighting jihad (based on Ibn al-Mubarak's *Kitab al-Jihad*) see Maher Jarrar, 'The martyrdom of passionate lovers: holy war as a sacred wedding', in H. Motzki (ed.), *Hadith: Origins and Developments* (Ashgate, 2004): 317–37.

29. A typical example can be found in those first century traditions praising the naval jihad and martyrdom as especially meritorious. See 'Shahidu 'l-bahri', in Wensinck, *Concordance*, Vol. 3: 199; and Juynboll, *Encyclopedia of Canonical Hadith*, p. 683. For a later example of this process aiming to provide frontier communities and/or ruling dynasties with a firm religious and ideological framework, see Sébastien Garnier, 'La sacralisation du littoral ifrîqiyen à l'époque hafside', *Revue des Mondes Musulmans et de la Méditerranée* 130 (2011/2): 103–30.

30. BU, *jihad*, 21. Compare also TIR, *jihad*, 13; *fada'il jihad*, 25; DA, *jihad*, 19; MU, *imara*, 108. See also a similar tradition featuring the Prophet himself as warmly desiring to die as a martyr (BU, *jihad*, 119).

31. Compare the view of Margoliouth cited in Ragnar Eklund, *Life between Death and Resurrection According to Islam* (Uppsala, 1941), p. 57 n. 3. On the image of Paradise according to hadith literature see Soubhi el-Saleh, *La Vie Future Selon le Coran* (Paris, 1971), pp. 29–43.

32. The martyr's body is the subject of several hadiths that underline its exceptional features in life as well as in death: the martyr will not feel the pain of being killed, except as the bite of an insect (cf. DA, *jihad*, 17); his body will remain uncorrupted (cf. BU, *jana'iz*, 78); on the Day of Judgement his wounds will have a ruby colour and the smell of musk (AD, *jihad*, 40; DA, *jihad*, 15).

33. This extremely interesting tradition is reported in Ibn al-Mubarak's *Kitab al-Jihad*, n. 63. On the book and its author see Michael Bonner, *Aristocratic Violence and Holy War: Studies in the Jihad and the Arab-Byzantine Frontier* (New Haven, 1966), esp. pp. 119–25; and Roberta Denaro, 'From Marw to the *tugur*: Ibn al-Mubarak and the shaping of a biographical tradition', *Eurasian Studies* 7 (2009/1–2): 125–43.

34. HAN, I, 266. On the bird tradition see Eklund, *Life between Death and Resurrection*, pp. 67–71 and 101–5.

35. Cf. Michael Bonner, 'Ja'a'il and holy war in early Islam', *Der Islam* 67 (1991): 45–64, esp. pp. 55–7, and Andrew Rippin, 'The commerce of eschatology',

in Stefan Wild (ed.), *The Qur'an as Text* (Leiden, New York and Köln, 1996), esp. pp. 131–3.

36. BU, *maghazi*, 36. The same narrative featuring 'Umar ibn al-Humam, martyred at Badr, can be found in Ibn Hisham, *Al-Sira al-Nabawiyya* (Cairo, 1375/1955), Vol. 1: 627.

37. In this respect we should not underestimate the role of the *qussas* (popular preachers and, later on, storytellers) in shaping the more detailed and fantastical hadiths on martyrdom. On *qussas* and their role see Khalil Athamina, 'Al-Qasas: its emergence, religious origin, and its socio-political impact on early Muslim society', *Studia Islamica* 76 (1992): 53–74; and Jonathan P. Berkey, *Popular Preaching & Religious Authority in the Medieval Islamic Near East* (Seattle and London, 2001). On the question of the presence of *qussas'* materials in non-legal hadiths (which applies to the majority of those on martyrdom), Ibn Hanbal's words on edifying traditions and pious tales transmitted (and forged) by *qussas* can be regarded as representative of the views of many hadith scholars: '[H]ow beneficial they are to common people even if what they tell is untrue!' Merlin L. Swartz (ed.), *Ibn al-Jawzi's Kitab al-Qussas wa-l-Mudhakkirin* (Beirut, 1986), pp. 105–6. Compare Denaro, *Dal Martire Allo Šahid*, pp. 89–90.

38. On Abbasid religious propaganda see Jacob Lassner, 'Propaganda in Early Islam: the Abbasids in the post-revolutionary age', *Israel Oriental Studies* 10 (1980): 73–85, and Denaro, *Dal Martire Allo Šahid*, pp. 116–21.

39. See Bonner, *Aristocratic Violence and Holy War*, esp. pp. 107–34.

40. See Farouk Omar, 'Some aspects of the Abbasid-Husaynid relations', *Arabica* 22/2 (1975): 170–9 (170).

41. See Jacob Lassner, *Islamic Revolution and Historical Memory: An Inquiry into the Art of Abbasid Apologetics* (New Haven, 1986), p. 55.

Bibliography

Hadiths

BU = al-Bukhari (d.870), *Sahih* (Leiden, 1862–8)

AD = Abu Dawud (d.889), *Sunan* (Cairo, 1928)

DA = al-Darimi (d.869), *Sunan* (Medina, 1966)

HAN = Ahmad ibn Hanbal (d.855), *Musnad* (Riyadh, 1998)

IM = Ibn Maja (d.887), *Sunan* (Cairo, 1952)

MU = Muslim (d.875), *Sahih* (Cairo, 2003)

NA = al-Nasa'i (d.915), *Sunan* (Cairo, [s.d.])

TIR = al-Tirmidhi (d.892), *Sunan* (Homs, 1965)

Athamina, Khalil, 'Al-Qasas: its emergence, religious origin, and its socio-political impact on early Muslim society', *Studia Islamica* 76 (1992): 53–74.

Ayoub, Mahmud, *Redemptive Suffering in Islam: A Study of the Devotional Aspects of 'Ashura' in Twelver Shi'ism* (The Hague, 1978).

Berkey, Jonathan P., *Popular Preaching & Religious Authority in the Medieval Islamic Near East* (Seattle and London, 2001).

Bonner, Michael, *Aristocratic Violence and Holy War: Studies in the Jihad and the Arab-Byzantine Frontier* (New Haven, 1966).

————, 'Ja'a'il and holy war in early Islam', *Der Islam* 68 (1991): 45–64.

Bosworth, C. E., 'Sabil', in P. Bearman, Th. Bianquis, C. E. Bosworth, E. van Donzel and W. P. Heinrichs (eds.), *Encyclopaedia of Islam*, 2nd ed. (Leiden, 1995), Vol. 8: 670.

Brown, Jonathan, *The Canonization of al-Bukhari and Muslim: The Formation and Function of the Sunni Hadith Canon* (Leiden and Boston, 2007).

Cook, David, *Martyrdom in Islam* (Cambridge, 2007).

Denaro, Roberta, *Dal Martire Allo Šahid: Fonti, Problemi e Confronti per Una Martirografia Islamica* (Roma, 2006).

————, 'From Marw to the *tugur*: Ibn al-Mubarak and the shaping of a biographical tradition', *Eurasian Studies* 7/1–2 (2009): 125–43.

Eklund, Ragnar, *Life between Death and Resurrection According to Islam* (Uppsala, 1941).

El Calamawy, Sahair, 'Narrative elements in the hadith literature', in A. F. L. Beeston, T. M. Johnstone, R. B. Serjeant and G. R. Smith (eds.), *The Cambridge History of Arabic Literature: Arabic Literature to the End of the Umayyad Period* (Cambridge, London and New York, 1983): 308–16.

Frolov, Dmitry V., 'Path or way', in *Encyclopaedia of the Qur'an* (Leiden and Boston, 2004), Vol. 4: 28–31.

Garnier, Sébastien, 'La sacralisation du littoral ifriqiyen à l'époque hafside', *Revue des Mondes Musulmans et de la Méditerranée* 130 (2011–2): 103–30.

Giffen, Lois, *Theory of Profane Love among the Arabs: The Development of a Genre* (New York, 1971).

Goldziher, Ignaz, 'Influences chrétiennes dans la littérature religieuse de l'Islam', *Revue de l'Histoire des Religions* 18 (1888): 186–7.

Günther, Sebastian, 'Fictional narration and imagination within an authoritative framework: Towards a new understanding of hadith', in Stefan Leder (ed.), *Story-telling in the Framework of non-fictional Arabic Literature* (Wiesbaden, 1998): 433–71.

Jacobi, Renate, 'The 'Udhra: love and death in the Umayyad period', in Friederike Pannewick (ed.), *Martyrdom in Literature: Visions of Death and Meaningful*

Suffering in Europe and the Middle East from Antiquity to Modernity (Wiesbaden, 2004): 137–47.

Jarrar, Maher, 'The martyrdom of passionate lovers: holy war as a sacred wedding', in Harald Motzki (ed.), *Hadith: Origins and Developments* (Ashgate, 2004): 317–37.

Jeffery, Arthur, *The Foreign Vocabulary of the Qur'an* (Baroda, 1938).

Juynboll, Gautier H. A., *Encyclopedia of Canonical Hadith* (Leiden and Boston, 2007).

Halevi, Leor, *Muhammad's Grave: Death Rites and the Making of Islamic Society* (New York, 2007).

Ibn Dawud, *Kitab al-Zahra* (Chicago, 1932).

Ibn Hisham, *Al-Sira al-Nabawiyya*, Part 1 (Cairo, 1955).

Ibn al-Mubarak, *Kitab al-Jihad* (Tunis, 1972).

Kassis, Hanna E., *A Concordance of the Qur'an* (Berkeley, 1983).

Kohlberg, Etan, 'Shahid', in P. Bearman, Th. Bianquis, C. E. Bosworth, E. van Donzel and W. P. Heinrichs (eds.), *Encyclopaedia of Islam*, 2nd ed. (Leiden, 1960–2002), Vol. 9: 203–7.

———, 'Medieval Muslim views on martyrdom', *Mededelingen der Koninklijke Nederlandse Akademie van Wetenschappen* 60 (1997): 281–307.

Lane, Edward W., *An Arabic-English Lexicon* (London and Edinburgh, 1865).

Lassner, Jacob, 'Propaganda in Early Islam: the Abbasids in the post-revolutionary age', *Israel Oriental Studies* 10 (1980): 73–85.

———, *Islamic Revolution and Historical Memory. An Inquiry into the Art of Abbasid Apologetics* (New Haven, 1986).

Leder, Stefan, 'The 'Udhri narrative in Arabic literature', in Friederike Pannewick (ed.), *Martyrdom in Literature: Visions of Death and Meaningful Suffering in Europe and the Middle East from Antiquity to Modernity* (Wiesbaden, 2004): 163–88.

Omar, Farouk, 'Some aspects of the Abbasid-Husaynid relations', *Arabica* 22/2 (1975): 170–9.

Pannewick, Friederike, 'Passion and rebellion: Shi'ite visions of redemptive martyrdom', in Friederike Pannewick (ed.), *Martyrdom in Literature: Visions of Death and Meaningful Suffering in Europe and the Middle East from Antiquity to Modernity* (Wiesbaden, 2004): 47–62.

Peeters, Paul, 'Les traductions orientales du mot martyr', *Analecta Bollandiana* 39 (1921): 50–64.

Raven, Wim, 'Martyrs', in *Encyclopaedia of the Qur'an* (Leiden-Boston, 2003), Vol. 3: 281–7.

Rippin, Andrew, 'The commerce of eschatology', in Stefan Wild (ed.), *The Qur'an as Text* (Leiden, New York and Cologne, 1996).

al-Saleh, Soubhi, *La Vie Vuture Selon le Coran* (Paris, 1971).

Smith, Jane I. and Haddad, Yvonne Y., *The Islamic Understanding of Death and Resurrection* (Albany, 1981).

Sublet, Jacqueline, 'La peste prise aux rêts de la jurisprudence. Le traité de Ibn Ḥağar al-'Asqalani sur la peste', *Studia Islamica* 33 (1971): 141–9.

Swartz, Merlin L. (ed.), *Ibn al-Jawzi's Kitab al-Qussas wa-l-Mudhakkirin* (Beirut, 1986).

Wensinck, Arent Jan, *The Oriental Doctrine of the Martyrs* (Amsterdam, 1921).

_____, *Concordance et Indices de la Tradition Musulmane* (Leiden, 1955).

Zammitt, Martin R., *A Comparative Lexical Study of Qur'anic Arabic* (Leiden, Boston and Cologne, 2002).

al-Zurqani, Muhammad, *Sharh 'ala Muwatta' al-Imam Malik*, Part 2 (Cairo, n.d.).

4

The Non-Military Aspects of *Kitab al-Jihad*

Mustafa Baig

The *Kitab al-Jihad*[1] (Book of Jihad) is a section in classical works of Islamic jurisprudence (*fiqh*) that primarily discusses the governance of a Muslim army entering non-Muslim territory (and vice versa). Legal literature sometimes refers to the same subject under the heading of *Kitab al-Siyar* (Book of Expeditions), using a term, *siyar*, sometimes rendered as 'Islamic international law' or 'Islamic law of nations' in modern usage.[2] Muslim jurists defined the *Kitab al-Siyar*'s content not only as 'ways of conduct of the warriors and what is incumbent on them and for them' but also as governing relations with a wide spectrum of groups ranging from non-believers and apostates to those with whom treaties have been made.[3] Hereafter, this section of Islamic jurisprudence, whether named *Kitab al-Jihad* or *Kitab al-Siyar* (or named with the joint heading of *siyar* and jihad), will be referred to simply as *kitab*.

The impression that jihad is confined to military struggle against an enemy seems confirmed by both the content and titles of this *kitab*. The *kitab* has subsections that largely cover aspects of warfare, imamate (leadership in war), taxation, treaties, spoils of war, rebels and apostasy. In Maliki works of law, the section on jihad is often called *bab al-muharaba* ('belligerency'). Perhaps the reason for such headings dominating the *kitab* is because the early contact Muslims had with non-Muslims was largely the result of warfare; hence the name, *Dar al-Harb*, given to non-Muslim territory. This feeds the impression that jurists only discussed jihad in reference to military struggles against the enemy. Although the term *Dar al-Harb* literally means 'Abode of War', it does not refer to a perpetual state of physical war, nor – as we shall see – does it preclude the possibility of peaceful Muslim abidance in non-Muslim territory. Thus the term will remain untranslated in this chapter.

I will argue that a closer examination of the *kitab* shows that Islamic jurists also covered a number of other wide-ranging subjects under the heading of jihad, reflecting a multifaceted body of literature within Islamic law. Further inspection of this *kitab* will reveal interesting points about non-belligerent ways of sojourn in non-Muslim territory, envisioned by classical Islamic jurists in terms of trade, imprisonment or conversion to Islam in non-Muslim territory.

Once this has been explored, the relationship of a Muslim (resident in non-Muslim territory) to the rest of the Muslim *umma* is established. Next, the discussions found in the *kitab* concerning the type of jurisdiction (*wilaya*) to be applied in non-Muslim lands is assessed by looking at the set of laws governing the legal affairs of a Muslim in non-Muslim territory (Islamic law versus the laws of the land). Studying key jurists' rulings on these topics therefore will help to widen our understanding of the full scope of the *kitab*. A key point that will be made is that while Muslims in non-Muslim territory are beyond Islamic jurisdiction, they are still under Islamic moral and religious obligations regardless of territorial status.

An analysis of these legal dictates will help to clarify some contemporary controversies in which debates surrounding the role of Islamic law in modern Western countries have surfaced more fervently over the last decade or so. Islamic law (shariah) has frequently been portrayed with negative characterisations and misrepresentations that are often delusory. An example can be seen in the 'knee-jerk reaction' (in the words of the Bishop of Hulme, Stephen Lowe) to a speech given by the then Archbishop of Canterbury Rowan Williams, 'Civil and religious law in England: a religious perspective' in 2008[4] by almost all parts of the media and a number of populist politicians, who construed his words to mean that he was calling for the adoption of shariah law in the UK.[5] In parallel, there are a very small number of radical voices who (while not recognising non-Islamic laws) call for the application of Islamic law in its entirety in non-Muslim countries, including criminal punishments (such as the now banned 'Islam4UK' group), as well as negating any obligations to live peaceably with non-Muslims.

Muslims Entering *Dar al-Harb* under a Security Covenant (*aman*) for Trade

Addressing Muslims in foreign lands as merchants was particularly pertinent for Muslim jurists, as trading was an important feature of Arab society even before the advent of Islam. Arab trade in the Malabar region of coastal India, South-East and East Asia is well-documented.[6] Such travels continued throughout the era of the Prophet and the early caliphate. Trade was hence an important means by which Islam was propagated outside the Arabian Peninsula.[7]

It is understandable, therefore, that the earliest Islamic jurists addressed Muslim traders in non-Muslim lands. This socio-economic phenomenon required legal rules to deal with the various particulars, even if that entailed devising hypothetical scenarios comparable to the discourse adopted in other specialisms within jurisprudence. No independent section of law was designated for the Muslim trader. Nevertheless, Muslim traders are mentioned in the context of the discussion of *isti'man* (claiming a security covenant), under the *kitab*, referring to when a Muslim enters non-Muslim lands with a security covenant. This shows that one could in fact enter *Dar al-Harb* in a peaceful state. Hence one cannot exclusively ascribe the connotation of war or belligerence to *Dar al-Harb*.

A standard foundational text (*matn*) of the Hanafi school, al-Quduri's *al-Mukhtasar*, which summarises the legal views of the school, clearly states:

> If a Muslim enters *Dar al-Harb* as a trader, it is not permitted for him to infringe on their property and life.[8]

Abu Bakr al-Yamani and al-Marghinani, in their commentaries on this statement, explain that this is because the Muslim is duty-bound to abide by the security covenant and that any infringement after obtaining it is a violation of the law (*ghadar*), and violation of the law is forbidden (*haram*).[9] Muslim jurists prohibited any kind of deceit in financial dealings or breaking of local law in *Dar al-Harb*. Such rulings dismiss the notion that Islam permits only hostile relations between Muslims and non-Muslims. Upon the obtaining of a security covenant, Islamic law does not allow a person to break any part of the law, let alone attack the property and persons living there.[10]

It is interesting to note that al-Marghinani and other jurists allocate a separate sub-heading (*bab*) within the *kitab* for the *musta'min* (he who claims a security covenant). This shows that the jurists distinguished between different ways of entering non-Muslim lands: through military expeditions or through peaceful means (trade). Both types are discussed under jihad.[11] Al-Maydani, in his gloss on al-Quduri's text above, adds other generic means of entry into *Dar al-Harb*, apart from those stemming from trade, but without specifying what these might be: 'by way of trade (or other means)'.[12]

This suggests that al-Quduri was not intending to limit purposes of travel to trade;[13] or, from a legal-historical point of view, it perhaps indicates and acknowledges a diversification in reasons why Muslims were travelling to non-Muslim lands. The obligation to uphold the security covenant is expressly mentioned by al-Mawardi:

> A Muslim who enters *Dar al-Harb* with a security covenant or is taken captive but then freed and given a security covenant is not permitted to attack them or their property, and has to guarantee them quarter.

Al-Mawardi states this without mentioning any difference among the four schools of law, pointing towards unanimity among the established schools on this issue.[14]

It is worth mentioning here that in contrast to the Hanafi texts, Maliki texts devote less attention to the case of a person claiming a security covenant or a Muslim trader in non-Muslim lands.[15] This is probably because the Maliki school was much more reluctant to permit Muslims to travel to non-Muslim lands in the first place.[16] However, the agreement of the jurists, if such a contract is made, still stands.

The Jurisdiction of *Dar al-Islam* (the Abode of Islam) in non-Muslim territory

Given the obligation to abide by the security covenant, the jurists then had to address the possibility of a Muslim contravening the law of the land and determine what type of law should be applied. This involved defining the extent of *Dar al-Islam*'s territorial jurisdiction. The Hanafis hold that Muslim jurisdiction cannot extend to non-Muslim territory. Abu Hanifa is reported to have responded thus to the question of crimes committed in non-Muslim territory and which system of punishment is applicable:

> I said: What is your opinion about this, that someone who goes in amongst them [in *Dar al-Harb*] with a security covenant, and then kills one of their men in *Dar al-Harb*, or seizes property or a slave and takes it to *Dar al-Islam*, then the inhabitants of [*Dar al-*] *Harb* convert to Islam or become a Protected Community (*dhimma*), would you return to them any of what this [person] took, or is there any liability for any of [the victim's] wealth or blood?
>
> He said: No
>
> I said: Why?
>
> He said: Because he carried out this act in *Dar al-Harb*, where rules for Muslims are not applicable.
>
> I said: Would you disapprove of this [action] of the man?
>
> He said: Yes – I would disapprove of it for him on the grounds of his religion to act perfidiously towards them.[17]

Behind this lies a larger concept of the inviolability and protection of life and property. The jurists discussed the case of a Muslim in a non-Muslim land who loans money or property (on credit) to a non-Muslim or is loaned something by a non-Muslim. If the two return to *Dar al-Islam* and one of them files a suit against the other in an Islamic court in the event of non-payment, then the Islamic sovereign (*hakim* or *qadi*) will not decree anything in this regard. The same applies if one embezzles the property of the other (*ghasab*).[18] The jurists maintain that jurisdiction (*wilaya*) is necessary for the enforcement of a decree. In this case the judge did not have jurisdiction at the time the debt took place (*la wilayata waqt al-iddana asl-an*)[19] as the judge is not able to adjudicate on those who are in *Dar al-Harb*.[20] The jurists also add that at the time of adjudication (*qada'a*), the judge does not hold jurisdiction over the non-Muslim since he had not committed himself to the jurisdiction of Islam in the past when the act had been carried out, but rather had committed himself to what will take place in the future.[21] Nevertheless, the judge will issue a fatwa to the Muslim that the property owed or embezzled should be returned; this is not a legally binding decree that will enforce the return of property but a verdict that states his religious obligation to abide by the security covenant.[22] Ibn Humam adds that, although the state will not enforce the return of the property, the fatwa will state that it is obligatory to return it as the matter remains between him and God.[23] Here we see the difference between a legal obligation (in terms of a state injunction) and a religious and moral obligation to return the property.

In the issue of owed property, the same ruling is given if two non-Muslims from non-Muslim territory file a case in *Dar al-Islam* because of the aforementioned reason (committing to Islamic rulings in the future).[24] The issue is somewhat different if both parties are non-Muslims but convert to Islam and enter *Dar al-Islam*. In this case the judge will decree that the property owed must be returned. Here the jurists hold that the occurrence of the debt is valid (jurisdictionally) as the occurrence took place with the agreement of both parties accepting the laws of Islam; hence the jurisdiction required for the judge to adjudicate is established at the time of pronouncing the decree, as both had committed (*iltizam*) themselves to the laws of Islam.[25]

In the interlocution with Abu Hanifa cited earlier, the issue of murder is also mentioned. Expounding the same principle, the jurists give the following details: if a Muslim who has obtained a security covenant takes the life of another Muslim with the same territorial status (in non-Muslim territory), whether it is murder (*'amad-an*) or manslaughter (*khata'-an*), in both cases it would be obligatory to pay the 'blood money' from his personal wealth; in the case of manslaughter an expiatory act (*kaffara*) is also required. The sentence is different from that which one would face in *Dar al-Islam*, where the sentence normally applied if murder is proven is retaliatory slaughter (*qawd/qisas*). For manslaughter, blood money must be paid by the tribe (*'aqila*),[26] because in *Dar al-Islam* the family is held partly responsible for the crime as they are required to know the perpetrator's whereabouts and restrain him from committing such an act. However, with a change in territory (*tabayan al-darayan*), the family cannot be held responsible for a crime that a family member committed in another land.[27]

Hanafis do not, however, excuse the expiatory act because the verse in the Qur'an pertaining to manslaughter ('Whoever kills another believer must free a believing slave')[28] is without restriction (*mutlaq*). Hence the ruling of the expiatory act would apply irrespective of location – whether the crime took place in *Dar al-Islam* or *Dar al-Harb*. As for the blood money, the jurists assert that a Muslim maintains the protection and inviolability of his life if he enters non-Muslim territory with a security covenant, because the inviolability here – even if to a lesser extent – is established from the protection of *Dar al-Islam*. Retaliatory slaughter, however, is impossible to execute except when the state has the power to do so. This can only exist with a Muslim sovereign in place who rules over Muslim subjects. Because this is not the case with *Dar al-Harb*, the ruling of retaliatory slaughter cannot be applied.[29] Some jurists draw a parallel between this and the fact that punishments for *hadd* (fixed Qur'anic prohibition) are nullified in the case of adultery and theft where there is no Muslim jurisdiction.[30]

If the case involves two Muslim prisoners in *Dar al-Harb*, where one takes the life of the other, or a Muslim trader (i.e. with a security covenant) takes the life of a Muslim prisoner, then the murderer will not be punished except that an expiatory act would be required in the case of manslaughter. The same ruling applies if a Muslim kills a Muslim who converted to Islam in non-Muslim territory.[31]

In these cases, we can observe the emphasis that the Hanafi school places on territory and jurisdiction. Here, the important concept of the inviolability ('*isma*) of life and property is highlighted in the juristic discussion of Islam in non-Muslim territory. The other schools (and also Abu Hanifa's two prime students), whilst recognising territorial jurisdiction and inviolability, give far less significance to its effect in non-Muslim territory. In the case mentioned above of the Muslim with a security covenant who kills another Muslim with the same territorial status, they state that retaliatory slaughter is obligatory in the case of murder. Al-Shafi'i, for example, argued that there should be no distinction between a Muslim killed in Muslim territory and one killed in non-Muslim territory.[32] The Hanafis, however, state that inviolability stems from territory, not from religion. They do, nevertheless, split inviolability into two categories: territorial/political (*al-'isma al-muqawwima*) and religious/moral (*al-'isma al-mu'aththima*). So where Abu Hanifa states that there is nothing due on a Muslim trader who kills a prisoner or Muslim convert, this is because the inviolability of life and property that *Dar al-Islam* offers him has been waived upon entering non-Muslim territory. However, the religious inviolability is not waived as long as he is a Muslim, meaning that the sin remains for committing the crime and contravening the security covenant, even though the Islamic punishment does not.[33] Hence the Hanafis differentiate between the legal obligation that is connected with *Dar al-Islam* and the moral obligation that is connected with Islam.

The above discussion on the jurisdiction of *Dar al-Islam* shows the complexity involved if someone violates the security covenant. A matter of particular importance that can be determined from this juristic discourse is that Muslim jurists envisaged Muslims sojourning in non-Islamic territory for temporary periods only. If we look at the case of a Muslim with a security covenant who murders another Muslim with a security covenant, a reason for maintaining the penalty of blood money is because the jurists treated his visit to non-Muslim lands as temporary with the idea that he would return to his homeland in the not-too-distant future; this can be discerned from al-Marghinani's use of the word 'contingency' ('*arid*), indicating a temporary cause for visiting non-Muslim territory.[34] This would also explain why Muslims in *Dar al-Harb* were often addressed as or assumed to be traders. Hence some jurists mentioned that since there is an intention of returning to *Dar al-Islam*, it is supposed (*taqdir-an*) that he was in *Dar al-Islam* as that is his permanent residence. *Dar al-Islam* is then able to fulfil some of its obligations to the murdered person.[35] The case of a Muslim who does not enter non-Muslim territory for temporary purposes but is rather a permanent resident in non-Muslim lands is not discussed by the jurists. One can only presume that, because the person in question has no legal connection with *Dar al-Islam*, the Islamic state would not be able to apply any of its rulings for crimes committed outside *Dar al-Islam* as the protection it offers to the life and property of Muslims would not exist.

Jurisdiction Outside *Kitab al-Jihad*

Many of these principles form the basis for spreading rulings across other sections of Islamic jurisprudence outside the *kitab*. In financial law, for example, the Hanafis rule that transactions that are otherwise prohibited in *Dar al-Islam* are permitted in *Dar al-Harb*. In standard Hanafi texts one can find the ruling (based on a prophetic tradition): 'There is no usury between a Muslim and a non-Muslim in *Dar al-Harb*.' This is because a Muslim sovereign cannot extend extra-territorial protection to those living outside *Dar al-Islam*; hence their property is violable and unprotected (*mubah, ghayr mahfuz*).[36]

Muslim jurists have also discussed independent jurisdiction within non-Muslim territory. The Hanafi jurists in particular state that it is permissible for Muslims to accept judicial positions from a non-Muslim authority as long as (according to most jurists) there is consensual agreement among the Muslims living there. These judges will be recognised under Islamic law and any rulings they make in determining the new Islamic months, dissolution of marriages (*khul'/faskh*), marriage of orphans and other areas of Islamic law that are not in conflict with the laws of the land are religiously binding, as are rulings made by an officially appointed judge in Muslim countries.[37]

Conclusion

This chapter has shown that the *Kitab al-Jihad* in Islamic jurisprudence should not be understood as a body of literature solely concerned with hostile relations between Muslims and non-Muslims. Instead, we can observe its multifaceted nature, in that the jurists discuss not only matters that regulate military warfare, but, in the same *kitab*, matters relating to peaceful abidance in non-Muslim territory. As well as entry into non-Muslim lands through warfare, Islamic law clearly envisages peaceful relations in non-Muslim lands. The fact that this guidance is in the *kitab* calls for a more panoptic understanding of what the *kitab* comprises. Because of issues arising from the wider context of jihad, discussions centred on jihad have a wider rubric than might be assumed.

Although legal manuals were predominantly designed to address Muslims living in *Dar al-Islam*, classical Islamic jurists codified complex and profound legal rulings pertaining to Muslims in non-Muslim lands too. In particular, we are able to discern the practical concerns of Hanafi jurists in extending the jurisdiction of Islam to non-Muslim lands. While judges in Muslim lands cannot enforce Islamic law for acts committed in non-Muslim lands owing to the lack of jurisdiction, Islamic law makes the subtle, yet important, qualification that a Muslim will not be relieved from the religious sin or his moral obligations in the event of breaking the law. Furthermore, although Hanafis stress that inviolability (of life and property) stems from territory, and not from religion, *Dar al-Islam* can still exercise some of its judicial authority. However, this is in view of the fact that Muslims were only conceived of as temporary sojourners to non-Muslim lands, and in the case of permanent residency, we can understand that there would be no question of applying Islamic law in non-Muslim lands.

Such a study therefore provides valuable information, resources and insights for approaching the contemporary debates mentioned earlier surrounding coexistence and Muslims living in non-Muslim lands, in which the question of legal affairs continues to feature prominently. Contrary to the rhetoric found in sections of the media, blogosphere and political sphere, Muslims are not commanded to implement penal law in non-Muslim jurisdictions. And contrary to claims made by certain radical groups, this chapter has shown that Muslims are not only obliged to observe the local law of the land (which includes not harming citizens and property), but – according to the dominant Hanafi school, at least – in the event of escaping justice for transgressing the law in a non-Muslim country (or being the victim of an offence), they will be deprived of all access or only receive limited access to Islamic justice if a case is brought to a Muslim country. All the while, Islamic law will continue to hold them responsible from a theological point of view.

This only serves to underline the point that Islamic law (and the *kitab*) incorporates the importance of having peaceful and pragmatic relationships with non-Muslims in non-Muslim lands, and provides the principles to enable such peaceful relations to be maintained for the benefit of Muslims and non-Muslims alike.

Notes

1. *Kitab* in works of classical Islamic jurisprudence and other Islamic texts refers to a chapter that has (or may have) subheadings (*abwab*) and sub-subheadings (*fusul*).
2. See for example Majid Khadduri, *The Islamic Law of Nations: Shaybani's Siyar* (Baltimore, 1966) and the Arabic edition by the same author *al-Qanun al-Dawli al-Islami: Kitab al-Siyar li-l-Shaybani* (Beirut, 1975).

3. Abu Bakr Muhammad ibn Ahmad al-Sarakhsi, *Kitab al-Mabsut* (Quetta, n.d.), vol. 10: 3.

4. Rowan Williams, 'Civil and religious law in England: a religious perspective', 7 February 2008 (text available at http://rowanwilliams .archbishopofcanterbury.org/articles.php/1137/, last accessed 24 December 2013).

5. A striking headline from the Sun newspaper reads: 'Williams: Victory for terrorism. The Archbishop argues for introduction of Sharia law in Britain'; the caption reads: '"They don't live in a Muslim country." SHARIA law – words that conjure images of stoning, amputations, lashings and executions. And coming soon to a court near you, according to the Archbishop of Canterbury, Dr Rowan Williams' (emphasis in original). *The Sun*, 'Williams: Victory for terrorism', 7 February 2008 (http://www.thesun .co.uk/sol/homepage/news/778163/Archbishop-of-Canterbury-Rowan-Williams-argues-for-introduction-of-Sharia-law-in-Britain.html, last accessed 15 December 2013). Such scaremongering has reached further heights with the rise of the 'anti-shariah movement', most prevalent in the USA; see, for example, Wajahat Ali, Eli Clifton, Matthew Duss, Lee Fang, Scott Keyes and Faiz Shakir, 'Fear, Inc.: The roots of the Islamophobia network in America', *Center for American Progress*, 26 August 2011 (http://www.americanprogress.org/issues/religion/report/2011/08/26/ 10165/fear-inc/, last accessed 27 December 2013).

6. Ira Lapidus, *A History of Muslim Societies* (Cambridge, 2002), p. 383; Hermanus, J. de Graaf, 'South-East Asian Islam to the eighteenth century', in P. M. Holt, A. K. S. Lambton and B. Lewis (eds.), *The Cambridge History of Islam* (Cambridge, 1984), Vol. 2A: 123; Raphael Israeli, *Islam in China* (London, 1994), pp. 2–3.

7. For more information on trade in early Islam see for example Maurice Lombard, *The Golden Age of Islam* (Amsterdam and Oxford, 1975).

8. Abu al-Hasan Ahmad ibn Muhammad al-Baghdadi al-Quduri, *al-Mukhtasar li-l-Quduri* (Lahore, n.d.), p. 296.

9. Abu Bakr ibn 'Ali al-Haddad al-Yamani, *al-Jawhara al-Nayyira 'ala Mukhtasar al-Quduri* (Multan, n.d.), Vol. 2: 373; Burhan al-Din Abu al-Hasan 'Ali al-Marghinani, *al-Hidaya Sharh Bidaya al-Mubtadi* (Cairo, n.d.), Vol. 2: 152.

10. The jurists state that this scenario is contrary to that of a prisoner of war (even if he was freed willingly) as he is not claiming a security covenant (*musta'min*). Al-Marghinani also adds that if the contract is contravened by the non-Muslim sovereign or by the consent of the sovereign then he is no longer responsible for upholding the security covenant.

11. The inverse case of a non-Muslim claiming a security covenant and entering Muslim territory is also discussed under this section, again signifying the provision in the law of a means of peaceful existence between Muslims and non-Muslims.

12. 'Abd al-Ghani al-Maydani, *al-Lubab fi Sharh al-Kitab 'ala al-Mukhtasar al-Mushtahir bi-Ism "al-Kitab" alladhi Sannafa-hu Abu al-Husayn Ahmad ibn Muhammad al-Quduri* (Beirut, n.d.), Vol. 4: 135. The words in parentheses are al-Maydani's.

13. In other words, it is not a precluding qualification (*qayd ihtirazi*) but an incidental one (*qayd ittifaqi/waqi'i*).

14. Abu al-Hasan 'Ali ibn Muhammad al-Mawardi, *al-Ahkam al-Sultaniyya* (Cairo, 1973), p. 141. Al-Mawardi (a Shafi'i jurist) on the regulations of governance mentions difference of opinion among the jurists if any exists. Here he only mentions al-Dawud (founder of the minority, now extinct, Zahiri school) as the only person to differ.

15. See for example Khalil ibn Ishaq al-Jundi's *Mukhtasar Khalil* (Cairo, n.d.) in which there is no mention of the security covenant (*aman*). This text is a core component of the *fiqh* syllabus of the Maliki School as is *al-Hidaya* for the Hanafis.

16. For Malik's disapproval see 'Abd al-Salam ibn Sa'id Sahnun, *al-Mudawwana al-Kubra* (Cairo, n.d.), Vol. 3: 278. The reason cited is that Muslims would be subjected to the 'laws of polytheism'.

17. Muhammad ibn al-Hasan al-Shaybani, in M. Khadduri, *al-Qanun al-Dawli al-Islami: Kitab al-Siyar li-l-Shaybani* (Beirut, 1975), p. 194.

18. Abu al-Barakat 'Abd Allah ibn Ahmad al-Nasafi, *Kanz al-Daqa'iq* (Karachi, 2004), Vol. 1: 593–4; Muhammad ibn 'Abd Allah al-Tamartashi, *Tanwir al-Absar* (printed with Sayyid Muhammad Amin ibn 'Abidin, *Radd al-Muhtar*), Vol. 6: 276; al-Marghinani, *Bidayat al-Mubtadi* (printed with its commentary *al-Hidaya*), Vol. 2: 153; 'Abd al-Latif Hasan 'Abd al-Rahman and Muhammad ibn al-Nizam (leading eds.), *al-Fatawa al-Hindiyya* (Beirut, 1997), Vol. 2: 257. See the following sources to see other ways in which this concept is expressed: Zayn al-Din ibn Ibrahim ibn Muhammad ibn Nujaym, *al-Bahr al-Ra'iq Sharh Kanz al-Daqa'iq* (Beirut, 1997), Vol. 5: 168; Badr al-Din al-'Ayni, *al-Binaya Sharh al-Hidaya* (Beirut, 2000), Vol. 7: 204; Fakhr al-Din 'Uthman ibn 'Ali al-Zayla'i, *Tabyin al-Haqa'iq* (Beirut, 2000), Vol. 4: 136.

19. al-Marghinani, *al-Hidaya*, Vol. 2: 153; Sayyid Muhammad Amin ibn 'Abidin, *Radd al-Muhtar 'ala Durr al-Mukhtar Sharh Tanwir al-Absar* (Beirut, 2003), Vol. 6: 276.

20. al-Zayla'i, *Tabyin al-Haqa'iq*, Vol. 4: 135; Ibn 'Abidin, *Radd al-Muhtar*, Vol. 6: 276.

21. al-Marghinani, *al-Hidaya*, Vol. 2: 153; al-'Ayni, *al-Binaya*, Vol. 7: 203–4; Ibn Nujaym, *al-Bahr al-Ra'iq*, Vol. 5: 167; al-Zayla'i, *Tabyin al-Haqa'iq*, Vol. 4: 135–6; Ibn 'Abidin, *Radd al-Muhtar*, Vol. 6: 276.

22. Muhammad 'Ala' al-Din al-Haskafi, *Durr al-Mukhtar* (printed with Sayyid Muhammad Amin ibn 'Abidin, *Radd al-Muhtar*) (Beirut, 2003), Vol. 6: 277; Ibn 'Abidin, *Radd al-Muhtar*, Vol. 6: 277; al-Marghinani, *al-Hidaya*, Vol. 2: 153. Al-'Ayni mentions that *mustaqbal* is in opposition to actions committed in *Dar al-Islam*, al-'Ayni, *al-Binaya*, Vol. 7: 204.

23. Kamal al-Din Muhammad ibn al-Humam, *Fath al-Qadir Sharh al-Hidaya* (Beirut, 2003), Vol. 6: 17–18; Ibn Nujaym, *al-Bahr al-Ra'iq*, Vol. 5: 167.

24. The same applies if a Muslim embezzles the property of a non-Muslim who then converts to Islam and files a case in *Dar al-Islam*; i.e. a fatwa will be issued but not a court decree.

25. al-Marghinani, *al-Hidaya*, Vol. 2: 153; Ibn Nujaym, *Bahr al-Ra'iq*, Vol. 5: 169; al-Zayla'i, *Tabyin al-Haqa'iq*, Vol. 4: 136–7; Ibn 'Abidin; *Radd al-Muhtar*, Vol. 6: 277.

26. *'Aqila* refers to the perpetrator's male relatives (or 'solidarity group') who are responsible for paying the blood money. See *Kitab al-Jinayat* in the aforementioned sources.

27. al-Marghinani, *al-Hidaya*, Vol. 2: 153; Ibn al-Humam, *Fath al-Qadir*, Vol. 6: 19; al-'Ayni, *al-Binaya*, Vol. 7: 205; Ibn Nujaym, *Fath al-Qadir*, Vol. 6: 19; al-Zayla'i, *Tabyin al-Haqa'iq*, Vol. 4: 137; Ibn 'Abidin, *Radd al-Muhtar*, Vol. 6: 277–8.

28. Q. 4:92.

29. al-Marghinani, *al-Hidaya*, Vol. 2: 153; Ibn al-Humam, *Fath al-Qadir*, Vol. 6: 19; al-'Ayni, *al-Binaya*, Vol. 7: 205; Ibn Nujaym, *Bahr al-Ra'iq*, Vol. 5: 169; al-Zayla'i, *Tabyin al-Haqa'iq*, Vol. 4: 137; Ibn 'Abidin, *Radd al-Muhtar*, Vol. 6: 277–8.

30. Ibn 'Abidin, *Radd al-Muhtar*, Vol. 6: 277.

31. al-Marghinani, *al-Hidaya*, Vol. 2: 153; Ibn al-Humam, *Fath al-Qadir*, Vol. 6: 20; al-'Ayni, *al-Binaya*, Vol. 7: 206; al-Nasafi, *Kanz al-Daqa'iq*, Vol. 1: 595; Ibn Nujaym, *al-Bahr al-Ra'iq*, Vol. 5: 169–70; al-Zayla'i, *Tabyin al-Haqa'iq*, Vol. 4: 138–9.

32. 'Ala' al-Din Abu Bakr ibn Mas'ud al-Kasani, *Bada'i' al-Sana'i' fi Tartib al-Shara'i'* (Beirut, 1998), Vol. 6: 69.

33. al-Sarakhsi, *al-Mabsut*, Vol. 10: 62; al-Zayla'i, *Tabyin al-Haqa'iq*, Vol. 4: 138–9; al-'Ayni, *al-Binaya*, Vol. 7: 206; Ibn 'Abidin, *Radd al-Muhtar*, Vol. 6: 278.

34. al-Marghinani, *al-Hidaya*, Vol. 2: 153.
35. Akmal al-Din Muhammad ibn Mahmud al-Babarti, *al-'Inaya Sharh al-Hidaya* (Beirut, 2007), Vol. 3: 311; al-'Ayni, *al-Binaya*, Vol. 7: 205.
36. See for example al-Marghinani, *al-Hidaya*, Vol. 3: 66.
37. Mu'in al-Din Mulla Miskin Harawi Farahi, *Sharh Mulla Miskin 'ala Kanz al-Daqa'iq* (photocopy without publisher information, printed with *Fath Allah al-Mu'in 'ala Sharh Mulla Miskin* of Abu al-Su'ud Sayyid Muhammad ibn 'Ali al-Husayni), Vol. 3: 26. Miskin's view is also mentioned by Ibn Nujaym (and others), *al-Bahr al-Ra'iq*, Vol. 6: 461. *Al-Fatawa al-Hindiyya* cites the view in reference to *al-Multaqat*, 'Abd al-Rahman and Ibn al-Nizam (leading eds.), *al-Fatawa al-Hindiyya*, Vol. 5: 108.

Bibliography

'Abd al-Rahman, 'Abd al-Latif Hasan and Ibn al-Nizam, Muhammad (leading eds.), *al-Fatawa al-Hindiyya* (complied by around 400 scholars) (Beirut, 2000).

Ali, Wajahat, Clifton, Eli, Duss, Matthew, Fang, Lee, Keyes, Scott and Shakir, Faiz, 'Fear, Inc.: The roots of the Islamophobia network in America', *Center for American Progress*, 26 August 2011 (http://www.americanprogress.org/issues/religion/report/2011/08/26/10165/fear-inc/, last accessed 27 December 2013).

al-'Ayni, Badr al-Din, *al-Binaya Sharh al-Hidaya* (Beirut, 2000).

al-Babarti, Akmal al-Din Muhammad ibn Mahmud, *al-'Inaya Sharh al-Hidaya* (Beirut, 2007).

de Graaf, Hermanus J., 'South-East Asian Islam to the eighteenth century', in P. M. Holt, A. K. S. Lambton and B. Lewis (eds.), *The Cambridge History of Islam*, vol. 2A (Cambridge, 1984).

Farahi, Mu'in al-Din Mulla Miskin Harawi, *Sharh Mulla Miskin 'ala Kanz al-Daqa'iq* (photocopy without publisher information, printed with *Fath Allah al-Mu'in 'ala Sharh Mulla Miskin* of Abu Su'ud Sayyid Muhammad ibn 'Ali al-Husayni).

al-Haskafi, Muhammad, 'Ala' al-Din, *Durr al-Mukhtar* (printed with Sayyid Muhammad Amin ibn 'Abidin, *Radd al-Muhtar*) (Beirut, 2003).

Ibn 'Abidin, Sayyid Muhammad Amin, *Radd al-Muhtar 'ala Durr al-Mukhtar Sharh Tanwir al-Absar* (Beirut, 2003).

Ibn al-Humam, Kamal al-Din Muhammad, *Fath al-Qadir Sharh al-Hidaya* (Beirut, 2003).

Ibn Nujaym, Zayn al-Din ibn Ibrahim ibn Muhammad, *al-Bahr al-Ra'iq Sharh Kanz al-Daqa'iq* (Beirut, 1997).

Israeli, Raphael, *Islam in China* (London, 1994).

al-Jundi, Khalil ibn Ishaq, *Mukhtasar Khalil* (Cairo, n.d.).

al-Kasani, 'Ala' al-Din Abu Bakr ibn Mas'ud, *Bada'i' al-Sana'i' fi Tartib al-Shara'i'* (Beirut, 1997).

Khadduri, Majid, *Islamic Law of Nations: Shaybani's Siyar* (Baltimore, 1966).

_____, *al-Qanun al-Dawli al-Islami: Kitab al-Siyar li-l-Shaybani* (Beirut, 1975).

Lapidus, Ira, A *History of Muslim Societies* (Cambridge, 2002).

Lombard, Maurice, *The Golden Age of Islam* (Amsterdam and Oxford, 1975).

al-Marghinani, Burhan al-Din Abu al-Hasan 'Ali, *Bidayat al-Mubtadi* (printed with its commentary *al-Hidaya*), *al-Hidaya Sharh Bidaya al-Mubtadi* (Cairo, n.d.).

al-Mawardi, Abu al-Hasan 'Ali ibn Muhammad, *al-Ahkam al-Sultaniyya* (Cairo, 1973).

al-Maydani, 'Abd al-Ghani al-Ghunaymi, *al-Lubab fi Sharh al-Kitab* (Beirut, n.d.).

al-Nasafi, Abu al-Barakat, 'Abd Allah ibn Ahmad, *Kanz al-Daqa'iq* (Karachi, 2004).

al-Quduri, Abu al-Hasan Ahmad ibn Muhammad al-Baghdadi, *al-Mukhtasar li'l-Quduri* (Lahore, n.d.).

Sahnun, 'Abd al-Salam ibn Sa'id, *al-Mudawwana al-Kubra* (Cairo, n.d.).

al-Sarakhsi, Muhammad ibn Ahmad Abu Bakr, *Kitab al-Mabsut* (Quetta, n.d.).

The Sun, 'Williams: Victory for terrorism', 7 February 2008 (http://www.thesun .co.uk/sol/homepage/news/778163/Archbishop-of-Canterbury-Rowan-Williams-argues-for-introduction-of-Sharia-law-in-Britain.html, last accessed 15 December 2013).

al-Tamartashi, Muhammad ibn 'Abd Allah, *Tanwir al-Absar* (printed with Sayyid Muhammad Amin ibn 'Abidin, *Radd al-Muhtar*) (Beirut, 2003).

Williams, Rowan, 'Civil and religious law in England: a religious perspective', Temple Lecture, Royal Courts of Justice, 7 February 2008 (http://rowanwilliams.archbishopofcanterbury.org/articles.php/1137/, last accessed 24 December 2013).

al-Yamani, Abu Bakr ibn 'Ali al-Haddad, *al-Jawhara al-Nayyira 'ala Mukhtasar al-Quduri* (Multan, n.d.).

al-Zayla'i, Fakhr al-Din 'Uthman ibn 'Ali, *Tabyin al-Haqa'iq* (Beirut, 2000).

5

Responses to the Almoravid Intervention in al-Andalus

Russell Hopley

The early twelfth century was a time of momentous change for the Muslims of the western Mediterranean. Sicily, an island that had entered the fold of Islam some four centuries earlier, had come under Norman rule in the final decade of the eleventh century.[1] Considerable territory in Islamic Spain had fallen prey to Christian re-conquest,[2] and sizeable tracts of land in North Africa, among them the vital metropolis of al-Qayrawan, were being plundered by Bedouin tribes as they embarked on their epic migration westward from Egypt.[3] The responses provoked by this traumatic series of events varied considerably, ranging from flight to a renewed call for jihad, a position advocated most strongly by the Almoravid emir Yusuf ibn Tashfin (r.1061–1106).[4]

The Almoravids crossed the straits from North Africa to al-Andalus on no fewer than three occasions in an effort to turn back the armies of Christian Iberia. The first of these three crossings occurred in 1086, in response to the seizure of Toledo by Alphonso VI of Castille the previous year. The decisive defeat Yusuf inflicted on Alphonso at the Battle of Zallaqa provided only temporary respite from the tide of Christian re-conquest, and Yusuf was to return to al-Andalus in 1088 and subsequently in 1091 in an effort to halt further Christian encroachment into the realm of the faith. On this latter occasion the Almoravid emir directed his armies to overthrow the numerous Muslim '*ta'ifa*' (small principality) kingdoms[5] that had sprung up throughout al-Andalus, and to establish in their stead direct rule of Islamic Iberia from the Almoravid capital in Marrakesh. This brought the Muslims of al-Andalus and much of North Africa under single rule, a status they had enjoyed only rarely since the period of the early Islamic conquests. However, the Almoravid overthrow of the *ta'ifa* kingdoms and annexation of al-Andalus was not without its critics. The jihad undertaken by Yusuf ibn Tashfin in al-Andalus was in many respects a highly problematic affair, since it entailed not only battle against the armies of Christian Iberia, but also, disconcertingly, armed confrontation with those *ta'ifa* rulers who refused to cede power to the Almoravids willingly. Yusuf ibn Tashfin's jihad was, therefore, one that held the potential of unleashing chaos as it turned one Muslim against another, and it undoubtedly appeared to more than a few observers at the time that the Almoravid state was attempting to conquer and annex a neighbouring Muslim territory under the pretext of jihad. This chapter will consider several signs that the Almoravid jihad in Muslim Spain was a highly contested undertaking, and it will explore the doctrinal basis upon which the Muslims of al-Andalus articulated their opposition to the Almoravid jihad in Iberia.

Perhaps the most significant expression of resistance to the Almoravid jihad in al-Andalus comes in the form of a brief missive penned by a legal scholar, Muhammad ibn Yahya ibn al-Farra', who served as *qadi* of the Andalusian city of Almeria at the time of the Almoravid intervention. The letter of Ibn al-Farra' is found in the text of a fatwa of the well-known Granadan jurist Abu al-Qasim al-Shatibi (d.1388).[6] The fatwa concerns the licit uses of money belonging to the public treasury, known in Arabic as the *bayt mal al-muslimin*. Al-Shatibi relates that Yusuf ibn Tashfin ordered the *qadi* from Almeria to oversee the collection and supply of provisions for the Almoravid jihad in al-Andalus. Ibn al-Farra' refuses, and when Yusuf is informed of the refusal he replies that he has taken counsel with his *fuqaha'* on the issue, and they have assured him that his demand for provisions is in fact the correct course of action. Bolstering his argument further, the Almoravid emir cites the example of 'Umar ibn al-Khattab, a close Companion of the Prophet and the second Rightly Guided Caliph (r.634–44), who, Yusuf observes, had mandated the supply of provisions for the sake of jihad.

Ibn al-Farra' replies that the *fuqaha'* who have provided counsel to Yusuf can, in short, 'go to hell', or *ila al-nar* as the Arabic reads. He points out that Yusuf ibn Tashfin is no 'Umar. 'Umar, the *qadi* remarks, possessed a just character that was beyond question: 'You', he says 'are no companion of the Prophet, and doubt has been cast on the justice of your actions.' If Yusuf is truly in need of additional provisions for his jihad, then he should enter the mosque and take an oath in person before the men of learning gathered there, swearing that the *bayt mal al-muslimin* has been depleted, and that there are no public funds remaining to support the Almoravid jihad. This, he contends, was the practice of 'Umar, an assertion that deftly turns Yusuf's mandate on its head and works quite effectively to undermine the Almoravid emir's attempt to portray himself as standard-bearer of 'Umar's *sunna*. Al-Shatibi concludes his discussion of this remarkable exchange between North African emir and Andalusian jurist by commenting that God admonished Yusuf ibn Tashfin through the *qadi*'s reply, and that the Almoravid emir pursued the matter no further.

The issue of oath-taking and the binding nature of oaths provided a potent weapon for those who opposed the Almoravid jihad in al-Andalus. It seems quite likely that Ibn al-Farra' refused to swear the oath of loyalty to Yusuf ibn Tashfin, and thus felt little compunction to contribute to his jihad. The emphasis on oath-taking in the *qadi*'s response is intended to underscore the problems Yusuf ibn Tashfin very likely experienced in this regard, particularly the difficulties he encountered in obtaining the oath of loyalty from the Muslim notables of al-Andalus. A missive to the esteemed eastern philosopher and jurist Abu Hamid al-Ghazali (d.1111) from the Sevillian *qadi* Abu Bakr ibn al-'Arabi (d.1147) noted that the leaders of the Andalusian *ta'ifa* states had rebuffed the Almoravid call for jihad in Iberia on the grounds that Andalusian Muslims had pledged the *bay'a* – a near-indissoluble oath of loyalty – to them and not to Yusuf ibn Tashfin.[7] The Almoravid emir was therefore in no position to demand that they participate in his jihad. The *ta'ifa* leaders further rejected Yusuf's call for jihad by pointing out that he was not of Qurayshi lineage, while many of them were (or at least claimed to be); he was thus unqualified to claim the mantle of leadership in jihad.

We might venture further that Yusuf ibn Tashfin withdrew his armies from Iberia following his first two incursions precisely because the challenge of revoking the *bay'a* sworn by the Andalusian notables to the various *ta'ifa* rulers was simply too daunting, if not insurmountable. If this was indeed the case, the Almoravid emir's response to this dilemma seems to have come following his third crossing into al-Andalus when he deposed the *ta'ifa* rulers wholesale, killing some and sending others into exile, presumably accompanied by those notables who had sworn the *bay'a* to them and were unwilling to rescind this binding act of fealty.

There was a further consequence of the Almoravid jihad in Iberia, one that undoubtedly exacerbated Andalusian opposition to the presence of Yusuf ibn Tashfin's armies in Muslim Spain. The incident in question involves a number of criminal gangs that had taken to impersonating the Almoravids in their distinctive dress and practice of wearing the veil.[8] Ibn 'Abdun al-Tujibi, a market inspector (*muhtasib*)[9] of Seville in the early twelfth century, reports that such gangs were able to operate with near impunity throughout the city when masquerading as Almoravids, their veils granting them anonymity whenever they appeared in public and their custom of moving about heavily armed going largely unquestioned by the authorities. Ibn 'Abdun reports that the criminal gangs wearing Almoravid dress were committing abuses and moral outrages that terrified the citizenry of Seville. Unfortunately he fails to specify what these crimes and outrages were, but he does note that many members of the gangs hailed from among the ranks of the servants and retinue, the *'abid* and *hasham,* who accompanied the Almoravids whenever they made an appearance in public. In this manner, Ibn 'Abdun remarks, men of questionable character were being conferred a dignity they scarcely deserved. The presence of the Almoravids in Seville, and presumably elsewhere in al-Andalus, thus presented a distinct challenge to the fabric of Muslim society. Alongside their wanton behaviour, these *false* Almoravids were, as the market inspector observes, effectively turning the social order of Islamic Spain on its head.

The Almoravid practice of wearing the veil in public undoubtedly served quite effectively to mark them as a distinct element in Andalusian society, one that had arrived in Islamic Spain specifically for the purpose of waging jihad. However, as Ibn 'Abdun's brief text makes apparent, the Almoravid veil, the sine qua non of jihad in early twelfth-century Iberia, was proving increasingly irksome to the Andalusian populace. Indeed, the insistence of the Almoravids upon wearing their veils at all times, especially during communal prayers in the mosques of Islamic Spain, prompted certain Andalusians to request a legal ruling on the licitness of this decidedly unorthodox custom. The fatwa handed down in response to this query is found among the legal opinions of the Cordoban jurist Ibn Rushd al-Jadd (d.1126),[10] grandfather of the eminent Muslim philosopher Averroes. Ibn Rushd ultimately ruled in favour of the Almoravid practice of wearing the veil during prayer, arguing that doing so was among the customs that the nomadic Berbers had handed down from father to son for countless generations. The jurist expounds upon this point by remarking that abandoning the veil would be detrimental not only to the Almoravids, but to the Muslims of Iberia as a whole. Indeed, by donning the veil in public amongst the Andalusian populace, Ibn Rushd argues that the Almoravids make known the legion of their number in Iberia; this, he affirms, is a source of strength for all Muslims, not just the Almoravids. Of equal importance, he notes, is the Almoravid veil's singular ability to strike fear in the hearts of the polytheists, a common byword in Islamic legal literature for the Christians of medieval Iberia.

Ibn Rushd remarks more pointedly that it is the Almoravids who have assumed the burden of jihad in the contested march areas of Iberia, and both they and their customs should thus be regarded with esteem by their Andalusian co-religionists. Indeed, this latter argument, namely that the Almoravids have taken it upon themselves to safeguard the survival of Islam in Iberia, seems marshalled in an effort to preempt any argument that might call into question the Almoravids' highly unusual dress, and, by extension, their presence in Islamic Spain.

In addition to the controversy surrounding the Almoravid veil, Ibn Rushd was also called upon to provide a fatwa concerning the merits of *hajj* (the pilgrimage to Mecca) versus jihad.[11] The petition for this fatwa specifies that the query concerning these two duties emanated directly from the Almoravid emir, 'Ali ibn Yusuf ibn Tashfin (r.1106–43), son of the aforementioned Yusuf ibn Tashfin, and the second Almoravid to govern al-Andalus. 'Ali ibn Yusuf assumed rule over al-Andalus at the outset of the twelfth century, a time that proved to be especially troublesome for Almoravid rule in the western Mediterranean; the young emir had to contend almost immediately with growing military pressure from the Christian kingdoms of northern Iberia, and the increasingly uncompromising criticism of Almoravid rule from the Mahdi ibn Tumart, a messianic figure who would very quickly attract a sizeable following among the Berber tribes in the mountainous regions south of Marrakesh.[12]

Of course, the primary concern underlying the emir's query involved the safety of Muslim pilgrims as they embarked on the journey to Mecca, very possibly exposing both their persons and their property to danger, particularly at sea, a tacit admission in itself that Muslim navies no longer commanded the sea lanes of the Mediterranean as they once had. Furthermore, it seems quite plausible that the Almoravid leader was concerned that pilgrimage to the sanctuary cities of Arabia was steadily draining al-Andalus of able-bodied men who could be called into military service. Indeed the likelihood that *hajj* now represented a means for young men to cool their heels in distant Mecca, far from the troubled shores of Muslim Spain, must have weighed heavily on the minds of the increasingly embattled Almoravids. On this latter point we should be attentive to the possibility that *hajj* presented an effective means for Andalusians to express their opposition to the Almoravid jihad in Iberia. Physically departing al-Andalus, with perhaps little intention of returning, gave voice to those who felt resentment at the Almoravids, allowing them to express their opposition to Yusuf ibn Tashfin's overthrow of the *ta'ifa* states. More specifically, embarking on *hajj* allowed those Andalusians who had pledged the *bay'a* to the now-deposed *ta'ifa* rulers an opportunity to depart Iberia without facing retribution from the new sovereigns of Islamic Spain.

It was in this atmosphere of disquiet that Ibn Rushd al-Jadd was asked to weigh *hajj* against jihad. Given the importance the Almoravid leadership attached to waging jihad in Iberia, his decision to argue in favour of the latter should come as no surprise. Indeed, the legal opinion that Ibn Rushd formulated represents something of a touchstone on the question; it is cited in at least three collections of Islamic legal opinions, both Andalusian and North African,[13] and it seems to have formed an important part of how Muslims of the medieval western Mediterranean viewed these two obligations. Ibn Rushd divides his fatwa into three parts. In the first part he states categorically that the duty of *hajj* is in abeyance, *saqit*, for Andalusians due to the potential danger Muslim pilgrims would face as they made the journey eastward. In place of going on *hajj*, Ibn Rushd wholeheartedly recommends jihad, the virtues of which, he contends, surpass enumeration. In fact, he asserts that the obligation to substitute jihad for *hajj* in such circumstances is so clear that it requires no further substantiation. It is highly ironic, of course, that a Muslim weakness – namely the inability to ensure the safety of the overland and sea routes to Mecca – represents, for Ibn Rushd, a point of strength for the Almoravids, presenting as it did something of a check against the emigration of young Andalusian males to Arabia.

In the second part of his response, Ibn Rushd restates the question, postulating in this second instance that the roadways to Mecca are secure and that Andalusian Muslims are able to embark on the pilgrimage without fear.[14] But Ibn Rushd again endorses jihad, due, as he says, both to its great inherent virtue and to the important consideration that the duty of *hajj* may be postponed to a later time, with Muslims expected to attend to more pressing matters before leaving for the pilgrimage. Indeed, appealing to the possibility of postponing an obligation, *tarakhi*, is central to Ibn Rushd's formulation, for it allows him to argue the merits of jihad and its superiority over *hajj* when more urgent needs are present.

In the third section of Ibn Rushd's fatwa the Almoravid emir asks the Cordoban jurist whether the same stipulations concerning *hajj* apply to North Africans as apply to Andalusians, namely that they should postpone pilgrimage and devote themselves to jihad if that is the more pressing need. In light of this second question from the Almoravid emir, it seems quite possible that Ibn Rushd's earlier reply may in fact have been a source of confusion for western Muslims, seemingly enjoining North Africans to undertake the pilgrimage to Mecca, while discouraging Andalusians from doing so in order to heed the call of jihad instead. Ibn Rushd's response undoubtedly made the emir's task of governing these two regions more difficult by placing him in the awkward position of applying one set of regulations to Andalusians and a second set to North Africans. This was undoubtedly a point of concern for the Almoravid leadership, as bringing doctrinal unity to the lands of the Islamic west had been among the earliest of the dynasty's stated goals. In response to this quandary, Ibn Rushd asserts that jihad takes precedence for North Africans, just as it does for Andalusians, even if the path to Mecca presents no danger to pilgrims. The jurist appeals once again to the concept of *tarakhi*, postponing an obligation to a later time, and states specifically, lest there be any doubt among Muslims of the western lands, that jihad is preferable even to postponing the pilgrimage to a later time. It bears pointing out that Ibn Rushd's opinion in this fatwa stands in marked contrast to the stance of earlier Maliki jurists, most notably the venerated Tunisian *faqih* Ibn Abi Zayd al-Qayrawani (d.996), who asserted that *hajj* should be undertaken at the earliest opportunity.[15]

A commentary appended to the fatwa of Ibn Rushd supplies some intriguing detail,[16] and it provides a sure indication that his preference for jihad over *hajj* was regarded with reservation by other jurists. The commentary is kept anonymous and offers no detail of when or where it might have been composed. It is introduced with little more than the impersonal expression '*qila*', 'it has been said', and observes, significantly, that it was common practice for Muslim pilgrims to rent ships from Christians in order to sail from Ifriqiya[17] to Alexandria, or from Ifriqiya to points farther west in North Africa, Sebta most probably, as they returned from the *hajj*. This, the commentary notes, is of minor importance if the emir of Tunis is strong and the Christians fear him. If this is indeed the case, Christian sailors would presumably do no harm to their Muslim passengers. However, if the emir is considered weak, the practice of renting ships from Christians presents a clear danger to Muslim pilgrims. The anonymous commentator notes further that he personally witnessed men of virtue and learning riding in ships in this fashion and that they did so out of necessity, meaning presumably that travel overland through the Muslim lands of North Africa presented a greater risk to pilgrims than travel by sea in Christian ships.[18]

The brief commentary concludes by noting that the *fuqaha'* of Fez and Bijaya have recommended this practice. The fact that these North African religious scholars were willing to ride roughshod over Ibn Rushd's contention that *hajj* is in abeyance for western Muslims, and that jihad may be licitly substituted for *hajj*, suggests a number of things. The North African jurists cited in the commentary may have sought guidance with the first generation of Maliki scholars, namely those like Ibn Abi Zayd al-Qayrawani who strongly recommended *hajj*,[19] and attached less importance to the rulings of later generations, including that of Ibn Rushd. This preference for *hajj* over jihad could likewise be a case of regionalism asserting itself in the field of legal practice, the jurists of Fez and Bijaya feeling more comfortable with the opinions of a fellow North African such as Ibn Abi Zayd than with those of Andalusian jurists who

were perhaps felt to be too far removed from North African concerns.
One might also speculate that North African jurists perhaps felt that
jihad was better left to their Andalusian co-religionists who were, in
any event, closer to *Dar al-Harb* than they.[20] Although the commentary
on Ibn Rushd's opinion is kept anonymous, it may plausibly be viewed
as representing a North African rejoinder to the legal opinion of the
Andalusian jurist, and it provides a sure indication that these two regions
of the Islamic west, neighbours by geography, could be quite distant from
one another in matters of basic doctrine.

The opinion of Ibn Rushd did not stem the flow of Muslim pilgrims
eastward, no matter the danger they might face. The jurist Ibn Talha
observes that he encountered many Muslims from North Africa during
his pilgrimage journey.[21] He registers some surprise at this, remarking
that his understanding was that *hajj* was not only in abeyance for western
Muslims, but that it had been deemed *haram*, 'forbidden', due to the
perilous nature of the journey. Popular pressure for the *hajj* must have
been strong enough to override the opinion of the venerable Ibn Rushd,
and his assertion that jihad is preferable to hajj for both Andalusians
and North Africans appears to have largely fallen on deaf ears. Perhaps
the best testimony to this is the travel narrative written by Ibn Jubayr
(d.1217), a native of Valencia who undertook the pilgrimage not long after
Ibn Rushd handed down his fatwa. Seen in this light, Ibn Jubayr's well-
known book of travels represents an outright rejection of any position
that emphasises the necessity of jihad over *hajj*.[22] One might say much
the same for that famous resident of Tangier, Ibn Battuta (d.1368 or
1377), and his extensive travels in the east, the initial impulse for which
was a desire to undertake the *hajj* to Mecca.

Another contemporary of Ibn Rushd, Abu Bakr al-Turtushi (d.1126),
also asserted that *hajj* was forbidden for the inhabitants of the Islamic
west.[23] Not content with declaring that *hajj* should be postponed to
a later time, Turtushi maintained that it was in fact sinful, *athim*, for
western Muslims to make the pilgrimage to Mecca. He says nothing,
however, on the question of substituting jihad for *hajj*. It is worthwhile
to reflect for a moment on the interesting case of al-Turtushi. A native
of the Iberian city of Tortossa, al-Turtushi made the pilgrimage early
in his life, and never set foot again in his native al-Andalus. Instead he

took up residence in Alexandria, where he wrote a number of important works, including the lengthy *Kitab al-Hawadith wa-l-Bida'* (*Treatise on Illegal Innovations in Islam*), and an influential fatwa condemning the works of al-Ghazali. Living in Alexandria, Turtushi was doubtless aware of the many Andalusian and North African pilgrims passing through the city on their way to the sanctuary cities of Arabia. Perhaps declaring the pilgrimage sinful was the only means he could find to stem the departure of Muslims from an increasingly troubled al-Andalus. One must, of course, overlook the inconvenient truth that he himself did that very thing.

If, as I have suggested above, the Almoravid jihad in Iberia was a highly contested affair, it is worthwhile to consider briefly how the jihad has been viewed in the modern period. In response to a question posed by the Algerian emir 'Abd al-Qadir (d.1883) regarding the licitness of waging jihad against the French forces occupying his country, the Moroccan jurist 'Ali ibn 'Abd al-Salam al-Tusuli (d.1842) cites the example of the aforementioned *qadi* of Almeria, Ibn al-Farra', and his opposition to the Almoravid jihad.[24] Al-Tusuli remarks to 'Abd al-Qadir that he should be mindful of the discord Yusuf ibn Tashfin provoked among Andalusians as he waged jihad on Iberian soil. This admonition was undoubtedly intended to caution the emir against being overly harsh in his treatment of the Algerian population. It further suggests that 'Abd al-Qadir may have been encountering difficulties not unlike those the Almoravids encountered in al-Andalus some seven centuries earlier, namely a hesitance on the part of the populace to participate wholeheartedly in jihad. Perhaps of most significance for this volume, the incident underscores the degree to which a jihad undertaken in Iberia in the medieval period was still felt to be of great relevance for a nineteenth-century jurist as he sought to formulate a doctrine for waging jihad at an especially critical moment for Islam in the western Mediterranean.

Notes

1. An account of the Norman conquest of Sicily is found in Donald Matthew, *The Norman Kingdom of Sicily* (Cambridge, 1992). See also Gordon Brown, *The Norman Conquest of Southern Italy and Sicily* (North Carolina, 2003).

2. Numerous contemporary histories of the Christian re-conquest of Islamic Iberia exist, e.g. Hugh Kennedy, *Muslim Spain and Portugal: A Political History of al-Andalus* (London, 1996), and Joseph F. O'Callaghan, *Reconquest and Crusade in Medieval Spain* (Philadelphia, 2003).

3. See Abu 'Abd Allah Muhammad al-Idrisi, *Nuzhat al-Mushtaq fi Ikhtiraq al-Afaq* (Beirut, 1989), Vol. 1: 280–5.

4. Biographical details for Yusuf ibn Tashfin and other significant North African figures mentioned in this chapter are supplied in Emmanuel K. Akyeampong and Henry Louis Gates, Jr. (eds.), *Dictionary of African Biography* (Oxford, 2012).

5. The *ta'ifa* kingdoms of al-Andalus arose following the demise of the Umayyad caliphate of Cordoba in 1033. Most prominent among the *ta'ifa* kingdoms was that of the Banu 'Abbad of Seville and Cordoba.

6. Al-Shatibi's fatwa is cited in Ahmad ibn Yahya al-Wansharisi, *Al-Mi'yar al-Mu'rib wa-l-Jami' al-Mughrib 'an Fatawa Ahl Ifriqiya wa-l-Andalus wa-l-Maghrib* (Rabat, 1981), Vol. 11: 132.

7. The text of Ibn al-'Arabi's letter to al-Ghazali is found in 'Ismat Dandash, 'Dirasa hawla rasa'il Ibn al-'Arabi', *Al-Manahil* 9 (1977): 149–90.

8. This incident is cited in Evariste Lévi-Provençal, 'Un document sur la vie urbaine et les corps de métiers à Séville au début du XIIe siècle: Le traité d'Ibn 'Abdun', *Journal Asiatique* (Avril-Juin 1934): 177–299.

9. The *muhtasib* was charged with overseeing and ensuring the legality of transactions that occurred in the marketplace, and would thus be responsible for verifying the soundness of all weights, measures and monies used in these transactions. The position also contained a moral component, as it was the duty of the *muhtasib* to see that the marketplace remained free of immoral behaviour.

10. Ibn Rushd's fatwa is given in Abu al-Walid Muhammad ibn Ahmad Ibn Rushd, *Fatawa Ibn Rushd*, ed. al-Mukhtar al-Talili, 3 Vols. (Beirut, 1984), Vol. 2: 963–5. See also al-Wansharisi, *al-Mi'yar*, Vol. 1: 225. Biographical details for Ibn Rushd are supplied in Vincent Lagardère, 'Abu 'l-Walid b. Rushd, Qadi al-Qudat de Cordue', *Revue des Études Islamiques* 54 (1986): 203–24.

11. The fatwa is given in Ibn Rushd, *Fatawa*, Vol. 2: 1021–6; al-Wansharisi, *al-Mi'yar*, Vol. 1: 432–7.

12. For a recent account of Ibn Tumart and the origins of the Almohad movement, see Allen Fromherz, *The Almohads: The Rise of an Islamic Empire* (London, 2010). Messianic dimensions of Almohad rule are discussed in Robert Brunschvig, 'Sur le doctrine du Mahdi Ibn Tumart', *Arabica* 2 (1955): 137–49.

13. The fatwa of Ibn Rushd is also cited by the Tunisian jurist Abu al-Qasim al-Burzuli (d.1438), in *Fatawa al-Burzuli: Jami' Masa'il al-Ahkam li-ma Nazala min al-Qadaya bi-l-Muftin wa-l-Hukkam* (Beirut, 2002), Vol. 1: 118.

14. A primary concern in this regard is that pilgrims have secure, unfettered access to *manahil* (sources of water) as they make their journey overland, both for consumption and for the maintenance of *tahara* (ritual purity).

15. See al-Wansharisi, *al-Mi'yar*, Vol. 1: 437.

16. The commentary is found in al-Wansharisi, *al-Mi'yar*, Vol. 1: 436.

17. Ifriqiyya is the medieval Arabic designation for the region encompassed today by Tunisia and northwestern Libya. The most common points of embarkation for pilgrims in medieval Ifriqiyya were the coastal cities of Tunis, Mahdia and Sfax.

18. This is a clear reference to the insecurity that prevailed in the North African hinterlands, especially in the region of Ifriqiya, following the Hilali Bedouin invasion of the 1050s. It should be noted that this invasion culminated in the sack of the venerated city of al-Qayrawan in 1057.

19. Ibn Abi Zayd al-Qayrawani's discussion of the topic is found in idem, *Fatawa Ibn Abi Zayd al-Qayrawani* (Beirut, 2004), pp. 130–2. Noteworthy is his use of the term *ghazw* in place of 'jihad'. A range of terms are found throughout Islamic legal literature that approximate jihad, including *ribat*, *ghazw* and *qufl*. For *hajj* we find the term *jiwar* frequently used to indicate a period of extended residence in the two sanctuary cities following the formal conclusion of the pilgrimage.

20. They would not have been mistaken in this judgement, as proximity to the contested areas is an important consideration in determining who is liable to shoulder the responsibility for waging jihad. *Dar al-Harb* (lit. 'Abode of War'), is a designation for those lands in which Islamic law does not hold sway and are thus subject to jihad.

21. This is most likely the Andalusian jurist and religious scholar Abu Bakr 'Abd Allah ibn Talha (d.1125). A native of Seville, Ibn Talha is best known for his commentary on the *Risala* of Ibn Abi Zayd al-Qayrawani.

22. Noteworthy in the travel narrative of Ibn Jubayr is the lengthy description of Sicily, a land lost to Islam a century and a half prior to his sojourn there. See idem, *Rihlat Ibn Jubayr* (Beirut, n.d.), pp. 252–71.

23. It should be noted that Turtushi also authored an epistle to Yusuf ibn Tashfin that was highly critical of the Almoravid emir's rule of al-Andalus following his overthrow of the numerous *ta'ifa* states in 1091.

24. The text of Tusuli's discussion of the Almoravid jihad is found in idem, *Ajwibat al-Tusuli 'an Masa'il al-Amir 'Abd al-Qadir fi al-Jihad* (Beirut, 1996), pp. 290–2.

Bibliography

Akyeampong, Emmanuel K. and Gates, Henry Louis, Jr. (eds.), *Dictionary of African Biography*, 6 Vols. (Oxford, 2012).

Balansi, Ibn Jubayr, *Rihlat Ibn Jubayr* (Beirut, n.d.).

Bonner, Michael, *Jihad in Islamic History: Doctrines and Practice* (Princeton, 2006).

Bosch-Vila, Jacinto, *Los Almoravides* (Tetuán, 1956).

Brown, Gordon, *The Norman Conquest of Southern Italy and Sicily* (North Carolina, 2003).

Brunschvig, Robert, 'Sur le doctrine du Mahdi Ibn Tumart', *Arabica* 2 (1955): 137–49.

Al-Bukhari, Muhammad ibn Isma'il, *Sahih al-Bukhari*, ed. 'Ali ibn Ahmad al-Hawari, 4 Vols. (Cairo, 1902).

Burzuli, Abu al-Qasim ibn Ahmad, *Fatawa al-Burzuli: Jami' Masa'il al-Ahkam li-ma Nazala min al-Qadaya bi-l-Muftin wa-l-Hukkam*, ed. Muhammad al-Habib Hilah, 7 Vols. (Beirut, 2002).

Dandash, 'Ismat, 'Dirasa hawla rasa'il Ibn al-'Arabi', *Al-Manahil* 9 (1977): 149–90.

De La Puente, Cristina, 'Vivre et mourir pour Dieu, œuvre et héritage d'Abu 'Ali al-Sadafi (m. 514/1120)', *Studia Islamica* 88 (1998): 77–102.

Fromherz, Allen, *The Almohads: The Rise of an Islamic Empire* (London, 2010).

Ibn Rushd, Abu al-Walid Muhammad ibn Ahmad, *Fatawa Ibn Rushd*, ed. al-Mukhtar al-Talili, 3 Vols. (Beirut, 1984).

Idrisi, Abu 'Abd Allah Muhammad, *Nuzhat al-Mushtaq fi Ikhtiraq al-Afaq* (Beirut, 1989).

Kennedy, Hugh, *Muslim Spain and Portugal: A Political History of al-Andalus* (London, 1996).

Khushani, Abu, 'Abd Allah Muhammad *Qudat Qurtuba*, ed. Ibrahim al-Abyari (Beirut, 1989).

Lagardère, Vincent, 'Abu 'l-Walid b. Rushd, Qadi al-Qudat de Cordue', *Revue des Études Islamiques* 54 (1986): 203–24.

———, Le Vendredi de Zallaqa (Paris, 1989).

———, Les Almoravides (Paris, 1989).

———, 'Évolution de la notion de *djihad* à l'époque almoravide (1039–1147)', *Cahiers de Civilisation Mediévale* 41 (1998): 3–16.

———, Les Almoravides, Le Djihâd Andalou (Paris, 1998).

Lévi-Provençal, Evariste, 'Un document sur la vie urbaine et les corps de métiers à Séville au début du XIIe siècle: Le traité d'Ibn 'Abdun', *Journal Asiatique* (Avril-Juin 1934): 177–299.

Matthew, Donald, *The Norman Kingdom of Sicily* (Cambridge, 1992).

Messier, Ronald, *The Almoravids and the Meanings of Jihad* (Santa Barbara, 2010).

O'Callaghan, Joseph F., *Reconquest and Crusade in Medieval Spain* (Philadelphia, 2003).

al-Qayrawani, Abu Muhammad 'Abd Allah ibn Abi Zayd, *Fatawa Ibn Abi Zayd al-Qayrawani*, ed. Hamid Lahmar (Beirut, 2004).

al-Tusuli, 'Ali ibn 'Abd al-Salam, *Ajwibat al-Tusuli 'an Masa'il al-Amir 'Abd al-Qadir fi al-Jihad* (Beirut, 1996).

Urvoy, Dominique, 'Sur l'évolution de la notion de Ǧihād dans l'Espagne Musulmane', *Mélanges de la Casa de Velazquez* 9 (1973): 335–71.

Wansharisi, Ahmad ibn Yahya, *Al-Mi'yar al-Mu'rib wa-l-Jami' al-Mughrib 'an Fatawa Ahl Ifriqiya wa-l-Andalus wa-l-Maghrib*, ed. Muhammad Hajji, 13 Vols. (Rabat, 1981).

Wensinck, Arent Jan, 'The refused dignity', in T. W. Arnold and R. A. Nicholson (eds.), *A Volume of Oriental Studies Presented to E.G. Browne* (Cambridge, 1922): 491–9.

Yaqut, Shihab al-Din Abi 'Abd Allah al-Hamawi, *Mu'jam al-Buldan*, ed. Farid 'Abd al-'Aziz al-Jundi, 4 Vols. (Beirut, 1990).

6

The 'Greater' Jihad in Classical Islam

Gavin Picken

Among the most intriguing debates regarding the subject of jihad is the dichotomous relationship between the so-called 'greater' jihad (*al-jihad al-akbar*) and 'lesser' jihad (*al-jihad al-asghar*). In this formulation, physical combat is deemed secondary to the higher purpose of disciplining one's negative character traits manifested in the soul. Indeed, due to the controversial nature of this 'greater' jihad, it was often rejected by many in Islam's mainstream 'orthodoxy' from the late medieval period onwards. Despite its repudiation by the majority, the 'greater' jihad maintained considerable currency amongst certain sections of Muslim society and in particular within the circles of Islam's mystics, the Sufis. Moreover, despite the general rejection of the notion of the 'greater' jihad, there would appear to be considerable evidence associated with it that corroborates Sufi claims regarding the validity of the concept. Consequently, Sufis utilised this evidence to elaborate the quintessential Sufi concept of combating the soul and the related concept of 'spiritual struggle' (*al-mujahada*), which constitutes a principal feature of the spiritual purification that may lead to mystical experience. This chapter, therefore, attempts to examine this controversy and the genesis of the Sufi idea of an esoteric form of 'spiritual combat'.[1]

The 'Greater' Jihad: Text and Controversy

The term 'greater' jihad and its antithesis 'lesser' jihad originate in a number of hadiths attributed to the Prophet Muhammad; the context of such hadiths is often given as the return from a military campaign, where the Prophet is said to have stated, 'You have returned in the best of ways and you have returned from the lesser jihad to the greater jihad – the devotee's opposition (*mujahada*) to his whimsical desires (*hawa-hu*)'.[2] Whereas the term 'lesser jihad' indicates physical combat, 'greater jihad' clearly does not mean engaging in military combat but rather, the spiritual struggle (*mujahada*) that each individual undertakes against one's lower ego and its desires (*hawa*, pl. *ahwa'*) and appetites (*shahwa*, pl. *shahawat*).

From the perspective of authentication, however, the vast majority of Muslim scholars deemed all of these hadiths to be inauthentic (*da'if*) and thus, they cannot be attributed to the Prophet. In further refutation of these hadiths and their implied purport, Ibn Taymiyyah (d.1328) states:

> As for the *hadith*, which some narrate, that he [the Prophet] said upon returning from the battle of Tabuk, 'You have returned from the lesser jihad to the greater jihad', this is baseless and no one who is knowledgeable regarding the Prophet's statements and actions has narrated it. Jihad against the unbelievers is one of the greatest of acts and indeed, it is the best action for which a person can volunteer.[3]

Consequently, it is not surprising that Cook observes:

> In reading Muslim literature – both contemporary and classical – one can see that the evidence for the primacy of spiritual jihad is negligible. Today it is certain that no Muslim, writing in a non-Western language (such as Arabic, Persian, Urdu), would ever make claims that jihad is primarily nonviolent or has been superseded by the spiritual jihad. Such claims are made solely by Western scholars, primarily those who study Sufism and/or work in interfaith dialogue, and by Muslim apologists who are trying to present Islam in the most innocuous manner possible.[4]

However, this perspective is contradicted by the fact that the notion of the 'greater' jihad is not entirely reliant upon the hadiths mentioned above but rather indicated and supported by a number of Qur'anic verses and alternative hadiths. Some commonly quoted Qur'anic verses include: 'And whosoever strives (*jahada*), strives (*yujahidu*) only for their own benefit; indeed, God is not in need of His creation' (Q. 29:6); 'Those who have striven for Our sake (*jahada fi-na*), indeed We will guide them to Our ways and surely God is with those who do good' (Q. 29:69); 'Have you seen the one who chooses his own desires as his deity?' (Q. 25:43); 'But as for one who feared to stand before his Lord and denied his soul its desires, indeed paradise is his abode' (Q. 79:40–1). One will notice that the two initial verses contain lexical cognates of jihad, namely *jahada* and *yujahidu*, whereas the second two verses contain reference to the necessity of reigning in the soul's lower desires. It is these two concepts that in combination indicate the concept of struggling against the negative potential inherent in the soul (*mujahadat al-nafs*).

This is further enhanced by the fact that Qur'anic verses 29:6 and 69, which contain conjugated verbal forms of the term 'jihad', are said to be from the Meccan period, long before the military connotation was legislated for in Q. 22:39–41 during the Medinan phase of the Prophet's mission.[5] Consequently, the reference to 'struggle' in such verses cannot refer to physical combat, as it had not been ordained up unto that point. Indeed, it is interesting to note, regarding Q. 29:6, that al-Hasan al-Basri (d.728) is reported to have said: 'A person may have performed jihad (*yujahid*) but have never raised a sword in battle.'[6] Similarly, commenting on Q. 29:69, Abu Sulayman al-Darani (d.830) stated:

> Jihad in this verse is not fighting against the unbelievers but rather support offered in the service of religion, refuting its detractors, restraining those who are oppressive and its most significant facet is commanding the good and forbidding the evil. It also includes the spiritual struggle against the soul (*mujahadat al-nufus*) and this is the greater jihad.[7]

Moreover, such Qur'anic verses are further substantiated by hadiths such as: 'The religious warrior (*al-mujahid*) is the one who struggles against his soul for the sake of God, the Mighty and Exalted', and: 'The religious warrior (*al-mujahid*) is the one who struggles against his soul in the obedience of God, the Mighty and Exalted.'[8] In addition, there are further rigorously authenticated hadiths that support this notion, for example: 'The best form of jihad is that a person struggle against his soul and his desires'[9] and also:

> The best of believers regarding Islam is a person from whom the Muslims are secure from their words and actions; the best of believers regarding faith (*iman*) is the best of them in moral behaviour (*khuluq*); the best

migrants (*muhajirun*) are those who turn away from what God the Exalted has forbidden and the best form of jihad is that a person struggle against his soul for the sake of God, may His majesty be glorified.[10]

Indeed, this understanding of jihad also appears to have been apparent among the Prophet's Companions (*al-sahaba*) since 'Abd Allah ibn 'Amr ibn al-'As (d.682 or 684), in response to someone who asked him about jihad, responded: 'Begin with your soul and struggle against it.'[11] This notion would appear to have been passed on to the subsequent generation of Muslims commonly referred to as the Successors (*al-tabi'un*) as one of them, Ibrahim ibn Abu 'Abla (d.769), when addressing a group returning from combat asked them:

'You have returned from the lesser jihad so what efforts have you made regarding the greater jihad?' They responded, 'O Abu Isma'il what is the greater jihad?' and he replied, 'It is the jihad of the heart (*al-qalb*).'[12]

Thus, we can observe that although the principal texts that mention the differentiation between the 'greater' and 'lesser' jihads are clearly problematic in terms of confirming their veracity, there are a number of other Qur'anic verses and Prophetic hadiths which – interpreted as a congruent whole – seem to indicate that jihad also involves a significant spiritual element. It is not surprising, therefore, that later scholars who were concerned with Islam's more esoteric facets focused their attention on such materials and developed a conceptual model for this form of spiritual 'combat'.

The 'Greater' Jihad in Sufism

Although the beginnings of Sufism are obscure and much debated, it would appear to have its primordial origins in the Prophetic period, which became that of the Companions and their followers, the early Successors.[13] However, it was during the Umayyad period that the signs of what would be recognised as Sufism were made manifest. Much like the development of jurisprudence (*fiqh*), regional schools sprang up, including the celebrated 'Baghdadi school'.[14] Much of Sufism's early tradition is described in hagiographical anecdotes recorded in biographical works, which provide a useful window on its nascent genesis.

The Formative Period

Of the early ascetical figures that are often quoted by Sufis as being representative of their tradition, Ibrahim ibn Adham (d.777) stands out as one of the most important.[15] It is interesting to note, therefore, that Ibn Adham is reported to have said: 'The most severe jihad is the jihad against one's desires. Whoever prevented his soul its desires has been freed of the world and its affliction and is protected and saved from its harm.'[16] In a similar vein, another noteworthy figure, Hatim al-Asamm (d.851), also states:

> There are three types of jihad: an internal jihad against Satan until you overcome him; an external jihad regarding fulfilling your compulsory duties until you perform them as God commanded and a jihad against God's enemies to bring glory to Islam.[17]

Therefore, it would appear that – despite the controversy surrounding the text advocating the 'greater' jihad – early Muslim spiritual and ascetical figures maintained a coherent theory of a spiritual jihad.

In addition to the extensive range of biographical anecdotes in this early period there were also a number of nascent discussions of spiritual theory and practice. Among these early works one of the most prolific and significant authors was al-Harith ibn Asad al-Muhasibi (d.857).[18] Although born in Basra, al-Muhasibi spent most of his life in Baghdad, where he wrote extensively on the nature of the soul and its purification.[19] It is significant, then, that when asked about the soul (al-nafs) al-Muhasibi responds:

> Haven't you heard God, the Exalted's statement, 'Indeed, the soul is prone to evil' [Q. 12:53]? And His, the Exalted's statement, 'As for the one who feared the position of his Lord and forbade his soul its desires' [Q. 79:40]? And in the story of the son of Adam, 'Then his soul made the murder of his brother seem appealing and so he killed him' [Q. 5:30]? 'He [Ya'qub] said: indeed your souls have enticed you to some matter, so patience is more befitting' [Q. 12:18]? 'He [Moses] said: And what have you to do with this O Samiri?' until His statement, 'Thus did my soul entice me' [Q. 20:95–6]? In addition, the Prophet, may the peace and blessings of God be upon him, said, 'You have returned from the lesser jihad to the greater jihad – the struggle against your souls.' A man asked the Prophet, 'What is

the best form of jihad?' and he replied, 'Your personal struggle against your
soul and your desires (*mujahadatu-ka nafsa-ka wa-hawa-ka*)'.[20]

It is clear from this quotation that not only was al-Muhasibi familiar with
the texts mentioned in the previous section but, indeed, that he understood them in a cohesive and cogent manner to deduce the necessity of
the concept of spiritual struggle and the combatting of the soul under
the term '*mujahada*'.[21]

These short excerpts, when taken as representative samples, strongly
suggest that the notion of the 'greater' jihad was further elaborated, both
in terms of implication and application, in this primary phase of Sufism's
genesis. In turn, this would supply scholars of the emerging tradition
with discussions that would underpin both future theory and praxis.

The Period of 'Consolidation'

Following the formalisation of various other Islamic disciplines up until
the tenth century, Sufism also underwent a period of consolidation and
codification and, consequently, many scholars term this period 'a period
of systemisation of the Sufi tradition'.[22] Within the next century, from
around 967 to 1074, we find that a myriad of treatises, biographical works
and manuals were produced to fulfil the apologetic purpose of introducing Sufism as a discipline or a science – termed '*ilm al-tasawwuf* – to
facilitate its integration and acceptance into the vista of Islamic learning.
It is such books that laid the foundations for future generations of Muslim mystics and it is therefore not surprising that many of them make
reference to the concept of 'spiritual struggle' (*al-mujahada*).

Of the early treatises on Sufi theory, one of the most noteworthy is
al-Ta'arruf li-Madhhab Ahl al-Tasawwuf (*Expounding the Sufi Path*) by
Abu Bakr al-Kalabadhi (d.990).[23] It is telling, therefore, that al-Kalabadhi
includes two chapters addressing the term '*mujahada*' in the plural and
relates it to both the early spiritual figures' acts of worship and their
scrupulousness in engaging with worldly affairs.[24] With regard to physical acts of worship such as prayer and fasting, the focus is not on the
outward facets of such pious actions as determined by the legal manuals,
or even the reward associated with them, but rather the perfection of
sincerity in performing them for God alone. Similarly, in discussing their
worldly engagements such as earning a living or inheriting wealth from

a relative, their main concern was ensuring the 'purity' of this worldly gain. Al-Kalabadhi portrays, through anecdotes related to Sufism's early personalities, the necessity of undertaking this spiritual struggle, or *mujahada*, in the engagement of the religious and worldly realms of experience.[25]

Perhaps the most significant Sufi text of the period is the *Risala fi al-Tasawwuf* (*Treatise on Sufism*) of Abu al-Qasim al-Qushayri (d.1074), since it combines the two genres of biographical hagiography and technical manual – a feature that no other text from the period displays.[26] In discussing a plethora of Sufi technical terms, unique to their spiritual vernacular, al-Qushayri also dedicates a section to a lucid and detailed account of *mujahada*.[27] Fittingly, al-Qushayri begins this entry by quoting Q. 29:69 and following it with the hadith: 'A man asked, "What is the best form of jihad?" to which the Prophet replied, "To speak the truth in front of an oppressive ruler"'.[28] It is evident, therefore, that al-Qushayri utilises these primary sources so as to emphasise the non-military nature of jihad.

Al-Qushayri goes on to interweave a variety of pious dicta from a number of early spiritual authorities such as Ibrahim ibn Adham (d.777), Abu Sulayman al-Darani (d.830), Abu Yazid al-Bistami (d.848), Dhu al-Nun al-Misri (d.860), Sari al-Saqati (d.867), Abu Hafs al-Haddad (d. between 874 and 869) and Abu al-Qasim al-Junayd (d.910), as well as quotations from his own Sufi mentors, Abu 'Ali al-Daqqaq (d.1015) and Abu 'Abd al-Rahman al-Sulami (d.1021). Among the most concise and telling quotations is that of Abu 'Uthman al-Maghribi (d.983), who is quoted as saying, 'Whoever thinks that some aspect of the [spiritual] path (*tariqa*) will be opened to him or some facet of it revealed to him without spiritual struggle (*mujahada*), he is sadly mistaken'.[29]

In addition to referencing historical antecedents, al-Qushayri also provides his own exposition of the subject matter, which tends to focus on the despicable nature of the soul, the subjugating of its desires, deterring its tendency to submerge itself in its appetites, overcoming its refusal to perform acts of obedience and, hence, the necessity of undertaking a multifaceted approach to spiritual self-discipline. Summarising this, al-Qushayri states: 'Know that the essence of spiritual struggle (*al-mujahada*) and its foundation is weaning the soul away from

its customary habits and forcing it to oppose its desires in every moment.'[30] Consequently, via these excerpts and an explication of his own
perspective upon the subject, al-Qushayri attempts to illustrate the authenticity of the concept of spiritual struggle by citations from authority
and, at the same time, to show that this idea has been diachronically and
systematically developed.

Conclusion

Observing the debate regarding the nature of jihad, Bernard Lewis comments: 'The overwhelming majority of classical theologians, jurists, and
traditionists, however, understood the obligation of jihad in a military
sense, and have examined and expounded it accordingly.'[31] Although
one may agree with this assessment in a general sense, it cannot be
overlooked that, in addition to military combat, there were other forms
of jihad to which Islam's source texts alluded.[32] Consequently, it is suggested that there is not only one form of jihad but rather four identifiable
major categories of jihad: jihad against one's soul and its negative facets
(*jihad al-nafs*); jihad of the tongue (*jihad al-lisan*); jihad of the hand (*jihad
al-yad*); and jihad of the sword (*jihad al-sayf*).[33]

Although combatting the soul and striving against its deleterious attributes is an identifiable facet of jihad that is supported by a range of
sources, the question remains: Is it the 'greater' jihad in comparison
with the other categories of jihad alluded to above? Muslim scholars
have clearly had two major concerns in this regard: first, what we may
refer to as 'textual misgivings', or in other words apprehension over the
veracity of the hadiths that depict the idea of the 'greater' jihad, and second, what we may refer to as 'conceptual misgivings', which relate to the
implications of such texts. The first was by far the easiest to deal with,
since all versions of the hadiths in question were quickly deemed 'inauthentic' according to the rigorous application of hadith methodology.
This would have meant by default that any consequent theoretical idea
produced by the text would have been rejected. This was equally important as their concern would have been that the practioners of faith may
have engaged with the spiritual inferences of jihad to the detriment of its
military application and thus perhaps put the security of the community
at risk.

The convenient relationship that stipulates that 'rejection of text is equal to rejection of concept' was clearly not convincing to everyone. Indeed, not only did the multivalent nature of the term 'jihad' imply a spiritual dimension, the subsidiary texts described above necessitated it. In addition, this 'spiritual jihad' may well have been deemed 'greater' due to the fact that, from the legal perspective, it is a compulsory duty on every individual (*fard 'ayn*). For no one is excluded from the necessity of struggling against one's lower self, whereas physical combat is usually perceived to be a duty laid upon the community at large (*fard 'ala al-kifaya*).[34] Moreover, the military struggle against physical enemies is primarily facilitated by them being visible and hence easier to engage as they constitute 'a clear and present danger'. On the contrary, the attempt to discipline the soul is a struggle that is 'unseen' and, consequently, much more difficult to enact. Similarly, in the 'theatre of war' there are occasions where there will be respite from engaging the enemy, but in contrast, there is no one who is without their soul for even a moment, and therefore, this is an encounter that takes place on an uninterrupted and continuous basis.

It is not surprising, then, that a group of pietistic practitioners of religion, seeking to implement the spiritual dimensions of their faith, not only pursued this based on a variety of textual references but also developed a conceptual model for its application under the rubric of the 'greater' jihad. In this context the famous Sufi luminary of Baghdad Abu al-Husayn al-Nuri (d.907) composed the following lines of poetry:

> I have no jihad other than the jihad against
> personal inadequacy and neglect;
> And my lack of fortitude in performing unceasing jihad is in itself a jihad.[35]

Notes

1. This chapter, due to considerations of space, only considers lexical cognates of 'jihad' and primarily the term '*mujahada*' in conjunction with '*al-nafs*', denoting the spiritual struggle against soul. It is worthy of note, however, that Sufis often used other synonymous terms and phrases such as 'opposing the soul' (*mukhalafat al-nafs*) and 'disciplining the soul' (*riyadat al-nafs*) to indicate similar conceptual notions.

2. Abu Bakr Ahmad ibn al-Husayn al-Bayhaqi, *Kitab al-Zuhd al-Kabir*, ed. 'Amir Ahmad Haydar (Beirut, 1987), p. 165; Muhammad Nasir al-Din al-Albani, *Da'if al-Jami' al-Saghir wa-Ziyadat al-Fath al-Kabir*, 3rd ed. (Beirut, 1990), p. 595; Abu Bakr ibn Ahmad ibn 'Ali [al-Khatib] al-Baghdadi, *Tarikh Baghdad – Madinat al-Salim*, ed. Mustafa 'Abd al-Qadir 'Ata', 24 Vols. (Beirut, 2004), Vol. 13: 498.

3. Ibn Taymiyyah, Ahmad ibn 'Abd al-Halim, *al-Furqan bayna Awliya' al-Rahman wa-Awliya' al-Shaytan*, ed. 'Abd al-Rahman al-Yahya (Riyadh, 2007), pp. 77–8.

4. David Cook, *Understanding Jihad* (London, Berkeley and Los Angeles, 2005), pp. 165–6.

5. Muhammad ibn Ahmad al-Qurtubi, *al-Jami' li-Ahkam al-Qur'an*, ed. 'Abd al-Razzaq al-Mahdi, 4th ed., 20 parts in 10 Vols. (Beirut, 2001), Vol. 12: 66–70 and 13: 286, 290, 324–5; Isma'il ibn 'Umar Ibn Kathir, *Tafsir al-Qur'an al-'Azim*, 4 Vols. (Beirut, 2008), Vol. 3: 1255–6, 1411 and 1426.

6. Ibn Kathir, *Tafsir al-Qur'an al-'Azim*, Vol. 3: 1411.

7. al-Qurtubi, *al-Jami' li-Ahkam al-Qur'an*, Vol. 13: 325.

8. al-Bayhaqi, *Kitab al-Zuhd al-Kabir*, p. 163; Abu Bakr 'Abd Allah ibn Muhammad ibn Abu al-Dunya, *Muhasabat al-Nafs*, ed. 'Abd Allah al-Sharqawi (Beirut, 1988), p. 72; 'Abd al-Rahman ibn Ahmad ibn Rajab, *Sharh Hadith Labbayk Allahumma Labbayk*, ed. Walid al-Farayyan (Mecca, 1996), p. 128; Muhammad ibn 'Isa al-Tirmidhi, *Jami' al-Tirmidhi*, (Riyadh, 1999), p. 392; Ahmad ibn Hanbal, *al-Musnad* (Riyadh, 1998), p. 1795; Yusuf ibn 'Abd al-Rahman al-Mizzi, *Tuhfat al-Ashraf bi-Ma'rifat al-Atraf*, ed. 'Abd al-Samad Sharaf al-Din, 16 Vols. (Beirut, 1999), Vol. 8: 262; Ahmad ibn Shu'ayb al-Nasa'i, *Kitab al-Sunan al-Kubra*, ed. Hasan 'Abd al-Mun'im Shibli, 12 Vols. (Beirut, 2001), Vol. 10: 386.

9. Muhammad Nasir al-Din al-Albani, *Sahih al-Jami' al-Saghir wa-Ziyadat al-Fath al-Kabir*, 2 Vols., 3rd ed. (Beirut, 1988), Vol. 1: 247.

10. Ibid., Vol. 1: 252.

11. Ibn Rajab, *Sharh Hadith Labbayk Allahumma Labbayk*, p. 128.

12. Yusuf ibn 'Abd al-Rahman al-Mizzi, *Tahdhib al-Kamal fi Asma' al-Rijal*, ed. Bashshar 'Awad Ma'ruf, 8 Vols. (Beirut, 1998), Vol. 1: 123.

13. Annemarie Schimmel, *Mystical Dimensions of Islam* (Chapel Hill, 1975), pp. 33–5; Julian Baldick, *Mystical Islam* (London, 1989), pp. 13–33.

14. Alexander D. Knysh, *Islamic Mysticism – A Short History* (Leiden, 1999), pp. 43–67.

15. Schimmel, *Mystical Dimensions of Islam*, pp. 36–8; Knysh, *Islamic Mysticism*, pp. 19–20.

16. al-Bayhaqi, *Kitab al-Zuhd al-Kabir*, p. 152.

17. Ibid., p. 286.

18. Gavin Picken, *Spiritual Purification in Islam: The Life and Works of al-Muhasibi* (London, 2011), pp. 67–122.

19. Ibid., pp. 168–215.

20. al-Harith ibn Asad al-Muhasibi, *Kitab al-Khalwa*, ed. al-Yasu'i (al-Mashriq, 1955), pp. 480–1.

21. For a more complete discussion of al-Muhasibi's elaboration of *mujahadat al-nafs* see Picken, *Spiritual Purification in Islam*, pp. 194–9.

22. Schimmel, *Mystical Dimensions of Islam*, pp. 77–97; Knysh, *Islamic Mysticism*, pp. 116–49.

23. Schimmel, *Mystical Dimensions of Islam*, p. 85; Knysh, *Islamic Mysticism*, pp. 123–4.

24. Muhammad ibn Ishaq al-Kalabadhi, *al-Ta'arruf li-Madhhab Ahl al-Tasawwuf*, ed. Ahmad Shams al-Din (Beirut, 1993), pp. 159–62 and 165–7.

25. Another major author of the period, Abu 'Abd al-Rahman al-Sulami (d.1021), also provides a similar exposition in his treatise *Jawami' Adab al-Sufiyya*. See Abu 'Abd al-Rahman al-Sulami, *Tis'a Kutub li-Abi 'Abd al-Rahman al-Sulami*, ed. Suleyman Ates (Ankara, 1981), pp. 41–2, 57, 82 and 86.

26. Knysh, *Islamic Mysticism*, pp. 131–2.

27. 'Abd al-Karim ibn Hawazin [Abu al-Qasim] al-Qushayri, *al-Risala al-Qushayriyya fi 'Ilm al-Tasawwuf*, ed. 'Abd al-Halim Mahmud (Damascus, 2003), pp. 189–95.

28. Ahmad ibn Shu'ayb al-Nasa'i, *Sunan al-Nasa'i al-Sughra* (Riyadh, 1999), p. 587.

29. Ibid., p. 189.

30. Ibid., p. 191.

31. Bernard Lewis, *The Political Language of Islam* (Chicago, 1988), p. 72.

32. See for example Muhammad ibn Isma'il al-Bukhari, *Sahih al-Bukhari* (Riyadh, 1999), pp. 461 and 1045–6.

33. Reuven Firestone, *Jihad: The Origin of Holy War in Islam* (Oxford, 1999), p. 17.

34. E. Tyan, 'Djihad', in Bernard Lewis, Charles Pellat and Josef Schacht (eds.), *Encyclopaedia of Islam*, 2nd ed., (Leiden, 1965), Vol. 2: 538–40.

35. al-Kalabadhi, *al-Ta'arruf li-Madhhab Ahl al-Tasawwuf*, p. 162.

Bibliography

al-Albani, Muhammad Nasir al-Din, *Sahih al-Jami' al-Saghir wa-Ziyadat al-Fath al-Kabir*, 2 Vols., 3rd ed. (Beirut, 1988).

———, *Da'if al-Jami' al-Saghir wa-Ziyadat al-Fath al-Kabir*, 3rd ed. (Beirut, 1990).

al-Baghdadi, Abu Bakr ibn Ahmad ibn 'Ali [al-Khatib], *Tarikh Baghdad – Madinat al-Salim*, ed. Mustafa 'Abd al-Qadir 'Ata', 24 Vols. (Beirut, 2004).

Baldick, Julian, *Mystical Islam* (London, 1989).

al-Bayhaqi, Abu Bakr Ahmad ibn al-Husayn, *Kitab al-Zuhd al-Kabir*, ed. 'Amir Ahmad Haydar (Beirut, 1987).

al-Bukhari, Muhammad ibn Isma'il, *Sahih al-Bukhari* (Riyadh, 1999).

Cook, David, *Understanding Jihad* (London, Berkeley and Los Angeles, 2005).

Firestone, Reuven, *Jihad: The Origin of Holy War in Islam* (Oxford, 1999).

al-Ghazali, Muhammad ibn Muhammad [Abu Hamid], *Ihya' 'Ulum al-Din*, 5 Vols. (Beirut, 2005).

Ibn Abu al-Dunya, Abu Bakr 'Abd Allah ibn Muhammad, *Muhasabat al-Nafs*, ed. 'Abd Allah al-Sharqawi (Beirut, 1988).

Ibn Hanbal, Ahmad, *al-Musnad* (Riyadh, 1998).

Ibn Kathir, Isma'il ibn 'Umar, *Tafsir al-Qur'an al-'Azim*, 4 Vols. (Beirut, 2008).

Ibn Rajab, 'Abd al-Rahman ibn Ahmad, *Sharh Hadith Labbayk Allahumma Labbayk*, ed. Walid al-Farayyan (Mecca, 1996).

Ibn Taymiyyah, Ahmad ibn 'Abd al-Halim, *al-Furqan bayna Awliya' al-Rahman wa-Awliya' al-Shaytan*, ed. 'Abd al-Rahman al-Yahya (Riyadh, 2007).

al-Kalabadhi, Muhammad ibn Ishaq, *al-Ta'arruf li-Madhhab Ahl al-Tasawwuf*, ed. Ahmad Shams al-Din (Beirut, 1993).

Knysh, Alexander D., *Islamic Mysticism – A Short History* (Leiden, 1999).

Lewis, Bernard, *The Political Language of Islam* (Chicago, 1988).

al-Mizzi, Yusuf ibn 'Abd al-Rahman, *Tahdhib al-Kamal fi Asma' al-Rijal*, ed. Bashshar 'Awad Ma'ruf, 8 Vols. (Beirut, 1998).

———, *Tuhfat al-Ashraf bi-Ma'rifat al-Atraf*, ed. 'Abd al-Samad Sharaf al-Din, 16 Vols. (Beirut, 1999).

al-Muhasibi, al-Harith ibn Asad, *Kitab al-Khalwa*, ed. al-Yasu'i (Beirut, 1955).

al-Nasa'i, Ahmad ibn Shu'ayb, *Sunan al-Nasa'i al-Sughra* (Riyadh, 1999).

———, *Kitab al-Sunan al-Kubra*, ed. Hasan 'Abd al-Mun'im Shibli, 12 Vols. (Beirut, 2001).

Picken, Gavin, *Spiritual Purification in Islam: The Life and Works of al-Muhasibi* (London, 2011).

al-Qurtubi, Muhammad ibn Ahmad, *al-Jami' li-Ahkam al-Qur'an*, ed. 'Abd al-Razzaq al-Mahdi, 4th ed., 20 parts in 10 Vols. (Beirut, 2001).

al-Qushayri, 'Abd al-Karim ibn Hawazin [Abu al-Qasim], *al-Risala al-Qushayriyya fi 'Ilm al-Tasawwuf*, ed. 'Abd al-Halim Mahmud (Damascus, 2003).

Schimmel, Annemarie, *Mystical Dimensions of Islam* (Chapel Hill, 1975).

al-Sulami, Abu 'Abd al-Rahman, *Tis'a Kutub li-Abi 'Abd al-Rahman al-Sulami*, ed. Suleyman Ates (Ankara, 1981).

al-Tirmidhi, Muhammad ibn 'Isa, *Jami' al-Tirmidhi*, (Riyadh, 1999).

Tyan, E., 'Djihad', in Bernard Lewis, Charles Pellat and Josef Schacht (eds.), *Encyclopaedia of Islam*, 2nd ed., (Leiden, 1965), Vol. 2: 538–40.

Part II

Jihad in Modern Politics and Society

7

Sectarian Violence as Jihad

Sami Zubaida

Sectarian divisions in any religion are mostly peaceful.[1] They become conflictual when politicised or when they coincide with other social or economic divisions and, in recent times, with geopolitical considerations. Each sect clearly believes that it is correct in its belief and practice and others more or less in error, but for the most part they live and let live. In Sunni Islam, the divisions between the legal doctrines are famously peaceful and tolerant of one another, and so are most divisions between Sufi orders. That is, except when you get fierce polemicists – like Ibn Taymiyyah in the fourteenth century – in contexts of social and military turbulence, when religious authority and social power are at stake as they were in the Mamluk sultanates under threats from Mongols, Shi'ites and Isma'ilis, as well as errant Sufis.[2] The Shi'ites, while implicitly questioning the legitimacy of Sunni rule and believing the Sunni to be in error, were, for most of their history, quiescent, and often dissimulated their dissent. The Sunni Muslims, for their part, would have rejected Shi'ite doctrines, but in most situations they were tolerant and their authorities may have tried to correct or re-interpret Shi'ite doctrines. These divisions became conflictual or violent when they coincided with antagonism between political entities, as in the case of the Ottomans and the Savafids, or when sectarian communities and their leaders were competing for power or resources, as happened at various points in Abbasid, Mongol and subsequent history. In modern times (since the nineteenth century), sectarian difference has often been read as dissent or subversion of emerging state powers. Ottoman Sultan Abdul Hamid II (r.1876–1909), adopting Sunni Hanafi Islam as the state religion, was uneasy about the Iraqi Shi'ites and tried to convert them, as he was less tolerant of rival Sunni legal schools. Yezidis and other esoteric religions, secure in their mountain strongholds for centuries, came under attack, as their resistance to military conscription was considered part of their heresy.[3] Wahhabis, on the fringe of the Ottoman dominion, were always fierce antagonists to 'the Turks' and their Islam, as were other fringe dissidents like the Sudanese Mahdi. It is in situations like this that sectarian jihad becomes plausible.[4]

If we follow the conventional division between church and sect (ignoring the problem of non-equivalence between Christian and Muslim terms for the purposes of the present discussion), then sectarians are typically more forthright about the righteousness of their creed and the (wilful) error of others. Evangelical Christians insist that they are just 'Christians' with no qualifications, implying that those who worship in other ways are not *really* Christian. Similarly, Wahhabis call themselves *muwahhidun*, monotheists, with the implication that other Muslims are *mushrikun*, taking other gods. It is these kinds of conviction which, when militant, can turn into sectarian jihad, as it did in the case of the eighteenth-century Wahhabis who launched their jihad: first against their compatriots in the Arabian Peninsula, converting them by the sword to the 'true' Islam; then against the 'Turks', considered heretics or apostates and, finally and famously, against the Shi'ites, their most consistent *bête noire*. The idea of jihad was much more ambiguous and ambivalent in Shi'ite discourse on their battles, as we shall see.

Wahhabi Jihads

Wahhabism as a doctrine of puritan Islam was first preached and enforced on the Bedouin of Arabia in the eighteenth century at the time of the eponymous founder and his political partner Muhammad ibn Saud and their alliance of the word and the sword.[5] The unconverted Arab was deemed not to be a proper Muslim, or perhaps any kind of Muslim at all: he was *jahil* (ignorant). He only became a Muslim when converted by a Wahhabi preacher to Hanbali doctrine as embellished by Ibn 'Abd al-Wahhab. Henceforth he was to abandon folk beliefs and practices such as the visitation of shrines, votive offerings, spells, rituals involving chanting and dancing and all the paraphernalia of magical and folk religion deemed to be 'superstition' and *shirk* (idolatry). He was then to observe all the orthodox obligations of prayers, fasting, almsgiving and pilgrimage. Those who were not thus converted were in a state of *jahl* (ignorance and error) and could be considered infidels, ripe for conquest and forced conversion. The confrontation of the Wahhabi kingdom with the Ottoman-Egyptian forces of Ibrahim Pasha, and their defeat in 1812–13, then cast the Ottomans ('the Turks') as the arch-enemy, foremost of the infidels under the guise of Islam. Thus the first targets of Wahhabi jihads were Sunni Muslims who, by virtue of following other paths of religion, were deemed infidels and confronted with violence. These acts mark Wahhabism out as a militant sect.

In the early twentieth century, the battles waged by 'Abd al-Aziz ibn Saud to regain the kingdom of his ancestors were fought with zealous religious warriors. The most renowned contingent was the Ikhwan: men drawn from among the nomadic Bedouin, converted by dedicated missionaries, then settled in *hujar*.[6] This is an interesting concept. *Hijra*, migration or flight, was the path taken by the Prophet and his Companions in departing from Mecca, then the abode of idolaters, to Medina where the faith was established. This concept of flight then became a metaphor for the determined renewal of the faith. Ibn 'Abd al-Wahhab interpretated *hijra* as the move from the lands of heresy to the lands of Islam. Conversion to Wahhabism then, is similar to the evangelical idea of 'being born again'. For the Ikhwan this metaphor became real in that they were nomads settled in special habitations called *hujar*, where the disciplines of the true religion were rigorously applied. For them, the outside world was the realm of *kufr* (heresy) and idolatry, to be constantly monitored and combated. The Sunni Muslims of the wider Sunni world were, as such, infidels, their life and property permitted to the believers. The lands of the Arabian Peninsula outside the Saudi domains of Najd were then *Dar al-Kufr* (the Abode of Heresy), their inhabitants and rulers subject to the sword or forced conversion in the course of a jihad. While the people of al-Hijaz and al-Hasa were ultimately subjugated, the zeal of the Ikhwan was an embarrassment to Ibn Saud, and they had to be subdued. This was especially the case after the bloody sacking of

Ta'if, when they slaughtered all the males, including children.[7] Ibn Saud then forbade the Ikhwan entry into the Hijazi cities that subsequently surrendered. Ultimately they rebelled against him when prevented from launching their raids into neighbouring Iraq, Kuwait ('sin city') and other British-protected territories, and were defeated with the aid of British arms.[8] The Ikhwan's main grievance was that Ibn Saud, in deference to Christian patrons, stopped their jihad and prevented the spread of God's word. The basic Wahhabi motif – that of conversion by the sword – endured, however, and was not only imposed on all the inhabitants of what became Saudi Arabia, but frequently repeated in the ideological polemics against various other Muslims, notably the Shi'ites.

The Shi'ites were to become the particular target of Wahhabi sectarian hostility. The Shi'ites sanctified their imams, attributing divine associa-tion and powers of intercession to individuals the Wahhabis considered mere men. For them, even the Prophet Muhammad only had sanctity in his capacity as God's messenger, and was otherwise only a man. By that logic, the dome over the tomb of the Prophet in Medina was levelled in the first Wahhabi raids, then in 1925 they destroyed Jannat al-Baghi ('Garden of Heaven') in Medina, which contained the tombs of the Prophet's daughter and other descendants sacred to the Shi'ites.[9] The Shi'ites held elaborate rituals in relation to their imams, especially the Muharram rites for Husayn. They maintained opulent shrines, decorated with fine fabrics, gold and images. In short, they were *mushrikun* (idol-aters) posing as Muslims. Add to that their challenge to Sunni authority and demonisation of the three first caliphs, and the Shi'ite becomes the antithesis of all Wahhabi virtues. The first wave of Wahhabi jihads at the turn of the nineteenth century included the raid into Ottoman Iraq targeting the holy shrine cities of Karbala and Najaf in 1801, sacking the cities, killing many of their inhabitants, destroying the opulent shrines of Imam 'Ali, Husayn and other descendants of the Prophet, and pillag-ing the gold and wealth. This became a traumatic memory for the Iraqi Shi'ites. It is thought to have stimulated their senior clerics to launch the successful missionary campaigns to convert the southern Iraqi Bedouin to Shi'ism, to act as defenders of the shrines. Ironically, this included part of a major Najdi tribe, the Shammar.[10]

These early nineteenth-century Wahhabi campaigns into Hijaz, Yemen, Iraq and Syria ultimately led to Ibrahim Pasha's Ottoman campaign which crushed the first Wahhabi/Saudi kingdom in 1812–13. During the Ikhwan conquest of al-Hasa, the region with the highest concentration of Shi'ites in what was to become Saudi Arabia, they demanded that Ibn Saud declare jihad against the Shi'ites, giving them the choice of converting to the true Islamic faith or being killed. Ibn Saud was reluctant, but the Ikhwan took matters into their own hands, and in 1926 massacred large numbers of the inhabitants of the region.[11] Within the Kingdom, which was consolidated in the 1930s, the Shi'ites became an inferior minority, often discriminated against, persecuted and prevented from public observation of their specific rituals, crucially the Muharram mourning for Husayn. Saudi clerics periodically issued fatwas against the Shi'ites. Ibn Baz (d.1999) famously denounced them as apostates, and following that logic, 'Abd al-Rahman al-Jibrin sanctioned the killing of Shi'ites, a call to arms which was repeated. The 1979 Iranian Revolution gave the Shi'ites confidence to express a defiance which, fuelled by the hostility to Iran and the ensuing Iran–Iraq war, sharpened Wahhabi and general Sunni antagonism. This was further intensified with the rise of Shi'ite power in Iraq after the 2003 invasion.

Sectarian jihads against Shi'ites were also waged in Afghanistan and Pakistan in recent years. The Taliban declared Afghan Shi'ites to be infidels, massacred some in Mazar-i Sharif and Bamiyan in 1997–8 and tried to forcibly convert others. In Pakistan, there are regular and repeated attacks by Sunni militants on Shi'ite mosques and processions, and occasional Shi'ite responses.

Iraq

The sectarian division in Iraq has had various social and political expressions over the course of its history.[12] For the most part the tensions, if any, were political and religious, with mutual denigration at times, but mostly mild. Under the Ba'th regime, the divide manifested itself in violence for the first time, mostly regime violence against Shi'ite targets. Public ideological discourse was rarely an attack on the Shi'ites as such, but always expressed through a denunciation of enemies with Iranian connections. As such, the state's own violent actions towards Shi'ites, and its attempts to stir others up to do the same, was never presented as sectarian jihad, and the retaliation equally avoided the sectarian terms. Saddam Hussein did not target the Shi'ites as such (although there was plenty of sectarian prejudice and discrimination). The regime was dominated by Sunni clans because those were Saddam's kin and allies: they did not represent the Sunni totality, which, in any case, did not exist. Individual Shi'ites held high positions in the regime, though not in the sensitive security apparatus. It was the Shi'ite institutions and loci of organised activity, especially those with political import, that were the particular targets for regime pressure and violence. The Ba'th had succeeded in eliminating or incorporating all centres of power, organisation and revenue in Iraqi society except for the Shi'ite institutions of *mujtahids* (legal authorities), schools, pilgrimage, prayer and assembly halls (*husayniyyat*) and rituals. Financed by independent channels of religious revenues, some of them from outside the country (Iran, the Gulf, India), these institutions – while under constant pressure, surveillance and harassment – were never successfully eliminated. The 1979 Iranian Revolution, followed by the war with Iran (1980–8), exacerbated this pressure on the Shi'ites, as the Revolution stimulated political confidence and action: membership of the da'wa party, the main Shi'ite political organisation, became a capital offence. Many prominent Shi'ite figures, notably Baqir al-Sadr and his sister, were imprisoned and executed in 1980.[13] Large numbers of Shi'ite communities and families were rounded up and expelled in several waves into the desert regions which border Iran, while their young men were incarcerated.[14] The ideological rationale of these persecutions was phrased in terms of combatting the Persian enemy: the Shi'ite victims were Iranians, not Arabs or Iraqis, not even Muslims. The racist abuses against Persians included questioning their faith and calling them '*majus*', 'magians' and fire-worshippers. These designations related to their Shi'ism, and could be (and were) read as including all Shi'ites. The explicit attack on Shi'ites, however, was to come during the uprisings in the south following the Iraqi defeat in the Kuwait war in 1991. The tanks that entered Karbala and attacked the shrines, massacring countless inhabitants, bore the slogan *la shi'a ba'da al-yawm* ('no Shi'ites after today').[15] The 1990s and early 2000s, up until the 2003 invasion, were years of great hardship for Iraqis, during which the regime's grip on society weakened.[16] It was then that the initially secular Ba'th and Saddam turned to tribe and religion to reinforce social control. Saddam launched *hamlat al-iman*, the faith campaign, which favoured Sunni, indeed Salafi, ulama and institutions. Iraqis, in their distress, turned increasingly to religion, with a sharpening of the sectarian lines. Salafi and Wahhabi networks, influences and finances played an important role in this re-Islamisation. These networks were sectarian in character, connecting Iraqi sentiments to the increasingly polarised sentiments of the region more broadly resulting from Iranian power, the increasing confidence and activism of the Shi'ites in Saudi Arabia and the Gulf and the rise in power and prestige of Lebanon's Hizbullah. This sectarianism was to be enhanced and sharpened after the American invasion, the removal of the Sunni regime and the rise of Shi'ite power.

The 2003 invasion removed Saddam's Ba'thist regime and, for the first time in its modern history, Sunni political and military dominance was removed. This was traumatic for many Sunni sectors, but primarily the inhabitants of the 'Sunni triangle' north-west of Baghdad, which was the heartland of the clans associated with Saddam's regime and family. The Shi'ite parties and institutions were, on balance, the beneficiaries of this redistribution of power. The Sunni insurgency and opposition that followed explicitly targeted the Shi'ites. The most vociferous were the jihadi groups under various banners, crystallising into al-Qa'ida in Iraq and the Islamic State of Iraq. The Shi'ites as such were the enemy, now identified as collaborators with the enemies of Arabs and Muslims: the American 'Crusaders' and the Iranian heretics. This rhetoric was also adopted by sundry Ba'thists and supported vociferously by Sunni governments and authorities in the region explicitly warning against resurgent Shi'ite power, such as King Abdullah of Jordan's famous warning about the 'Shi'ite crescent' from Tehran to Beirut. Iraqi Sunni leaders, notably the Association of Muslim Clerics, alternately supported or kept silent on the anti-Shi'ite rhetoric and the calls for jihad.[17] Saddam, soon after the invasion, invoked a supposed historical precedent, that of al-Alqami, a Shi'ite wazir of the last Abbasid caliph, who is supposed to have handed the keys of Baghdad to the besieging Mongolian forces under Hulago during the thirteenth-century sacking of the city. This was to be repeated by many Sunni detractors; one Saudi cleric supported the Zarqawi group's attacks on 'the symbol of heresy and the sons of al-Alqami'.[18] By this time the denunciation of the Shi'ites in the region as agents of the USA and Iran, heretics and traitors to the Arabs, had become widespread. This condemnation on explicitly sectarian grounds was not generally reciprocated by Shi'ite leaders or ideologues, though it was probably in the sentiments of many.

Shi'ite Positions

In the course of the twentieth century and the contexts of wars and rebellions, Shi'ite clerics and leaders in Iraq and Lebanon were prominent in nationalist and pan-Islamic rhetoric. During the First World War Iraqi *mujtahids* declared jihad in support of the Ottomans against the infidel powers. They were also instrumental in instigating and leading the 1920 revolution, a major insurrection against the British occupation.[19] Many of them were supporters of Islamic reform movements coming from Egypt and Syria, equally those rooted in the Constitutional Revolution in Iran. Sectarian jihad, then, was far from the thoughts of the Shi'ites, though they often complained of sectarian attitudes and discrimination by the mainly Sunni authorities. Those authorities, by contrast, whether Sunni sectarians or pan-Arab nationalists, continued to impugn the Arab credentials and Iraqi loyalties of the Shi'ites and hint or explicitly state that their main affiliation and loyalty was to Iran. As we have seen, these accusations would only became more potent after the Iranian Revolution and the war with Iraq.

The Shi'ite Logic of Jihad

The key narratives of Shi'ism are those of the martyrdom of Husayn and the disappearance and future apocalyptic reappearance of the Twelfth Imam al-Mahdi, both of which involved themes of jihad. The narrative of Husayn has had multiple ideological constructions under different historical circumstances, with reactions ranging from apolitical mourning rituals to political constructions of activism and jihad, as at the time of the 1979 Revolution and the war with Iraq.[20] In this latter construction, it is Husayn's role as a fighter and martyr for righteousness and justice against the godless Yazid which is highlighted and becomes an example for believers to emulate: hence jihad in the path of the martyrs. Equally, in this mode, the return of the Mahdi will initiate a jihad against tyranny and injustice and establish a world of bliss. For most Shi'ites throughout their history, the response was to wait passively for the apocalypse. But in activist and revolutionary situations, the Mahdi's return is to be aided by the active anticipation and militancy of the believers (common to millenarian movements), hence jihad.

The activist narrative of Husayn and of the Mahdi both came into play during the 1979 Revolution and subsequent war with Iraq: first the Shah, then Saddam were identified as modern-day counterparts of Yazid, and the fighters as seekers of martyrdom in the path of Husayn, who when martyred would join the imams in Paradise. It was also suggested that the fight might also hasten the return of the Mahdi. These themes were deliberately articulated by Khomeini and other leaders against the Americans and Saddam, but the two were identified together.[21] The pan-Islamic and anti-imperialist rhetoric of the Revolution forbade identifying the enemies in sectarian terms as Sunnis, an inhibition not always shared by the other side. 'The road to Jerusalem passes through Karbala' was a popular war slogan which implicitly identified Saddam with the USA and Israel, and the war against Iraq as part of the anti-imperialist struggle. This rhetoric continues to present times, from Ahmadinejad (President of Iran 2005–13) to Hizbullah in Lebanon: the Arab enemies are not identified as Sunnis but as corrupt rulers acting as agents of imperialism and Israel. Popular sentiment among Iranians and Shi'ites, however, indicates a somewhat different view of the matter.

In recent years, especially after the 2003 invasion of Iraq, the sectarian divisions within Islam have acquired ever greater significance, within particular countries as well as where the geopolitics of the region are concerned. Iraq after 2003 saw Shi'ite political parties rise to government power. While these parties are divided and fractious they nevertheless have a definite sectarian identity, and the various struggles in the country have also been clearly sectarian. Ironically, contrary to American designs, post-invasion Iraq has become a sphere of strong Iranian influence and power-broking among the factions, adding to Iranian power in the region. These developments have worried the Sunni Arab world, especially Saudi Arabia and the Gulf states which harbour considerable Shi'ite populations, repressed and now increasingly restive; indeed, in open rebellion in Bahrain at the time of writing in 2012. In Syria, too, the ongoing rebellion has acquired definite sectarian dimensions, with a strongly Sunni tinge against the Alawite ruling clique. Iran supports the regime, while Saudi Arabia and the Gulf support the opposition, with barely hidden sectarian allegiances. Wahhabi proselytising, including its anti-Shi'ite preaching, with Saudi institutions and money, now reaches all corners of the Muslim lands. The sectarian dimension now engulfs both internal struggles and rebellions and international relations: ours is becoming the era of sectarian jihads.

Notes

1. This chapter was finalised in December 2012.
2. On Ibn Taymiyyah, see Henri Laoust, *Essai sur les doctrines sociales et politiques de Taki-d-din Ahmad b. Taymiya* (Cairo, 1939); Sami Zubaida, *Law and Power in the Islamic World* (London, 2003), pp. 93–103; Antony Black, *The History of Islamic Political Thought: From the Prophet to the Present* (Edinburgh, 2001), pp. 154–9.
3. Selim Deringil, 'The struggle against Shi'ism in Hamidian Iraq', *Die Welt des Islams* 30 (1990): 45–62.
4. For a general account of Islamic sects, see Sami Zubaida, 'Sects in Islam', in Peter B. Clarke (ed.), *The Oxford Handbook of the Sociology of Religion* (Oxford, 2009): 545–61.
5. On Wahhabism and Saudi Arabia, see Madawi al-Rasheed, *A History of Saudi Arabia* (Cambridge, 2010); and J. S. Habib, *Ibn Sa'ud's Warriors of Islam: The Ikhwan of Najd and Their Role in the Creation of the Sa'udi Kingdom, 1910–1930* (Leiden, 1978).
6. Habib, *Ibn Sa'ud's Warriors of Islam.*
7. al-Rasheed, *A History of Saudi Arabia*, pp. 43–8.
8. Ibid., pp. 49–71.
9. Ibid., pp. 44–8.
10. Yitzhak Nakash, *The Shi'is of Iraq* (New Jersey, 1994), pp. 28–30.
11. Al-Rasheed, *A History of Saudi Arabia*, pp. 44–8.
12. For a general overview of Iraqi Shi'ites, see Nakash, *The Shi'is of Iraq*; on the more recent sectarian and Shi'ite politics, see Faleh Jabar, *The Shi'ite Movement in Iraq* (London, 2003).
13. Jabar, *The Shi'ite Movement in Iraq.*
14. Jens-Uwa Rahe, 'La deportation des chiites en Iran', in Chris Kutschera (ed.), *Le Livre Noir de Saddam Hussein* (Paris, 2005): 255–68.
15. Fanar Haddad, *Sectarianism in Iraq: Antagonistic Visions of Unity* (London, 2011), pp. 65–76.
16. Charles Tripp, *A History of Iraq*, 3rd ed. (Cambridge, 2007), pp. 239–50.
17. Ibid., pp. 303–16; Haddad, *Sectarianism in Iraq*, pp. 179–204.

18. Seyyed Vali Reza Nasr, *The Shia Revival: How Conflicts within Islam Will Shape the Future* (New York, 2006), p. 246.
19. Tripp, *A History of Iraq*, pp. 39–44.
20. Mary Hegland, 'Two images of Hussein: Accommodation and revolution in an Iranian village', in Nikki Keddie (ed.), *Religion and Politics in Iran* (New Haven, 1983): 218–35; Michael Fischer, *Iran: From Religious Disputes to Revolution* (Cambridge, MA, 1980).
21. Fischer, *Iran: From Religious Disputes to Revolution*; Yann Richard, *Shi'ite Islam*, trans. Antonia Nevill (Oxford, 1995).

Bibliography

Black, Antony, *The History of Islamic Political Thought: From the Prophet to the Present* (Edinburgh, 2001).

Deringil, Selim, 'The struggle against Shi'ism in Hamidian Iraq', *Die Welt des Islams* 30 (1990): 45–62.

Fischer, Michael (1980), *Iran: From Religious Disputes to Revolution* (Cambridge, MA, 1980).

Habib, J. S., *Ibn Sa'ud's Warriors of Islam: The Ikhwan of Najd and Their Role in the Creation of the Sa'udi Kingdom, 1910–1930* (Leiden, 1978).

Haddad, Fanar, *Sectarianism in Iraq: Antagonistic Visions of Unity* (London, 2011).

Hegland, Mary, 'Two images of Hussein: Accommodation and revolution in an Iranian village', in Nikki Keddie (ed.), *Religion and Politics in Iran* (New Haven, 1983): 218–35.

Jabar, Faleh, *The Shi'ite Movement in Iraq* (London, 2003).

Laoust, Henri, *Essai sur les doctrines sociales et politiques de Taki-d-din Ahmad b. Taymiya* (Cairo, 1939).

Nakash, Yitzhak, *The Shi'is of Iraq* (New Jersey, 1994).

Nasr, Seyyed Vali Reza, *The Shia Revival: How Conflicts within Islam Will Shape the Future* (New York, 2006).

Rahe, Jens-Uwa, 'La deportation des chiites en Iran', in Chris Kutschera (ed.), *Le Livre Noir de Saddam Hussein* (Paris, 2005): 255–68.

al-Rasheed, Madawi, *A History of Saudi Arabia* (Cambridge, 2010).

Richard, Yann, *Shi'ite Islam*, trans. Antonia Nevill (Oxford, 1995).

Tripp, Charles, *A History of Iraq*, 3rd ed. (Cambridge, 2007).

Zubaida, Sami, *Law and Power in the Islamic World* (London, 2003).

———, 'Sects in Islam', in Peter B. Clarke (ed.), *The Oxford Handbook of the Sociology of Religion* (Oxford, 2009): 545–61.

8

The New Qa'ida Wahhabists and the Revival of Jihad in Saudi Arabia

Mansour Alnogaidan

Fifteen of the 19 individuals who hijacked planes in the USA on 11 September 2001 were from Saudi Arabia. Despite being a state with an unambiguously conservative religious identity, Saudi Arabia gave rise to the first global jihadist movement, in the form of al-Qa'ida. The group that was formed and until 2011 led by the wealthy Saudi Osama bin Laden comprises a diffuse network of jihadists that declare war not only on the USA and its allies, but also on the Saudi regime, whose legitimacy they reject. The role played by Saudi Arabia in both the genesis of Salafi jihadism and the war of ideas against al-Qa'ida and other jihadist groups is of paramount importance. As this chapter will show, it needs to be understood in the context of the evolution and transformation of the Saudi state since the eighteenth century, a process in which jihad as an ideological and religious phenomenon has occupied centre stage.

The Covenant

In the mid-eighteenth century Sheikh Muhammad ibn 'Abd al-Wahhab and Muhammad ibn Saud forged a covenant to establish an Islamic emirate in al-Dir'iyya, in the middle of the Arabian Peninsula. Expansionist wars and jihad against those who refused to submit to the new ideology in the different villages and metropolises of Arabia were widespread as the movement emerged. Ibn 'Abd al-Wahhab would contact the emirs of towns, as well as chiefs of villages and tribes, asking them to embrace the new movement and pledge allegiance to Ibn Saud, Prince of al-Dir'iyya, or else have their populations declared as heretics who renounced the religion of Islam (*kuffar*). Upon the Sheikh's approval, armies were raised in preparation for violent jihad and looting the property of the 'enemy'. During Ibn 'Abd al-Wahhab's lifetime, political decisions were made jointly by himself and the ruling prince. The title of imam bestowed on Ibn Saud privileges such as the power to declare jihad, enforce almsgiving and execute the penalties of Islamic law.[1]

During this period in al-Dir'iyya, two types of jihad against the enemy were adopted. The first type was the jihad against rejectionists, that is, those who refused to pledge allegiance to Imam Ibn Saud. People in this category were considered to be apostates and non-believers. The second type was jihad against the rebels, or those who opposed the political influence of al-Dir'iyya, even if they had submitted to the call of Ibn 'Abd al-Wahhab and adopted his beliefs from the very beginning. In the First Saudi State, no distinction was made between those who rejected the teachings of the new movement and those who opposed the authority of Imam Ibn Saud, Prince of al-Dir'iyya. In Sunni jurisprudence, fighting against rebels is not specifically considered a form of jihad. In either case, a theological justification was required to motivate fighters and volunteers to embark upon a holy war.[2]

In 1788, after the death of Ibn 'Abd al-Wahhab, Muhammad ibn Saud murdered Muhammad ibn Ghurayb, a young scholar who was related by marriage to Ibn 'Abd al-Wahhab, for daring to raise doubts about the legality of attacking and looting the property of the Bedouin. This was the first instance of Wahhabi teachings being called into question. In the early nineteenth century, other voices emerged among those Wahhabi scholars who were more open-minded, having been influenced by their debates with scholars from Hijaz, Iraq and Syria. They posed questions and put forward ideas about the validity of considering those who disagreed with them over interpretations of Islam as apostates whose blood could be shed and property looted. This ultimately led to questioning the legitimacy of declaring jihad against opponents. Proponents of such views, who tended to come from remote areas far from the centre of al-Dir'iyya, were demonised and declared to be apostates by more militant

Wahhabi peers, such as the sons and grandsons of Ibn Saud and their supporters. Despite these divisions, however, there was unanimous agreement that decisions of war and the declaration of jihad, as well as of peace, rested solely in the hands of the imam.

The First Saudi State's power reached its heyday after the annexation of Mecca and Medina and their subjugation to the rule of the imam in Najd in 1814. With the destruction of al-Dir'iyya in 1818 at the hands of the Egyptian leader Muhammad Ali Pasha's armies, the Wahhabi state fell into ruin. After its collapse, the Wahhabi state's legacy was divided among its more powerful opponents until the Saudi dynasty reclaimed tenuous power in Najd. The majority of the urban dwellers of Najd remained loyal to the principles of the Wahhabi movement, which partially explains why the Sauds managed to stage a quick comeback. It also explains their ability to restore most of their spheres of influence, with the exception of Mecca and Medina, which were ruled by nobles supported by Muhammad Ali and later by the Ottoman sultan's armies.

Despite the fact that many sought power and influence in the Arabian Peninsula, no one could rival the sway of the Sauds over the hearts and souls of people. The covenant forged between Ibn Saud and Muhammad ibn 'Abd al-Wahhab left a deep impression in people's hearts even when their power was decaying. The Wahhabis alone claimed the legitimate right to declare jihad.

After Riyadh became the capital of the Saudi dynasty, the Sauds waged military campaigns to subdue those precincts that had escaped their hegemony. The Wahhabis, in turn, conferred on these campaigns the distinction of 'fighting in the path of Allah'. However these battles did not stir as much religious fervour and enthusiasm as did the first wars of conquest. This was because occasional disputes occurred among the champions of Wahhabism themselves and among the members of the House of Saud. Wars erupted between the two sons of Faysal ibn Turki, 'Abd Allah and Saud, in 1866. The struggle between the two brothers sparked off contradictory stances and fatwas from partisans of each side, with each declaring a holy war against the other.

Takfir (excommunication) fatwas issued by ulama (religious scholars) in Riyadh against those who interpreted the imam's teachings in ways contrary to theirs had lost their former appeal and influence. After the restoration of the Saudi state following the destruction of al-Dir'iyya, the

Sauds entered into more pragmatic alliances with influential groups, in which they showed leniency over adherence to the Wahhabi teachings. The religious fervour that marked the beginnings of the First Saudi State was at a low ebb and the logic of expedience began to govern the choice of allies. After 1843, the reign of Faysal ibn Turki, who had maintained excellent relations with the pasha in Egypt and avoided the adventurous policies of his predecessors, reflected an open-minded atmosphere. In this atmosphere some religious scholars found an outlet for views that it had previously been impossible for them to express, including those that criticised the intolerant religious views of Riyadh's ulama, and challenged the validity of deploying *takfir* and jihad against opponents of the Wahhabi movement.[3]

We cannot understand the Sauds' jihad doctrine without comprehending their stances toward the Ottoman caliph who was, in the eyes of the majority of Muslims and their religious leaders, the imam and possessed the exclusive right to declare jihad. The Wahhabis' attitude towards the Ottoman caliph was ambiguous and shrouded in mystery. Though the letters sent by Sauds to their opponents libeled the Sultanate, to the point of accusing it of heresy, they did not allude to the sultan's entitlement to the caliphate and did not challenge his claim to the title of Guardian of the Two Holy Mosques. However, Ibn Saud conferred upon himself the title of imam, which runs counter to that of caliph. Up until the 1920s, the Wahhabis' religious rulings and literature often included references to *takfir* against the Ottomans, branding the latter infidels and heretics who worshipped the tombs of the dead. After the annihilation of al-Dir'iyya, it was revealed that Wahhabi scholars used to refer to *both* Turkish and Byzantine armies in their correspondence as armies of the infidel states.

Jihad in the Third Saudi State

By 1902, teachings of Wahhabism were already deep-rooted in all the areas that had been governed by the Sauds for the previous 150 years. In that year, 'Abd al-'Aziz ibn 'Abd al-Rahman al-Faysal took control of Riyadh. The pretext he cited to go to war against Ibn Rashid, the governor of Ha'il, was to restore the dominions of his predecessors. To achieve this end, 'Abd al-'Aziz drew on the loyalty of individuals united in their hatred of Ibn Rashid's despotic rule and hopeful of playing a new role under a victorious Saudi prince. Fighting in the path of Allah – jihad – was not among 'Abd al-'Aziz's declared aims. At that time, the influence of the descendants of Sheikh Muhammad ibn 'Abd al-Wahhab, who constituted the mainstay of the Wahhabi movement, was in decline. There were other luminaries in Najd who surpassed them in learning and charisma, and who declared allegiance to the Ottoman caliph. With the appearance of 'Abd al-'Aziz, hopes of the Wahhabi movement for a revival of the covenant flourished. Religious fervour revived, and 'Abd al-'Aziz benefited from the fatwas circulated by Riyadh's ulama concerning the apostasy and infidelity of the Ottoman dynasty and Ibn Rashid and his followers.

In 1913, 'Abd al-'Aziz discovered great potential in the tribesmen among whom Wahhabi teachings had been propagated by roaming Wahhabi preachers. He encouraged the religious enthusiasm of disparate elements from the tribes and towns known as the Ikhwan (Brotherhood), who nurtured hopes of restoring the old glory of the time of 'Abd al-'Aziz ibn Muhammad ibn Saud. The ulama encouraged the Ikhwan to volunteer in the conquering armies of Imam 'Abd al-'Aziz, to whom thousands proclaimed allegiance. In 1915, 'Abd al-'Aziz signed the Saudi–British treaty in Qatif, through which – in line with other British agreements with Gulf emirates – Ibn Saud renounced relations with other foreign powers in return for British protection.[4]

King 'Abd al-'Aziz surrounded himself with an entourage of Arab advisors who had received a modern education. He also struck up friendships with Western politicians and travellers. He aspired to establish a modern state that commanded the respect of its neighbours and the great powers. In the early 1920s, 'Abd al-'Aziz publicly relinquished the title of imam in an assembly with his Ikhwan commanders. He informed them that he was an emir aiming to restore the stolen domains of his ancestors and not a caliph.[5] Having annexed Mecca and Medina, he declared himself Sultan of Hijaz and Najd.

The establishment of the state was preceded by a long struggle with some of his army commanders who insisted on pursuing expansionist battles to the north and east, which encroached on British interests in Iraq, Kuwait and the Levant. Ulama loyal to 'Abd al-'Aziz tried repeatedly to win over the Ikhwan. Most importantly, they argued that jihad was contingent upon the orders of the Muslims' leader, who had the right to make agreements and peace treaties in accordance with the public interest. They also argued that 'enjoining good and forbidding wrong' (*al-amr bi-l-ma'ruf wa-l-nahy 'an al-munkir*) and peacefully promoting Wahhabi teachings could be considered a form of jihad.[6]

'Abd al-'Aziz quelled the mutiny in 1927 in a decisive battle at Sabla, in the heart of Saudi Arabia. He managed to subdue the Ikhwan, killing hundreds of them and taking the survivors prisoner. After uniting the land, 'Abd al-'Aziz declared the Kingdom of Saudi Arabia in 1932. Religious teachings and fatwas were then focused on the jihad of self-defence, the reform of the faith and obedience to the ruler.

Jihad After the Foundation of Saudi Arabia

The establishment of the state of Israel in 1948 heralded the re-emergence of the idea of jihad as fighting for God. Some Western ambassadors reported King 'Abd al-'Aziz as saying: 'It would be an honour for me to be martyred on the battlefield in defense of Palestine against the Jews.' Saudi scholars in Hijaz and Najd wrote that they would call for jihad if a partitioning policy was applied in Palestine. Subsequently, Saudi forces participated in the 1948 war.[7]

During the 1950s, King 'Abd al-'Aziz and his entourage came to the conclusion that the hard-line attitude of the Ikhwan no longer posed a threat to the regime, since it was directed against misguided innovations and the temptations of modern life. The authorities instead paid closer attention to Bedouin recruits and formed a reserve contingent whose members received annual stipends. In 1954 the Saudi government set up the National Guard Forces, which absorbed the remaining Ikhwan guerillas. Sheikhs of tribes became chiefs of the brigades, with each brigade comprising individuals belonging to one single tribe. In 1962, one year after Prince 'Abd Allah ibn 'Abd al-'Aziz – the future King of Saudi Arabia – assumed the stewardship of the National Guard, the Saudi Ministry of the Interior established the Mujahidin Forces. Rather than fighting wars against non-believers and apostates, their work was restricted to guarding government buildings, supporting the army, patrolling city streets at night and escorting princes.[8]

In the late 1950s, Wahhabism reached a turning-point. It started to flourish outside Saudi borders and to garner new supporters.

'Abd al-'Aziz was the inspiration behind this expansion. However, the strict Hanbali nature of Wahhabism was becoming diluted as Wahhabism became restricted to only a few specific domains. An influx of immigrants, including scientists and teachers, filled huge gaps in educational institutions. The reservoir of ideas that had shaped the movement of Ibn 'Abd al-Wahhab was running dry and giving way to the burgeoning ideas of leftist, nationalist and communist movements, a tide that the religious establishment appeared powerless to stem.[9]

In 1960, the Islamic University was established in Medina. The Syrian hadith scholar, Nasir al-Din al-Albani, wielded great influence over his university students. He criticised political Islam and the Muslim Brotherhood and preached loyalty to the government in religious sermons and books. Four years later, he was deported from the country due to the machinations of his university colleagues. But through his many books, he helped lay the foundations of a new theory about the first generation of Muslims (the Salaf) based on the purification of the faith and the soul. At the same time, fugitive groups of the Muslim Brotherhood from Egypt and Syria were starting to enter the Kingdom in large numbers. They were welcomed by King Faysal as a weapon against the Nasserists and communists.

The idea of jihad was revived, this time with King Faysal as its driving force. For Faysal, jihad meant fighting for freedom and liberating Palestine from Jewish occupation. The October 1973 War was considered the archetype of the kind of jihad to which King Faysal aspired, and Faysal called on his people to embark on jihad in Palestine. Newspapers also published appeals for volunteers to enlist. In one of his famous speeches, King Faysal inflamed passions when he said that he would rather die immediately than live a single day if he were not destined to be martyred in the land of Palestine.[10] Yet this aura of enthusiasm which rekindled sentiments of solidarity in the Islamic world in general, and in Saudi Arabia in particular, did not result in the formation of a real jihadist organisation, whether official or secret, in Saudi Arabia.

Return of the Ikhwan

One reason why no real jihadist organisation ever materialised is that the logical consequence of such a group's existence would call into question the legitimacy of the Saud regime itself, in part by discrediting its devotion to Islam and commitment to applying Islamic law. Following the death of King Faysal, this danger inherent in jihadism became a tangible reality in the form of the fundamentalist group known as the Muhtasiba Group, members of which stormed the Holy Mosque in 1979. This was linked to the Utaybi group, whose roots go back to the late 1960s when a group of self-appointed moral inspectors (*muhtasibin*) raided some photography studios and shops. A member of the royal family, together with some militants, attacked the Television Building in Riyadh in 1966 and was killed by the police. The group represented the core of the fundamentalist Muhtasiba Group, which later grew into a larger group supported by the government and nurtured by one of its loyal ulama, Sheikh 'Abd al-'Aziz ibn Baz. The memory of these early jihadists would prove to be a major factor in shaping the worldview of the followers of the Muhtasiba Group and their leader Juhayman al-'Utaybi, whose father had been a fighter in the Ikhwan army. Juhayman himself, and many other followers of the group, had also previously served in the National Guard. From the 1970s, members of the group had been gripped by feelings of nostalgia for the golden age of the Ikhwan.

The breakdown of the alliance between 'Abd al-'Aziz and the Ikhwan was one of the major issues on Juhayman's mind, as manifested in literature authored by the group, including the so-called 'Seven Letters'. Prior to their occupation of the Holy Mosque, the group's literature called for reviving the tradition of jihad, which had been suspended by the political will of 'Abd al-'Aziz ibn Saud. They called for jihad against the non-believers and Shi'ites. This was the first time King 'Abd al-'Aziz had been subject to open criticism of this kind, and this occurred despite the fact that the ulama were apparently unified, well-established and capable of responding to any challenge.

After the death of King Faysal, divisions arose within the group. When some of the group's followers raised doubts about the state's adherence to Islam, the Islamic establishment rose to the challenge. Juhayman and other members of the group were students of 'Abd al-'Aziz ibn Baz, President of the Islamic University, who became the Kingdom's leading Islamic scholar from 1970. Al-Albani also commanded the respect of the group and his books were well received by its members. After 1977, the group was further strengthened by new Egyptian members who were already active in jihadist groups such as al-Takfir wa-l-Hijra (Excommunication and Holy Flight).

In November 1979, 250 guerillas led by Juhayman al-'Utaybi stormed the Holy Mosque and declared the imminent return of the Mahdi (redeemer). Juhayman and his colleagues gave sermons in front of tens of thousands of worshippers in the mosque in which they explained the basic ideas of the group and the circumstances leading up to the occupation of the mosque. Two weeks later, the revolt was put down by the Saudi government.

Fundamentalist Jihadism

In the 1980s, thousands of Saudis joined their Arab Afghan brothers in jihad against the USSR. The political debates taking place in the Pakistani city of Peshawar resulted in a reformulation of the concept of jihad that entailed designating Arab governments, including that of Saudi Arabia, as apostate. Saudis bore the brunt of these theoretical innovations whose architects were Egyptian and Syrian theorists involved with the Jihad Group and al-Gama'a al-Islamiyya. These activists also took part in the Afghan war, which gave rise to the so-called Peshawar formula, which was headquartered in the Sweden District in Riyadh. The ideas of Juhayman al-'Utaybi flourished again during the 1980s, thanks to those members of the group who survived in Kuwait and Yemen. In the late 1980s, a Jordanian named 'Isam al-Barqawi (alias Abu Muhammad al-Maqdisi), who spent his formative years in Kuwait and was closely acquainted with Juhayman's group, was studying the Wahhabi heritage and the fatwas of Wahhabi scholars for issues related to *takfir* (excommunication) and precedents for turning against the ruler. Thanks to al-Maqdisi, ideas that had long seemed obsolete were revived. Al-Maqdisi blended the ideas of the first Wahhabis and those of the Muhtasiba Group with the Salafi (purist) trend of al-Albani. He crowned his visit to Pakistan in 1990 with his famous book, *The Clear Proof in the Excommunication of the Saudi State*.

By the end of the 1980s, two fundamental principles of the traditional concept of jihad were falling into abeyance. These were the imam's monopoly on the authority to declare jihad and the esteem in which the ulama were held. These intellectual developments reached their apex at the time of the Iraqi occupation of Kuwait and the concomitant disillusionment with the ulama. Islamists were particularly disappointed that the ulama did not play their expected role. This deterioration in the spiritual influence of the ulama coincided with the emergence of a new generation of preachers who were trying to strike a balance between the Islamic creed and Wahhabi theology, on the one hand, and the ideas of the Muslim Brotherhood, on the other. They discredited the authenticity of the ulama, thus stirring grave concern among members of the royal family.

In 1994, the Saudi government discovered the nucleus of the first Salafi jihadist organisation on its soil. In November of the following year, al-Qa'ida carried out the first attack on Western expatriates via an explosion in Riyadh. Jihadist thought, which is based on *takfir*, took the Saudi religious sphere by storm. The change came in two forms: first, it took the form of dubbing King Fahd himself a *kafir* (non-believer) and branding his government apostate. Second, jihadists deemed the official bodies of ulama to be mere government officials who had relinquished their sacred mission and were loyal only to the monarch. The loss of the prestige previously enjoyed by the ulama paved the way for various new interpretations of the concept of jihad by theorists and researchers who did not belong to the official religious establishment and attached no value to the blessing of the established ulama.

These transformations led to the erosion of the classical jihad theology taught in religious institutes and universities. New ideas and theories emerged in the form of hybridised models constructed by those who did not belong to official religious institutions. Such models constituted amalgams of obsolete and new ideas. New concepts and schools of thought emerged outside the sphere of academic jurisprudence, influenced by nostalgia for the Islamist movements of the 1930s. The gulf between contemporary jihadist thought and the theology of the past was reflected in the initiative of 'Abd al-Muhsin al-Abikan, a Saudi scholar who entered into a live debate on MBC television with those who disagreed with him about jihad and the legitimacy of the US occupation of Iraq.

Saudi Arabia is now engaged in a war of ideas against al-Qa'ida. The Kingdom is a major battlefield for this struggle, and any inroads it makes against violence and its underlying ideology, however slow, have considerable significance due to Saudi Arabia's extensive influence on the Islamic world in general and on Sunni Islam in particular.

Notes

1. Husayn Ibn Ghannam, *Rawdat al-Afkar wa-l-Afham* (*The Pasture of Ideas and Concepts*, Cairo, 1948).
2. 'Abd al-Rahman ibn Qasim, *al-Durar al-Saniyya fi al-Ajwiba al-Najdiyya* (*The Sparkling Pearls in Najdi Responses*, Riyadh, 1964).
3. Hafiz Wahba, *Khamsun 'Am-an fi Jazirat al-'Arab* (*Fifty Years in the Arabian Peninsula*, Cairo, 1960).
4. Muhammad Jalal Kishk, *al-Sa'udiyyun wa-l-Hall al-Islami* (*Saudis and the Islamic Solution*, Cairo, 1982); John Habib, *al-Ikhwan al-Sa'udiyyun fi 'Aqdayn 1910–1930* (*The Saudi Brethren Over Two Decades*, Riyadh, 1998).
5. Wahba, *Khamsun 'Am-an*.
6. Ibn Qasim, *al-Durar al-Saniyya*.
7. Falah Khalid 'Ali, *Filastin wa-l-Intidab al-Britani 1939–1948* (*Palestine and the British Mandate 1939–1948*, Riyadh, 1999). Isma'il Ahmad Yaghy, *al-Malik 'Abd al-'Aziz ibn 'Abd al-Rahman al-Sa'ud wa-Qadiyyat Filastin 1936–1948* (*King 'Abd al-'Aziz ibn 'Abd al-Rahman al-Saud and the Question of Palestine 1936–1948*, Riyadh, 1999).
8. John Habib *al-Ikhwan al-Sa'udiyyun*. See also Nawal al-Rashid, 'al-Qita' al-amni fi 'ahd al-Malik 'Abd al-'Aziz yashadu tatawwur-an marhaliyy-an li-hifz al-amn' ('The security sector under King 'Abd al-'Aziz witnesses transformative change to maintain security'), *al-Riyadh*, 23 September 2003.
9. Alexei Vassiliev, *The History of Saudi Arabia* (London, 1998).
10. Hazim al-Samira'i, *al-Malik Faysal ibn 'Abd al-'Aziz al-Sa'ud* (*King Faysal ibn 'Abd al-'Aziz al-Saud*, London, 2001).

Bibliography

'Ali, Falah Khalid, *Filastin wa-l-Intidab al-Britani 1939–1948* (*Palestine and the British Mandate 1939–1948*, Riyadh, 1999).

Habib, John, *al-Ikhwan al-Sa'udiyyun fi 'Aqdayn 1910–1930* (*The Saudi Brethren Over Two Decades*, Riyadh, 1998).

Ibn Ghannam, Husayn, *Rawdat al-Afkar wa-l-Afham* (*The Pasture of Ideas and Concepts*, Cairo, 1948).

Ibn Qasim, 'Abd al-Rahman, *al-Durar al-Saniyya fi al-Ajwiba al-Najdiyya* (*The Sparkling Pearls in Najdi Responses*, Riyadh, 1964).

Kishk, Muhammad Jalal, *al-Sa'udiyyun wa-l-Hall al-Islami* (*Saudis and the Islamic Solution*, Cairo,1982).

al-Rashid, Nawal, 'al-Qita' al-amni fi 'ahd al-Malik 'Abd al-'Aziz yashadu tatawwur-an marhaliyy-an li-hifz al-amn' ('The security sector under King 'Abd al-'Aziz witnesses transformative change to maintain security'), *al-Riyadh*, 23 September 2003.

al-Samira'i, Hazim, *al-Malik Faysal ibn 'Abd al-'Aziz al-Sa'ud* (*King Faysal ibn 'Abd al-'Aziz*, London, 2001).

Vassiliev, Alexei, *The History of Saudi Arabia* (London, 1998).

Wahba, Hafiz, *Khamsun 'Am-an fi Jazirat al-'Arab* (*Fifty Years in the Arabian Peninsula*, Cairo, 1960).

Yaghy, Isma'il Ahmad, *al-Malik 'Abd al-'Aziz ibn 'Abd al-Rahman al-Sa'ud wa-Qadiyyat Filastin 1936–1948* (*King 'Abd al-'Aziz ibn 'Abd al-Rahman al-Saud and the Question of Palestine*, Riyadh, 1999).

9

The Muslim Brotherhood and Jihad

Hossam Tammam[1]

At the beginning of 2010, Abu al-'Ala' Madi, Islamist leader and co-founder of Hizb al-Wasat (the Centre Party), alluded to the Brotherhood's role in jihadist action in Chechnya in the mid-1990s, a time when separatist unrest was at its height in the region. This caused controversy in relation to the Muslim Brotherhood's stance on violence and armed action. Madi also referred to comments made by the fifth Supreme Guide, Mustafa Mashhur, dating to the late 1970s, in which he alleged the presence of a secret Brotherhood cell within the army, poised to seize power.

The Muslim Brotherhood's discourse on armed action was supposed to have been phased out on the basis that violence was a thing of the past. However, a number of developments and debates strengthened the hegemony of the conservative trend within the Brotherhood. Most of the movement's leaders, at the time of writing, belonged to this trend, including the Supreme Guide Muhammad Badi', known for forming part of the '1965 organisation' that aimed to overthrow the Nasser regime.

The Brotherhood's history of violence raises the important question of what conditions support the use of violence as part of the programme of an Islamist social movement. Theoretical considerations on the place of violence in political Islam fall broadly within two approaches. The first relies on jurisprudential texts, some of which constitute literature that is central to the Islamic movement, as well as related verses on jihad from the Qur'an and hadith. From this perspective, Islamic doctrine encourages the framing of individual and group behaviour in conformity with the teachings of Islam, even if that requires the use of violence.[2] A second, more sociological, approach focuses on the social background, class and occupation of those whom the Islamist group is successful in recruiting.[3] Recruits generally belong to marginalised groups in society, often from rural areas and living at the boundaries of urban centres. They are more familiar with violence because of these characteristics, which cause them to feel like outsiders in the context of rapid modernisation.

Neither approach is sufficient on its own for drawing conclusions on the use of violence to effect change. Categorical references to jihad in the shariah, which are employed by Islamist movements to justify their opposition to 'the other' both domestically (the regime) and externally (Western forces), do not give us enough information about the reasons and conditions that lead to jihad in a particular historical period. Nor do they explain changes and revisions which take place in other phases. Likewise, the sociological approach does not offer an explanation as to why only some movements resort to violence as a means for change. Some jihadist movements prefer working within states and target governing structures, whilst others favour global jihad. Still others espouse both of these approaches.

Egypt offers an important case study for exploring the above questions. Whilst the Jihad Organisation (Tanzim al-Jihad) and the Islamic Group (al-Gama'a al-Islamiyya) evolved toward jihadism in the 1970s, the Muslim Brotherhood opposed violence. But important shifts within the Brotherhood in the aftermath of internal elections in 2008 and 2009 led it to become more conservative, in line with a growing Salafist element within its ranks and in Egyptian society more generally. Furthermore, the movement's relationship with the Egyptian regime has altered since the fall of Mubarak. This chapter thus explores the Muslim Brotherhood's position on jihad from both theoretical and sociological perspectives, in order to assess the potential for its transformation into a jihadist movement, in the sense of employing armed violence to achieve its political goals.

The Brotherhood's idea of jihad oscillates between the 'foundational' orientation of its founder, Hasan al-Banna, and a more universalist orientation associated with Sayyid Qutb. This tension can also be conceived as one between a theory of the state and a utopian vision of the Islamic community (*umma*). The internal composition of the Brotherhood has arguably played the most significant role in influencing the movement's understanding of jihad, which shifts between these two propositions.

The concept of jihad has evolved since its adoption by Islamist movements in the twentieth century, partly due to the expansion of the religious realm beyond the sphere of scholars and official religious institutions, which had historically been responsible for explaining the concept of jihad to the Muslim public. Interaction with Western civilisation from the nineteenth century stimulated religious reform. With the growth of educational movements, religious knowledge, including on the subject of jihad, came to be imparted beyond official religious institutions. The growing use of the media and modern communications technology helped generate and disseminate information on religion. Throughout the twentieth century, the actors involved in defining jihad proliferated, with Islamist movements becoming its most influential articulators. New conceptions of jihad emerged, from 'civil jihad' to 'electronic jihad'.

Disagreement among Islamist movements arose on a number of issues. Should the focus of jihad be primarily national or international? Was the decision of the ruler (*wali al-amr*) binding and exclusive for all sections of the *umma* or were other groups permitted to give opinions on and call for jihad? Many Islamists decided on the latter, in line with their conviction that parts of the Muslim world had been occupied by outsiders and the Islamic credentials of rulers were in doubt. Jihad shifted from being an obligation for those in the *umma* who could engage in it if Muslim lands were occupied, as outlined in traditional Sunni teachings, to an obligation that, if ignored, amounted to neglecting a basic pillar of religion. The focus thus inexorably shifted from confronting an external enemy to dealing with an internal one. This interpretation was particularly prominent in Egypt during the 1970s and 1980s.

The founder of the Muslim Brotherhood, Hasan al-Banna, had placed the issue of force at the forefront of the Brotherhood's thinking. Al-Banna formed groups called 'rovers', mainly focusing on training and athleticism. The absence of an explicitly military entity within the Brotherhood, however, reflected al-Banna's preference for gradualism. The rovers, which aimed to recruit and reform young people, were part of the National Scouts Association, the only militaristic entity that was permitted in Egypt at the end of the 1930s. Even though political organisations were formally prohibited from possessing military wings, the rovers were excluded from the prohibition, as were similar appendages of the Wafd party, Misr al-Fata and other emerging nationalist groupings.[4]

The Secret Apparatus (al-Tanzim al-Sirri) that Hasan al-Banna later created was more overtly violent. The political context played a role in its creation at the end of the 1940s. As 'Abd al-Halim Mahmud notes, the Secret Apparatus emerged during a specific historical moment dominated by the desire to defend the Brotherhood's missionary work in the absence of an independent authority to tackle the weakness of the state and the Egyptian army at the time. It was also the time when the Palestinian question became part of the Egyptian Brotherhood's agenda. Furthermore, the Second World War transformed Egypt's western border – with Libya – into a combat front, which facilitated the acquisition of weapons needed for military training camps. As well as receiving military training, members of the Secret Apparatus studied the jurisprudence of jihad and correct practices of worship such as prayer and fasting, and learnt the need for patience and endurance.[5]

The Brotherhood's ideas on jihad should be approached within their historical context. In the 1930s and 1940s al-Banna viewed jihad as a way of combating the British presence in Egypt and the Jewish presence in Palestine. Jihad was not yet directed internally towards the state or regime. The formation of the Secret Apparatus was related to the intensification of the pressure of British occupation and the latter's role in encouraging Jewish migration to Palestine, as well as to the activities of Zionist organisations in Palestine. For this reason, the organisation engaged in acts of resistance against Zionist groups in Palestine.

The Muslim Brotherhood participated in the Palestine War of 1948 as a militia tolerated by the state. But defeat focused attention on the army, whose weakness the Brotherhood equated with the weakness of the state itself. It is unclear whether the operations of the Secret Apparatus against the Brotherhood's political opponents in Egypt – the most prominent being the assassinations of Judge Ahmad al-Khazandar and Prime Minister Mahmud Fahmi al-Naqrashi – were carried out with the knowledge of the Supreme Guide, or were organisational or individual decisions taken within the Secret Apparatus. But such operations led to a quick response to neutralise and ban the Brotherhood in the wake of the assassination of al-Banna in 1949. From this point the Brotherhood sought to distance itself from the Secret Apparatus, directly and candidly condemning the initiative as a deviation from the general direction of the Brotherhood. Al-Banna himself had declared: 'They are neither Brothers nor Muslims.' Through this statement, al-Banna disassociated himself from the assassins, from those who supported violence against the regime as a strategy, and from those who rationalised violence as a necessary phase in the national struggle.

Given that the British occupation constituted an enemy that was at once internal and external, al-Banna and the Brotherhood accepted the need for a militia in the form of the Secret Apparatus. Following the departure of the British and the consolidation of an independent state, however, the existence of a sub-state military organisation became untenable. In the context of Nasser's repression of the Brotherhood, however, the impulse for violence embodied in the Secret Apparatus was revived and legitimised by the ideas of Sayyid Qutb. The '1965 organisation' can be considered a continuation of the Secret Apparatus during the Qutb era. This poses an important question: was it Qutb's ideas that led the Brotherhood back towards violence, or the organisation's own characteristics?

Qutb's ideas imbued the Secret Apparatus with an ideological rationale that it had lacked under al-Banna. Qutb's ideas of *hakimiyya* (sovereignty of God) and *jahiliyya* (pre-Islamic 'ignorance') drew sharp distinctions between legitimate and illegitimate leaders and authentic and inauthentic Muslims in society, and were interpreted by many to oblige violence to upset the status quo. Qutb's 'Qur'anic generation' was to be the believers' vanguard for establishing the Islamic state. This meant the removal of government by man (for example, the removal of the Nasser regime)[6] and the restoration of rule by God via the implementation of Islamic law.

Between 1954 and 1965 Qutb brought the ideological and organisational trends together. Brotherhood members who were imprisoned by Nasser, especially the youth and members of the Secret Apparatus, played an important role in defining what had remained undefined during al-Banna's time. Resisting a regime now considered infidel became the priority. The Brotherhood's clandestine activity was underpinned by a comprehensive ideology aimed at the consolidation of a believers' vanguard able to demonstrate the superiority of faith and maintain emotional isolation from the state and un-Islamic societal values. Qutb's teachings provided the organisation with a utopian universal vision of 'us' versus 'them', and an identity forged upon these ideas as well as a sense of shared suffering. This reinforced the choice of violence as a means of Islamising the state and society.

At the same time, Brotherhood leaders attempted to curb the influence of Sayyid Qutb's ideas in the late 1960s. The leadership issued a famous letter, 'Preachers not Judges', heavily qualifying the notion of *takfir* (excommunication) promoted by Qutb. But this effort failed to prevent the violent interpretations of Qutb's work that emerged during the Sadat period. At this time the majority of the Islamist movement did not oppose the principle of armed violence, but differed on the extent of its usefulness and the appropriate timing for it.

In 1974 the first Islamist coup movement in Egypt's history, the so-called Military Technical College group, emerged and many jihadist insurrectionary organisations subsequently sprang up, most prominently the Jihad Organisation and the Islamic Group. The Brotherhood was not isolated from these developments. But experience had given it a greater capacity for realism and caution. The Brotherhood viewed violence against the state as a 'lost cause', having borne the brunt of repression at the hands of the regime in the late 1940s and during the Nasser period. The Brotherhood in the 1970s, rather than confronting the state, aimed to build a hierarchical organisation that was beyond state control and surveillance. This strategy, importantly, was followed despite the fact that the leaders who launched and guided it were those who had been associated with the Secret Apparatus before the revolution.[7] The Muslim Brotherhood was not involved in violent operations during this period, and probably had not established a cell in the army, as Mustafa Mashhur reputedly claimed. But the interconnections within the Islamist movement between Brotherhood and jihadist figures kept the idea of violence on the Brotherhood's radar.

The success of the operation to assassinate President Sadat in 1981 prompted the Brotherhood to clarify its stance vis-à-vis violence. The Jihad Organisation and the Islamic Group, in killing the head of state, raised the spectre of renewed confrontation with the regime. Under pressure to declare its position within the Islamist movement the Brotherhood opted to become part of the 'moderate' camp. This choice reflected not only the Brotherhood leaders' ideological assessment that this was the line closest to that of al-Banna, but also the pragmatic aim of securing legitimacy for the Brotherhood in the eyes of the regime, which sought the Brothers' support in its confrontation with jihadism.

The Brotherhood took part in the 1984 parliamentary elections in coalition with the liberal Wafd Party. This further encouraged the Brotherhood's 'moderation' through peaceful political action within the professional syndicates, local councils and the Parliament. But despite this moderation, an ideological 'predisposition' for violence remained latent within the movement, rooted in books and writings which the movement was reluctant to revise and criticise intellectually, including some of Qutb's pieces that remained on the educational curriculum of the Brotherhood.

The international context played an important role in framing the Brotherhood's stance toward violence and jihad. From its inception the Brotherhood had global aspirations and a vision of creating a comprehensive Islamic community. The International Organisation (al-Tanzim al-Duwali) had been an important component of the Brotherhood since al-Banna's creation of the Department of Communications with the Islamic World in the 1930s with the strategy of establishing parallel entities in other Arab countries. Nevertheless, nationalism was more prominent during the formative years for two reasons. First, the Brotherhood sought to penetrate all state and society institutions in Egypt, from the universities to the army. It was successful in attracting religious members of the army who later formed the Free Officers Movement that led the July revolution. Second, the Brotherhood was first and foremost a reformist, and not revolutionary, movement. Its priority was to reform the state from within, rather than to destroy and rebuild it. This domestic focus is highly significant when looking at the shift that happened following the confrontation with the regime.

Indeed, Qutb's universalist revolutionary project, which considered the entire Islamic community to be in a state of *jahiliyya* (or willful ignorance of Islamic principles), paralleled Nasser's expansionist Arab nationalist foreign policy during the 1960s. Qutb's thinking reflected the same public dissatisfaction with the nation-state framework as did Arab nationalism. The Brotherhood's practical stance towards armed violence and jihad was, like the regime's foreign policy, pulled in two directions: internally toward reform and consolidation within the state and externally toward the concept of the *umma*. These two tendencies were encapsulated in the thought of al-Banna and Qutb respectively.

The Brotherhood beyond Egypt

Just as the Brotherhood in Egypt reached a rapprochement with the regime, Brotherhood branches elsewhere adopted conciliatory postures towards state authorities. In Algeria, the Brotherhood joined the government in confronting both the Islamic Salvation Front and the Armed Islamic Group, and played the role of providing Islamic support to the army in its campaign against Islamic insurgency. The Brothers in Iraq (the Islamic Party) became part of the political process within the Transitional Council. The Brotherhood abandoned armed resistance against occupation in favour of repentance, as was recorded in the Islamic Party's slogan: 'Resist occupation through repentance in Ramadan.' Even though a section of the Brotherhood took part in the creation of a resistance movement, Harakat Jami' (Mosque Movement), the movement's majority preferred political action to secure a place in post-Saddam Iraq.

The Brotherhood provided weapons to the Yemeni Islah Bloc during the war of defence in 1994 under the umbrella of the state. In Somalia the Brotherhood preferred political action over the formation of an armed resistance movement, and in clashes between armed Islamists, the Brotherhood leaned towards Sheikh Sharif and his wing in power in preference to the jihadist movements. The Muslim Brotherhood branch in Lebanon, al-Gama'a al-Islamiyya (The Islamic Group) founded Quwwat al-Fajr (The Forces of Dawn) to fight against the Israeli occupation of Lebanon. However, despite the involvement of its leadership in armed action, the experiment remained on the margins and did not represent a fundamental shift towards resistance. In Gaza, Hamas, which was considered the only military manifestation of the Brotherhood, did not pursue an overt military policy against the ruling Fatah faction in the Palestinian Authority until it was symbolically protected by its legitimacy as an elected authority in 2006. It was only then that Hamas formed an internal police force (the Executive Force) subordinate to the Ministry of Interior.

The Syrian Muslim Brotherhood was, perhaps, the exception when it rebelled militarily against the Alawite Ba'th regime in a battle that ended in the bloody massacre of thousands of Brothers in Hama in 1982. But violence did not reflect the mainstream view of the Brotherhood in Syria but rather that of the growing influence of a jihadist nucleus within the organisation represented by the 'fighting vanguard'. Thereafter, this nucleus was joined by the mainstream leadership and subsequently adopted by the whole of the Brotherhood. These actions apparently received approval from the international leadership after they were convinced of the possibility of victory. But the confrontational faction ultimately yielded to those favouring political action. This came too late as, in the wake of the Hama massacre, the Brotherhood in Syria was almost totally wiped out.

It is difficult to find other models similar to Syria's Brotherhood, which turned to armed confrontation against the state. Although Tunisia's al-Nahda movement accepted responsibility for violent incidents in the 1980s, these may have been isolated cases, and al-Nahda was in fact the most definite of the Brotherhood's organisations in rejecting the use of violence against the state. In Libya, some have implicated the Brotherhood in the incident in the barracks of Bab al-'Aziziyya in the 1980s, which had aimed to assassinate Colonel Gaddafi. However, it is likely that any involvement was the personal initiatives of individual members rather than a matter of Brotherhood-sponsored policy.

The Brotherhood is not opposed to armed jihad in fighting against occupation or confronting a non-Islamic state. However, they tend to support others rather than engage in such jihad themselves. For this reason, the Brotherhood decided, after much disagreement, to limit such involvement to providing materials and logistical support to the anti-Soviet jihad movement in Afghanistan. This decision was taken by the committee in charge of the Afghan jihad portfolio at the time, headed by Dr Ahmad Malat, and it reflected the Brotherhood's fear that Arab regimes supporting the jihad would turn against the fighters and that the Brotherhood would be held to account. The Brotherhood supported those who wanted to participate in armed jihad, but stopped short of building military capability and forbade any of its own members from taking part.

This pattern repeated itself in the Bosnia-Herzegovina war, where the Brotherhood's role was limited to material support and relief efforts, and they had no direct involvement in military action or the provision of ammunition. This logic guided all of the Brotherhood's relations with Islamic separatist movements, whether in Kashmir, the Philippines or Chechnya. The Brotherhood supported separatist movements in these countries, but without direct military involvement. Even in cases where they were implicated in armed jihad, as happened with the Chechnya Separatist Movement, these were individual instances that had not been centrally approved and were at odds with the Brotherhood's declared stance. The Brotherhood paid the price for this situation when Russia placed it on its list of terrorist organisations.

Between the Brotherhood's long-standing commitment to the Islamic *umma* and its legacy of historical experience, its internal composition stands as a mediating variable in culturally framing the idea of jihad. Many times it meant giving priority to the complexities of the national arena rather than getting dragged into conflicts and alliances alongside international jihadist movements.

During the 1980s and up until the mid-1990s when Egypt's political spaces began to open up, the Brotherhood's relationship with the state and society changed. The Brotherhood's political imagination also shifted, albeit gradually, within a new social context that placed constraints on its ability to resist in any other way than by launching a full-scale rebellion. This reality affected not only the Brotherhood but all political forces in the country. The Brotherhood also strove to develop the organisation as an umbrella for a broad spectrum of Egyptian society, from cities and rural areas, and across all social classes and generations. This regional, social and generational diversity increased the risk to the organisation's cohesion yet encouraged a more inclusive approach.

There is great diversity of thought within the Muslim Brotherhood. The only common denominator is an intellectual belief in the comprehensiveness of Islam and a rigorous organisational umbrella. Intellectual plurality produces contradictions within the Brotherhood, including orientations ranging from the Salafist all the way to religious liberalism. The Brotherhood does not endorse a specific jurisprudential doctrine and prefers to avoid deliberating on intellectual matters such as excommunication and violence unless obliged to do so. This characteristic allows it a high degree of flexibility as long as it does not compromise obedience to its leadership.

In its intellectual composition and political orientation, the Brotherhood became an umbrella for Islamic movements. It has encompassed a variety of members, including al-Azhar scholars, the 'official' Salafi bodies Ansar al-Sunna and al-Jam'iyya al-Shar'iyya as well as the broader Salafi movement, former jihadists, politicians who originated in other political parties, workers from different sectors and peasants. This diversity makes it difficult for the group to advance a cohesive political agenda, establish a long-term struggle for its causes or support any jihad. As such, the Brotherhood's approach to jihad depends on calculations of political and social costs and benefits. The Brotherhood's ideology reflects this social spectrum which encompasses the devout bourgeoisie in cities and new generations of recruits who vary in their religious fervour. New preachers, popular since the mid-1990s, have espoused the notion of 'civil jihad', which challenges the approach of jihadist thinkers and groups. The level of political stability and inclusion on which the Brotherhood as an umbrella grouping depends is unlikely to be compatible with jihadist views. Nevertheless, as noted at the beginning of this chapter, the Brotherhood has moved increasingly towards conservatism and Salafism, in line with growing religious feeling in Egypt in general. If we assume that Egypt's Salafism differs from other Salafi currents by dint of the predominance of an activist component and a contemporary Egyptian context in which everybody is demanding change, then the pursuit of a violent strategy will remain a distinct possibility in the years to come.

Notes

1. This chapter was written by Hossam Tammam shortly before his untimely death in 2011.
2. Mohammed M. Hafez and Quintan Wiktorowicz, 'Violence as contention in the Egyptian Islamic movement', in Quintan Wiktorowicz (ed.), *Islamic Activism: A Social Theory Approach* (Bloomington, 2004): 61–88.
3. Saad Eddin Ibrahim, 'Anatomy of Egypt's militant Islamic groups: Methodological note and preliminary findings', *Journal of Middle East Studies* 12 (1980): 423–53.

4. For more detail, see 'Abd al-Halim Mahmud, *al-Ikhwan al-Muslimun: Ahdath Sana'at al-Tarikh*, Part 1 (*The Muslim Brotherhood: Events that Shaped History*, Alexandria, 2004), pp. 162–5.
5. Ibid., pp. 167, 253 and 258.
6. Ibid., pp. 97–8.
7. The most prominent were Mustafa Mashhur, Ahmad al-Malat, Husni 'Abd al-Baqi, Kamal al-Sananiri and Ahmad Hasanayn, who soon became part of the Guidance Bureau.

Bibliography

Hafez, Mohammed M. and Wiktorowicz, Quintan, 'Violence as contention in the Egyptian Islamic movement', in Quintan Wiktorowicz (ed.), *Islamic Activism: A Social Theory Approach* (Bloomington, 2004): 61–88.

Ibrahim, Saad Eddin, 'Anatomy of Egypt's militant Islamic groups: Methodological note and preliminary findings', *Journal of Middle East Studies* 12 (1980): 423–53.

Mahmud, 'Abd al-Halim, *al-Ikhwan al-Muslimun: Ahdath Sana'at al-Tarikh* (*The Muslim Brotherhood: Events that Shaped History*, Alexandria, 2004).

10

Jihad Discourse in Egypt under Muhammad Mursi

Ewan Stein

Jihad has occupied a prominent position in the worldview, political strategy and foreign policy of the Muslim Brotherhood, which enjoyed a brief taste of power from 2012–13. Muhammad Mursi was Egypt's first freely elected, and first Islamist, president. He was removed from power on 3 July 2013 by a military coup backed by large sections of Egyptian society. Mursi and the Brotherhood had many enemies and detractors at home and abroad. For some, the Brotherhood was an irredeemably radical Islamist group that used elections to seize control of the state, but which would use this power to enforce its ideological vision on Egyptian society and declare a jihad against Israel and the West.[1] Others saw the Brotherhood as having sold out to a US–Israeli agenda in the Middle East. Al-Qa'ida, for example, accused Mursi of having 'abandoned' jihad.[2]

Each of these interpretations fundamentally misrepresents the way the Muslim Brotherhood has conceptualised jihad throughout its history. Jihad, as Rudolph Peters has observed, 'is a concept with a wide semantic spectrum, and its actual meaning differs from organization to organization'.[3] Often translated in the Western media as 'holy war', jihad has connotations inclusive of, but broader than, violence. In the case of the Muslim Brotherhood, this chapter aims to show that the organisation's understanding of jihad has remained relatively consistent over time; where it has engaged with jihad discourse, it has done so to serve its overall purpose of establishing and consolidating a mass movement in Egypt oriented towards the gradual Islamic reform of state and society. This chapter also demonstrates that, contrary to common perceptions, jihad discourse can constitute a means for Islamist social and political actors to legitimise, rather than overturn, the status quo. This broader perspective evolves from a general examination of the Brotherhood's approach to jihad in the decades prior to the election of Muhammad Mursi before focusing more closely on the Mursi and immediate post-Mursi periods.

The Muslim Brotherhood's Jihad before Mursi

An appreciation of the modern historical context is essential to understanding the meaning and salience of jihad for the Muslim Brotherhood in the twenty-first century. The Muslim Brotherhood has interpreted jihad, primarily, as the process of striving toward the Islamisation of society and the establishment of an Islamic state governed by shariah. Jihad, in this iteration, is a mechanism for advancing social and political reform. The Brotherhood has also advocated military jihad in support of Muslim struggles against occupation or invasion, foremost of which has been the Palestine cause. But, as Yusuf al-Qaradawi, one of the Brotherhood's key intellectual allies, notes: '[I]n our era only the armed forces have the authority over jihad of action (*jihad bi-l-yad*), and these are in the hands of governments.'[4] Military jihad, for the Brotherhood, must be sanctioned by a legitimate Muslim ruler.[5] The Brotherhood's direct experiences with military jihad – against the Zionist forces in Palestine prior to the establishment of the State of Israel, against British colonialism in Egypt and providing logistical support to jihadists fighting the USSR in Afghanistan – formally took place under the aegis of the Egyptian state. As such they can be considered 'orthodox' interpretations and manifestations of jihad, as opposed to more radical versions that direct violence against, or without the sanction of, the state.

Having fought alongside the Egyptian army in Palestine in 1948, the Brotherhood was suppressed by Gamal Abdel Nasser in 1954. A minority trend of the Brotherhood came to identify the Egyptian regime as a legitimate target of jihad. For Hossam Tammam, this represented a continuation of the so-called 'Secret Apparatus' that had targeted the colonial presence in the pre-1952 period. Violence directed against the monarchy during this phase of the Brotherhood's history was disowned by Hasan al-Banna, the group's founder and Supreme Guide.[6] An alleged plot against Nasser was uncovered and in 1966 Sayyid Qutb, the chief theoretician of jihad as insurrectionary violence, was executed. In the 1970s, while jihadist groups sought to put Qutb's ideas into practice, the Brotherhood followed the more accommodationist, or 'moderate', line of Supreme Guide Hasan al-Hudaybi and sought reform within the existing system.[7] Since the 1970s, and arguably since its inception, the Brotherhood has constituted a societal bulwark for the Egyptian regime by absorbing more radical opposition. Despite being formally proscribed, it has not overtly challenged the legitimacy of the regime and has 'played by the rules' of quasi-democratic politics.[8] It has avoided radical forms of political action, such as strikes and demonstrations criticising the regime, and presented itself as a 'moderate' Islamist alternative that can draw support away from militant jihadist groups.

Although adopting a 'moderate' stance toward domestic political change, the Brotherhood, in line with the overall political consensus in Egypt up until the 1970s, remained 'radical' in its foreign policy positions. It has opposed US influence in the Middle East and supported Palestinian liberation from Israeli occupation. During the 1970s, the Brotherhood's newspaper, *al-da'wa*, promoted Palestine, and particularly Jerusalem, as Islamic causes and called for the liberation of Palestine via jihad.[9] Following President Anwar Sadat's address before the Knesset in November 1977, calling for war with Israel became an oppositional and, from the regime's perspective, impermissible, stance. Militant jihadist groups viewed the peace process and resultant treaty between Egypt and Israel as symptoms of the unbelief of the Egyptian regime and proof that the only way to liberate Palestine was first to overthrow the 'near enemy'.[10] The road to Jerusalem, for the militant jihadists, passed through Cairo.

The Brotherhood, in contrast, campaigned for jihad under the auspices of the existing regime. Supreme Guide 'Umar al-Tilmisani was elected leader of the newly formed Permanent Islamic Congress for the Propagation of Islam, which organised public meetings and rallies in opposition to the Camp David accords and 'called for the recovery of Jerusalem by the Muslims'.[11] Sadat responded to this, and many other forms of supposedly threatening activity, with harsh repression. Not distinguishing between this criticism of Egyptian foreign policy and more fundamental rejections of the regime's legitimacy, Sadat failed to realise that pro-Palestine rallies organised by the Brotherhood were 'an attempt by the Brotherhood to absorb the extremist danger to the regime'.[12] Reflecting its broader goal of consolidating its societal presence through reconciliation with the regime, the Brotherhood tempered its criticism of Camp David from this point onwards.

Downplaying the Israel–Palestine issue to avoid provoking the regime did not mean the Muslim Brotherhood had 'abandoned' jihad. The signing of the Egypt–Israel peace agreement in 1979 coincided conveniently with the Soviet invasion of Afghanistan in the same year. In what became a key turning point in the Cold War, the USA and its allies embarked upon a decade-long campaign of military, financial and logistical support for the Afghan mujahidin against the Soviet Union. Sadat saw Afghanistan as an ideal opportunity to prove that Egypt was a worthy ally for the USA. The regime facilitated – or at least permitted – the emigration of Egyptian jihadists to fight in Afghanistan, provided bases for the US military and supplied Soviet-made weaponry to the mujahidin.[13] In this way, Egypt became a key regional partner – alongside Israel and Saudi Arabia – of the USA. Although demanding jihad in Palestine became riskier, the Brotherhood could throw its weight wholeheartedly behind the jihad against the Soviet Union.[14] On this issue the Muslim Brotherhood was moving in lockstep with a regime keen to establish its role as a useful partner of the USA in the war against communism. The Brotherhood was thus able to use the idea of jihad not only as a way of bolstering the status quo in Egypt but a means of aiding the consolidation of the West's post-Cold War security arrangement in the Middle East.

In the context of growing anti-Israeli sentiment and the outbreak of the Palestinian Intifada in 1987, the Brotherhood revived its calls for military jihad against Israel. As with its rallies in the early 1980s, the jihad the Brotherhood had in mind was 'orthodox' in the sense that it was contingent upon authorisation by the Mubarak regime. For the Brotherhood, the strategy of calling for jihad against Israel represented an opportunity to raise its public profile and establish its Islamic and patriotic credentials, rather than a genuine desire to mobilise fighters for war against Israel. It also represented an implicit confirmation of the regime's legitimacy and a diversion of 'jihadist' sentiments away from the 'near enemy' (the Mubarak regime) toward the 'far enemy' (Israel). Whereas the militant jihadist groups seized upon the Egyptian regime's failure to act against Israel to justify their strategy of violent regime change, the Brotherhood was urging the regime to allow Egyptians to fight the Jews in Israel.[15] The Brotherhood was again playing the role of helping to absorb anti-regime sentiments and bolster the status quo.

Popular mobilisation in support of the Palestinians resumed during the Second, or 'Al-Aqsa', Intifada, which began in 2000. This time, demonstrations were mainly coordinated by leftist groups, with the Brotherhood taking a back seat. As Carrie Rosefsky Wickham observes, 'the Brotherhood was quick to denounce Israel's actions and to express solidarity with the Palestinian people. Yet it was small, grassroots networks on the left . . . and not the Brotherhood – that "broke the sacred red lines" and called protestors into the streets.'[16] Islamist activists, including those connected to the Brotherhood, became more involved in these protests as time went on, but although some called for jihad against Israel, the process of coordination with leftist groups had the effect of reducing the prevalence of specifically Islamist discourse. As Maha Abdelrahman notes, 'the famous slogan of the Islamists: "Khaibar Khaibar, Oh Jews, Mohammed's army will be back" . . . [was] discarded by the organizers at every demonstration', as was support for Palestinian suicide operations.[17] Despite the participation of Brotherhood members in the protests, moreover, the Brotherhood leadership baulked at endorsing domestic demands. Solidarity protests quickly became indictments of the Mubarak regime, which constituted a 'red line' for the Brotherhood, one not to be crossed lightly if at all. As then Supreme Guide Ma'mun al-Hudaybi explained:

> We shouldn't fight over secondary issues and leave the major causes. We shouldn't break our ranks. Instead, we have to unite the front against the external aggression. We are careful that the popular support for the intifada would never be directed toward confronting the regime. No one benefits from that but the enemy.[18]

To summarise the foregoing historical discussion, before the fall of Mubarak, jihad for the Muslim Brotherhood had two primary dimensions. On the one hand, jihad encompassed the entirety of the Brotherhood's domestic struggle to establish an Islamic state and society, including by raising awareness about Islamic causes overseas. On the other hand, the Brotherhood supported military action against enemies of Islam in Palestine and elsewhere, and supported the active participation of Egyptian Muslims in such external jihads under the umbrella of the Egyptian state. The Brotherhood's own involvement in the Afghan jihad took place on this basis, and its calls for jihad in Palestine were addressed to the regime as the body authorised to judge on matters relating to war and peace. In this sense the Brotherhood's jihad has been 'orthodox', in contradistinction to that of the more militant jihadists who sought the overthrow of the regime as a precondition to liberating Palestine and other occupied parts of the *umma* (Islamic community).

Jihad Discourse under Mursi

As James Piscatori has argued, while Islam plays a contextual role in the formulation of foreign policy in Muslim states, Islamic ideals and solidarities are trumped by pragmatism and *raison d'état*.[19] This is the case for Muslim regimes (whether or not they are 'Islamist'), and arguably it is also the case for Islamist social movements that seek to thrive under the auspices of those regimes. Islamism in principle aspires to re-draw the map of the Muslim world, liberating those parts occupied by infidels and unifying the *umma* in a caliphate governed according to shariah. Muhammad Mursi, a leader from within the Muslim Brotherhood, conducted his presidential campaign on an explicitly Islamist ticket. In speeches he repeated well-known Brotherhood slogans, such as 'the Qur'an is our constitution' and 'jihad is our path' (*al-jihad sabilu-na*).[20] Following Mursi's election, many Egyptians and others expected to see a qualitative foreign policy change, particularly where Israel was concerned, as the Brotherhood put its principles into practice.[21]

It is important to bear in mind that the Brotherhood was never in control of the Egyptian state. It is thus not possible to draw conclusions about the behaviour of an Islamist group 'in power' based on Mursi's time in office. The 25 January 2011 'revolution' had by no means dislodged the incumbent regime. The security forces, large parts of the bureaucracy, judiciary and media, and of course the military all remained in place and influential. In many ways the Brotherhood continued to behave like a loyal opposition movement despite having won both parliamentary and presidential elections. The engagement of the Brotherhood, as well as that of other newly prominent parts of the Islamist spectrum, with the issue of jihad, reflects this structural continuity. The discussion that follows focuses on the issue of jihad in political discourse in relation to three key issues: first, Egypt's policy towards Israel; second, the civil strife in Syria and third, the military coup directed against Mursi in July 2013.

Under Mursi, the Brotherhood's position vis-à-vis Israel was broadly continuous with its previous stance, with one important exception. In the past, it will be recalled, the Brotherhood had called upon Sadat and Mubarak to 'open the door of jihad' against Israel. From 2012, however, the Brotherhood's position vis-à-vis the state shifted due to Mursi's position as president, and it naturally refrained from undermining Mursi's diplomatic approach. In an official statement following Israel's bombardment of Gaza in November 2012, the Brotherhood called on 'Arab and Muslim leaders and rulers as well as all official diplomatic institutions [to] do their duty, to champion the cause of their nation and apply all pressure to stop the shedding of Palestinian blood, and put an end to Israeli arrogance'.[22] Mu'adh 'Abd al-Karim, a young Brotherhood activist, described Mursi's diplomatic approach at this time (the latter had demanded an emergency session of the security council and lodged a protest with the Israeli ambassador) as 'relatively positive and good' compared with that of Mubarak. 'Abd al-Karim noted that although Mursi should also act on the humanitarian front, by opening the Rafah crossing and accepting refugees, diplomatic activity was the best the president could do at this stage.[23]

To the extent that jihad constituted an element of foreign policy toward Israel, it was conceptualised as moral and political effort in support of the Palestine cause, on the one hand, and support for the Palestinians' right to armed resistance on the other. As such, the Brotherhood called upon

all national political forces [to] consider all ways and procedures to support our Palestinian brothers, such as economic boycott, popular rejection, increasing public awareness of the truth about the Palestinian issue, and supporting the resistance alternative and the right of return of all Palestinian refugees.[24]

Mursi insisted that the state and the people would act together, 'al-sha'b wa-l-qiyada', in solidarity with the people of Gaza, but the Brotherhood nevertheless retained the conception that state and society had different roles to play in relation to Israel. The following remarks by Mahmud Husayn, General Secretary of the Muslim Brotherhood, are particularly revealing about the extent to which the Brotherhood continued to focus on social and public relations activism rather than on changing Egyptian foreign policy. Husayn commented after revelations that Mursi had sent a standard diplomatic, but nevertheless warm, letter to Israeli president Shimon Peres:

> The relations that we have and the attitude we adopt towards Israel are well known and will remain unchanged. We consider Israel to be an enemy to Egypt and we want to see Palestine liberated from occupation. The Hamas movement is considered part of the Muslim Brotherhood organization. We have no connection with the position taken by the Egyptian state in this regard, even if the president of the republic is a member of the Muslim Brotherhood. The state is sometimes governed by considerations that do not concern us.[25]

The Brotherhood's new role within the state, and organic connection to the office of the president, militated against publicly demanding that Mursi authorise jihad. But other parts of the Islamist movement were not bound by such ties and called instead for jihad and martyrdom. Thus the imam of the 'Umar Makram mosque in Cairo, Mazhar Shahin, promised that no less than one million Egyptian youth and women would volunteer to liberate Jerusalem: '[I]f Israel has a nuclear bomb, then we have a creed stronger than a million nuclear bombs.'[26] Similar sentiments were voiced by demonstrators from the Gama'a Islamiyya during a march to Tahrir: 'ya hukkam al-bilad, iftah bab al-jihad!' ('oh leaders throughout the land, open the door of jihad!').[27] The Brotherhood, and intellectuals sympathetic to it, were able to channel such demands into their broader conception of jihad, which centred on the need to Islamise Egyptian state and society. Yusuf al-Qaradawi, for example, used the Gaza episode as an opportunity to emphasise once again the necessity of implementing shariah in Egypt, 'which would enable us to confront the West and defeat it'.[28] Chants during a march following al-Qaradawi's sermon at al-Azhar also called for implementing shariah as a way of defeating the West and 'liberating all Islamic lands'.[29]

The demand that Mursi 'open the door of jihad' and call up volunteers should be seen in a similar light to the Brotherhood's own calls for jihad against Israel prior to the January 2011 Revolution. Salafis and other non-Brotherhood Islamists played a legitimising role for Mursi comparable to the one the Muslim Brotherhood played for Sadat and Mubarak. The clamour of other parts of the Islamist movement for jihad affirmed the legitimacy of the president and his right to decide on matters of war and peace. It also demonstrated a reservoir of respect for Mursi's authority via rallies and demonstrations, and undermined more fundamental opposition to his rule. Those calling for jihad were not serving Mursi with an ultimatum to authorise jihad or else stand down, and Mursi's refusal to 'open the doors' was not interpreted, except perhaps in the most extremist of circles, as evidence of non-belief or illegitimate rule. Whereas the most prominent rejectionists under Sadat and Mubarak were militant jihadists, those who sought to delegitimise and unseat Mursi were the broadly secular (liberal, leftist) opposition and elements of the old regime.

The second issue that arose during Mursi's presidency to bring the issue of jihad to the fore was the civil war in Syria. The Syrian imbroglio was increasingly being cast in sectarian terms. The manipulation of sectarian sentiments was certainly not a new phenomenon, as Sami Zubaida discussed in Chapter 7. In the Egyptian context Hosni Mubarak was certainly not innocent of stoking Sunni fears of what Jordanian King Abdullah, in 2004, had termed an emerging 'Shi'ite crescent' in the Middle East.[30] Although sectarian discourse predated Mursi's election as president, the open involvement of Hizbullah in the Syrian conflict in 2013 marked a palpable escalation in Sunni–Shi'ite sectarianism. On 31 May 2013 Yusuf al-Qaradawi used his Friday sermon in Doha to call on all Muslims able to do so to travel to Syria and fight jihad in support of the rebels. Al-Qaradawi chose his words carefully, and left some scope for interpretation, but his speech was broadly interpreted as a call for sectarian jihad:

> Tens of thousands of people came from Iran, and came from Iraq, and came from Lebanon and came from the lands of the Shi'a everywhere to fight the

Sunnis and those who are with them: Christians, Kurds and others. I do not accuse the Shi'a as a whole. There are good Shi'a including many friends of mine, in Iran, Iraq and Lebanon that refuse this dreadful iniquity. We don't condemn them, just everyone that stands with Hizbullah and supports this party.[31]

Al-Qaradawi was not alone in calling on Muslims to fight jihad in Syria. His stance was endorsed by the Grand Mufti of Saudi Arabia, Sheikh 'Abd al-'Aziz ibn 'Abd Allah al-Shaykh.[32] Muhammad al-'Arifi, a leading Saudi cleric, called for jihad 'in every way possible' during a sermon in a Cairo mosque.[33] And in Egypt, an aide to President Mursi, while not endorsing Egyptian participation in the Syrian jihad and stressing the need for a political solution, remarked that Egyptians were free to travel as they pleased.[34]

But the Saudis, as well as rulers of other Arab states, were nevertheless concerned that the kind of 'blowback' produced by the jihad in Afghanistan might be repeated in Syria. Before al-Qaradawi made his speech in Qatar (a rival of Saudi Arabia), a member of the official Saudi religious establishment had issued a fatwa stating that any jihad would have to take place 'under the authority of the guardian' (i.e. responsible authorities) and in accord with a nation's foreign policy: 'Everything is linked to a system and to the country's policies and no person should be allowed to disobey the guardian and call for jihad.'[35] Prince Turki al-Faisal, the Saudi intelligence minister, later remarked: 'No Saudis will be trained to fight in Syria. In fact, we don't want any Saudis there at all.'[36] Jordan, similarly, was uneasy about the prospect of its citizens travelling to fight in Syria and had arrested and jailed three for attempting to join the jihadist Nusra Front in June 2013.[37] Mursi's position was arguably also less permissive than the reported comments of his aide suggested. When asked, during a conference of ulama (religious scholars) held in Cairo on 14 June 2013, if the Brotherhood supported the idea of jihad in Syria, Brotherhood spokesman Ahmad 'Arif simply indicated that they would support the outcome of the conference, which, as we shall see, did not endorse foreign participation in the jihad.

The conference brought together almost 500 ulama from over 70 Islamic associations, including the Sheikh of al-Azhar, Ahmad al-Tayyib and Yusuf al-Qaradawi. It must be assumed, given the conference's location, participants and the extreme sensitivity of the issue, that the Brotherhood would have been aware of, and perhaps helped to shape, the conference declaration in advance. The statement echoed al-Qaradawi's call for jihad in support of the Syrian people, calling for a boycott of Iranian goods and 'financial, moral, and military jihad (*bi-l-nafs wa-l-mal wa-l-silah*) and all kinds of jihad and support in order to rescue the Syrian people'. The enemies, according to the statement, were the 'sectarian' regime in Syria, with its allies in Iran, Iraq, Hizbullah 'and others among the *rawafid* and *batiniya*'.[38] *Rawafid*, literally 'those who refuse', is a derogatory term for Shi'ites, while *batiniya* refers to Isma'ilis and other 'mystical' sects associated with Bashar al-Asad's supposedly 'Alawite' regime. It stopped short, however, of calling on able-bodied Muslims to travel to Syria in order to fight jihad. Al-Qaradawi's own statement at this conference was more explicitly sectarian than his Doha sermon. He insisted: '[T]his war is not [a] civil [one]. It is rather a war against Islam and Sunnis. My call to all the Muslims in the world is to protect their brothers.'[39] But this time al-Qaradawi also refrained from demanding that Muslims travel to Syria to fight jihad.

It is perhaps a reflection of growing fears of 'blowback' across the region and in the USA (as well as the potential diminution of Qatar's regional aspirations and influence) that calls for arming and dispatching jihadists from other Arab countries were absent from official discourse, even if the sectarian dimensions of the jihad discourse grew increasingly pronounced. The day after the conference, Mursi attended and spoke at a rally in support of the Syrian uprising. Among the speakers at the televised rally, before a capacity crowd in Cairo Stadium, was the well-known Salafi preacher Muhammad Hasan. Hasan called on Mursi to implement the recommendations of the conference of ulama that had taken place in Cairo and also urged him 'not to open Egypt's door to *rafida* (Shi'ites)'.[40] Mursi's attendance at this rally has been singled out as a step too far for an Egyptian military nervous of Islamic radicalism and foreign policy adventures.[41] But Hasan's discourse was consistent with the regional trend identified above, which was to keep the Syria issue sectarian but to minimise the export of jihadists from other Arab countries. Like the ulama statement, to which he was a party, Hasan did not call for Muslims outside of Syria to travel there to fight; nor did he call on Mursi to 'open the doors of jihad'. Hasan chose his words carefully:

> Jihad is a duty of the soul, of money and arms, everyone according to his abilities. Defensive jihad (*jihad al-daf'*) now, against the suffering and bloodshed, is an individual obligation (*wajib 'ayni*) for the Syrian people. And it is a collective duty (*wajib kifa'i*) for Muslims throughout the world.[42]

Expressed in this way, it is clear that while providing military, financial or moral support is an obligation for Muslims, it is 'collective', meaning it is not obligatory for everyone. The intent seems to be to affirm, in line with the Saudi fatwa cited above, that it is the 'guardian' (*wali*) who decides on whether and how jihad is to be pursued. Hasan was careful to emphasise that any support offered to the Syrian people under the rubric of jihad would depend on authorisation from the president:

> Excellency Mr. President: The recommendations and decisions of these conferences will never be implemented other than under your authority. We call on you – you and your brothers among the rulers, kings and presidents of Arab and Islamic states – to lose no time . . . in implementing these recommendations. We call on you to implement the recommendations and these conferences [*sic*] to apply pressure to the rulers of the Western world to supply weapons to the sons of those now being slaughtered in Syria.[43]

Not only does Hasan imply that any jihad activity outside of the president's authority would be illegal, but he specifies that the jihad he would like to see Mursi take forward should focus on pressuring the West to adequately arm the rebels. Hasan's speech, in the presence of President Mursi, was seized upon by much of the media and non-Islamist actors in Egypt as evidence that Mursi was pandering to dangerous jihadists. But Hasan's stance was fully in accordance with the USA's own decision to arm the opposition in Syria as well as the stance of the Arab League as announced at its summit in Doha in March 2013.[44] Although virulently sectarian, the Salafi cleric was participating in a much broader regional discourse of demonisation toward Shi'ites that was being stoked by Western-aligned Sunni Arab states.

Mursi, in his own speech at this rally, avoided any mention of the word 'jihad'. Instead, he declared that 'Egypt supports the struggle of the Syrian people materially and morally (*madiyy-an wa-ma'nawiyy-an*)' and that the 'Egyptian leadership, people and army (*Misr qiyadat-an, sha'b-an, wa-jaysh-an*) would not leave the Syrian people until they gain their rights, dignity and sovereignty in its unified territory'.[45] Despite the fact that both Mursi's speech and that of Muhammad Hasan were clearly calibrated to chime with Saudi and Western positions on Syria, the rally was portrayed as evidence of the Brotherhood's radicalism. One report notes that 'clerics at the rally urged Mursi to back their calls for jihad to support rebels' and quotes Brotherhood specialist Khalil al-Anani opining: 'Mursi's endorsement of jihad in Syria was a strategic mistake that will create a new Afghanistan in the Middle East.'[46] Such readings misinterpret the dynamics at play. Neither Hasan, nor the conference of ulama whose recommendations Hasan called on Mursi to implement, demanded the participation of non-Syrian Muslims in military jihad. Mursi's reference to the military as a supporter of the Syrian people may best be interpreted not, as in some quarters, as evidence of an intention to dispatch the Egyptian army to Syria, but as a reassurance that it was the army, and not private jihadists, that had the responsibility for waging war.

The third instance in which jihad acquired political salience for the Muslim Brotherhood was the reaction to Mursi's removal from power by the military under the command of General 'Abd al-Fatah al-Sisi. The coup was carried out following large-scale popular demonstrations organised by the Tamarrud (Rebel) campaign. The Brotherhood and other supporters of the ousted president staged counterdemonstrations in cities throughout the country. In the months following the coup, until the time of writing in early November 2013, some 1,300 protesters were killed and much of the Brotherhood's leadership arrested and imprisoned.[47] Although violence against police and military targets was perpetrated in the name of restoring Mursi to power, most intensely by jihadist groups in the Sinai, the Brotherhood and other key Islamist formations called for civil resistance and other forms of non-violent protest.

That the Brotherhood has termed its campaign of non-violent resistance 'jihad' is consistent with the movement's historical understanding of jihad as integral to the Islamisation and reform of state and society. Thus the writer Fajr Atif Sahsah, in an article posted on the website of the Brotherhood's Freedom and Justice Party, seeks to outline the various forms of civil disobedience and creative resistance people can pursue in order to 'break the coup'. For Sahsah all such strategies, which begin with purifying the self, constitute jihad: 'Jihad is not a singular duty that leads to an end. It is a path that passes through many other stations and includes other forms of jihad. It includes reforming the self and bowing at the altar of prayer and obedience.'[48] A similar perspective is shared by the Salafi preacher Muhammad 'Abd al-Maqsud, who announced in an address broadcast on his YouTube channel on 15 September 2013 that demonstrating against the military coup was a jihad that should be pursued until victory. He insists that the 'leaders of the coup bear responsibility for the blood and suffering of Muslims in Sinai' and that they have dealt with the people of Sinai in a more brutal fashion than did the Israelis.[49] It is significant that although Maqsud is describing the act of demonstrating as a 'jihad', he is not pronouncing *takfir* (excommunication) on General al-Sisi or the military leadership, which would legitimise a violent insurrection against them.

The Brotherhood's jihad following the ousting of Mursi is thus not a military one against al-Sisi, something which would require the generals to be labelled as *kuffar* (non-believers) and thus legitimate targets of violence. That the Brotherhood and its supporters have not, at least until the time of writing in December 2013, pursued this 'Qutbist' line tells us much about the overall strategy of the Muslim Brotherhood, which has remained consistently 'moderate' over time. This may be due, as Hossam Tammam argues in Chapter 9, to the fact that militant jihadism is not compatible with the Brotherhood's strategy of building a mass movement with broad support across the classes. The Brotherhood leadership's moderation contrasts sharply with the 'radical' discourse of the Egyptian military leadership and many of its supporters in civil society and the media. Since the ousting of Mursi in July 2013, the coup leaders and their supporters have framed their vendetta against the Brotherhood in the language of the West's 'War on Terror'.

This has constituted a form of secular nationalist '*takfir*', in which Brotherhood members and Mursi supporters have been categorised as 'non-Egyptians' and terrorists with the transparent purpose of legitimising violence against them. As one Egypt observer remarked about the evolution of this discourse following the coup:

> The pro-Morsi [sic] protesters were no longer just a bunch of skin-disease ridden, cult supporting lunatics, but also terrorists. Again, this happened almost seamlessly. Television presenters indulged themselves in the vilest xenophobia against Palestinians and Syrians, who they claimed were camped out in pro-Morsi sit-ins and meddling in Egyptian affairs . . . The aim, of course, was two-fold: firstly, to support the claim that the Brotherhood has links with Hamas and other foreign groups involved in acts of insurgency in Sinai; and secondly, to isolate the Brotherhood even further, turn it into a 'them' separate from the rest of the population.[50]

Brotherhood spokespersons, for their part, have made a concerted effort to debunk the myth that all supporters of Mursi are jihadist terrorists, which has included the use of democratic, rather than Islamic, language in promoting their cause. Demonstrations and other forms of non-violent resistance against a military coup are fully compatible with the Brotherhood's long-standing understanding of jihad as a process of striving for justice and reform. And Brotherhood and others have, as in the examples above, described these strategies as part of their jihad. But in general, the Brotherhood has preferred instead to use a concept that resonates in a far more favourable way among the public. In exhorting Egyptians to participate in an 'intifada' ('uprising'), rather than a jihad, against the coup the Brotherhood avoids the terroristic connotations of the word 'jihad' while also linking its cause to that of the Palestinians and the original uprising of 25 January 2011.[51]

Conclusion

This chapter has shown that the Muslim Brotherhood's conception of jihad has remained consistent over time. It has approached jihad as a mechanism for domestic reform, and as military action conducted under the authority of the state. This conception has related to the Brotherhood's historical desire to build a mass movement for Islamic reform without provoking state repression and has thus also functioned to absorb more radical opposition to the Egyptian regime. Under Mursi, the

Brotherhood and its allies in the Salafi movement continued to behave like a loyal opposition in light of the fact that they did not manage to achieve control over the state. This helps account for the continuity in Islamist discourse on jihad in the post-Mubarak era.

The Brotherhood's discourse on jihad has also reflected the influence of regional and international factors and the group's desire to remain within the US-led security arrangement in the Middle East. Syria became, though not in the military sense, Mursi's Afghanistan. President Sadat was able to use support for the jihad in Afghanistan as a way both of pleasing his key international sponsors (mainly the USA and Saudi Arabia) and of appeasing the Islamist movement at home. In a distinctly less radical way Mursi could use the jihad against the Asad regime in Syria as a way of aligning Egypt with the West and other Arab states, while also mobilising support among his Islamist base at a time when his position was under intense pressure from domestic opponents. It is instructive to draw a further parallel between other parts of the Islamist movement, particularly Salafis, during Mursi's tenure, and the role the Muslim Brotherhood played under Sadat and Mubarak. The Brotherhood from the late 1970s had helped to divert domestic jihadism by supporting the jihad in Afghanistan and staging pro-Palestine rallies. Some Salafis, by affirming Mursi's legitimacy as ruler and participating in a regionally resonant sectarian discourse on Syria, sought – unsuccessfully it turned out – to demonstrate a depth of support for Islamist rule and thereby strengthen Mursi's position vis-à-vis the secular opposition that sought his removal.

It is finally worth stressing that Tamarrud and the secular opposition in 2013 came to play a role similar to, but infinitely more effective than, that played by the militant jihadist groups in earlier years. Rejecting the legitimacy of Mursi's leadership, this popular movement was able to mobilise the kind of groundswell of opposition of which jihadist movements could only have dreamed. This success may at least in part have been due to the fact that Tamarrud did not take aim at – indeed, it came to draw support from – the Egyptian military, which remained the primary focus of Egyptian nationalism. Since Mursi's ouster large parts of the 'army and the people' have waged a kind of sectarian jihad against the Brotherhood and its supporters, a jihad waged by 'secularists' in which violence against parts of Egyptian society deemed to be outside the fold has been accepted as legitimate. The vendetta against the Muslim Brotherhood provides a stark reminder of the need to think twice before attributing violence and radicalism in the Muslim world to the Islamic concept of jihad.

Notes

1. See, for example, Sharona Schwartz, 'Egyptian Muslim Brotherhood's leader says jihad on Israel is every Muslim's duty', *The Blaze*, 8 July 2012 (http://www.theblaze.com/stories/2012/07/08/egyptian-muslim-brotherhood%e2%80%99s-leader-says-jihad-on-israel-is-every-muslim%e2%80%99s-duty/, last accessed 30 December 2013).

2. Maamoun Youssef, 'Al Qaeda leader Ayman Al-Zawahri: Morsi ouster in Egypt is proof that democracy is corrupt', *Huffington Post*, 3 August 2013 (http://www.huffingtonpost.com/2013/08/03/ayman-al-zawahri-egypt _n_3701385.html, last accessed 30 December 2013).

3. Rudolph Peters, 'The political relevance of jihad doctrine in Sadat's Egypt', in E. Ingram (ed.), *National and International Politics in the Middle East: Essays in Honour of Elie Kedourie* (London, 1986): 252–71 (270).

4. Yusuf al-Qaradawi, *Al-Ikhwan Al-Muslimun: 70 Am-an fi al-da'wa wa-l-Tarbiya wa-l-Jihad (The Muslim Brothers: 70 Years of Preaching, Education and Jihad)* (Cairo, 1999), p. 286.

5. Peters, 'The political relevance of jihad doctrine in Sadat's Egypt'.

6. See Hossam Tammam, Chapter 9 of this volume.

7. Barbara Zollner, *The Muslim Brotherhood: Hasan al-Hudaybi and Ideology* (New York, 2008).

8. Mona al-Ghobashy, 'The metamorphosis of the Egyptian Muslim Brothers', *International Journal of Middle East Studies* 37/3 (2005): 373–95; Jason Brownlee, 'The Muslim Brothers: Egypt's most influential pressure group', *History Compass* 8/5 (1 May 2010): 419–30; Holger Albrecht, 'How can opposition support authoritarianism? Lessons from Egypt', *Democratization* 12/3 (June 2005): 378–97.

9. Ewan Stein, *Representing Israel in Modern Egypt: Ideas, Intellectuals and Foreign Policy from Nasser to Mubarak* (London and New York, 2012).

10. Johannes J. G. Jansen and Muhammad 'Abd al-Salam Faraj, *The Neglected Duty: The Creed of Sadat's Assassins and Islamic Resurgence in the Middle East* (New York, 1986).

11. John Cooley, *Unholy Wars: Afghanistan, America and International Terrorism* (Pluto Press, 2002), p. 25.

12. Ibid.

13. Ibid.

14. BBC Radio 4, *Koran and Country: How Islam Got Political*, 10 November 2005 (http://news.bbc.co.uk/nol/shared/spl/hi/programmes/analysis/transcripts/10_11_05.txt, last accessed 30 December 2013).

15. Saad Eddin Ibrahim, 'Domestic developments in Egypt', in William B. Quandt (ed.), *The Middle East: Ten Years after Camp David* (Washington DC, 1988): 19–63.

16. Carrie Rosefsky Wickham, *The Muslim Brotherhood: Evolution of an Islamist Movement* (Princeton, 2013), p. 99.

17. Maha Abdelrahman, 'With the Islamists? Sometimes. . . With the State? Never!: Cooperation between the left and Islamists in Egypt', *British Journal of Middle Eastern Studies* 36/1 (April 2009): 37–54.

18. Quoted in Wickham, *The Muslim Brotherhood*, p. 100.

19. James P. Piscatori, *Islam in a World of Nation-States* (Cambridge, 1986).

20. *YouTube*, 'Mohamed Morsi – the Koran is our constitution – the Prophet Muhammad is our leader, jihad is our path', 11 July 2012 (http://www.youtube.com/watch?v=g8NtiUMOFFg&feature=youtube_gdata_player, last accessed 30 December 2013).

21. Qadri Hifni, 'Istratijiyyatu-na hiya al-salam ma' Isra'il' ('Our strategy is peace with Israel'), *al-Ahram*, 21 November 2012 (http://www.ahram.org.eg/1090/2012/11/21/4/184363/219.aspx, last accessed 6 November, 2013).

22. Ibid.

23. Riham Sawud, 'Jum'at ghadab al-yawm tahtif "Salli fajr al-milyuniyya wa-dakk husun al-Sahyuniyya"' ('Today's Friday of Anger cries out "Pray the million-man dawn prayer and destroy the bastions of Zionism"'), *al-Shuruq*, 16 November 2012: 6.

24. Muslim Brotherhood, 'Muslim Brotherhood statement on Israeli aggression against Gaza', *Ikhwan Web* n.d. (http://www.ikhwanweb.com/article.php?id=30376, last accessed 9 December 2012).

25. *Al-Sharq al-Awsat*, 'Khitab taklif al-safir al-Misri lada Isra'il yuthiru jadal-an siyasiyy-an' ('Letter commissioning the Egyptian ambassador to Israel causes political controversy'), *al-Sharq al-Awsat*, 19 October 2012 (http://aawsat.com/details.asp?section=4&issueno=12379&article=700429&feature=#.UnI2aVNH58E, last accessed 30 December 2013).

26. *Aswat Misriyya*, 'Tazahurat fi al-Qahira wa-l-Iskandriyya wa-iddat muhafazat tadamun-an ma' ahali Qita' Ghazza' ('Demonstrations in Cairo, Alexandria and a number of governorates in solidarity with the people of the Gaza Strip'), 16 November 2012 (http://aswatmasriya.com/news/view.aspx?

id=40dc4a4d-c330-4adf-99b7-36b5afe671e6, last accessed 30 December 2013).

27. Ibid.

28. Isma'il al-Ashwal, 'al-Qaradawi min fawq minbar al-Azhar yad'u 'ala Isra'il wa-Bashshar. . . wa-yashkur Mursi wa-Qatar' ('Al-Qaradawi from the pulpit of al-Azhar calls against Israel and Bashar . . . and thanks Mursi and Qatar'), *al-Shuruq*, 17 November 2012: 7.

29. Ibid.

30. Vali Nasr, *The Shia Revival: How Conflicts Within Islam Will Shape the Future* (New York, 2006).

31. *YouTube*, 'al-Maqta' al-a'naf fi khutbat al-jum'a li-l-Shaykh Yusuf Al-Qaradawi yasif Hizb Allah bi-hizb al-Shaytan' ('The most violent section in the Friday sermon of Sheikh Yusuf al-Qaradawi describes Hizbullah as the party of Satan'), 31 May 2013 (http://www.youtube.com/watch?v=J-npCduuHNw&feature=youtube_gdata_player, last accessed 30 December 2013.

32. *Gulf News*, 'Grand Mufti says opposition to Hezbollah is right', 6 June 2013 (http://gulfnews.com/news/gulf/saudi-arabia/grand-mufti-says-opposition-to-hezbollah-is-right-1.1193838, last accessed 30 December 2013).

33. *YouTube*, 'al-'Arifi yu'lin al-jihad fi Suriya min Misr' ('al-'Arifi declares jihad in Syria from Egypt'), 2013 (http://www.youtube.com/watch?v=dvZkqGq1A54&feature=youtube_gdata_player, last accessed 6 November, 2013).

34. *GlobalPost*, 'Thousands of Egypt Islamists rally for Syria jihad', 14 June 2013 (http://www.globalpost.com/dispatch/news/afp/130614/thousands-egypt-islamists-rally-syria-jihad, last accessed 30 December 2013).

35. Jamestown Foundation, 'Fatwa wars continue as Saudi cleric bans jihad in Syria', *Ecoi.net*, 15 June 2012 (http://www.ecoi.net/local_link/223589/331126_en.html, last accessed 30 December 2013).

36. *Gulf News*, 'Dependent Saudi Arabia has few options on Syria', 26 October 2013 (http://gulfnews.com/news/gulf/saudi-arabia/dependent-saudi-arabia-has-few-options-on-syria-1.1247309, last accessed 6 November, 2013).

37. *Gulf News*, 'Jordan jails three for Syria jihad', 11 June 2013 (http://gulfnews.com/news/region/jordan/jordan-jails-three-for-syria-jihad-1.1195828, last accessed 30 December 2013).

38. *Nashwan News*, 'Nuss bayan ulama' al-umma bi-l-da'wa ila al-jihad fi Suriya' ('Text of the clerics' statement on calling for jihad in Syria'), 13 June 2013 (http://nashwannews.com/news.php?action=view&id=26492, last accessed 30 December 2013).

39. *Al-Qaradawi*, 'Al-Qaradawi: al-harb fi Suriya didd al-umma kulla-ha wa-Iran laysa la-ha min al-Islam shay'' ('Al-Qaradawi: The war in Syria is against the entire *umma* and Iran has nothing to do with Islam'), 15 June 2013 (http://http://iumsonline.org/ar/Default.asp?ContentID=6474&menuID=6, last accessed 30 December 2013).

40. *YouTube*, 'Aqwa kalima li-l-ra'i' Muhammad Hasan amam Muhammad Mursi wa-hushud al-jamahir li-l-jihad fi Suriya' ('The strongest speech of the great Muhammad Hasan before Muhammad Mursi and the masses for jihad in Syria'), 16 June 2013 (http://www.youtube.com/watch?v=n6h6eYVob_E&feature=youtube_gdata_player, last accessed 30 December 2013).

41. *Irish Times*, 'Morsi role at Syria rally seen as tipping point for Egypt army', (http://www.irishtimes.com/news/world/africa/morsi-role-at-syria-rally-seen-as-tipping-point-for-egypt-army-1.1450612, last accessed 6 November 2013).

42. *YouTube*, 'Aqwa kalima li-l-ra'i' Muhammad Hasan amam Muhammad Mursi wa-hushud al-jamahir li-l-jihad fi Suriya' ('The strongest speech of the great Muhammad Hasan before Muhammad Mursi and the masses for jihad in Syria').

43. Ibid.

44. The Arab League statement stressed 'the right of each member state, in accordance with its wish, to provide all means of self-defence, including military support to back the steadfastness of the Syrian people and the free army'. It also 'called on all regional and international institutions to provide all forms of assistance and support to enable the Syrian people defend themselves and continue their struggle to establish justice and rule of law in their country'. Ministry of Foreign Affairs, 'Crown Prince and Arab leaders wrap up the work of the Arab summit in its twenty-fourth session with Doha declaration', 27 March 2013 (http://www.mofa.gov.sa/sites/mofaen/ServicesAndInformation/news/statements/Pages/ArticleID2013327141220927.aspx, last accessed 30 December 2013).

45. *YouTube*, 'Khitab al-ra'is Mursi fi mu'tamar al-umma al-misriyya li-da'm al-thawra al-Suriyya' ('The speech of President Mursi in the conference of the Egyptian nation in support of the Syrian revolution'), 15 June 2013 (http://www.youtube.com/watch?v=9WS52JBnqSE&feature=youtube_gdata_player, last accessed 30 December 2013).

46. *Gulf News*, 'Egypt acquiesces on jihadis for Syria', 18 June 2013 (http://gulfnews.com/news/region/syria/egypt-acquiesces-on-jihadis-for-syria-1.1198653, last accessed 30 December 2013).

47. Human Rights Watch, 'Egypt: protester killings not being investigated: impunity encourages excessive force', *Human Rights Watch*, 2 November 2013 (http://www.hrw.org/news/2013/11/02/egypt-protester-killings-not-being-investigated, last accessed 30 December 2013).

48. Fajr Atif Sahsah, 'al-mas'uliyya al-fardiyya fi qasr al-inqilab... wajibat wa-ibda' ('Individual responsibility in breaking the coup: duties and creativity'), *Bawabat al-Hurriyya wa-l-Adala (Freedom and Justice Portal)*, 8 September 2013 (http://fj-p.com/article.php?id=83761, last accessed 30 December 2013).

49. Muhammad 'Abd al-Maqsud, "Abd al-Maqsud: al-Tazahur didd "al-inqilab al-fajir"; "jihad" hatta tahqiq al-nasr' ("Abd al-Maqsud: Demonstrating against "the obscene coup" is a "jihad" until victory'), *al-Masri al-Yawm*, 15 September 2013 (http://www.almasryalyoum.com/node/2119451, last accessed 30 December 2013).

50. Sarah Carr, 'The Popular War on Terror', 25 July 2013, *Jadaliyya.com* (http://www.jadaliyya.com/pages/index/13192/the-popular-war-on-terror-, last accessed 30 December 2013).

51. William Booth, Michael Birnbaum and Abigail Hauslohner, 'Egypt's Muslim Brotherhood calls for "uprising" after troops shoot protesters', *Washington Post*, 8 July 2013 (http://wapo.st/183k23p, last accessed 30 December 2013).

Bibliography

'Abd al-Maqsud, Muhammad, "Abd al-Maqsud: al-Tazahur didd "al-inqilab al-fajir"; "jihad" hatta tahqiq al-nasr' ("Abd al-Maqsud: Demonstrating against "the obscene coup" is a "jihad" until victory'), *al-Masri al-Yawm*, 15 September 2013 (http://www.almasryalyoum.com/node/2119451, last accessed 30 December 2013).

Abdelrahman, Maha, 'With the Islamists? Sometimes... With the state? Never!: Cooperation between the left and Islamists in Egypt', *British Journal of Middle Eastern Studies* 36/1 (April 2009): 37–54.

Albrecht, Holger, 'How can opposition support authoritarianism? Lessons from Egypt', *Democratization* 12/3 (June 2005): 378–97.

al-Ashwal, Isma'il, 'al-Qaradawi min fawq minbar al-Azhar yad'u 'ala Isra'il wa-Bashshar... wa-yashkur Mursi wa-Qatar' ('Al-Qaradawi from the pulpit of al-Azhar calls against Israel and Bashar... and thanks Mursi and Qatar'), *al-Shuruq*, 17 November 2012: 7.

Al-Sharq al-Awsat, 'Khitab taklif al-safir al-Misri lada Isra'il yuthiru jadalan siyasiyy-an' ('Letter commissioning the Egyptian ambassador to Israel causes political controversy'), 19 October 2012 (http://aawsat.com/details.asp?section=4&issueno=12379&article=700429&feature=#.UnI2aVNH58E, last accessed 30 December 2013).

Aswat Misriyya, 'Tazahurat fi-l-Qahira wa-l-Iskandriyya wa-iddat muhafazat tadamun-an ma' ahali Qita' Ghazza' ('Demonstrations in Cairo, Alexandria and a number of governorates in solidarity with the people of the Gaza Strip'), 16 November 2012 (http://aswatmasriya.com/news/view.aspx?id=40dc4a4d-c330-4adf-99b7-36b5afe671e6, last accessed 30 December 2013).

BBC Radio 4, *Koran and Country: How Islam Got Political*, 10 November 2005 (http://news.bbc.co.uk/nol/shared/spl/hi/programmes/analysis/transcripts/10_11_05.txt, last accessed 30 December 2013).

Booth, William, Birnbaum, Michael and Hauslohner, Abigail, 'Egypt's Muslim Brotherhood calls for "uprising" after troops shoot protesters', *Washington Post*, 8 July 2013 (http://wapo.st/183k23p, last accessed 30 December 2013).

Brownlee, Jason, 'The Muslim Brothers: Egypt's most influential pressure group', *History Compass* 8/5 (1 May 2010): 419–30.

Carr, Sarah, 'The popular War on Terror', *Jadaliyya.com*, 25 July 2013 (http://www.jadaliyya.com/pages/index/13192/the-popular-war-on-terror-, last accessed 30 December 2013).

Cooley, John, *Unholy Wars: Afghanistan, America and International Terrorism* (Pluto Press, 2002).

al-Ghobashy, Mona, 'The metamorphosis of the Egyptian Muslim Brothers', *International Journal of Middle East Studies* 37/3 (2005): 373–95.

Global Post, 'Thousands of Egypt Islamists rally for Syria jihad', 14 June 2013 (http://www.globalpost.com/dispatch/news/afp/130614/thousands-egypt-islamists-rally-syria-jihad, last accessed 30 December 2013).

Gulf News, 'Grand Mufti says opposition to Hezbollah is right', 6 June 2013 (http://gulfnews.com/news/gulf/saudi-arabia/grand-mufti-says-opposition-to-hezbollah-is-right-1.1193838, last accessed 30 December 2013).

———, 'Jordan jails three for Syria jihad', 11 June 2013 (http://gulfnews.com/news/region/jordan/jordan-jails-three-for-syria-jihad-1.1195828, last accessed 30 December 2013).

———, 'Egypt acquiesces on jihadis for Syria', 18 June 2013 (http://gulfnews.com/news/region/syria/egypt-acquiesces-on-jihadis-for-syria-1.1198653, last accessed 30 December 2013).

———, 'Dependent Saudi Arabia has few options on Syria', 26 October 2013 (http://gulfnews.com/news/gulf/saudi-arabia/dependent-saudi-arabia-has-few-options-on-syria-1.1247309, last accessed 6 November 2013).

Hifni, Qadri, 'Istratijiyyatu-na hiya al-salam ma' Isra'il' ('Our strategy is peace with Israel)', *al-Ahram*, 21 November 2012 (http://www.ahram.org.eg/1090/2012/11/21/4/184363/219.aspx, last accessed 6 November 2013).

Human Rights Watch, 'Egypt: Protester killings not being investigated: Impunity encourages excessive force', *Human Rights Watch*, 2 November 2013 (http://www.hrw.org/news/2013/11/02/egypt-protester-killings-not-being-investigated, last accessed 30 December 2013).

Ibrahim, Saad Eddin, 'Domestic developments in Egypt', in William B. Quandt (ed.), *The Middle East: Ten Years after Camp David* (Washington DC, 1988): 19–63.

Irish Times, 'Morsi role at Syria rally seen as tipping point for Egypt army', 4 July 2013 (http://www.irishtimes.com/news/world/africa/morsi-role-at-syria-rally-seen-as-tipping-point-for-egypt-army-1.1450612, last accessed 6 November 2013).

IUMS Online, 'Al-Qaradawi: al-harb fi Suriya didd al-umma kulla-ha wa-Iran laysa la-ha min al-Islam shay'' ('Al-Qaradawi: The war in Syria is against the entire Islamic community and Iran has nothing to do with Islam'), 15 June 2013 (http://iumsonline.org/ar/Default.asp?ContentID=6474&menuID=6, last accessed 9 November 2014).

Jamestown Foundation, 'Fatwa wars continue as Saudi cleric bans jihad in Syria', *Ecoi.net*, 15 June 2012 (http://www.ecoi.net/local_link/223589/331126_en.html, last accessed 30 December 2013).

Jansen, Johannes J. G. and Faraj, Muhammad 'Abd al-Salam, *The Neglected Duty: The Creed of Sadat's Assassins and Islamic Resurgence in the Middle East* (New York, 1986).

Ministry of Foreign Affairs, 'Crown Prince and Arab leaders wrap up the work of the Arab summit in its twenty-fourth session with Doha declaration', 27 March 2013 (http://www.mofa.gov.sa/sites/mofaen/ServicesAndInformation/news/statements/Pages/ArticleID2013327141220927.aspx, last accessed 30 December 2013).

Muslim Brotherhood, 'Muslim Brotherhood statement on Israeli aggression against Gaza', *Ikhwan Web*, n.d. (http://www.ikhwanweb.com/article.php?id=30376, last accessed 9 December 2012).

Nashwan News, 'Nass bayan ulama' al-umma bi-l-da'wa ila al-jihad fi Suriya' ('Text of the clerics' statement on calling for jihad in Syria'), 13 June 2013 (http://nashwannews.com/news.php?action=view&id=26492, last accessed 30 December 2013).

Nasr, Vali, *The Shia Revival: How Conflicts within Islam Will Shape the Future* (New York, 2006).

Peters, Rudolph, 'The political relevance of jihad doctrine in Sadat's Egypt', in E. Ingram (ed.), *National and International Politics in the Middle East: Essays in Honour of Elie Kedourie* (London, 1986): 252–71.

Piscatori, James P., *Islam in a World of Nation-States* (Cambridge, 1986).

al-Qaradawi, Yusuf, *Al-Ikhwan al-Muslimun: 70 Am-an fi al-Da'wa wa-l-Tarbiya wa-l-Jihad* (*The Muslim Brothers: 70 Years of Preaching, Education and Jihad*) (Cairo, 1999).

Sahsah, Fajr Atif, 'Al-mas'uliyya al-fardiyya fi qasr al-inqilab. . . wajibat wa-ibda' ('Individual responsibility in breaking the coup: duties and creativity'), *Bawabat al-Hurriyya wa-l-'Adala* (Freedom and Justice Portal), 8 September 2013 (http://fj-p.com/article.php?id=83761, last accessed 30 December 2013).

Sawud, Riham, 'Jum'at ghadab al-yawm tahtuf "Salli fajr al-milyuniyya wa-dakk husun al-Sahyuniyya"' ('Today's Friday of anger cries, "Pray the million-man dawn prayer and destroy the bastions of Zionism"'), *al-Shuruq*, 16 November 2012: 6.

Schwartz, Sharona, 'Egyptian Muslim Brotherhood's leader says jihad on Israel is every Muslim's duty', *The Blaze*, 8 July 2012 (http://www.theblaze.com/stories/2012/07/08/egyptian-muslim-brotherhood%e2%80%99s-leader-says-jihad-on-israel-is-every-muslim%e2%80%99s-duty/, last accessed 30 December 2013).

Stein, Ewan, *Representing Israel in Modern Egypt: Ideas, Intellectuals and Foreign Policy from Nasser to Mubarak* (London, 2012).

Wickham, Carrie Rosefsky, *The Muslim Brotherhood: Evolution of an Islamist Movement* (Princeton, 2013).

Youssef, Maamoun, 'Al Qaeda leader Ayman Al-Zawahri: Morsi ouster in Egypt is proof that democracy is corrupt', *Huffington Post*, 3 August 2013 (http://www.huffingtonpost.com/2013/08/03/ayman-al-zawahri-egypt_n_3701385.html, last accessed 30 December 2013).

YouTube, 'Mohamed Morsi – The Koran is our constitution – The Prophet Muhammad is our leader, jihad is our path', 11 July 2012 (http://www.youtube.com/watch?v=g8NtiUMOFFg&feature=youtube_gdata_player, last accessed 30 December 2013).

––––––, 'Al-maqta' al-a'naf fi khutbat al-Jum'a li-l-Shaykh Yusuf Al-Qaradawi yasif Hizb Allah bi-hizb al-Shaytan' ('The most violent section in the Friday sermon of Sheikh Yusuf al-Qaradawi describes Hizbullah as the party of Satan'), 31 May 2013 (http://www.youtube.com/watch?v=J-npCduuHNw&feature=youtube_gdata_ player, last accessed 30 December 2013).

––––––, 'Khitab al-ra'is Mursi fi mu'tamar al-umma al-Misriyya li-da'm al-thawra al-Suriyya' ('The speech of President Mursi in the conference of the Egyptian nation in support of the Syrian revolution'), 15 June 2013 (http://www.youtube.com/watch?v=9WS52JBnqSE&feature=youtube_gdata_player, last accessed 30 December 2013).

_____, 'Aqwa kalima li-l-ra'i' Muhammad Hasan amam Muhammad Mursi wa-hushud al-jamahir li-l-jihad fi Suriya' ('The strongest speech of the great Muhammad Hasan before Muhammad Mursi and the masses for jihad in Syria'), 16 June 2013 (http://www.youtube.com/watch?v=n6h6eYVob _E&feature=youtube_gdata_player, last accessed 30 December 2013).

_____, 'Al-'Arifi yu'lin al-jihad fi Suriya min Misr' ('Al-'Arifi declares jihad in Syria from Egypt'), 2013 (http://www.youtube.com/watch?v= dvZkqGq1A54&feature=youtube_gdata_player, last accessed 6 November, 2013).

Zollner, Barbara, The Muslim Brotherhood: Hasan Al-Hudaybi and Ideology (New York, 2008).

11

Jihad as a Form of Struggle in the Resistance to Apartheid in South Africa

Na'eem Jeenah

Muslim opposition to colonialism and apartheid in South Africa began soon after the arrival of the first Muslims in the Cape Colony in the mid-seventeenth century. Various acts of resistance through the centuries highlighted the Muslim community's opposition to the oppression it faced and, in the latter part of the twentieth century, to the oppression faced by it and its black compatriots. From the late 1960s onwards, Muslims began playing a role in the struggle against apartheid in excess of what their numbers might suggest. Many joined the various national liberation movements: the African National Congress (ANC), the Pan Africanist Congress (PAC), the Black Consciousness Movement (BCM), the South African Communist Party (SACP) and other socialist or nationalist organisations. Some Muslims in the Cape Town area joined the struggle from the 1950s *as Muslims* and considered their involvement an Islamic duty. The number and spread of these Muslims expanded from the early 1970s. They characterised the anti-apartheid struggle as a jihad and an Islamic duty upon all Muslims – a stance which contradicted the position taken by the majority of their co-religionists. This increase in Muslim participation was mainly as a result of the emergence of new organisations in other parts of the country and their national recruitment of members. The South African anti-apartheid struggle thus resulted in the development of novel conceptions of jihad and martyrdom, with South African Muslim activists adopting as *their* martyrs not only Muslims but also non-Muslims who were killed in the course of the struggle.

A brief account of South Africa's history will place this phenomenon in context. Resistance to colonialism in South Africa began in 1652 with the establishment of the first 'refreshment station' by the Dutch East India Company (VOC) in the 'Cape of Good Hope' (now Cape Town). The refreshment station became a colony and expanded eastwards and northwards. In this period of colonisation through to the beginning of the twentieth century, there was substantial – though not united – armed resistance by the indigenous population. Despite some successful encounters, the resistance was mostly outmanoeuvred by more sophisticated weaponry. In 1910, the Union of South Africa was formed within the dominion of the British Empire, unifying the colonies of Cape Province, Transvaal, Natal and Orange Free State. This period saw new forms of struggle being used by black people whose strategy shifted from military confrontation as a way to repel foreign colonisers to attempts at obtaining more justice within new political and economic structures. Organisations such as the African People's Organisation (APO) and the South African Native Convention (a precursor to the South African Native National Congress, which later became the ANC) emerged to fight for the rights of black South Africans. Their demands included the right to vote and be elected to Parliament.

The electoral victory (through a white electorate) of the Afrikaner-based National Party in 1948 signalled the beginning of the policy of apartheid that discriminated against people on the basis of their 'race', which also determined their rights and privileges (including citizenship). Disadvantaging and dehumanisation of the Black majority – which had been practised for three centuries – became government policy and was systematically implemented. By 1961, when South Africa was proclaimed a republic, numerous resistance movements actively opposed apartheid, including the ANC, PAC and SACP. In 1960, these and other organisations were banned and driven underground and into exile. In the 1970s, the Black Consciousness Movement (BCM) was formed and was for a long while the largest liberation movement within the country.

The 1980s saw a vigorous increase in resistance activity within the country and the formation or rise of new anti-apartheid organisations such as the United Democratic Front (UDF – aligned to the ANC), the National Forum (which united Africanists, Black Consciousness adherents and various leftist organisations), the Federation of South African Trade Unions (FOSATU – founded in 1979), the Congress of South African Trade Unions (COSATU – formed in 1985 as a merger of FOSATU and other unions) and a number of other community, youth, religious, cultural and sports organisations. The increasing mobilisation of people, various creative forms of resistance and the international isolation of the apartheid state ultimately led to the unbanning of liberation movements, the release of most political prisoners and the beginning of negotiations between the state and the liberation movements in the early 1990s, and South Africa's first democratic elections in 1994.

Muslims in the Struggle

Although Muslims form a small part of the South African population – around one million out of a total of 48 million people, making up about 2 per cent of the population – the community and its individuals have played significant roles in South African society for the past three and a half centuries. The first Muslims in the southern part of Africa were taken there from Bengal, Indonesia and Java by the Dutch as slaves and political exiles barely a decade after the VOC set up its refreshment station. Their arrival heralded the beginning of Muslim resistance in southern Africa, which took various forms including, for example, the smallpox protests of 1840 and the cemetery uprising of 1886 which demanded the preservation of the Tana Baru cemetery.[1] Such uprisings were not, however, the only acts of resistance. As Robert Shell showed, just the practice of their religion and its rituals (which were proscribed until 1794) and being able to survive as a Muslim in the early Cape Colony were in themselves acts of resistance.[2] The injustices with which Muslims were confronted included restrictions on their religion, movements and right to own property.

Yet Muslim resistance had, by the turn of the twentieth century, virtually disappeared. Most Muslims attempted, rather, to be accommodated and accepted by the authorities – especially in the northern Natal and Transvaal provinces where the vast majority of Muslims were of Indian origin and came to South Africa as indentured labourers or traders in the nineteenth century. This is not to suggest that Muslims were not involved in any resistance activities, but rather that Muslim involvement in anti-colonial, anti-racist and anti-apartheid activities was not on the basis of their religious affiliation. So, for example, Muslims such as Dr Abdullah Abdurrahman were involved in the APO (Abdurrahman became its president) at the turn of the century and Muslim merchants were involved in the formation of the Natal and Transvaal Indian Congresses (NIC and TIC), as well as in the passive resistance campaigns in the early twentieth century.[3]

By the middle of the twentieth century, as black resistance to apartheid intensified, a number of Muslims were to be seen in prominent positions in various resistance organisations. These included people such as Dr Yusuf Dadoo who became General Secretary of the South African Communist Party (SACP), ANC activists Ahmad Timol and Babla Saloojee who were killed in detention, Azanian People's Organisation (Azapo) leader Abu Bakr Asvat, and Azapo and Workers' Organisation for Socialist Action (WOSA) leader Haroon Patel (before he joined the Muslim Youth Movement in the 1990s). In the main, these activists engaged in their political activity outside of the Muslim community and with no (stated) political inspiration from their religious background.[4] Hardly any of them suggested that Islam had played a role in developing their political consciousness. Indeed, many had been forced by the community to make a choice: either be part of the Muslim community or be involved in politics; it was not possible to do both. This was imposed through intolerance, tinged with a degree of racism, in both religious and communal discourse regarding political involvement. In particular, there was a strong discourse within the Muslim community labelling political involvement – especially of the anti-apartheid variety – as '*kufr* politics' (the politics of disbelief).

There were exceptions. For example, Ismail Meer – a member of the SACP and the NIC – always maintained that his activism was inspired by his Islamic faith and identity. He saw no contradiction in being a politically involved Communist and a devout Muslim. He emphasised:

> The only political party which I could belong to as a devout Muslim, deeply immersed in the Quranic teaching, was the Communist Party of South Africa, which had no segregation and which was promoting the interests of all South Africans on a non-racial democratic basis.[5]

Another example of a Muslim activist whose involvement in the liberation movement was inspired by Islam was the indomitable clergyman Maulvi Ismail Mohamed Cachalia, a leading member of the TIC and the ANC.[6] Although trained as a traditionalist scholar at the Darul Uloom in Deoband in India, and at a time when Deobandi scholars in South Africa were opposing Muslim involvement in politics, Cachalia's 'efforts can be principally regarded as a contextualization of Koranic political maxims for seeking liberation for disenfranchised South Africans'.[7]

The trend of Muslims having to distance themselves from or leave Islam in order to oppose apartheid began to change in the 1950s, a decade that might be regarded as the beginning of what we now call 'political Islam' in South Africa. The Muslim Teachers' Association, founded in Cape Town in 1951, protested against the apartheid state and, in 1952, called on Muslims not to participate in Voortrekker celebrations held to commemorate Afrikaner expansionism into the north of South Africa. The Claremont Muslim Youth Association and the Cape Muslim Youth Movement – both established in the late 1950s – launched a declaration in 1961 that called on Muslims and other South Africans to unite to 'rid our beloved land of the forces of evil and tyranny'.[8] Referring to this declaration, known as the 'Call of Islam', Tamara Sonn points out:

> While Muslims had protested interference with their religious practice in earlier years, this call for Islamic resistance was unique in a number of ways. First, unlike earlier protests, the new resistance was not against specific rulings, but was aimed against an entire system deemed essentially unjust. Second, and more significantly, the injustices being suffered were not those suffered by Muslims alone, but by all victims of oppression, regardless of religious affiliation.[9]

It was a significant development that struggling for the rights of all people – including non-Muslims – was regarded as an Islamic duty.

A driving force behind the new movement and leader of the Claremont Muslim Youth Association was Imam Abdullah Haron, the imam of Masjid al-Jamia or Stegman Road Mosque in Claremont. Although linked to the Pan-Africanist Congress, Haron saw his politics and his anti-apartheid activities as being founded on, inspired and guided by Islam; his Islamic activism was influenced by and inseparable from his anti-apartheid activism. His association's newsletter, *Islamic Mirror*, carried political articles by leaders of the Muslim Brotherhood such as Sayyid Qutb. Haron's murder in detention by security police in 1969 was a milestone in Islamic resistance in South Africa.

Soon after Haron's murder, the Muslim community witnessed the establishment of two Muslim resurgence organisations: the Muslim Students Association (MSA – formed in 1969 in Cape Town and launched nationally in 1974) and the Muslim Youth Movement (MYM – formed in 1970). Both were destined to become national organisations which would significantly influence the development of anti-apartheid Islam.

The MSA remained politically inactive for almost the entire first decade of its existence, even through national student uprisings in 1976. The MYM – initially a socio-religious organisation – changed its orientation in 1977 when it was inspired by foreign Islamist movements such as Egypt's Muslim Brotherhood and Pakistan's Jamaat-e-Islami and began referring to itself as an 'Islamic movement'. Armed with a new ideology, the MYM insisted that Islam was a 'comprehensive way of life' and that politics was an important component of Islamic belief and practice (almost as important as spirituality). From the late 1970s its discourse increasingly included political rhetoric. Although the MYM began describing the apartheid state as 'satanic' and compared it to the regime of the Pharaoh during the Jewish exodus from Egypt, it did not immediately involve itself in anti-apartheid activity. In its new training programmes and study groups (*halaqat*), many sessions featured discussions on jihad and martyrdom (even referring to the struggle against apartheid as a jihad), but the movement found it difficult immediately to apply these concepts to the South African context. It continued to search for an 'Islamic paradigm' with which to respond to the apartheid state.[10]

This search delayed the MYM's entry into practical anti-apartheid engagement. The sought-for paradigm was never developed, but after national student uprisings erupted in 1980 and the subsequent influx of politically conscious students into the MSA and the MYM, both organisations were dragged into anti-apartheid political activity by their younger, more radical members. The Iranian Revolution of 1979 also identified these organisations as a new source of inspiration.

While admiration for Iran soon waned for most MSA and MYM members, the revolution inspired the formation of another, more radical, Muslim organisation in 1981. Qibla was founded by Achmad Cassiem, a former schoolteacher who, by then, had spent ten years in the infamous Robben Island prison for PAC-related activities. He had attended a national MYM 'Islamic Training Programme' in 1977 and had left disillusioned because of the MYM's unwillingness to engage in armed struggle. Many early members of Qibla were recruited from the MSA. Taking its lead from the Iranian Revolution, Qibla's main slogan – even after South Africa's first democratic election in 1994 – was 'One Solution, Islamic Revolution'.

Qibla regarded South African Muslims as having the solution for apartheid's injustices. Their understanding of Islam was a normative description of the Muslim community. Qibla thus asserted:

> Islam declares war on racism and racialism. This is more than a mere battle of words. As proof we offer Muslims as the only truly consolidated anti-racist force in the country. This has been historically maintained for three hundred years because it is an ideological unit and not a nationality, tribe and race or class.[11]

The organisation expressed a strong dislike for any alternative to Islam. Some of its bitterest vitriol was reserved, for example, for the Call of Islam because of the latter's affiliation to the ANC's internal wing, the United Democratic Front (UDF). Nevertheless, and despite its uncompromising position on Islamic revolution, Qibla was closely aligned to the PAC and, to a lesser extent, the BCM in the form of Azapo. The PAC's Tehran office was staffed in the 1980s by a Qibla exile; Cassiem was often invited to address PAC meetings after the latter was unbanned in 1990; political prisoners from Robben Island claimed Cassiem had been part of the Africanist group on the Island; Qibla leader Yusuf Patel was active in the BCM; and another senior Qibla member, Hassan Ghila, was part of the original group that left the ANC to form the PAC. Qibla also sometimes used the PAC salute, used the name 'Azania' to refer to South

Africa and employed Africanist slogans in its meetings.[12] Apart from the development of a small cadre of Muslim anti-apartheid activists, Qibla also had a programme of armed struggle. A number of its members left South Africa for military training (often in PAC camps) and, upon their return, undertook sabotage operations against the state.

The 1980s was the main period of political activity for the MYM, Qibla and the Call of Islam (COI or the Call), which emerged in 1983–4, when four senior members of the MYM/MSA – Farid Esack, Ebrahim Rasool, Adli Jacobs and Shamiel Manie – broke away to form a new organisation called Muslims Against Oppression. In its subsequent incarnation as the Call of Islam, the organisation aligned itself with the UDF. The MYM/MSA firmly refused to align to any particular tendency of the liberation movement, preferring to adopt what it called 'positive neutrality' – not aligning itself with any tendency but willing to work with all anti-apartheid movements.[13]

The Call regarded itself as 'a South African phenomenon owing little or nothing to the international developments in the Muslim world'.[14] Furthermore, Esack argued that the only reason the Call had organised or participated in international solidarity efforts – such as its protest against the bombing of Libya by the USA in 1986 – was to show that American aggression in Southern Africa was as abominable as that in Northern Africa. Despite this self-proclaimed notion of South Africanness, however, the reality was that the Call's senior members were all schooled in the ideology of Islamist Brotherhood politics during their period in the MYM and MSA.

The Call argued that its understanding of Islam and its engagement in the anti-apartheid struggle mutually influenced each other. For Esack, theology was fundamentally rooted in the basic experiences of the people, no matter where else it might also be located. The organisation saw itself as a radically new phenomenon on the South African scene. Explaining the organisation's involvement in the UDF, Ebrahim Rasool illustrated this point.

> The UDF taught us that it takes a lot of grassroots organization and a regular presence in the community to create, in turn, the conditions whereby Muslims will be able to take their place in the struggle. It does not simply take

an appeal for revolution from the Quran to create revolutionaries among Muslims. That creation is the product of social conditions, theological reflection and organization.[15]

The Call also described the anti-apartheid struggle as a jihad. As part of its contribution to this jihad, some of its members joined the ANC's armed wing, Umkhonto we Sizwe ('Spear of the Nation', abbreviated to MK), and engaged in sabotage actions against the state.[16]

These organisations – the MSA/MYM alliance, the Call of Islam and Qibla – were the main Muslim groups involved in the anti-apartheid struggle in the 1980s which claimed Islam, the Qur'an or the life of the Prophet Muhammad as their inspirations. A fifth organisation was a small Shi'ite group in Cape Town called al-Jihad, headed by former MK soldier Ismail Joubert who was given the nickname '*Tatamkhulu Afrika*' ('the Great Father of Africa') in the MK camps. Except for the Call, all these groups held to the ideal of an Islamic state at some point. Qibla – which is now virtually non-existent – continued to promote the 'Islamic state' as an ideal for South Africa well into the twenty-first century. The MYM and MSA abandoned the idea in 1989.

Apart from armed action in the case of Qibla and the Call, these organisations were involved through the 1980s and 1990s in mass mobilisation within Muslim and non-Muslim communities, building campaigns (often together with other organisations such as the UDF, BCM and PAC) and in strengthening mass movements in the country. The MSA, MYM and the Call also worked with the trade union movement – FOSATU and then COSATU – on various campaigns and were at the forefront of actions against the racist tricameral Parliament that was formed in 1983 to co-opt sections of the black community – so-called 'Indians' and 'Coloureds' – into the apartheid system. Muslim involvement in the struggle reached its height in the mid-1980s and was especially visible in the Western Cape province where Muslim political funerals mobilised Muslims and non-Muslims alike, *Allahu Akbar* became a nationalist slogan shouted by Muslim and non-Muslim activists, and the Palestinian keffiyeh and other paraphernalia of these Muslim organisations were banned. A number of Muslim activists from these organisations were detained while others went underground for periods of time.

Anti-Apartheid Struggle – Jihad and Martyrdom

These organisations regarded activities against the apartheid system and state as a jihad. At the height of negotiations with the apartheid govern-ment, in 1992, Achmad Cassiem articulated the position thus:

> There should be an intensification of revolutionary violence to counter and stamp out the other forms of violence. Muslims have contributed in the ideological sense the concept of Jihad which means that they exert themselves to the utmost in order to attain a just social order and therefore would have no truck with compromise with the enemy. For them every day is a good day to die – to achieve martyrdom is to achieve a victory. We are not talking at all of suspending the armed struggle . . . because that is proscribed in the Quran.[17]

In explaining Qibla's ideology in *Quest for Unity*, Cassiem wrote: 'The essence of Jihad is sacrifice and it is necessary because a revolutionary is not merely an exponent of revolutionary rhetoric but one who attacks what is oppressive and exploitative in order to destroy and eradicate it.'[18]

The terms 'jihad' and 'martyrdom' were also used extensively in the speeches and publications of the Call, MSA and MYM, which regarded their commitment to the anti-apartheid struggle as a religious obligation. MYM and MSA meetings were usually characterised by the shouting of the Muslim Brotherhood slogans '*al-jihad sabilu-na*' ('jihad is our path') and '*al-mawt fi sabil Allah asma amani-na*' ('death in the path of God is the highest of our aspirations'). It was clear that these slogans – especially for younger members of these organisations – referred to the anti-apartheid struggle. The jurisprudential niceties of jihad that classical Islamic scholars have detailed and debated – such as the question of who has the power to declare a jihad or what the conditions might be for it – were irrelevant for these Islamist anti-apartheid activists. Irrelevant, too, was any notion that jihad might be a struggle waged on behalf of Muslims. That 98 per cent of the South African population was non-Muslim, that many of those alongside whom these Islamists marched and fought the security forces were Christians or Communists, did not lessen their zeal for the struggle as jihad. Indeed, many of their publications referred to the anti-apartheid struggle as a whole – whether prosecuted by Muslims or not – as jihad. These Muslim activists based their perspective on particular (often quite literalist) interpretations of Qur'anic verses and hadiths.

In promoting the fight against apartheid, their publications, speeches, and sermons were peppered with verses such as:

And fight them on until there exists no tumult and oppression and there prevails justice and faith in God. . . [19]

And why should you not fight in the cause of those who, being weak, are ill-treated and oppressed; men, women and children whose cry is, 'Our Lord, rescue us from this land whose people are oppressors, and raise for us from among you one who will help, and raise for us from among you one who will protect'.[20]

The story of Moses in the Qur'an was seen as especially poignant and descriptive of apartheid, and verses quoted in this regard included: 'And we wished to be gracious to those who were being oppressed in the land, to make them leaders and to make them heirs'[21] and '[t]ruly Pharaoh elated himself in the land and broke up its people into sections, oppressing a small group among them: their sons he slew, but he kept alive their females'.[22]

Since jihad had been redefined to include the anti-apartheid struggle, it was logical that the notion of martyrdom would also be redefined since martyrs are generally regarded as those who are killed in the course of jihad. From the late 1970s, Muslim anti-apartheid activists from these organisations began referring to Muslims killed in the anti-apartheid struggle (including those from outside their ranks and who were killed by the state for their membership of organisations such as the ANC) as martyrs. Imam Haron, for many Muslim activists, epitomised martyrdom in the cause of the anti-apartheid struggle. Yet he and other Muslims killed in the struggle were not the only ones to whom the epithet *al-shahid* (the martyr) was applied. By the 1980s, it was also used in reference to non-Muslim martyrs such as Black Consciousness leader Steven Bantu Biko. Throughout the 1980s, organisations such as Qibla and the MSA often commemorated September as 'Martyrs' Month' and remembered the deaths of Haron, Biko and Ikhwan ideologue Sayyid Qutb simultaneously.

While the particular coinage and usage of these terms can be attributed to these organisations, they also attained wider currency – sometimes beyond the Muslim community. The so-called 'renaming' of a street in Cape Town as 'Jihad Street' – as brief as it was – during the 1985 uprisings was one indication of this.

Other Forms of South African Jihad

As apartheid approached its last days and as use of the term 'jihad' for the anti-apartheid struggle had gained wide currency, MYM and Call activists in particular extended the term to refer to other social justice struggles as well. For example, Rashied Omar, a former MYM president, coined the term 'gender jihad' in 1995 to refer to the struggle of Muslim women (and men) for women's rights and equality. The term was popularised within South Africa by another MYM activist, Shamima Shaikh, head of the organisation's Gender Desk from 1993, and it subsequently became a popular term among Islamic feminists around the world (especially after its global popularisation by Amina Wadud).[23] On other occasions, 'jihad' was also used in the context of racism ('jihad against racism') and South Africa's socio-economic woes ('jihad for reconstruction and development' and 'jihad against poverty').

Conclusion

The terms 'jihad' and '*shahada*' (martyrdom) have specific meanings given to them by Muslim jurists, and their legitimate use in any context is loaded with nuance and dependent on a number of conditions. Furthermore, the contemporary usage of the terms is loaded with political agendas and posturing, which often distorts the original meanings of the terms in rather ugly ways. The South African anti-apartheid struggle saw both terms being redefined by Muslims in a way that subverted the more rigid definitions of jurists and, at the same time, ensured that both terms earned a positive acceptance and respectability that is unusual in the contemporary context. For South African Muslim anti-apartheid activists (and some non-Muslim activists too), jihad and martyrdom are all about struggling for justice and fairness – irrespective of whether or not the strugglers or the beneficiaries are Muslim. These redefinitions began to be developed in the 1950s and increased in popularity from the 1970s as organisations such as the MYM and the MSA were formed and became national. Later, these ideas were entrenched with the formation of Qibla and the Call of Islam. Apart from these organisations, a small number of individual Muslim activists who were involved in nationalist liberation organisations also regarded their involvement a result of their commitment to Islam.

Notes

1. See Achmat Davids, *The History of the Tana Baru: The Case for the Preservation of the Muslim Cemetery at the Top of Longmarket Street* (Cape Town, 1985) and *The Mosques of the Bo-Kaap* (Cape Town, 1980), pp. 62–84.
2. Robert C. H. Shell, 'Between Christ and Mohammed: Conversion, slavery, and gender in the urban Western Cape', in Richard Elphick and Rodney Davenport (eds.), *Christianity in South Africa: A Political, Social and Cultural History* (Berkeley, 1997): 268–77.
3. See Maureen Swan, *Gandhi: The South African Experience* (Johannesburg, 1985).
4. See, for example, Essop Pahad, 'A proud history of struggle', *The African Communist* 78 (1979) (http://www.sacp.org.za/people/dadoo.html, last accessed 30 December 2013); Yusuf Dadoo, 'Articles, Statements and Speeches', 22 May 2000 (http://www.sacp.org.za/docs/history/dadoo00.html, last accessed 30 December 2013); E. S. Reddy, 'India and South Africa: New challenges', press statement (April 1995) (http://www.anc.org.za/show.php?id=6853, last accessed 30 December 2013).
5. See, for example, Ismail Meer, *A Fortunate Man* (Cape Town, 2002), p. 272.
6. See, for example, Yusuf Dadoo, 'Maulvi Cachalia: The contributions of a thinker-activist in the political liberation of South Africa', *Journal of Muslim Minority Affairs* 16/1 (1996): 129–33.
7. Ibid., p. 129.
8. Farid Esack, *Qur'an, Liberation & Pluralism: An Islamic Perspective of Interreligious Solidarity Against Oppression* (Oxford, 1997), p. 47.
9. Tamara Sonn, 'Muslims in South Africa: A very visible minority', in Yvonne Yazbeck Haddad and Jane I. Smith (eds.), *Muslim Minorities in the West: Visible and Invisible* (Walnut Creek, 2002): 255–65 (257).
10. Abdulkader Tayob, *Islamic Resurgence in South Africa: The Muslim Youth Movement* (Cape Town, 1998), p. 19.

11. 'Revolution Today, Justice Tomorrow', Qibla publication quoted in Farid Esack, 'Rejoinder to Nkrumah', *Review of African Political Economy* 53 (March 1992): 75–8 (78).
12. Farid Esack, 'Three Islamic strands in the South African struggle for justice', *Third World Quarterly* 10/2 (1988): 473–98.
13. Muslim Youth Movement of South Africa, 'General Assembly Minutes' (1989).
14. Esack, 'Three strands', p. 491.
15. Ebrahim Rasool, 'Muslims Mobilize', *New Era* (March 1988): 33–4 (33).
16. Jill E. Kelly, '"It is *because* of our Islam that we are there": The Call of Islam in the United Democratic Front era', *African Historical Review* 41/1 (2009): 118–39 (129–31).
17. Zubeida Jaffer, 'Muslims are becoming a political force', *Work in Progress* 80 (1992): 36.
18. Achmad Cassiem, *Quest for Unity* (Cape Town, 1992), p. 68.
19. Q. 8:39.
20. Q. 4:75.
21. Q. 28:5. See, for example, an MSA poster and T-shirt with this verse: http://www.aluka.org/action/showMetadata?doi=10.5555/AL.SFF.DOCUMENT.POS00000000.043.053.0465 (last accessed 30 December 2013).
22. Q. 28:4.
23. See Amina Wadud, *Inside the Gender Jihad* (Oxford, 2006).

Bibliography

Cassiem, Achmad, *Quest for Unity* (Cape Town, 1992).

Dadoo, Yusuf, 'Maulvi Cachalia: The contributions of a thinker-activist in the political liberation of South Africa', *Journal of Muslim Minority Affairs* 16/1 (1996): 129–33.

Davids, Achmat, *The Mosques of the Bo-Kaap* (Cape Town, 1980).

———, *The History of the Tana Baru: The Case for the Preservation of the Muslim Cemetery at the Top of Longmarket Street* (Cape Town, 1985).

Esack, Farid, 'Three Islamic strands in the South African struggle for justice', *Third World Quarterly* 10/2 (1988): 473–98.

———, 'Rejoinder to Nkrumah', *Review of African Political Economy* 53 (March 1992): 75–8.

———, *Qur'an, Liberation & Pluralism: An Islamic Perspective of Interreligious Solidarity Against Oppression* (Oxford, 1997).

Haddad, Yvonne Yazbeck and Smith, Jane I. (eds.), *Muslim Minorities in the West: Visible and Invisible* (Walnut Creek, 2002).

Jaffer, Zubeida, 'Muslims are becoming a political force', *Work in Progress* 80 (1992): 36.

Kelly, Jill E., '"It is *because* of our Islam that we are there": The Call of Islam in the United Democratic Front era', *African Historical Review* 41/1 (2009): 118–39.

Meer, Ismail, *A Fortunate Man* (Cape Town, 2002).

Muslim Youth Movement of South Africa, 'General Assembly Minutes' (1989).

Pahad, Essop, 'A proud history of struggle', *The African Communist* 78 (1979) (http://www.sacp.org.za/people/dadoo.html, last accessed 30 December 2013).

Rasool, Ebrahim, 'Muslims Mobilize', *New Era* (March 1988): 33–4.

Reddy, E. S., 'India and South Africa: New challenges', press statement (April 1995) (http://www.anc.org.za/show.php?id=6853, last accessed 30 December 2013).

Shell, Robert C. H., 'Between Christ and Mohammed: Conversion, slavery, and gender in the urban Western Cape', in Richard Elphick and Rodney Davenport (eds.), *Christianity in South Africa: A Political, Social & Cultural History* (Berkeley, 1997): 268–77.

Sonn, Tamara, 'Muslims in South Africa: A very visible minority', in Yvonne Yazbeck Haddad and Jane I. Smith (eds.), *Muslim Minorities in the West: Visible and Invisible* (Walnut Creek, 2002): 255–65.

Swan, Maureen, *Gandhi: The South African Experience* (Johannesburg, 1985).

Tayob, Abdulkader, *Islamic Resurgence in South Africa: The Muslim Youth Movement* (Cape Town, 1998).

Wadud, Amina, *Inside the Gender Jihad* (Oxford, 2006).

12

Women, Islam and War in Lebanon and the Palestinian Territories

Maria Holt

Umm Salim is a 53-year-old widow; she lives in the village of Ayta al-Sha'b on the Lebanese-Israeli border.[1] When Israel invaded Lebanon in the summer of 2006, one of her sons was wounded and her house badly damaged; the family was inside the house when it was bombed, she said, but they managed to get away to a neighbouring village. It was a bad experience, she recalled, but she and others in the village were helped by the Islamic resistance, which she described as 'a matter of pride'.[2] Many people in southern Lebanon refer to the Islamic resistance movement, Hizbullah, in similarly glowing terms; they have been supported in rebuilding their homes and lives in defiance of Israeli invasion and occupation. For Umm Salim, as for many other Lebanese who see themselves as having nowhere to turn, Islam, as an authentic expression of resistance, has become increasingly attractive. Her sentiments are echoed by Palestinians in the West Bank who regard the resistance as an important tool in their struggle against the Israeli occupation of their land, not only because of its perceived success as a military force but also as a result of the vision it espouses.

This raises the question of exactly how women fit into this vision of a resistance which, in Alastair Crooke's words, is 'centred not on killing but on ideas and principles'.[3] The word 'jihad' is often used to refer to the resistance. While this term tends to have negative connotations in the west, Lebanese Shi'ites and Palestinian women see it as having broader, less pejorative meanings. For them, jihad is associated with 'struggle'. Lara Deeb argues that jihad describes women's work within the community and also, more generally, public piety; it is a particular responsibility of pious women, she notes, 'with regard to the markers of piety they carried and their centrality in signifying modern-ness'.[4] Amina Wadud, too, defines jihad as 'effort' or 'exertion'. The gender jihad, she argues, 'is a struggle to establish gender justice in Muslim thought and praxis'.[5] This more inclusive notion of jihad informs the practice of Islamic resistance and women's role in it.

This chapter will take Crooke's argument as a starting point in understanding whether Islamic resistance incorporates or excludes women. While Crooke is correct that killing is not the sole or primary aim of resistance movements, militant activism has played a controversial role in the struggle, leading to the question of 'how violence produces and enhances social solidarity in [a] group's quest not only for recognition but also for entitlement to rights'.[6] The outbreak of violence between Israel and the Palestinian Islamist party Hamas, which started at the end of December 2008, highlighted again, in the eyes of the international community, the face of Islamic resistance as that of a young man, usually described as a 'terrorist'. As during the July 2006 war between Israel and Hizbullah, the resistance was vilified by many Western observers as male, violent and irrational. There are a number of reasons why this image has taken hold of the popular imagination, which this chapter will explore, but it will also argue that this image fails to do justice to Islamic resistance movements in Lebanon and the Palestinian territories. In reality, these movements reflect the diversity and complexity of Palestinian and Lebanese societies, including – importantly – the voices and activities of women.

In 2007, I conducted a research project into the effects of Islamic resistance on women in Lebanon and Palestine, for the purposes of which over 100 women were interviewed, including some who support and are part of the resistance, others who are more critical and many who have no strong opinion, other than a desire to live in peace and security.[7] The interviews took place in the woman's home or workplace, or in a community centre or office of a non-governmental organisation. They were mostly conducted on an individual basis, although a few took the form of group discussions; most were in Arabic, with the help of an interpreter. This research raised a number of questions: how does Islamic resistance reflect the aspirations of its female constituency? Is it possible to conceptualise 'resistance' beyond the arena of conflict? What implications does the involvement of women in Islamic resistance movements have for future models of 'modernity' in Lebanon and Palestine?

In order to answer these questions and to gain a deeper appreciation of the impact of Islamic resistance on the lives of Shi'ite Muslim women in Lebanon and Palestinian (Sunni Muslim) women in the West Bank, this chapter discusses, firstly, the gendered nature of national identity, with specific reference to the various forms of violence experienced by women during processes of nation-building and conflict. Next, it considers theories and understandings of 'resistance', broadly defined, by challenging the automatic linking of Islamic resistance with violence and non-democratic tendencies. Finally, with reference to interviews carried out in Lebanon and the West Bank, it analyses the 'plurality' of women's 'resistances'. This chapter will argue that Islamic resistance movements have sought to mobilise *all* segments of society, although men and women have usually been allotted different responsibilities. The efforts of women have been critical to the success of these movements and, far from being solely a male endeavour, Islamic resistance should be regarded as an unsurprising reaction to the perceived powerlessness caused by Israeli invasion and occupation.

The 'Gendered Nature' of National Identity

The global political system has traditionally paid little attention to the factor of gender, focusing instead on predominantly 'male' concerns of the state, war and national security. There is a similar lack of awareness of gender in theories of nation-making. As Dibyesh Anand argues, it 'is not so much that women are absent in nationalist thinking, but while symbolically very important, their role as agents is at best supportive of men as primary actors'.[8] In the Arab world, too, nationalist sentiments arose within a context of occupation and change; it was a response to the fragmentation of colonialism and to an ideological crisis, which originated 'in the intensification of the contradictions and the accumulation of conflictual situations in Arab society'.[9] The nation-state became a 'compulsory' model for newly independent former colonies.[10] But nationalists also drew inspiration from the *umma* (Islamic community). They claimed that, since Arabs possessed a common history, language and religion, it was 'natural' that they should form one nation. From the start, however, Arab nationalism was an ideology mired in contradiction. Power, as Fouad Ajami notes, 'engenders resistance. In this context, the power of the West, of an ascendant civilizational model, often forces others to look for means of resistance.'[11]

Since both nationalists and colonialists lacked an awareness of 'the gendered nature of colonialism and decolonialism', patriarchal ideas 'articulated in the language of Islam have subverted the practice of gender equality and social justice' set out in the Qur'an, and created a notion of nationalism that is based on masculine attributes and values.[12] Women's relationship with 'the nation' is complex; their national identity is often symbolic, closely associated with the preservation of cherished traditional values and the protection of a respectable image. However, it is also linked to notions of modernity, in the sense both of women as agents of progress and the counter-argument that 'the status of women in the Middle East delays the "modernization" and "liberation" of societies'.[13] For nationalist elites involved in the anti-colonial struggle, the creation of a 'new Arab woman' was regarded as part of the modernising project. But this woman frequently occupies an uncomfortable position, resented by the traditional classes, struggling to balance a public role with the responsibility of running her home and dismissed by some as a tool of decadent Western feminism. In the Middle East, as Evelyne Accad suggests, 'nationalism and feminism have never mixed very well. Women have been used in national liberation struggles ... only to be sent back to their kitchens after "independence" was gained.'[14]

Lebanese and Palestinian nationalisms developed along different trajectories in the twentieth century. For the Palestinians, nationalism flourished 'not only because Palestinians have been attached to their territory and because they have shared religion, language and customs and other nationalist symbols, but because their history of expulsion, of dispossession and, more recently, the Israeli Occupation, have sharpened and heightened their nationalistic feelings', whereas modern Lebanon has been described as 'not a nation but an uneasy association of communities and classes'.[15] The Lebanese Shi'ites are part of that 'uneasy association', and the global communal solidarity of the Shi'ites, as a minority Islamic sect and an oppositional movement, is part of their identity. Like the Palestinians, the nationalism of Lebanese Shi'ites was forged in defiance and adversity. Perceiving themselves as a disadvantaged minority in their own country, the Shi'ites turned to communal activism to enhance their position within the larger Lebanese nation and, in response to Israeli aggression in Lebanon, Shi'ite nationalism developed particular modes of heroism.

Both the Lebanese Shi'ites and the Palestinians have remained steadfast in their determination to end the Israeli occupation and liberate their land; this is a matter of honour for women as much as men. As diplomacy and passive resistance were perceived to have failed, militant confrontation was adopted as a more realistic tactic. Despite the success of Hizbullah's guerrilla campaign against Israel in southern Lebanon (1982–2000), Palestinians and Lebanese Shi'ites regard themselves as oppressed by a far more powerful enemy, one which appears vindictive and seems to respond only to force. These perceptions have created an expression of nationalism which is linked to masculine notions of action, confrontation and defence.

Since the liberation struggle is so closely linked to the protection of 'the nation', and nationalism, as Joseph Massad says, tends to be 'masculine-based' and also relies on violence, it would appear to exclude women.[16] But how accurate is this picture? Taking into consideration Crooke's suggestion that the resistance is concerned not only with violence, it is too simplistic to reduce the complex dynamics of these two societies to an association between 'men', 'the nation' and war. For both, Islamic resistance is creating a more complex modernity.

Although national liberation movements aim to modernise their societies, their egalitarian instincts are often limited by a preoccupation with continuity and traditional values and, as a result, women have often felt excluded by the nationalist project. The assumption is that women will be 'better off', in terms of rights and entitlements, once independence has been won, but very often real improvements either fail to materialise or fall short of expectations. Male modes of action, because they are associated with victory, have a tendency to remain unexamined, and the role of women to be idealised since, historically, 'women have been regarded as the repositories, guardians, and transmitters of culture'.[17] However,

this symbolically ambivalent role is likely to constrain women's involvement in violent conflict and post-conflict reconstruction, and raises the
question of agency.

Nonetheless, women do find ways of participating, and both Palestinian and Lebanese women have played innovative roles. They support
the male fighters in a variety of ways, protect their children as best they
can and attempt to maintain the integrity of their communities. The majority of women regard violence, directed against an unprincipled foe, as
unavoidable, and it would be overly simplistic in both cases to link women
automatically with peace and men with war. If we examine the sorts of
activities in which women engage during national liberation struggles,
we discover both diversity and creativity. During the First Palestinian
Intifada (1987–93), for example, women in the West Bank and Gaza
Strip established alternative educational and economic structures; they
engaged in non-violent protest against the occupation and devised inge-
nious methods of avoiding Israeli interference in order to carry on with
their normal lives and form effective political organisations. During the
Lebanese civil war (1975–90), women of different religious confessions
engaged in courageous peace-building activities, such as publicly meeting at the 'Green Line' dividing East and West Beirut in order to express
their opposition to violence.

'A Plurality of Resistances': Effects of Violence on Women's Participation

In order to construct a more nuanced challenge to Western claims of
universality, I have adopted Michel Foucault's suggestion of 'taking the
forms of resistance against different forms of power as a starting point'
from which to analyse relations of power.[18] According to Foucault, 'there
is a plurality of resistances' which, by definition, 'can only exist in the
strategic field of power relations'.[19] In this instance, 'power relations'
refers to the immediate condition of Israeli occupation and also the supporting environment of Western hegemonic and cultural power. It is
necessary to look at 'the resistances resulting from . . . various antagonistic interactions' in order to understand how power relations work.[20]

To contextualise the concept of 'resistance' and the position of women
within this framework, we need to be clear, firstly, about what is being

resisted; and, secondly, about the scope of the resistance project. As noted, the Arabic word 'jihad' means 'striving'. It has also been 'a potent system for popular mobilization'.[21] As Crooke argues, it is not solely linked to violence but, rather 'the resurgence of Islamic forms of sociability... within a range of Muslim societies is best understood as an expression of resistance against Western politico-cultural domination as well as a form of social protest against the failed modernizing project of postcolonial Muslim regimes'.[22] The origins of resistance, according to Frantz Fanon, are to be found in the 'imposed guilt and inferiority that those deemed "backward" and "culturally primitive" are forced to assume because of their powerlessness against an overbearing system ... those who are demonised as having no values and therefore no identity can liberate themselves through armed resistance'.[23] For Khalid Mish'al, the leader of Hamas, 'resistance' means 'struggle against the enemy who steals our land and destroys our houses, commits sacrilegious acts against our holy places, assaults children and women and kills people. It is our normal, natural right to resist, to struggle against them.'[24] However, as Bill Ashcroft puts it, 'the post-colonial strategy of transformation turns resistance from a simple opposition to a control of the means of representation'.[25] Arabs are weary of being 'spoken for'; they feel compelled to reclaim their own voice against Western hegemony and overbearing power. Not only has their land been stolen or occupied, but 'their loss and catastrophe have been covered up, hidden away, and systematically erased'.[26]

Thus, 'resistance' is linked to claims for power and identity. It operates on several levels, not only against Israeli power and violence, but also as a means of rejecting the neo-imperialism of the West; it is used as 'a tool with which to control and direct the powerful feelings which occupation and humiliation have unleashed ... [and] has objectives tied to the principle of refusing subservience'.[27] For purposes of resistance, Islam is used 'as a symbolic point of reference which functions as an icon from which both the nationalist and Islamist call to resistance is derived'.[28]

In the Lebanese and Palestinian cases, the Islamists' power is not only a reaction to state power; it also embodies resistance against the power of the Israeli occupation and, therefore, places a strong emphasis on violent activism, which tends to complicate the position of women. As members of victimised populations, many women support and admire the activities of Islamic resistance movements as they appear to signal a refusal to acquiesce to loss and humiliation. Yet there are additional factors that make the position of women more precarious. In situations of enemy penetration into public and private spaces, women are seen as particularly vulnerable and in need of protection. A report by the International Committee of the Red Cross notes that the 'vulnerability of women often derives from the fact that armed conflicts today have changed in such a way that civilians are increasingly caught up in the fighting and that women bear the brunt of the burden of ensuring the day-to-day survival of their families'.[29]

As a result of their vulnerability, the position of women as subjects has also been questioned. Are they colluding, as some have suggested, in their own oppression or are they at the forefront of resistance against Western forms of 'modernisation'? Given their role in the project of nation-making and the responsibilities this entails, Lebanese and Palestinian women occupy a protected position; on the one hand, Islamist movements recognise that women are also suffering the effects of Israeli aggression and 'share in a conviction of the need for resistance'; on the other hand, Islamists sometimes have another agenda: they seek to consolidate or recreate a more 'moral' society, which often results in greater control of women.[30]

Women and Islamic Resistance in the West Bank

The tradition and practice of resistance has a long history in the Palestinian territories. Since the start of the British occupation in the 1920s, Palestinians have sought to protect their land and their national identity, and women have been full and active participants. Palestinians living in the West Bank and Gaza Strip say that, in response to their dispossession by the newly created state of Israel in 1948, they had no choice but to engage in active resistance. Yet their fear of Israeli brutality 'committed against them, is transformed by the colonizer into a fear *of* them, the victims of colonial violence', thus demonising what Palestinians regard as a quest for justice and international legitimacy.[31] As a result of the Israeli occupation in 1967, the colonisation project began to invade the private space and to threaten the integrity of women and families.

In the wake of the Second Intifada, which started in September 2000, women and girls have faced particular risks and indignities; for example, early marriage for girls is rising; women's mobility has been curtailed by Israeli practices such as checkpoints and the 'separation wall' in the West Bank and, therefore, many young women have been forced to give up their education.

One way of asserting agency has been through an Islamisation of the conflict. Islah Jad argues that 'the defeat of the nationalist movement in Palestine ... allowed the Islamist movement Hamas to take on the nationalist struggle to achieve Palestinian national rights'.[32] She suggests that the popularity of Islamist parties resulted, firstly, from 'the failure of the peace process and the spread of corruption in the Palestinian Authority'; and, secondly, 'because of the institutions they ran which provided services and care to a large number of people, particularly women'.[33] After September 2000, violence rapidly escalated on both sides, and Palestinians felt increasingly desperate. Additionally, we saw the acceleration of militant activities by Islamist groups such as Hamas and Islamic Jihad, the apparently indiscriminate use of violence by the Israeli army and, in January 2006, Hamas's resounding victory in the Palestinian parliamentary elections, which led to the withdrawal of international support. As a result, the position of women was seriously undermined.

In the early days of the struggle, the 'large-scale political mobilization of Palestinian women was not perceived as a challenge to social stability but rather as a necessary and valuable contribution' to the struggle for independence.[34] However, 'a gendered distinction appears in the practice of violence'; while women certainly participated in the First and Second Intifadas, their roles and responsibilities have differed from those of men.[35] Hanadi, a professional women in her fifties, said that she does not believe in Islamic resistance. Everyone is struggling for an independent Palestinian state, she said, 'but it should not be an armed struggle'.[36] Mervat in Ramallah agreed; the way Hamas does 'resistance', she said, 'makes the Palestinian cause unclear; although it is against what Israel is doing and against the occupation, this will achieve nothing, and will only help the Israelis'.[37]

At the same time, having experienced mounting Israeli violence and repression since 2000, many Palestinians – including women – have come to regard violent resistance that has the support of religion as being one of the few options available to them. Their resolve was reinforced by the electoral success of Hamas and also the Palestinian 'victory' over Israel in the 2008 Gaza war. In the opinion of Rasha, a student at Birzeit University, people voted for Hamas because they need to see changes in all aspects of life. Islamic movements, she added, look at a woman in a different way to others; they look beyond her body to her mind, and this is attractive to women.[38] Suwad, a journalist, was of the same opinion. In her view:

> Israel will never accept any peace agreement that threatens its security, so it is a waste of time to keep negotiating. The Israelis know they are occupying Palestinian land but they will never give the Palestinians anything. It is a war and the Palestinians have the right to defend themselves in order to go back home.[39]

Islamic organisations in the West Bank and Gaza Strip have actively recruited and mobilised women. For example, they have established programmes to instruct women 'in Islamic culture, philosophy, law and religion', and 'to educate women in proper Islamic behaviour and the running of an Islamic home'.[40] It is likely that such activities permit women living in harsh and fearful conditions to feel they have some control over their lives.

There is a tension between the empowerment that Islamist movements seem to offer and the conservative nature of their social vision, especially with regard to women. This was constantly reiterated in women's narratives. Umm 'Adil, a retired teacher, said that some years ago, she used to work in a college; then only one of the teachers wore the hijab, but now the overwhelming majority wear it; it has become familiar. The Hamas movement, she added, 'claim they are religious, but they must learn how to live together; they should not impose anything'.[41] Her words illustrate the complexity of a relationship which, while asserting Palestinian dignity, has sometimes adopted coercive measures towards women.

Women and Islamic Resistance in Lebanon

For the Lebanese Shi'ites, resistance through Islam has proved similarly attractive, although there are significant differences between the two case studies. While Palestinians living under Israeli occupation have seen scant return for the sacrifices they have made, members and supporters of Hizbullah interviewed for this chapter all insisted that the resistance was responsible for the historic defeat of the militarily more powerful Israel. In 2007, women in southern Lebanon were interviewed about their participation in and feelings about the resistance, particularly in light of the unexpected war between Israel and Hizbullah the previous year, during which many southern villages suffered damage and loss of life. Muna in Nabatiyya, for example, said that, because the resistance defended and liberated Lebanon, it is supported by many people with different beliefs.[42] 'Amal in the same town said that the resistance is an integral part of life in the south.[43] Umm Wissam, who lives in a village on the border and whose home was destroyed in the 2006 war, described the resistance as a 'crown on our head'.[44]

Wafa' is 33 years old and works as a university lecturer in Beirut. She is part, she said, of the Islamic resistance and believes that all Lebanese should respect the resistance that 'protects the honour and dignity of Lebanon'. Wafa spoke of the importance of living and witnessing humiliation, insisting that 'it is a great honour to have the resistance'. She added that women make a difference and that Islam enjoins women to be active in society and also in jihad.[45]

Women, as Wafa' said, are taking part in the defence of their country. Maha, a Hizbullah activist in Beirut, explained that men bear the primary responsibility for waging war. But, if the enemy enters one's country, the Qur'an allows all members of the community to resist.[46] Hizbullah leader Hasan Nasr Allah agreed with this, but he added that there was an 'avoidance of the military participation of women' during the civil war and Israeli occupation of Lebanon and that this was 'in line with the traditions and customs of Shi'a culture in Lebanon'. The reasons for the non-participation of women, he said, were as follows: '[F]irstly, there was no need; and secondly, it was important to keep women away from Israeli military retaliation; for the Israelis to harm women would be very cruel.'[47] His concern is similar to that of Hamas and illustrates a resistance that both needs and encourages women's participation and, at the same time, seeks to project a more moral vision of society.

Conclusion

The above research seeks to challenge notions of Islamic resistance as an exclusively male form of activism, firstly, by suggesting reasons for the marginalisation of women, such as the evolution of a masculine-based nationalism in Lebanon and Palestine and the effects of violence on women's ability to participate; secondly, by describing 'the pluralities of resistance' practised by women; and, finally, by referring to the narratives of Lebanese and Palestinian women who admire or are critical of Islamic resistance against Israeli invasion and occupation. Many support the resistance out of a desire for survival and justice. But they also share the vision of a resistance based on ideas and principles. Their activities take place within an admittedly strongly traditional and patriarchal framework, but one that is adjusting to take account of women's skills and aspirations. Rather than dismissing Islamic resistance as violent terrorism, it is worth listening more carefully to the voices of women such as Umm Salim in southern Lebanon and Suwad in Ramallah who see Islamic resistance movements as promoters of dignity, self-defence and the rights of women.

Notes

1. The names of all women interviewed for this article have been disguised.
2. Interview, Ayta al-Sha'b, 2 May 2007.
3. Alastair Crooke, *Resistance: The Essence of the Islamist Revolution* (London, 2009), p. 16.
4. Lara Deeb, *An Enchanted Modern: Gender and Public Piety in Shi'i Lebanon* (Princeton and Oxford, 2006), p. 204.
5. Amina Wadud, *Inside the Gender Jihad: Women's Reform in Islam* (Oxford, 2006), p. 10.
6. Madawi al-Rasheed and Marat Shterin, 'Introduction: Between death of faith and dying for faith: Reflections on religion, politics, society and violence', in Madawi al-Rasheed and Marat Shterin (eds.), *Dying for Faith: Religiously Motivated Violence in the Contemporary World* (London, 2009): xvii-xxx (xx).
7. I interviewed 60 women in the West Bank and 46 women in Lebanon. My research was funded by the United States Institute of Peace.

8. Dibyesh Anand, 'Nationalism', in Laura J. Shepherd (ed.), *Gender Matters in Global Politics: A Feminist Introduction to International Relations* (London, 2010): 280–92 (285).

9. Issa J. Boullata, *Trends and Issues in Contemporary Arab Thought* (Albany, 1990), p. 152.

10. Sami Zubaida, *Islam, the People, and the State* (London, 1988), p. 121.

11. Fouad Ajami, *The Arab Predicament: Arab Political Thought and Practice Since 1967* (Cambridge, 1981), p. 16.

12. Marnia Lazreg, *The Eloquence of Silence: Algerian Women in Question* (London and New York, 1994), p. 3; Margot Badran, *Feminism in Islam: Secular and Religious Convergences* (Oxford, 2009), p. 284.

13. Nadera Shalhoub-Kevorkian, 'Counter-narratives of Palestinian women: The construction of Her-story and the politics of fear', in Moha Ennaji and Fatima Sadiqi (eds.), *Gender and Violence in the Middle East* (London, 2011): 29–60 (39).

14. Evelyne Accad, 'Sexuality and sexual politics: Conflicts and contradictions for contemporary women in the Middle East', in Chandra Talpade Mohanty, Ann Russo and Lourdes Torres (eds.), *Third World Women and the Politics of Feminism* (Bloomington and Indianapolis, 1991): 237–51 (238).

15. Michael C. Hudson, *Arab Politics: The Search for Legitimacy* (New Haven and London, 1977), p. 281.

16. Joseph Massad, 'Conceiving the masculine: Gender and Palestinian nationalism', *Middle East Journal* 49/3 (Summer 1995): 467–83 (469).

17. Arati Rao, 'The politics of gender and culture in international human rights discourse', in Julie Peters and Andrea Wolper (eds.), *Women's Rights Human Rights: International Feminist Perspectives* (London and New York, 1995): 167–76 (169).

18. Hubert Dreyfus and Paul Rabinow, *Michel Foucault: Beyond Structuralism and Hermeneutics* (Chicago, 1982), p. 211.

19. Michel Foucault, *The Will to Knowledge, The History of Sexuality: Vol. 1* (London, 1976), p. 96.

20. Azza M. Karam, *Women, Islamisms and the State: Contemporary Feminisms in Egypt* (Basingstoke, 1998), p. 4.

21. Crooke, *Resistance*, p. 69.

22. Saba Mahmood, *Politics of Piety: The Islamic Revival and the Feminist Subject* (Princeton, 2005), p. 24.

23. Frantz Fanon, *The Wretched of the Earth* (New York, 1963), p. 16.

24. Khalid Mish'al, interviewed by Huw Spanner, 21 May 2008 (http://www.spannermedia.com/interviews/Mish%27al.htm, last accessed 10 Feb 2014).

25. Bill Ashcroft, 'Representation and its discontents: Orientalism, Islam and the Palestinian crisis', *Religion* 34 (2004): 113–21 (113).

26. Haim Bresheeth, 'The continuity of trauma and struggle: Recent cinematic representations of the Nakba', in Ahmad H. Sa'di and Lila Abu-Lughod (eds.), *Nakba: Palestine, 1948, and the Claims of Memory* (New York, 2007): 161–91 (162).

27. Crooke, *Resistance*, p. 197.

28. Islah Jad, *Feminism between Secularism and Islamism: The Case of Palestine (West Bank and Gaza)* A Conflicts Forum Briefing (July 2010) (http://conflictsforum.org/briefings/CaseOfPalestine.pdf, last accessed 10 February 2014), p. 3.

29. International Committee of the Red Cross, *Women in War: A Particularly Vulnerable Group?*, 1 March 2007 (http://www.icrc.org/Web/Eng/siteeng0.nsf/html/women-vulerability-010307, last accessed 30 December 2013).

30. On the 'need for resistance': Jad, *Feminism between Secularism and Islamism*, p. 4.

31. Shalhoub-Kevorkian, 'Counter-narratives of Palestinian women', p. 35.

32. Jad, *Feminism between Secularism and Islamism'*, p. 4.

33. Ibid., p. 10.

34. Simona Sharoni, 'Gendering conflict and peace in Israel/Palestine and the north of Ireland', *Millenium* 27/4 (1998): 1061–89 (1064).

35. Julie Peteet, 'Male gender and rituals of resistance in the Palestinian Intifada: A cultural politics of violence', in Mai Ghoussoub and Emma Sinclair-Webb (eds.), *Imagined Masculinities: Male Identity and Culture in the Modern Middle East* (London, 2000): 103–26 (116).

36. Interview, Abu Diss, 18 June 2007.

37. Interview, Ramallah, 3 November 2007.

38. Interview, Birzeit University, 3 November 2007.

39. Interview, Ramallah, 31 October 2007.

40. Sara Roy, *Failing Peace: Gaza and the Palestinian-Israeli Conflict* (London, 2007), pp. 178–9.

41. Interview, Ramallah, 13 June 2007.

42. Interview, Nabatiyya, 2 May 2007.

43. Interview, Nabatiyya, 28 April 2007.

44. Interview, Ayta al-Sha'b, 2 May 2007.

45. Interview, Beirut, 3 May 2007.

46. Interview, Beirut, 26 January 1993.

47. Interview, Sayyid Hasan Nasr Allah, Beirut, 9 June 2003.

Bibliography

Accad, Evelyne, 'Sexuality and sexual politics: Conflicts and contradictions for contemporary women in the Middle East', in Chandra Talpade Mohanty, Ann Russo and Lourdes Torres (eds.), *Third World Women and the Politics of Feminism* (Bloomington and Indianapolis, 1991): 237–51.

Ajami, Fouad, *The Arab Predicament: Arab Political Thought and Practice Since 1967* (Cambridge, 1981).

Anand, Dibyesh, 'Nationalism', in Laura J. Shepherd (ed.), *Gender Matters in Global Politics: A Feminist Introduction to International Relations* (London, 2010): 280–92.

Ashcroft, Bill, 'Representation and its discontents: Orientalism, Islam and the Palestinian crisis', *Religion* 34 (2004): 113–21.

Badran, Margot, *Feminism in Islam: Secular and Religious Convergences* (Oxford, 2009).

Boullata, Issa J., *Trends and Issues in Contemporary Arab Thought* (Albany, 1990).

Bresheeth, Haim, 'The continuity of trauma and struggle: Recent cinematic representations of the Nakba', in Ahmad H. Sa'di and Lila Abu-Lughod (eds.), *Nakba: Palestine, 1948, and the Claims of Memory* (New York, 2007): 161–91.

Crooke, Alastair, *Resistance: The Essence of the Islamist Revolution* (London, 2009).

Deeb, Lara, *An Enchanted Modern: Gender and Public Piety in Shi'i Lebanon* (Princeton and Oxford, 2006).

Dreyfus, Hubert and Rabinow, Paul, *Michel Foucault: Beyond Structuralism and Hermeneutics* (Chicago, 1982).

Fanon, Frantz, *The Wretched of the Earth* (New York, 1963).

Foucault, Michel, *The Will to Knowledge, The History of Sexuality: Vol. 1*, trans. Robert Hurley (London, 1976).

———, *The History of Sexuality, Vol. 1: An Introduction* (New York, 1978).

Hudson, Michael C., *Arab Politics: The Search for Legitimacy* (New Haven and London, 1977).

International Committee of the Red Cross, *Women in War: A Particularly Vulnerable Group?*, 1 March 2007 (http://www.icrc.org/eng/resources/documents/feature/2007/women-vulnerability-010307.htm, last accessed 30 December 2013).

Jad, Islah, *Feminism between Secularism and Islamism: The Case of Palestine (West Bank and Gaza)*, A Conflicts Forum Briefing (July 2010) (http://conflictsforum.org/briefings/CaseOfPalestine.pdf, last accessed 10 February 2014).

Karam, Azza M., *Women, Islamisms and the State: Contemporary Feminisms in Egypt* (Basingstoke, 1998).

Lazreg, Marnia, *The Eloquence of Silence: Algerian Women in Question* (London and New York, 1994).

Mahmood, Saba, *Politics of Piety: The Islamic Revival and the Feminist Subject* (Princeton, 2005).

Massad, Joseph, 'Conceiving the masculine: Gender and Palestinian nationalism', *Middle East Journal* 49/3 (Summer 1995): 467–83.

Mayer, Tamar (ed.), *Women and the Israeli Occupation: The Politics of Change* (London and New York, 1994).

Peteet, Julie, 'Male gender and rituals of resistance in the Palestinian Intifada: A cultural politics of violence', in Mai Ghoussoub and Emma Sinclair-Webb (eds.), *Imagined Masculinities: Male Identity and Culture in the Modern Middle East* (London, 2000): 103–26.

Rao, Arati, 'The politics of gender and culture in international human rights discourse', in Julie Peters and Andrea Wolper (eds.), *Women's Rights Human Rights: International Feminist Perspectives* (London and New York, 1995): 167–76.

al-Rasheed, Madawi and Shterin, Marat, 'Introduction: Between death of faith and dying for faith: Reflections on religion, politics, society and violence', in Madawi al-Rasheed and Marat Shterin (eds.), *Dying for Faith: Religiously Motivated Violence in the Contemporary World* (London, 2009): xvii–xxx.

Roy, Sara, *Failing Peace: Gaza and the Palestinian-Israeli Conflict* (London, 2007).

Shalhoub-Kevorkian, Nadera, 'Counter-narratives of Palestinian women: The construction of Her-story and the politics of fear', in Moha Ennaji and Fatima Sadiqi (eds.), *Gender and Violence in the Middle East* (London, 2011): 29–60.

Sharoni, Simona, 'Gendering conflict and peace in Israel/Palestine and the north of Ireland', *Millenium* 27/4 (1998): 1061–89.

Spanner, Huw, Interview with Khalid Mish'al, 21 May 2008 (http://www.spannermedia.com/interviews/Mish%27al.htm, last accessed 10 Feb 2014).

Wadud, Amina, *Inside the Gender Jihad: Women's Reform in Islam* (Oxford, 2006).

Zubaida, Sami, *Islam, the People, and the State* (London, 1988).

Interviews conducted by the author

Abu Diss, 18 June 2007

Ayta al-Sha'b, 2 May 2007

Beirut, 26 January 1993
Beirut, 9 June 2003 (with Sayyid Hasan Nasr Allah)
Beirut, 3 May 2007
Birzeit University, 3 November 2007
Nabatiyya, 28 April 2007
Nabatiyya, 2 May 2007
Ramallah, 13 June 2007
Ramallah, 31 October 2007
Ramallah, 3 November 2007

13

Al-Qa'ida, Jihad and the 'Surge'

Lt. Gen. Sir Simon Mayall

By the time I landed in Baghdad in autumn 2006 to take up the appointment of Deputy Commanding General for Multi-National Corps – Iraq (MNC-I), the full scale of the security problems the USA had unleashed by its invasion of Iraq in 2003 was all too clear.[1] However, the sheer complexity of what constituted the main elements of the burgeoning chaos was only just being properly understood, and the strategy to address them was only just slowly unfolding. An old expression has it: 'When you are up to your arms in alligators it is sometimes difficult to remember that your original plan had been to drain the swamp'.[2] That was the situation in 2006, when the intensity of the violence and its multiple sources threatened to overwhelm the capacity of the Coalition Forces (CF) and the nascent Iraqi Security Forces (ISF) either to deal with it, or to step back to analyse it properly, in order to construct a new, coherent and relevant strategy. Sun Tzu, famously, is supposed to have said: 'Strategy without tactics is the slowest path to victory. Tactics without strategy is the drumbeat before defeat.'[3]

The Sunni Arab minority dictatorship of Saddam Hussein had been replaced by a Western 'occupation force'. As far as many Sunnis across the Muslim world were concerned, this 'occupation force', in the name and through the mechanisms of 'democracy' was, de facto, going to institutionalise Shi'ite-dominated governments in the heart of the ancient seat of the Abbasid Sunni caliphate. Since this would also guarantee an inevitable degree of Iranian influence, this combination had provoked an incendiary situation. Despite a widespread dislike of Saddam Hussein, all the USA's Sunni Arab interlocutors, even the Kuwaitis, had cautioned against large-scale intervention in Iraq. Into this mix were thrown the centuries-old and violently competitive instincts of a number of other conflicts: the factional Sunni–Shi'ite rivalry; the historical Arab–Persian antagonism, further complicated by the large Iraqi Kurdish population in the North; the clash between secular pragmatism and religious fundamentalism; and the intra-Sunni divisions between an Arab nationalism of a state-centric nature, and those strategists and operators whose inspiration was drawn from the ancient 'golden age' of the caliphate and the universal Muslim identity of the *umma*. In the latter category were Osama bin Laden and Layman al-Swahili, the architects of 9/11, and Ahmad Fadil al-Khalayilah, better known as Abu Mus'ab al-Zarqawi, the most zealous and unrestrainedly violent of those who fought in Iraq under the jihadist banner.

The situation of jihad in Iraq at that time might best be described as a 'Clash within Civilisation'[4] rather than the more popular notion touted by Samuel Huntington in his seminal work *The Clash of Civilizations*.[5] While the concept and language of jihad, and the religious underpinning of historical antagonism and conflict between Islam and Christianity based on the concept of the 'infidel', were well understood and documented, they drew attention away from a much wider set of historical and violent rivalries that exist within the Muslim world. This conflict manifested itself far more widely than the division between Sunni and Shi'ite. It went to the heart of the origins of Islam and its historical experience of early Arab dominance, the usurpation of the caliphate by the Turks, the dominance of the West from the eighteenth century onwards and the shattering of the integrity of the *umma* (Islamic community) with the collapse and fragmentation of the Ottoman Empire. This was further exacerbated with the abolition of the universal caliphate by Kemal Ataturk. The language of jihad was also used in the internal competition for the soul and leadership of the Islamic world, but in this context it identified the 'enemy', against whom 'the struggle' must be conducted, as those labelled as 'heretics' and 'apostates' – internal to the Muslim world, in other words, as opposed to hostile forces from outside. The jihadist narrative deemed Muslim challengers to their extreme aspirations to be, in many ways, more dangerous opponents than the external 'infidels'. In language, thought and action those jihadists who used the argumentation of orthodoxy to combat heterodoxy would have been very recognisable to the Catholic and Protestant zealots of the European Reformation and Counter-Reformation in the sixteenth and seventeenth centuries.

One of Karl von Clausewitz's most enduring observations is that 'the first, the supreme, the most far-reaching act of judgement the statesman and commander have to make is to establish the kind of war . . . on which they are embarking; neither mistaking it for, nor trying to turn it into, something that is alien to its nature'.[6] Having worked closely with so many brave, intelligent and selfless Americans over so many years, and counting so many close friends among them, it pains me to be critical of the USA. However, the violence in Iraq in 2006, and the grim statistics of military and civilian casualties, revealed that US strategic thinkers, operational commanders and tactical leaders did not heed Clausewitz's sage advice from 2003 until 2006. While intervention in Afghanistan in 2001 had a clear logic and an easily explicable narrative, the political and legal argumentation for action in Iraq had as much to do with internal US dynamics between the White House, the State Department and the Pentagon as it did with the stated *casus belli* regarding weapons of mass destruction (WMD) and Saddam Hussein's links to al-Qa'ida. Not only was the invasion mired from the outset in a controversy that alienated domestic public opinion, it squandered the support of those in the Muslim world whose broad interests aligned with the USA and its allies, and who loathed Saddam. In addition, it usefully fed the jihadist narrative of Osama bin Laden, and helped to fulfil his stated objective to commit the West to a major conflict on Muslim soil.

Early problems were compounded by a lack of clarity over the aims of the occupation, and haphazard mismanagement from the outset. Revealing a catastrophic lack of feel for the people of Iraq and the fine balance of interest and power, the Coalition Provisional Authority (CPA) disbanded the Ba'th Party, making redundant all those members who were indispensable for the conduct of almost all important administrative functions, and the Armed Forces, who could, and should, have been co-opted into a security solution that the USA and its allies had neither the strength nor relevant capabilities to deliver. In addition, the actions of the military, schooled in the Colin Powell doctrine of overwhelming

force and 'decisive victory', quickly alienated the bulk of the Iraqi population, of all persuasions, even those who had most to gain from the
overthrow of Saddam. Humiliation is a dangerous game in the Middle
East. 'Abd al-Bari Atwan cites an Iraqi, living abroad and no friend of
Saddam, as saying: 'The sense that our people, our erstwhile leaders, our
country, our culture and our history were being spat on by US soldiers,
themselves pitifully lacking in history, education, culture and respect,
was too much to bear.'[7]

By 2006 there were three major and identifiable groups of insurgent opposition.[8] The most obvious was the large contingent of secular
Sunnis. These comprised disenfranchised Ba'thists, ex-Iraqi Army per-
sonnel, ex-members of Saddam's security forces and radicalised citizens,
grouped under the umbrella organisation of the National Council for the
Resistance (NCR), all united in their targeting of the Coalition Forces
(CF) and the newly empowered Shi'ites. In the Sunni majority areas of
Anbar and the Euphrates valley, and the Saddam heartlands of Tikrit,
they had early on infiltrated the re-forming Iraqi Security Forces, particularly the police; and, although divided by ideology, they had formed
ad hoc coalitions with the jihadist and Islamist groups that had begun to
pour in through the porous Syrian border, financed and facilitated by a
range of sympathisers. Resistance was inflamed by feelings of dishonour
and calls for retribution and retaliation, especially in the tribal areas of
Anbar in West Iraq. It was too easy either to ignore the strength of this
feeling of humiliation or, unhelpfully, to confuse or conflate it with the
ideological zealotry of the jihadists.

The second group were the Islamists and jihadists themselves, many
of them foreign fighters, who coalesced around al-Zarqawi and his 'al-
Qa'ida in the Land of the Two Rivers', all of them broadly committed to
the establishment of an Islamic 'caliphate' in Iraq, having first expelled
the 'occupiers'. Al-Zarqawi had given his *bay'a* (oath of allegiance) to
Osama bin Laden late in 2004, but his ambition was too obvious and
by 2006 he had been instructed by bin Laden to confine himself to
military matters, and not to try to usurp the ideological leadership. His
overall strategy appeared to have four strands: isolate the USA from its
allies and erode its legitimacy, by attacking international bodies (the
UN), non-governmental organisations (NGOs) and US allies (al-Qa'ida
took up this cue with its attack in Madrid); prevent any Iraqis from

cooperating with the occupiers with a series of attacks on army and police recruitment centres, and targeted assassinations and bombings of those to whom the CPA planned to transfer power; commit atrocities to drive out foreigners and hamper attempts to reconstruct Iraq; and foment sectarian conflict by targeting the Shi'ites.[9]

In all this al-Zarqawi had been murderously successful in making life for the Coalition a poisoned chalice, and comprehensively dashing whatever hopes the USA had for a swift and clean extraction.[10] His disdain for the Americans, Shi'ites, Persians and secularists was matched by his contempt for the US goal of 'democracy', which he saw as not just empowering the Shi'ite 'heretics' but heresy in its own right, with its espousal of freedom of choice. His operations in Iraq, although they had within them the seeds of his own destruction, dovetailed well with Osama bin Laden's wider, global jihadist agenda, set out in 2005 in a document titled 'al-Qa'ida's Strategy to the Year 2020' and published in *al-Quds al-Arabi*.[11]

How much of this strategy was the result of pre-9/11 thinking, and how much *ex post facto* explanation, is difficult to discern, but the document posited five distinct stages. The first was to provoke the USA into invading Muslim lands. This had been achieved in Afghanistan, although it had cost al-Qa'ida its safe havens, and was now underway in Iraq. The second phase was to incite the Muslim world, the *umma,* to outrage, and to raise a new generation of mujahidin to fight the USA and its allies. The third stage was to expand this conflict throughout the Muslim world. The fourth stage was to restructure and reorganise al-Qa'ida, to make it an international ideology, transcending national boundaries through the application of broad guiding principles and the internet, and to inspire and enable a range of franchised operations that would put pressure on Western security forces and populations. The fifth stage was to cause the US to 'implode' under the financial and military pressures of prosecuting the wars and conflicts that al-Qa'ida had provoked them into initiating. From the perspective of the Operations Room in HQ MNC-I it was sometimes tempting to feel that the opposition strategy was on a better trajectory than our own.

The third group comprised the Shi'ite resistance movements. In US planning the Shi'ites had been seen as the net beneficiaries of the invasion, and those who should have had most reason to cooperate and ally with the Coalition. A mixture of Iraqi nationalism, Shi'ite disdain for the USA's Sunni friends in the Gulf states, Iranian influence and US miscalculations led to a stand-off with the Sadrists.[12] This put the Coalition and the Mahdi army – *Jaysh al-Mahdi* (JAM) – into a state of persistent confrontation that made establishing a common front against the Sunni insurgents and jihadists difficult. The status, role and influence of JAM was further complicated by the tendency of the Shi'ite-dominated government, led by Nouri al-Malaki, to see only threats from Sunni groups and to restrain Coalition operations against the malign activities of Shi'ite militias.

Around and among these violent groups and seething tensions were large numbers of Iraqis who simply sought to keep their heads below the parapet, while trying to steer clear of the compound violence of attacks aimed at the Coalition Forces, the US-led counter-insurgency campaign, the battles between competing Sunni and Shi'ite militias and the increasingly fractious relationship between the al-Zarqawi jihadists and the indigenous Sunni insurgents. Only the Kurds, in their mountain fastnesses in the north, were relatively immune from this witch's brew of violence. However, their ambitions for a Greater Kurdistan brought them into sporadic conflict with the Shi'ite-dominated government and the Sunni insurgents, both of whom contested their aspirations. Nor were they immune from the suspicions and interventions of their northern neighbours, the Turks, who had their own long-standing problems with the contiguous Kurdish minority in their own country.

Although al-Zarqawi himself was killed in June 2006, his masterminding of the bombing of the Golden Mosque in Samarra in February of that year had catalysed an even more virulent round of Sunni and Shi'ite violence. Within this cycle of terror, indiscriminate Sunni car and suicide bombs provoked Shi'ite militia retaliation that sought to ethnically cleanse the formerly Sunni or mixed areas of Baghdad. Samarra acted as an accelerant for all the violent tensions competing for prominence in Iraq at that time, inspiring a security situation that teetered on the brink of all-out civil war. While acts of violence and casualties rose inexorably through 2006, the Coalition Forces continued to try to prosecute a counter-insurgency campaign, to protect civilians, to stand between the competing militias and 'death squads', to support reconstruction and to build the new Iraqi Security Forces. The Coalition Forces were increasingly only the USA and UK, as other allied contingents either withdrew from Iraq or hunkered down in their fortified outposts, reflecting their governments' lack of enthusiasm for an operation that had started controversially and had then gone wildly off script. In many cases the ISF, notably the army, acted bravely and admirably, but their patchy performance understandably reflected their short independent existence, the speed of their expansion, their lack of capability and the complexity of the sectarian soup in which they were swimming. In some instances, particularly in the case of the National Police (NP), the ISF acted in a thoroughly sectarian manner, bringing their loyalty into question, alienating the Sunni population, damaging the credibility of the government and feeding the jihadist narrative.

By late 2006, identifying a revised and coherent military strategic framework that would underpin the political policy of supporting a new, democratic Iraqi government that would govern in the interests of all its citizens and not be a threat to the region was the highest political and military priority for the US government. This became even more urgent as the Bush presidency moved towards its last quarter. Such a framework would need to address all the constituent elements of Sunni Arab and jihadist threats and violence, while keeping the JAM at arm's length yet within the wider political tent, and mitigating the worst and most malign elements of Iranian influence. The reality was that the USA felt it was facing a strategic defeat deemed to be potentially greater than that of Vietnam.[13] Public support had plummeted; US casualties were now measured in the thousands; the financial burden, even for the USA, was huge; Iran was emboldened, not cowed; and the global reputation of the USA had been severely damaged. In addition, the campaign in Afghanistan against the Taliban and the damaged remnants of al-Qa'ida, the original reason for military action in 2001, had been allowed to become a subsidiary theatre. All excuses had been exhausted. The language of 'victory' had been dropped in favour of the lower ambitions of 'sustainable security' and 'withdrawal with honour'.

However, through the gloom, some elements of the campaign gave cause for hope. The USA has a commendable capacity for self-reflection and self-criticism. In 2001, General Rick Shinseki, who had led the US Army Transformation Programme, had warned: '[I]f you don't like change, you are going to like irrelevance even less.'[14] President Bush now reluctantly admitted the current strategy was not succeeding, and the US military acknowledged its own mistakes and its failure to use tactics relevant to the reality of the situation on the ground. The higher leadership of the US military, most notably General David Petraeus, but also many of the junior commanders, demanded – and got – a complete overhaul of the doctrine for dealing with an insurgency crisis on the scale of that facing the USA in Iraq in 2006.

Poring over historical examples, accepting a brutally honest assessment of the situation in Iraq and taking into account his own experiences as a divisional commander in North Iraq, Petraeus and a broad-based, multidisciplinary team ruthlessly examined the US experiences over three years, from the successes in Tal Afar and Ramadi to the scandals of the Haditha massacre and the Abu Ghraib abuses. In reassessing operational design, training, tactics and equipment, Petraeus's team set out a doctrine in which were discerned the outlines of a military strategy that would, in time, give the US administration the confidence to remain politically committed to seeing the operation in Iraq through to a more positive outcome than appeared possible in 2006.[15] It was against this background that the recommendations of the Baker-Hamilton Report, to wind down the US operation as soon as possible, were superceded by the decision to 'surge' a further five brigade combat teams (BCTs) into Iraq, while pursuing ever closer partnership with the ISF, in order to grow them in numbers, capability and confidence faster, so that transition, when it came, would be more sustainable.[16]

The UK was a bystander in terms of the debate over the 'surge', both because Washington did not seek to engage London in the debate and also because the British government was, by this time, largely set on a path of withdrawal out of an increasingly unpopular conflict, whatever the circumstances, and the shifting of focus to the neglected campaign in Afghanistan. However, the UK's influence through this period was significant in two respects, irrespective of the level of US reinforcement. First, Lieutenant General Graeme Lamb, the Multi-National Force – Iraq (MNF-I) deputy to Generals Casey and then Petraeus, argued strongly and effectively for physical barrier measures akin to those used in Northern Ireland, to reduce the opportunities for, and effect of, violence against civilians in Baghdad. Second, and more importantly, he convinced the US high command, and even the Shi'ite-dominated government, that despite their distaste for the prospect, opportunities existed to engage with elements of the Iraqi Sunni insurgency, particularly among the tribes of Anbar, and to exploit their disaffection with the Zarqawists and jihadists.

My own contribution at the Corps level, working for Generals Chiarelli and then Odierno, was to advocate that a better use of even the extant US force levels would be to hug the ISF ever closer by embedding in, and partnering with, their units and formations at every level. Given the inevitability of eventual security transition, either via a US 'surge' or not, I argued that the ISF would grow more quickly in confidence and competence by closer proximity to the US troops. Thus their capabilities would develop faster, and we could more effectively instil a sense of national responsibility, while limiting any capacity, or inclination, to act in a sectarian manner.

The new strategy straddled politics and reconstruction but had at its heart the concept that 'the people were the prize', and that the right combination of understanding, tactics and narrative would remove many of the insurgents from the field of their own volition. It acknowledged that a one-dimensional reliance on 'kill or capture', where feelings of dishonour, humiliation and revenge would inevitably breed countless new opponents, was fundamentally counterproductive. The key was to focus on 'protecting the people'.[17] 'Security', as an objective, needed to be interpreted in the widest possible sense. The 'surge', along with the growth of the ISF, was clearly a critical element in giving the population, particularly in Baghdad, a greater sense of security. This was accompanied by major projects to give physical protection to sectarian communities by erecting barriers and checkpoints, which made the job of the car and suicide bombers more difficult, deterred the militia death squads and acted as a check on ethnic and confessional cleansing. A clear-out of many of the senior leaders of the NP removed much of their propensity for sectarian activity. The renewed US commitment gave confidence to the government of Iraq, and it also allowed the US to put increasing pressure on them to act in the national interest and reach out to those elements of the Sunni population that sought political accommodation.

Of vital importance was the recognition that, if the Shi'ite majority could be protected against Sunni and jihadi violence, Shi'ite militias could be persuaded into an uneasy, but real, state of truce with CF, leaving the US and ISF to concentrate on al-Qa'ida, who represented the mutual enemy. The second key strand was the recognition and acknowledgement that Sunni resistance and violence were not monolithic, and that there were significant and expanding fault lines between Iraqi Sunnis on the one hand and the jihadists and foreign fighters on the other. Under al-Zarqawi the latter had embarked on a spree of violence that drew no distinction between the CF, Shi'ites or Sunni 'compromisers', and was indiscriminate in the killing of men, women and children. In order to keep the Sunni tribes of Anbar in line, as their enthusiasm for violence ebbed, the jihadists had resorted to ever more grisly control measures and retribution. In Ramadi the USA had identified this and, by protecting the local population, had set the conditions for a local rejection of the jihadists which in time grew into the 'Sunni Awakening' and the Sunni 'Sons of Iraq'.[18]

In the face of this setback, al-Qa'ida launched a ferocious counter-offensive in early 2007. As more and more areas of insurgent control were now contested, violence continued to rise, testing the nerves of politicians and military alike. However, a potent combination of high-tech intelligence gathering, well-targeted special forces' operations, growing cooperation with the Sunni tribes and partnered operations with an increasingly confident ISF led to a rapid decimation of al-Qa'ida's leadership, and the destruction of its networks in western Iraq throughout 2007. With this came the important, albeit reluctant, agreement of the Iraqi government to the recognition, and bankrolling, of the 'Sons of Iraq', previously seen as the enemy. The combination of these actions and initiatives increased the credibility of the Iraqi government, as it did that of the ISF, and with it came a greater confidence among the people, of all parts of Iraqi society, in supporting the legitimate power bases. Suddenly, in mid-2007, the levels of violence plummeted, and remained consistently low as the jihadist campaign culminated, faltered and largely died, while the JAM remained in an uneasy, but sustained truce.

Therefore, by 2007, although many of the strategic objectives of the US-led invasion of Iraq had already been fatally undermined – not least that of reversing Iranian regional and nuclear ambitions – the new US 'strategy' had at least now given the operations and tactics on the ground the context, coherence, relevance and focus that had previously been lacking. The effect on the overall campaign was transformative in scale and nature. At the same time the jihadist strategy, with its emphasis on violence and maximalist agenda, had catalysed a fault line in the overall Sunni insurgency, allowing the CF and ISF to exploit it to the advantage of the Coalition and all Iraqi citizens. Violence by no means stopped, but the beneficial outcome of success in this 'clash of strategies' led to the measurable levels of operational success that permitted an orderly transition of security responsibility in the 2010–12 period, and a well-managed withdrawal of US and Coalition troops.

Notes

1. This chapter was written in May 2012.
2. Attributed to President Ronald Reagan, 1982.
3. This is often attributed to Sun Tzu, but is not found in his classic book *The Art of War*. It is probably apocryphal, but nonetheless highly instructive.
4. Simon Mayall, *Jihad: The Clash within Civilization* (Seaford House Papers, 2003).
5. Samuel P. Huntington, *The Clash of Civilizations and the Remaking of the World Order* (London, 1997).
6. Karl von Clausewitz, *On War* (Princeton, 1976), p. 54.
7. 'Abd al-Bari Atwan, *The Secret History of al-Qa'ida* (London, 2006), p. 197.
8. Ibid., pp. 199–206.
9. Ibid., p. 200.
10. US planning predicted forces levels dropping from c.140,000 to c.30,000 by October 2003. During the 'surge' of 2007 they actually rose to c.160,000.
11. Atwan, *The Secret History*, p. 252.
12. Sadrists took their name from the Shi'ite radical cleric Muqtada al-Sadr, whose father, the Grand Ayatollah Muhammad al-Sadr, had been killed by Saddam Hussein in 1999. JAM was set up in 2003 as a response to the US invasion.
13. Thomas E. Ricks, *The Gamble: General David Petraeus and the American Military Adventure in Iraq, 2006–2008* (London, 2009), p. 53.
14. General Eric Shinseki, quoted in Mackubin Thomas Owen, 'Marines Turned Soldiers', *National Review Online*, 10 December 2001 (http://old.nationalreview.com/comment/comment-owens121001.shtml,

last accessed 10 February 2014). Shinseki eventually fell out with Bush, Wolfowitz and Rumsfeld when he recommended far higher troop numbers to achieve strategic success in Iraq.

15. Ricks, *The Gamble*, p. 76.

16. Baker-Hamilton Report, named after the Chairmen of the Iraq Study Group (ISG), set up on 15 March 2006 and reporting to President George W. Bush on 6 December 2006.

17. General David Petraeus, 'Learning Counterinsurgency: Observations from Soldiering in Iraq', *The Military Review* 86 (January/February 2006): 2–12. In December 2006 *Counter Insurgency FM3–24* was published.

18. Ricks, *The Gamble*, pp. 202–8.

Bibliography

Atwan, 'Abd al- Bari, *The Secret History of al-Qa'ida* (London, 2006).

von Clausewitz, Karl, *On War* (Princeton, 1976).

Huntington, Samuel P., *The Clash of Civilizations and the Remaking of the World Order* (London, 1997).

Mayall, Simon, *Jihad: The Clash within Civilization* (Seaford House Papers, 2003).

Owens, Mackubin Thomas, 'Marines Turned Soldiers', *National Review On-line*, 10 December 2001 (http://old.nationalreview.com/comment/comment-owens121001.shtml, last accessed 10 February 2014).

Petraeus, David, 'Learning Counterinsurgency: Observations from Soldiering in Iraq', *The Military Review* 86 (January/February 2006): 2–12.

Ricks, Thomas E., *The Gamble: General David Petraeus and the American Military Adventure in Iraq, 2006–2008* (London, 2009).

Part III

Representations of Jihad
in Modern Culture

14

Yemen's Al-Qa'ida and Poetry as a Weapon of Jihad

Elisabeth Kendall

Throughout history, poetry has played a central role in Arab culture, punctuating a broad range of activities, from tribal occasions and political events through to the simple get-togethers of everyday life. The power of poetry to move Arab listeners and readers emotionally, to infiltrate the psyche and to create an aura of tradition, authenticity and legitimacy around the ideologies it enshrines make it a perfect weapon for militant jihadist causes. Osama bin Laden himself composed poetry, including, perhaps most famously, his ode celebrating the destruction of the USS *Cole* in 2000, which he recited at his son's wedding. Another of bin Laden's poems was found in an abandoned safehouse in Kabul following al-Qa'ida's withdrawal, having been distributed among trainee jihadists as a powerful propagandist exhortation to fight.[1]

Over the last three decades, several Islamic extremist magazines (paper and digital) have regularly featured poetry extolling the virtues of, and rewards for, militant jihad. However, scholars and analysts alike have almost entirely neglected contemporary Arabic jihadist poetry, skipping over it in favour of more direct pronouncements, rulings and position statements. Yet poetry can carry messages to a broader audience as it plugs naturally into a long tradition of oral transmission, particularly on the Arabian Peninsula, spreading ideas through repeated recitation and chanting and through conversion into anthems (*nashid, nasha'id*). This is particularly important in regions where internet, photocopying and printing facilities are either difficult or prohibitively expensive to access. From an analyst's perspective, poetry also reveals clues about jihadist motivation, group dynamics and cultural concerns, which can help to illuminate the contemporary political landscape in which it is deployed. In the quest to understand the hearts and minds of those who practise militant jihad, neglecting to interrogate the poetry that speaks to both would seem a fundamental oversight.

This chapter, therefore, explores the functions and characteristics of the Arabic poetry deployed by jihadists. First, it situates the practice of exploiting poetry for political and religious purposes in its historical continuum. Next, it interrogates the continuing relevance of such poetry today using original primary survey research and relates this specifically to the new al-Qa'ida heartland, Yemen. Finally, the chapter explores the various functions of jihadist poetry today. The main source of the poetry used for these investigations is the Arabic-language magazine of 'Qa'idat al-Jihad in the Arabian Peninsula' (often referred to as al-Qa'ida in the Arabian Peninsula or AQAP). This is the Yemeni-based journal *Sada al-Malahim* (*The Echo of Epic Battles*), released online 2008–11. Given that this investigation focuses more on the socio-political role of poetry than on its aesthetics, mining jihadist magazines rather than poetry anthologies reaps several added benefits: the poetry can be observed within its functioning context; there is a greater immediacy to its inclusion and role, as opposed to the more studied selection involved in compiling an anthology; and, in addition to the publication of whole poems, magazine articles are themselves studded with a great many isolated verses. The chapter concludes with observations regarding the importance of poetry as a resource, not just for cultural and literary analysis, but also for political and counter-terrorism analysis.

Jihadist Poetry in Historical Context

The use of Arabic poetry by today's jihadists comes at the end of a long tradition of poetry employed as a cultural tool to win social and political capital, dating back to pre-Islamic times in Arabia. The annual market at 'Ukaz, just outside Mecca, 'was as much about poetry as about trade'.[2] At this and others of the dozen or so major markets in pre-Islamic

Arabia, including the one in Mahra (now eastern Yemen) which served as an important forum for the southern Arabian tribes, old epics were recited alongside new poems aimed at elevating leaders or denigrating opponents, often accompanying political agendas such as the settling of blood feuds or the celebration of an alliance.[3] This poetic tradition continued to thrive into Islamic times.

The evidence does not support the notion – still held in some quarters[4] – that the Prophet Muhammad reviled poets as liars or magicians. This notion probably springs from the story that Muhammad himself was so shocked by the experience of receiving the first revelations that he worried that he might be a madman or a poet under demonic influence and considered killing himself. The Angel Gabriel intervened to convince him that his inspiration came from a divine source. Naturally, Muhammad's fellow Meccans also associated his revelations with their experiences of poetry, particularly given that the revelations were in rhymed prose (*saj'*). It was therefore natural for the Qur'an to address these accusations by clarifying that Muhammad was not a poet, for his revelations came directly from Allah.[5] Taken in context, therefore, it is clear that poetry and poets per se were not outlawed. The point was simply that Muhammad was to be considered a prophet, not a poet. Poetry was deemed acceptable, indeed actively useful, as long as it was Islamic rather than emanating from a demonic source.[6]

There is much evidence that Muhammad understood well the potential power of poetry and actively deployed it to spread the new religion. Ibn Kathir (d.1373) – a medieval historian upon whom Osama bin Laden drew extensively in his speeches – mentions that the Prophet welcomed poets who came to him with compositions praising him and celebrating Islam's early battle campaigns.[7] Ibn Rashiq (d.c.1070), in his famous medieval work on poetry, reports:

> Concerning the poets who supported him and parried against the polytheists on his behalf, like Hassan ibn Thabit, Ka'b ibn Malik and 'Abd Allah ibn Rawaha, the Prophet used to say: 'Indeed this group inflicts more damage on the people of Mecca than a hail of arrows could do!'[8]

This suggests that deploying poetry was a conscious strategy adopted by Muhammad. Today's jihadists have adopted the same strategy. Indeed, verses from all three of 'the Prophet's poets' named above are included in the Yemeni jihadist journal *Sada al-Malahim*.[9] Thus in January 2011, we find a pep talk addressed to the jihadists, advising them to draw strength by chanting the following verses by 'Abd Allah ibn Rawaha:

> But I ask the Merciful for forgiveness
> and for a fearful blow that will make my blood gush out,
> or to be stabbed by zealous hands armed
> with a spear that will rip through the bowels and liver.[10]

This demonstrates the intention to use poetry to strengthen resolve. It also hints at a possible weakening of morale among the jihadists, perhaps owing to President Obama's launch of a concerted campaign of drone strikes against them. In fact, this turned out to be al-Qa'ida's final issue of the Yemen-based magazine, indicating that the jihadists were indeed under real pressure.

The deployment of poetry as an auxiliary weapon in militant campaigns did not lie dormant from the time of Muhammad until being picked up by today's jihadists but, again, research into this phenomenon is sparse. There is abundant evidence of poetry composed to inspire, impassion, console or intimidate during the Crusades. Carole Hillenbrand writes of '[scholarly] neglect of a whole corpus of jihad poetry, which is scattered through Muslim chronicles, biographical dictionaries and medieval anthologies'.[11] Greater attention has, however, been given to the earlier uses of poetry by the Kharijites, a radical militant group that emerged within 30 years of Muhammad's death and believed in killing anyone who did not share their beliefs regarding leadership.[12] This doctrine has led to some obvious comparisons between Kharijites and today's jihadists, although the latter vehemently reject the Kharijite label and have issued numerous rebuttals, including in their magazine *Sada al-Malahim*.[13] In fact, one rebuttal is actually communicated using poetry, in a verse from a contemporary ode (*qasida*) called 'Qissat Mujahid' ('The Jihadist's Story') composed by Sheikh Abu al-Bara' al-Awlaqi. This jihadist poet was one of the perpetrators of two ambushes on security patrols in Shabwa that killed 11 Yemeni soldiers in the space of three days in July 2010, and his verses likely commemorate his fellow jihadists who were 'martyred' in the second of the ambushes:

> They accused him unjustly of being one of the Kharijites; if he were,
> then would that all God's servants were Kharijites emulating him.

Would that he who lampoons him time and again
would [instead] lampoon and denounce apostasy and belittle it.[14]

Despite such rebuttals, Osama bin Laden quoted Kharijite poetry in several of his speeches, and there is even a verse in *Sada al-Malahim* that, although unattributed in the jihadist magazine, can in fact be identified as poetry composed by the brutal Kharijite leader, Qatari ibn al-Fuja'a (d. *c.*698).[15] Hence jihadist poetry today fits into a long tradition of poetry composed and deployed to support the Islamic faith and rally the believers. But does today's continuation of the poetic tradition by jihadists simply spring from the desire to emulate their pious warrior forebears in as many ways as possible, or does poetry retain genuine popular relevance in their contemporary world?

Is Poetry Still Relevant in the Arabia of Today?

The publication recently of collections of poems penned by Guantanamo prisoners and the Afghan Taliban[16] has surprised many western commentators who perhaps considered the art of poetry to be at odds with the stereotypical image of the hardened jihadist.[17] Both the Guantanamo and the Taliban volumes focus on the lyrical qualities of the poetry, so neither showcases the kind of aggressive messages and violent imagery that abound in the poetry of Yemen's jihadists published in *Sada al-Malahim*. However, at the very least they highlight the continuing role of poetry in providing solace, emotional release and spiritual sustenance.

But how popular is poetry? To gain an insight into the contemporary importance of poetry in al-Qa'ida's Yemen heartlands, and in the absence of any existing data, this author asked a scientifically randomised sample of over 2,000 inhabitants of eastern Yemen for their views.[18] A question about the importance of poetry in contemporary cultural life was inserted discreetly amid a battery of socio-economic questions in a general survey to avoid any overt focus that might skew results towards a positive outcome. The survey was conducted in December 2012 by local fieldworkers, men and women, face to face to capture illiterate respondents of both genders. A startling 74 per cent of respondents believed that poetry was either 'important' or 'very important' in their culture today. This accords with the impression of popularity conveyed by Flagg Miller's detailed research into audio-cassette poetry in the Yafi' region

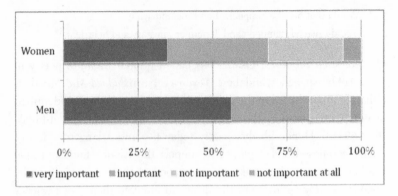

Figure 1 The importance of poetry in contemporary culture in eastern Yemen.

spanning the al-Qa'ida heartlands of Lahij and Abyan governorates in the 1990s.[19] To put the survey result in a broader context, a similar question asked in Egypt in late 2011 yielded a result of only 6 per cent.[20] In order to understand more about the audience for poetry in eastern Yemen, this result was correlated with other questions. Poetry was found to be very slightly more important among the desert tribes than along the more sedentary coast, among those in the poorest economic group and among those who carry a gun (a result which was not explained simply by any greater prevalence of guns in desert locations). Surprisingly perhaps, the presence of a television and level of education made no discernible impact, and the importance of poetry was only very weakly correlated to increased age. Finally, poetry was found to be more important among men (82 per cent) than women (69 per cent). This is not surprising since it is the men who mainly recite at formal gatherings (see Figure 1).

In Yemen, the capacity of poetry to spread ideas is particularly relevant, given the persistence of oral tradition. Poetry is therefore likely to endure beyond the lifetime of the other contents of a jihadist magazine since it is easily memorised and passed on orally. Reading jihadist magazines aloud was one of the strategies recommended by Abu Mus'ab al-Suri, al-Qa'ida's erstwhile propagandist in London, in his plans for the propagation of a jihadist agenda.[21] This is especially important in Yemen where internet penetration is extremely low. Statistics are difficult to come by, but in the easternmost Mahra governorate, for example, only 3 per cent of the population has internet access.[22] Anwar al-Awlaqi (d.2011 in a drone strike), a US-born member of al-Qa'ida in Yemen, recognised this when he encouraged poets and singers to engage their talents to spread militant jihadist messages in his booklet '44 Ways to Support Jihad'.[23] The fact that contemporary jihadist journals use poetic verses directly alongside quotations from the Qur'an and hadith to illustrate points demonstrates how deep-rooted and revered the poetic tradition remains, particularly in tribal areas of Yemen.[24]

But does the listener or reader understand the poetry? This question about language necessarily arises, given the jihadist predilection for the use of classical Arabic despite the prevalence of regional dialects and, in some areas of Yemen, separate South Arabian languages.[25] Only one of the 172 poems and isolated verses in the jihadist journal *Sada al-Malahim* is composed in colloquial Arabic. To understand this seeming mismatch, one must appreciate the sacred nature and beauty of classical Arabic and its effect on the listener or reader. The language of poetry emulates the language in which the Qur'an was revealed; and, much like the Qur'an, the poetic language with its musicality, rhymes and rhythms can speak to listeners on a subliminal level, even when – in the most classical verses – little more than the keywords and stock phrases and themes are actively understood. Jihadist publications make liberal use of poetry from the classical heritage (which they largely fail to attribute), but which listeners might find faintly familiar from oral tradition. Contemporary compositions, whilst overwhelmingly adopting the form of the classical *qasida* with its double hemistich verses and monorhyme, tend to offer shorter lines with a simpler grammatical structure and more accessible vocabulary than those appropriated from the literary heritage. The beauty of the language, solemn intonation, pattern and rhythms found in more classical poems could not fail to impress, as is clear from the large number of YouTube hits that some of these poems receive.[26] This is particularly apparent when the poems are set to images (often of jihadists training or dead children in Iraq and Gaza) with faint background music and a 'reverb effect' that emphasises the monorhyme and heightens the sense of gravitas in the apocalyptic battle between good and evil that is the underlying theme running through most poems. Hirschkind's research into Islamic cassette sermons in Cairo similarly corroborates the theory that the emotional effects of sound can have more of an impact than the meanings of the words themselves.[27] And the auditory impact of rhymed and chanted poetry is likely to be even greater than that of a sermon.

Throughout the period (2008–11) that Yemen's *Sada al-Malahim* continued to publish, only 11 per cent of the contemporary poems showcased failed to adopt the classical *qasida* form. Such poems tend to be simpler than the *qasida* poetry, with punchy economical lines that would facilitate memorisation and be highly suitable for conversion into *nashid*s (jihadist anthems). Take the following example, which comes at the end of an article emphasising the USA's weakness exacerbated by the financial crisis in what the article perceives to be the imminent collapse of capitalism:

> I will fasten my explosive belt,
> I will shudder like a lightening bolt
> and rush by like a torrential stream
> and resound like stormy thunder.
> In my heart is the heart of a volcano.
> I will sweep through the land like a flood.
> For I live by the Qur'an
> as I remember the Merciful.
> My steadfastness lies in faith
> so let the day of the Qur'an come.
> For I live by the Qur'an
> as I remember the Merciful.
> My steadfastness lies in faith
> so let the day of the Holy Book come
> to demolish the thrones of the tyrant.
> My voice is the loudest voice
> for I do not fear false clerics.
> I will live and die for Allah.[28]

This kind of poem would be considerably more comprehensible than those appropriated from the classical heritage, yet it retains an aura of historical authenticity despite the clearly modern message of a suicide bomber employing relatively modern technologies of destruction (the 'explosive belt'). It achieves this through strategies such as relaying natural images – torrential streams, stormy thunder, floods, volcanoes.

Such references to nature were a common feature of traditional desert poetry dating back to the pre-Islamic period. It also strikes a note of authenticity and symbolically sanctifies the content by vocalising the Arabic text. Vowels are not marked in modern Arabic texts (including contemporary poetry), but they are a notable feature of the Qur'an and of much of the religious literature surrounding it. These strategies, together with the frequent references to Allah and the Qur'an, imbue the poem with a historicity that legitimates its message. This leads us to consider our final question regarding the functions of contemporary jihadist poetry.

What are the Functions of Jihadist Poetry Today?

Since this research seeks to illuminate the uses of jihadist poetry, rather than its aesthetics, this section will analyse the poetry by function and point out some of the literary devices exploited to fulfil these functions, rather than taking a more traditional typological approach that discusses the literary components of each type. The functions of jihadist poetry can be divided into three broad and interlocking categories – practical, ideological and emotional – which will be dealt with in turn. Some of the practical functions of the poetry, such as the easy, inexpensive and powerful propagation of ideas through oral transmission, have already been raised. Another practical function is to set the scene or clinch an argument by strategic placement of isolated verses of poetry in articles, often near the beginning or the end. For example, al-Qa'ida in Yemen put out a call in 2008 for skilled professionals such as doctors, engineers and those with some knowledge of chemistry, physics or journalism to join the jihadist cause. The interest and emotions of the targeted professionals are engaged through the inclusion of a poetic verse mid-article to encapsulate the broad problem they are being asked to address. Namely, Islam needs (their) help to restore its glory so that it can rise again to its former heights:

> Wherever you turn to Islam in any country,
> you find it like a bird with its wings clipped.[29]

Perhaps surprisingly, the jihadists are comfortable relying on poetry directly alongside citations from the Qur'an or hadith to illustrate the same point. The above verse is sandwiched between two passages of the Qur'an.

In the practical function of argument, poetry has the added advantage of papering over cracks in logic or avoiding the necessity of providing evidence by guiding an argument into an emotional rather than intellectual crescendo. In making the case in 2009 for a revolution against the Yemeni regime, the manifold problems with the ruling Salih family are summarised simply by a line of poetry:

> They govern mankind without a heart;
> their interests are served and they are called leaders.

Similarly, rather than making an argument for militant action as the best route for wresting the land from the regime, this is simply given as the stated solution and placed beyond argument by being enshrined in poetry:

> That land will not be mighty
> until its people fight its rulers.[30]

Many of the poems also provide a vital documentary function. Hungarian sociologist Karl Mannheim argues that there are three levels of meaning in a cultural act: objective, expressive and documentary.[31] The objective meaning is inherent in the act itself (for our purposes, a bombing or ambush, for example). The expressive meaning involves the intention behind the act (here, the expression of power for the jihadists and glory for Allah). The documentary meaning is considered by Mannheim as the most important because it relates the act to its broader context. It is here that poetry can play a crucial role, for it provides a credible format for documenting the unseen elements of jihadist acts, particularly suicide operations, which cannot be documented objectively. Poems construct an attractive image of the suicide bomber being welcomed and seen to by the virgins of Paradise in green meadows with rivers. His body is whole and smells of musk, rather than mutilated and blackened. He died calmly with a smile on his lips, rather than sweating and petrified. This kind of mythologising documentary would help to encourage a steady stream of recruits. We find the following verses among readers' contributions in 2010, in the context of praise for martyrdom operations conducted by their brothers in the Maghreb. The mention of Abu al-Bara'

Abd al-Malik indicates that these verses were inspired by the escalation of jihadist operations in Algeria in 2008 under al-Qa'ida in the Islamic Maghreb.

> The virgins of Paradise dressed up and shone with radiance
> hoping to meet the knights who strike fear.
> They spoke softly and smiled,
> 'Is there any lion who has ascended to be united in love?
> Is there a loved one who is a reverent jihadist
> who is gaining entry to the gardens of Paradise and hope?
> Is there any fiancé (for us) who is a knight and a warrior,
> advancing and diving among the blades (of swords)?
> Is there any martyr whom we desire to be united with us in love,
> and whose dowry is a flowing ocean of blood?'[32]

However, poetry does not just document and report (what cultural theorists call 'constative'), it also creatively brings to life the contents of the poem (what cultural theorists call 'performative'), and it is through the symbolic performance of conflict that cultures of resistance are most effective.[33] In other words, poetry is a means of reinforcing fundamental jihadist messages by 'performing' them. Here the function is at once practical, ideological and emotional. For example, the previous verses perform the scene of virgins primping themselves in Paradise in eager anticipation of intercourse with the next martyr, thus reinforcing messages to would-be jihadists about the route to reward, happiness and sexual gratification. Jihadist poetry provides a vehicle for enacting various different aspects of the overarching struggle between good and evil. It performs various routes to happiness, reward, honour, victory and salvation and, conversely, the routes to misery, oppression, corruption, punishment, shame and damnation. Not only does poetry function as a site of symbolic struggle, its effect turns it into a catalyst for real struggle as it inspires its listeners. Thus the poem is a living, active and reproductive event that will itself be repeated and passed on, rather than remaining merely a passive report. The following verses perform the act of a suicide bomber, recreating both the fear of potential victims and the rush of the power 'high' felt by the bomber:

> I am among them, a ghost exacerbating their torture.
> They will know nothing of my coming and going

until destruction looms in their public spaces
and they fall in throngs.[34]

Moving now to more overt ideological functions, jihadist poetry plays a major role in helping to produce a jihadist identity. There is no clear original jihadist identity, only a constantly repeated imitation of the idea of the original. Poetry helps to create this, for example, by referencing heroic figures from Islamic history, employing well-known tropes (such as referring to jihadists as lions and warriors), employing hyperbole when mentioning contemporary jihadist acts, eulogising martyrs and mythologising their virtues. Consolidation of the jihadist identity is facilitated by constructing it against an 'other' through a process of essentialism. Just as English literature helped to construct a British imperialist identity that portrayed Africans as ignorant savages that needed to be saved and taught, jihadist poetry helps to construct a pure Islamic identity against an 'other'. Western countries are blurred together and stigmatised, generally using the terms Zionists, Crusaders, Americans and English,[35] while the regimes that collaborate with them, especially Arab, are denounced as allies, clients and dogs of these Zionist Crusaders. Constructing a coherent enemy 'other' helps to produce a sense of identity and common global cause for jihadist struggles that may in fact be fuelled in large part by local and regional concerns.[36] The USA itself contributed to this process when it constructed named entities out of loose concepts with the barest of common denominators in order to fulfil its own need for a coherent enemy: al-Qa'ida, the 'Axis of Evil' and the 'War on Terror' are all in reality opaque and diffuse ideas.

The polarisation of the jihadist and his enemy is thus achieved through essentialising their respective positions. This is aided by a strategy of binary opposition, meaning that the interpretation of one term is generated by reference to another term. This steers and manipulates the reader/listener's perception of the world. The poetry is replete with oppositions leading from the basic countering of jihadists (*mujahidun*) against infidels (*kuffar*). The effect of this opposition (or juxtaposition) is to stretch the meaning of the latter term – 'infidels' – to include anyone who does not support the jihadists, thus including even nominal Muslims. Cultural Studies scholars Andrew Edgar and Peter Sedgwick confirm that 'the analysis of such series of oppositions provides a crucial insight into the working of ideology'.[37] In fact, ideology spreads and takes effect to the degree that binary oppositions are taken for granted, for they appear to be reflecting the world whereas in reality they are actively structuring it. What is particularly interesting is to note how the overarching binary oppositions (good/evil, jihadist/infidel, believer/apostate) in global jihadist ideology can be flexed to suit the local context. In the Yemen-based *Sada al-Malahim* magazine, for example, we find 'lions', referring to the Yemen-based jihadists, versus 'ants' – referring not just to Jews, but to anyone aligned with them. The following non-consecutive verses are from a *qasida* tellingly attributed to Hadi al-Jihad, a pseudonym literally meaning 'The Inducer of Jihad':

> So they called the Jews with their cunning and their retinue
> ants crawling in the forest of lions.
> O He who submits to Allah, O Servant to Him,
> Behind me is a Jew, the brother of hatred.
> So kill him, purge our land of his filth
> so that no abodes of apostasy remain.[38]

We also find the jihadists – significantly including all those who support them, not just the active fighters – placed in binary opposition to infidels – also significantly now implicating unsympathetic Yemeni sheikhs – in the following non-consecutive verses:

> We are the men of al-Qa'ida, we are the supporters (*ansar*),
> we are your troops, O Osama bin Laden.
> We are the men of war and noble heroes,
> and with us are those who give full support and those who display courage.
> The Crusaders and anyone allied with them are infidels,
> [Even] if he be a sheikh wearing his turban.[39]

We find several other oppositions constructed through a local lens, such as supporters (*ansar*) versus procrastinators (*murji'un*, referring to those individuals and tribes who are sympathetic to but not actively joining the jihad); true clerics (those who support the Yemeni jihadists) versus false clerics (those who condemn their acts as un-Islamic); and loyal Muslims versus al-Aswad al-Unsi (a false seventh-century Yemeni prophet who is used as a euphemism for then Yemeni President Ali Abdullah Salih). This local flavour that the poetry helps to infuse into the global jihadist binary opposition of good versus evil supports the view of Laurent Bonnefoy, who argues that jihad in Yemen is largely a product of locally generated context and contingencies, onto which ideologies of global jihad are grafted.[40]

The use of poetry, given its status as an ancient and revered cultural practice on the Arabian Peninsula, in and of itself lends credibility to the jihadist movement. The use of the respected *qasida* form and sacred classical language in particular help to legitimate the ideologies contained in the poetry, as mentioned above. However, a further and perhaps equally powerful strategy for ideological validation is the reconstruction of a tradition, into which contemporary acts are situated. Jihadist acts thus become the natural culmination of a long chain of seemingly comparable acts from Islam's glorious past. In other words, legitimacy is established through the impression of continuity, as contemporary acts and ideals are back-projected onto an existing historical lineage. The following verses demonstrate this historical continuum in action through their construction of contemporary jihadist operations both as an extension of Islam's earliest battles for survival and as an apocalyptic struggle that is destined to continue until the end of time:

> The greatness of the umma lies in a blend of blood and dust
> at Badr and al-Yarmuk and the Battle of al-Yamama.
> Our jihad will not be stopped by the many dangers,
> our jihad from the past until the Day of Judgment.[41]

The jihadists' use of the poetry genre and their appropriation of historical figures and events into the poetry can be seen as part of a bid to win what French sociologist Pierre Bourdieu would term cultural capital.[42] Like economic capital, cultural capital is a resource to be exploited in the pursuit of power. Al-Qa'ida in the Arabian Peninsula is culturally constructed as the contemporary manifestation of an epic struggle for Islam that dates back to the earliest days of the Prophet.

One contemporary poem entitled 'The Voice of Osama to the People of *Shahama* (Gallantry)' likewise invokes the early Islamic Battle of Badr in 624 and heroic deeds of the Prophet Muhammad's Companions, in an attempt to persuade more men to take up militant jihad. The poem throws down a direct challenge to Yemeni tribesmen to live up to Islam's early heroes, invoking famous names that would be especially aspirational for a largely impoverished generation with an otherwise bleak future:

> Our sheikh [Osama bin Laden] is calling the tribes to
>   follow the example of the Beloved,
> Support Islam, O people of guns and rifles.
> . . .
> Why is there no one like Mus'ab and Khalid and al-Khabib
> and Ibn Abu al-Waqqas who led the young warrior-knights?
> If only among you were the likes of Hamza and the
>   intelligent Abu Bakr.[43]

History is an effective tool, since no Muslim, even those who are not supportive of modern-day militant jihad, can argue with the acts of Islam's early martyrs. Therefore, identifying modern-day operations with early Islam's acts of martyrdom provides powerful justification.

Finally, poetry's most intrinsic function lies in its emotional power to move people to feel, think or act in a certain way. There is an abundance of verses designed to prepare listeners psychologically to undertake jihad. This might be done relatively discreetly by inspiring outrage through the description of injustices, or it may be achieved through overt incitement, as in the following example. The following lines from the same contemporary composition demonstrate how the jihadist appeal is directed at entrenched tribal values of honour and shame, but these are then situated within the broader loyalty framework of Islam:

> Where are you, O virile men, O poison of war?
> Where are you as apostasy violates the holy places of the Arabs?
> Where are you and where is the audacity that seems to be absent in you?
> Where are you as Muhammad's community burns in flames?
> Where are you as dignity screams at the Sons of the Cross?
> Where are you as Jerusalem lies captured and is plundered time and again?[44]

Poetry also provides a powerful emotional means of reassuring current and future recruits by confirming the worth of recent martyrs, praising their virile qualities and celebrating their achievements at the same time as mourning their loss. Such compositions play on traditional types of Arabic poetry by combining the well-known functions of *madh* (praise), *ritha'* (lament) and *hija'* (lampooning the enemy).

Conclusion

Despite significant differences among leading theorists on many issues pertaining to jihad theory and practice, all agree that ideological indoctrination and spiritual preparation should take precedence over military training.[45] For militant jihadists, poetry is key to achieving this, through the practical, ideological and emotional functions outlined above. Given that grass-roots recruits tend to be shaped as much by passion as by ideology, it is worth studying the poetry that sparks and fuels passion. The above investigation has shown how poetry can inject ideas into the deep psyche through a cocktail of techniques: powerful images, historical allusions and parallels, linguistic beauty, rhyme or rhythm and metre. All are framed within the broader apocalyptic struggle between good and evil and imbued with a long sense of tradition, both religious and literary (oral). This lends authenticity to the messages conveyed, using the genre of poetry, whose widespread popularity is proven still to persist today.

It therefore seems surprising that counter-terrorism efforts have not yet made full use of poetry as a vehicle for counter-propaganda. Thomas Johnson of the US Naval Academy suggested that the USA should retaliate against Taliban poetry with compositions of its own,[46] but Afghanistan scholars Alex Strick van Linschoten and Felix Kuehn have dismissed this idea as inappropriate. This dismissal may perhaps be correct with regard to Taliban poetry, given that its content appears significantly more human and personal than that of contemporary jihadist poetry in Yemen.[47] The latter's highly aggressive content, militant tone and propagandist function make it a natural priority for cultural counter-propaganda. Moreover, competing for hearts and minds through poetry has a long history in Arab culture that stretches back to pre-Islamic times. One poet would champion one side of an argument, and another would compose a verse to challenge it in a back-and-forth poetic joust. This jousting tradition has continued into modern-day Yemen, both verse-by-verse and poem-by-poem, as observed, for example, in the struggles between conservatives and reformers during the first half of the twentieth century that were articulated popularly through poetry.[48] It is therefore unsurprising to find jihadists, in Yemen but also elsewhere, releasing poetry to spread their worldviews and win support. In the words of Saudi jihadist Ibrahim Rubaysh, who became a spiritual leader of al-Qaʻida in

Yemen following his release from Guantanamo, and whose poetry appears in *Sada al-Malahim*: 'The poet's words are the font of our power.'[49] And yet poetry remains almost universally overlooked by analysts, both as a source of insight into hearts and minds and as a potential vehicle for counter-propaganda. In short, poetry as a weapon is currently being stockpiled in only one arsenal: that of the jihadists.

Notes

1. David Rohde and C. J. Chivers, 'Al Qaeda's grocery lists and manuals of killing', *New York Times*, 17 March 2002.
2. Barnaby Rogerson, *The Prophet Muhammad: A Biography* (London, 2004), p. 18.
3. Rogerson, *The Prophet Muhammad*, p. 19.
4. A typical example of the polemical Western literature is Richard Gabriel's work on Muhammad, which asserts: 'Muhammad seems to have possessed an acute sensitivity to personal ridicule. He hated poets and singers... Muhammad seems to have had a deep loathing for poets per se.' *Muhammad: Islam's First Great General* (Norman, 2007), p. 65.
5. Q. 36:69 and Q. 69:41.
6. A useful discussion can be found in Michael Zwettler, 'A mantic manifesto: the sura of "The Poets" and the Qur'anic foundations of Prophetic authority', in James L. Kugel (ed.), *Poetry and Prophecy: The Beginnings of a Literary Tradition* (New York, 1990): 75–119 (81–2).
7. Ibn Kathir, *Mawlid*, p. 30. See: http://sunnah.org/publication/mawlid.htm (last accessed 31 January 2014).
8. Ibn Rashiq, *al-'Umda fi Mahasin al-Shi'r wa-Adabi-hi wa-Naqdi-hi* (Beirut, 1972), Vol. 1, p. 40. This is also cited in J. C. Bürgel, 'Qasida as discourse on power and its Islamization: some reflections', in Stefan Sperl and Christopher Shackle (eds.), *Qasida Poetry in Islamic Asia and Africa: Classical Traditions and Modern Meanings* (Leiden, 1996), Vol. 1: 451–74 (453).
9. See *Sada al-Malahim* 12 (Jan/Feb 2010): 32 for Hassan ibn Thabit; 16 (Jan 2011): 30 for Ka'b ibn Malik; 11 (Sept/Oct 2009): 18; and 16 (Jan 2011): 12 for 'Abd Allah ibn Rawaha.
10. Shakir Ahmad ibn Hamil, 'Hakadha tantasir al-'aqa'id' ('In this way, beliefs will be victorious'), *Sada al-Malahim* 16 (Jan 2011): 12.
11. Carole Hillenbrand, 'Jihad poetry in the age of the Crusades', in Thomas F. Madden, James L. Naus and Vincent Ryan (eds.), *Crusades – Medieval*

Worlds in Conflict (Aldershot, 2010): 9–24 (13). Elements of this corpus have also been examined in Hadia Dajani-Shakeel, 'Jihad in twelfth-century Arabic poetry: a moral and religious force to counter the Crusades ', *Muslim World* 66 (1976): 96–113.

12. Tarif Khalidi, 'The poetry of the Khawarij: violence and salvation', in Thomas Scheffler (ed.), *Religion between Violence and Reconciliation* (Beirut and Würzburg, 2002): 109–22; Ihsan 'Abbas, *Shu'ara' al-Khawarij: Dirasa Fanniyya Mawdu'iyya Muqarana* (Amman, 1986); Azmi Muhammad Shafiq al-Salihi, 'The society, beliefs and political theories of the Kharijites as revealed in their poetry of the Umayyad era', PhD thesis, University of London (SOAS), 1975.

13. *Sada al-Malahim* 2 (March 2008): 13; see also Nelly Lahoud, *The Jihadis' Path to Self-Destruction* (London, 2010), especially pp. 31–43; and Joas Wagemakers, '"Seceders" and "postponers"?: an analysis of the "khawarij" and "murji'a" labels in polemical debates between quietist and jihadi-salafis', in Jeevan Deol and Zaheer Kazmi (eds.), *Contextualising Jihadi Thought* (London, 2012): 145–64.

14. These are verses 17 and 18 of a 31-verse ode entitled 'Qissat Mujahid', *Sada al-Malahim* 14 (June/July 2010): 66–7.

15. al-Jahjah, 'Ghuraba'' ('Strangers'), *Sada al-Malahim* 6 (Nov 2008): 32.

16. Alex Strick van Linschoten and Felix Kuehn (eds.), *Poetry of the Taliban* (London, 2012); Marc Falkoff (ed.), *Poems from Guantanamo: The Detainees Speak* (Iowa City, 2007).

17. Some of the reactions are recounted in Laura King, '*Poetry of the Taliban* elicits both anger, astonishment', *Los Angeles Times*, 7 July 2012 (http://articles.latimes.com/2012/jul/07/world/la-fg-taliban-poetry-20120708, last accessed 18 December 2013), as well as in the introductions to the books themselves.

18. The survey was undertaken in December 2012 by this author with the assistance of the locally based Mahra Youth Unity Organisation, an independent non-governmental body. The survey was conducted throughout the nine provinces that comprise Yemen's geographically huge but sparsely populated Mahra governorate rather than directly in al-Qa'ida strongholds for security reasons. The sample distribution was weighted for gender and location based on official census data.

19. Flagg Miller, *The Moral Resonance of Arab Media* (Cambridge, MA, 2007).

20. In a mass survey conducted in Egypt by this author and colleagues, only 6 per cent of respondents were found to read or listen to poetry. See Mazen Hassan, Elisabeth Kendall and Stephen Whitefield, 'Media, cultural consumption and normative support for democracy in post-revolutionary Egypt' (forthcoming).

21. Jarrett M. Brachman, *Global Jihadism: Theory and Practice* (New York, 2009), Kindle loc. 3360.

22. From the scientifically randomised survey of over 2,000 inhabitants conducted in December 2012 by this author in association with the Mahra Youth Unity Association.

23. Point 40 in Anwar al-Awlaqi, '44 Ways to Support Jihad'. Available online at http://www.youtube.com/watch?v=hwEsd76kXbU (last accessed 30 January 2014). For a rare analysis of the power of *nashids*, see Benham Said, 'Hymns (nasheeds): a contribution to the study of the jihadist culture', *Studies in Conflict & Terrorism* 35/12 (2012): 863–79.

24. The highly revered status of poetry among tribal communities is also amply demonstrated in Steven C. Caton, *Peaks of Yemen I Summon: Poetry as Cultural Practice in a North Yemeni Tribe* (Berkeley and Los Angeles, 1990).

25. Samuel Liebhaber has demonstrated, for example, how tenaciously the Mahra tribes in eastern Yemen have clung to their language, particularly in poetry, by looking at how popular forms of Arabic sung-poetry from other parts of Yemen have been adapted to the Mahri language. Samuel Liebhaber, 'The Humayni pulse moves east: Yemeni nationalism meets Mahri sung-poetry', *British Journal of Middle Eastern Studies*, 39/2 (August 2011): 249–65.

26. For example, although the YouTube links to several poems have now been blocked owing to their virulent content, the poem 'Mutafa'il wa-l-ya's bi-l-mirsad' ('Optimistic as despair lies in wait') in *Sada al-Malahim* 1 (January 2008), 22, quoted later in this article, appears in several forms on YouTube as a *nashid*, one of which has received just under 49,000 hits (as of 7 November 2013). It includes remarks encouraging listeners to kill Jews: http://www.youtube.com/watch?v=xL1xfMkbDMA (last accessed 18 December 2013).

27. Charles Hirschkind, *The Ethical Soundscape: Cassette Sermons and Islamic Counterpublics* (New York, 2006).

28. *Sada al-Malahim* 8 (March 2009): 29.

29. Ibrahim al-Hadrami, 'al-Mujahidun wa-l-taqa al-kamina' ('The jihadists and hidden power'), *Sada al-Malahim* 5 (Sept 2008): 22. This line is unattributed but can be traced to a poem by Mahmud Ghunaym (1902–72), an Egyptian elementary school teacher with a traditional religious education who was awarded an Egyptian state prize in 1963 in recognition of his poetic talents.

30. Both verses here are unattributed. I have traced the first to the Abbasid poet Abu al-'Ala' al-Ma'arri (d.1058) and the second to the Lebanese poet Amin Taqi al-Din (d.1937). 'Fi al-Aqsa naltaqi: sinariyu inhiyar al-nizam al-hakim'

('We will meet in al-Aqsa: scenario of the fall of the ruling regime'), *Sada al-Malahim* 9 (May 2009): 28.

31. Karl Mannheim, *Essays on the Sociology of Knowledge* (London, 1952), pp. 43–7.

32. *Sada al-Malahim* 13 (April/May 2010): 54. These verses are unattributed but can be traced to a longer poem. The earliest version I found online was cached from 1999 and the longest version ran to 78 verses.

33. See Peter Stallybrass and Allon White, *The Politics and Poetics of Transgression* (London and New York, 1986).

34. *Sada al-Malahim* 13 (April/May 2010): 54.

35. Linschoten and Kuehn state that the international forces are the group most often mentioned in Taliban poetry. Foreigners are referred to generically and Americans are not particularly singled out. Linschoten and Kuehn (eds.), *Poetry of the Taliban*, p. 44. This differs from my findings from Yemeni jihadist poetry, where Americans are often mentioned explicitly as the enemy, along with their associates.

36. See Laurent Bonnefoy, 'Jihadi violence in Yemen: dealing with local, regional and international contingencies', in Jeevan Deol and Zaheer Kazmi (eds.), *Contextualising Jihadi Thought*: 243–58.

37. Andrew Edgar and Peter Sedgwick, *Cultural Theory: The Key Concepts* (London and New York, 2007), Kindle loc. 893.

38. 'Mutafa'il wa-l-ya's bi-l-mirsad' ('Optimistic as despair lies in wait'), *Sada al-Malahim* 1 (Jan 2008): 22. This is commonly found sung as a *nashid* on YouTube.

39. Abu Hajir al-Ma'ribi (pseudonym), 'Hanna junudu-ka ya Usama' ('We are your troops, O Osama'), *Sada al-Malahim* 6 (Nov 2008): 30.

40. Bonnefoy, 'Jihadi violence in Yemen', pp. 244–5. Akbar Ahmad makes a related point that tribal codes of honour and revenge motivate acts of terror at least as much as any broader global notion of jihad. Akbar Ahmed, *The Thistle and the Drone: How America's War on Terror Became a Global War on Tribal Islam* (Washington DC, 2013).

41. al-Ma'ribi, 'Hanna junudu-ka ya Usama'.

42. Pierre Bourdieu, *The Field of Cultural Production* (Cambridge, 1993), Part I.

43. The names mentioned are all Companions of the Prophet. Abu al-Bara', 'Sawt Usama li-ahl al-shahama' ('The voice of Osama to the people of gallantry'), *Sada al-Malahim* 4 (July 2008): 25. In this respect, jihadist poetry differs from Taliban poetry, which reveals a more nuanced perspective on the past. Taliban poetry traces parallels to Biblical prophets and to Afghanistan's past military heroes, rather than focusing solely on Islamic religious figures. Linschoten and Kuehn (eds.), *Poetry of the Taliban*, pp. 18–19.

44. Abu al-Baraʾ, 'Sawt Usama li-ahl al-shahama' ('The voice of Osama to the people of gallantry'), *Sada al-Malahim* 4 (July 2008): 26.

45. This conclusion is based on in-depth analysis of jihadist discourse on terrorist training by Brynjar Lia, 'Doctrines for jihadist terrorist training', *Terrorism and Political Violence* 20 (2008): 518–42.

46. Jeffrey Brown and Daniel Sagalyn, 'Poetry as a weapon of war in Afghanistan' (an interview with Thomas Johnson), *PBS Newshour Art Beat*, 25 March 2011 (http://www.pbs.org/newshour/art/blog/2011/03/taliban-poetry.html, last accessed 18 December 2013).

47. Linschoten and Kuehn (eds.), *Poetry of the Taliban*, p. 47. More examples of Taliban poetry, including an interesting basic content analysis, can be found in Michael Semple, 'Rhetoric of resistance in the Taliban's rebel ballads', Carr Center Paper for Harvard University, March 2011. The latter creates a distinct category for works used for propaganda purposes.

48. One such poetry battle took place between conservatives and reformers regarding modernisation of the dress code in Yemen. Al-Baradduni, *al-Thaqafa wa-l-Thawra fi al-Yaman* (n.p.: 1991), pp. 152–5. Cited in Lucine Taminian, 'Persuading the monarchs: poetry and politics in Yemen, (1920–1950)', in Remy Leveau, Franck Mermier and Udo Steinbach (eds.), *Le Yemen Contemporain* (Paris, 1999): 2013–19 (212).

49. Ibrahim Rubaysh, 'Ode to the Sea', in Falkoff (ed.), *Poems from Guantanamo*, p. 66. The continuing relevance of verse-by-verse battle is analysed in chapter 4 of Caton, *Peaks of Yemen*.

Bibliography

'Abbas, Ihsan, *Shu'ara' al-Khawarij: Dirasa Fanniyya Mawdu'iyya Muqarana* (Amman, 1986).

Ahmed, Akbar, *The Thistle and the Drone: How America's War on Terror Became a Global War on Tribal Islam* (Washington DC, 2013).

al-Awlaqi, Anwar, '44 Ways to Support Jihad' (http://www.youtube.com/watch?v=hwEsd76kXbU, last accessed 30 January 2014).

Bonnefoy, Laurent, 'Jihadi violence in Yemen: dealing with local, regional and international contingencies', in Jeevan Deol and Zaheer Kazmi (eds.), *Contextualising Jihadi Thought* (London, 2012): 243–58.

Bourdieu, Pierre, *The Field of Cultural Production* (Cambridge, 1993).

Brachman, Jarret M., *Global Jihadism: Theory and Practice* (New York, 2009).

Brown, Jeffrey and Sagalyn, Daniel, 'Poetry as a weapon of war in Afghanistan' (an interview with Thomas Johnson), *PBS Newshour Art Beat*, 25 March 2011 (http://www.pbs.org/newshour/art/blog/2011/03/taliban-poetry.html, last accessed 18 December 2013).

Bürgel, J. C., 'Qasida as discourse on power and its Islamization: some reflections', in Stefan Sperl and Christopher Shackle (eds.), *Qasida Poetry in Islamic Asia and Africa: Classical Traditions and Modern Meanings* (Leiden, 1996), Vol. 1: 451–74.

Caton, Steven C., *Peaks of Yemen I Summon: Poetry as Cultural Practice in a North Yemeni Tribe* (Berkeley and Los Angeles, 1990).

Dajani-Shakeel, Hadia, 'Jihad in twelfth-century Arabic poetry: a moral and religious force to counter the Crusades', *The Muslim World* 66/2 (April 1976): 96–113.

Edgar, Andrew and Sedgwick, Peter, *Cultural Theory: The Key Concepts* (London and New York, 2007).

Falkoff, Marc (ed.), *Poems from Guantanamo: The Detainees Speak* (Iowa City, 2007).

Gabriel, Richard, *Muhammad: Islam's First Great General* (Norman, 2007).

Hassan, Mazen, Kendall, Elisabeth and Whitefield, Stephen, 'Media, cultural consumption and normative support for democracy in post-revolutionary Egypt' (forthcoming).

Hillenbrand, Carole, 'Jihad poetry in the age of the Crusades', in Thomas F. Madden, James L. Naus and Vincent Ryan (eds.), *Crusades – Medieval Worlds in Conflict* (Aldershot, 2010): 9–24.

Hirschkind, Charles, *The Ethical Soundscape: Cassette Sermons and Islamic Counterpublics* (New York, 2006).

Khalidi, Tarif, 'The poetry of the Khawarij: violence and salvation', in Thomas Scheffler (ed.), *Religion between Violence and Reconciliation* (Beirut and Würzburg, 2002): 109–22.

King, Laura, '*Poetry of the Taliban* elicits both anger, astonishment', *Los Angeles Times*, 7 July 2012 (http://articles.latimes.com/2012/jul/07/world/la-fg-taliban-poetry-20120708, last accessed 18 December 2013).

Lahoud, Nelly, *The Jihadis' Path to Self-Destruction* (London, 2010).

Lia, Brynjar, 'Doctrines for jihadist terrorist training', *Terrorism and Political Violence* 20/4 (2008): 518–42.

Liebhaber, Samuel, 'The Humayni pulse moves east: Yemeni nationalism meets Mahri sung-poetry', *British Journal of Middle Eastern Studies* 39/2 (August 2011): 249–65.

Linschoten, Alex Strick van and Kuehn, Felix (eds.), *Poetry of the Taliban* (London, 2012).

Mannheim, Karl, *Essays on the Sociology of Knowledge* (London, 1952).

Miller, Flagg, *The Moral Resonance of Arab Media* (Cambridge, MA, 2007).

Rogerson, Barnaby, *The Prophet Muhammad: A Biography* (London, 2004).

Rohde, David and Chivers, C. J., 'Al Qaeda's grocery lists and manuals of killing', *New York Times*, 17 March 2002.

Said, Benham, 'Hymns (nasheeds): a contribution to the study of the jihadist culture', *Studies in Conflict & Terrorism* 35/12 (2012): 863–79.

al-Salihi, Azmi Muhammad Shafiq, 'The society, beliefs and political theories of the Kharijites as revealed in their poetry of the Umayyad era', PhD thesis, University of London (SOAS), 1975.

Semple, Michael, 'Rhetoric of resistance in the Taliban's rebel ballads', Carr Center Paper for Harvard University, March 2011.

Stallybrass, Peter and White, Allon, *The Politics and Poetics of Transgression* (London and New York, 1986).

Taminian, Lucine, 'Persuading the monarchs: poetry and politics in Yemen, (1920–1950)', in Remy Leveau, Franck Mermier and Udo Steinbach (eds.), *Le Yemen Contemporain* (Paris, 1999): 2013–19.

Wagemakers, Joas, '"Seceders" and "postponers"?: an analysis of the "khawarij" and "murji'a" labels in polemical debates between quietist and jihadi-salafis', in Jeevan Deol and Zaheer Kazmi (eds.), *Contextualising Jihadi Thought* (London, 2012): 145–64.

Zwettler, Michael, 'A mantic manifesto: the sura of "The Poets" and the Qur'anic foundations of Prophetic authority', in James L. Kugel (ed.), *Poetry and Prophecy: The Beginnings of a Literary Tradition* (New York, 1990): 75–119.

15

Poetics of Martyrdom in Early Modern Palestine

Rana Issa

The role of poetry in 'awakening' a national Arab sentiment in the first decades of the twentieth century has long been a marvel to historians.[1] Writers such as Talal Asad,[2] George Antonius[3] and Albert Hourani[4] attest with some disbelief that poetry, in the region, was the major vehicle for instilling in the people 'the pride of race' necessary for an anti-imperial revolt. The consensus on the role of poetry in nation-building has not, however, generated literary studies that can account for the phenomenon of so-called 'nationalist poetry'. Perhaps the difficulty lies in the almost impossible double vision these poets possessed. They were Arab poets writing in the classical styles of the eleventh-century zenith of Islamic rule; they were also Syrian, Palestinian, Egyptian poets who reflected the local concerns of their nations emerging in the wake of Western imperialism. The relationship of poetry to Arab nationalism can be envisioned in different ways. Tarif Khalidi remarks that in early Palestinian modernity, 'the stirrings of nationalism, in the form of the rediscovery of the classical Arab literary heritage, coincided with a slow but steady influx of Jewish immigrants, many of whom were Zionists'.[5] Khalidi's comments preserve the spatial unfolding of modernity while describing how literature functioned as a coping strategy in a changing landscape. This chapter attempts to explore this intersection between poetry and emerging Palestinian nationalism.

Like other Arab nationalisms, Palestinian nationalism was forged on the battlefield. However, unlike other colonised nations, where the local populations battled for sovereignty over their lands, and categories such as 'native' and 'settler' were clearly defined, the Palestinians suddenly found themselves attempting to prove their indigenous status in the face of Zionism's claims that the Jews emigrating from Europe were the natives. The role of British imperial forces in facilitating the prevalence of this discourse is well known.[6] After the Balfour Declaration in 1917, the British utilised their military resources to ensure a solid grafting of this resolution onto the Palestinian terrain. Nationalist Palestinian poetry became the voice of the ensuing intense political revolts against British policies of displacement, which replaced Palestinians with another people, European Jews.

Palestinian revolt against the British Mandate officially started in 1923. It climaxed in the 1936–9 popular uprising that ended with a crushing defeat for the Palestinians at the hands of British soldiers and Zionist militias. The Palestinian memory recalls these events with such gloom that the Palestinian writer Ghassan Kanafani claims that by 1939, 5 per cent of male Palestinians perished,[7] leaving the resistance in a state of total disarray and inertia.[8] As the British Royal Air Force disciplined the Palestinians with aerial bombardment, poetry flourished to such an extent that the poets have since been known as the fathers of Palestinian literature.

Poetry defined its role through the rhetorical transformation of military defeat into a moral victory. The proliferation of the martyrdom trope clearly defined the role of poetry in imagining the nation. Yet, while many scholars have traditionally focused on the role of post-*Nakba* poetry in the formation of Palestinian nationalism, few have tried to explore the literary history of Palestine prior to the *Nakba*. Some Arab scholars justify the neglect of earlier poetry by citing its lack of aesthetic merit,[9] while others are eager to celebrate it for its closeness to the struggle and its construction of the martyrdom trope. Both perspectives, however, leave out important questions about the function of this poetry and the consequences of its proximity to what the Palestinians perceived as their war for independence.

Written in the classical style of the Arabic *qasida*, early Palestinian poetry contextualised its role vis-à-vis a larger Arab literary revival. Arabic poetry conveyed racial pride only to the extent that it signified *national* identity. Put differently, Palestinians attested to their *Arabness* by submitting to certain poetic forms, but the content remained locally implicated in the urgency of struggle. This double vision was resolved through the artificial split of form from content, with little attention paid to how form ultimately shapes the content.[10] By reading the works of 'Abd al-Rahim Mahmud (1913–48) and Ibrahim Tuqan (1905–41), the two most famous poets from that period, I will question how the tropes of martyrdom and jihad unfolded in a poetry that remained classical in form. As I show, these fathers of Palestinian poetry were paradoxically secularising Palestinian identity through deploying a cultural repertoire that was becoming increasingly defined as Islamic.

The proliferation of martyrdom tropes in poetry attempted to address the malaise experienced under British colonial policies. In the poetry, the disenfranchisement of Arab Christians and Muslims evolved into a shared sense of nationalism that was quickly secularised. The poetry derived its formality from an Islamic tradition but articulated an emerging secularity of the nation-state. Martyrdom, the supreme sacrifice of a citizen, borrowed from the Islamic tradition only what suited the demands of modern nationalism. In his insistence on underscoring the martyr as a man of faith, Khalid Karaki risks covering up the paradox that ensues from entwining the Islamic tradition with modern nationalism. In his exploration of pre-modern and early modern poetry, Karaki concludes:

> The concept of martyrdom in modern poetry was linked to the Islamic image of the martyr ... the martyr is not a man coming from legend and History but he is a person who believes and who is fully conscious of his decision.[11]

Yet, in spite of its perceived heroism, martyrdom is traditionally a notion that can only derive meaning from its historical context.[12] This means that for an emerging Palestinian nationalism that included both Muslim and Christian as well as secular adherents, the Islamic import of martyrdom remained linked to the demands of the struggle and not to the precepts of faith.

Prior to 1923, political concerns were also manifest in Palestinian poetry. The number of poets who took the glorification of British rule as their subject matter is remarkable. All this would soon change.[13]

What is more remarkable is that Palestinian poetry, unlike the competing Palestinian political parties, quickly matured into a more unified political identity. The Palestinian poets echo the people's realisation that Britain was not their ally but had independent territorial interests. A strong sense of nationalism was poetically asserted and voiced the people's responses to British policies. During the Great Arab Revolt, or the Great Strike of the 1930s, Palestinians staged a major uprising against the British forces for aiding and facilitating the influx of thousands of Jewish immigrants to the 'promised land'. This poetry supported the uprising and was unified in rejecting British rule and Zionist colonialism.

As Rashid Khalidi writes, the basis of Mandate rule in Palestine 'was specifically designed by its British architects to exclude national-self determination for the Arab majority, even while facilitating the same end for the Jewish minority'.[14] Palestinians responded with demonstrations and strikes against the British and Zionists. In these demonstrations and national assemblies, new poetry was chanted to infuse people with revolutionary enthusiasm and motivate them to join the resistance.

Following 1917, the religious content of much of the poetry was used to construct an inclusive secular Palestinian identity that could withstand the influx of Jews.[15] The Qur'an and the Bible were woven into an emerging secular vision of Palestine inclusive of Christian and Muslim citizens. As Sa'di Abu Shawir observes, 'the impact of the Qur'an was especially clear in the work of Ibrahim Tuqan . . . and Wadi' Bustani . . . and Iskandar al-Baytjali'.[16] One ought to mention that while Tuqan was a Muslim, Bustani (1886–1952) and al-Baytjali (1890–1973) are Christians. Abu Shawir's findings are reiterated by Khalid Sulaiman, who argues that 'poets paid great attention to the religious status of Palestine and its significance to both Muslims and Christians'.[17]

Al-Baytjali is one example of the prioritisation of nation over religious community. Despite his Christian faith, he rejects the conduct of the western leaders of the Greek Orthodox Church – the largest Christian community in Palestine at the time – whom he accuses of indifference to the political well-being of their Palestinian Christian parish. He accuses them of selling church lands to Jewish newcomers:

> We accepted them as our own
> priests and we even named patriarchs.
> Once they became many they performed

for themselves a power that was ours.
They dispensed with our inheritance to their clients
and they pretended that they came as monks.[18]

Al-Baytjali's rejection of the sale of Palestinian land leads him to reject the Greek Orthodox Church as an institution that advances British Imperial interests rather than the political and civil rights of Palestinians.

This polemic is repeated in the letters of another Christian, Khalil Sakakini (1878–1953), sent to his son Sari. Sakakini criticised the Egyptian Ahmad Amin's lecture in Nablus:

> He was unable to shed his Islamism, and what becomes apparent is that it is difficult for the individual to shed his biases. Therefore attaining truth in such endeavors becomes impossible . . . who can stand in the midst of an Islamic society and say to people that religion has little to offer humanity?[19]

At the start of the revolution in 1936, Sakakini writes in another letter,

> A sheikh in Nablus declared holy jihad in the Muslim way. Some hapless youth and naïve individuals followed him with banners and said to him, let us declare holy jihad and advance to Jaffa . . . Yes this small revolt unnerved the spiritual strength of the Jews.[20]

Sakakini's ambivalence is visible through his use of terms like *naive* and *hapless* to describe those who succeeded in demoralising the Jewish immigrants, even as he emphasises that jihad is an Islamic category of war. As the war progressed, Sakakini became more inclined to use jihad unreservedly to mean the revolution of the Arab natives of Palestine against Zionists and the British. In another letter, he writes:

> The nation continues its strikes, and not a day passes that does not add new strength to the strike. Demonstrations are more frequent, settlements are being burned, and trees uprooted, and if all this is not effective the situation will certainly come to a crossroads: either the declaration of holy jihad, or the formation of armed groups that fight according to the Irish model.[21]

For Sakakini, Palestine's liberation is crucial, even if he is not convinced that Islam is the most effective ideology in the struggle.

The British-sponsored Islamic Council, headed by the Mufti Hajj Amin al-Husayni, was careful to avoid hostilities with Christians. On the ground, Husayni, who found the Nashashibi family and the Hadi family a greater threat to his rule than the Christians, administered a rough and violent policy against his political rivals. Under the Great Strike, the major political families in Palestine were caught up in eliminating their political rivals rather than in fighting the Mandate laws, and soon enough the population began to look for alternative means to organise itself. Several parties were founded, armed and eager for the fight. Such was the case of The Chief Leadership of the Holy Jihad for the Rescue of Palestine,[22] an Islamic group that was not among the top three political parties, yet was quite active on the battlefront. It distributed a pamphlet in 1936 articulating its aims: '[T]o thwart the partition project *or* to realize our national pact that Palestine become an Arab, democratic, united nation'.[23] Nowhere in the document do the words 'Islam' or 'Muslim' appear. Instead 'Arab' signifies the people whose homeland is Palestine. As in this pamphlet, the propagation of the term 'jihad' in the poetry subordinates it to cultural and religious histories. Poetry followed suit and reinvented jihad as the national revolt of Palestine. The call to jihad found in early Palestinian poetry was the central aim of the martyr poem. In his poem '*da'wa ila al-Jihad*' ('A Call to Jihad'), 'Abd al-Rahim Mahmud writes:

> 'My people, the day of sacrifice has arrived
> and blazed honor in the Promised Land.
> My people, awaken from a sleep
> for after tyranny there is no sleep.[24]

Like his compatriots, Mahmud engaged with the broader paradigm of Arabic literature. Through his choice of the classical poetic form, Mahmud communicated a pride in Arab history, yoking it to modern concepts, such as the nation-state, imperialism and class struggle. Arabic poetry was becoming Egyptian, Tunisian or Iraqi, not through its form but through its content. To be accepted in the echelons of Arabic poetry and to have one's poems published in various Arabic newspapers was a national achievement. Through newspapers, poetry compensated for the fragmentation of Arab domains under colonialism. Importantly, an assertion of an autonomous Palestinian nationalism rested on the ability of Palestinian poets to produce Arabic poetry in the classical *khalili* structure,[25] and publish it in Arab newspapers. By publishing martyrdom poetry in various Arab newspapers, Mahmud, Tuqan and others stirred the sympathies of their Arab brethren for the Palestinian cause.

Mahmud, who died on the battlefront, believed Palestine was a cause worth fighting for. What makes his death so unnerving for Palestinians is that his martyrdom poetry had been written in the first person; as if this poet mujahid predicted his own death. By dedicating his pen to battles and heroes, Mahmud also restored poetry's ancient function as a *diwan* or record. In the modern context, the record appropriates new meanings by turning the poet into a witness defending the legality of Palestinian narrative. As a witness, the poet authors an alternative legality strengthened by the generation of metaphor. The poet claims authority of witness, as in a court of law. Such metaphoric authority posits knowledge against power. Acting as witness, Palestinian poetry implicitly rejects British judicial hegemony in Palestine. In this way, poetic memory defies discourses of power. Through witnessing, poetry relies on memory in its struggle against the forgetfulness of power.

Therefore, at the height of the Palestinian uprising in the early 1970s, Jabra Ibrahim Jabra singles out Mahmud as the inspirational cultural and political figure of the period. His article *'al-Faris al-Sha'ir'* ('The Poet Knight') focuses on the uniqueness of Mahmud within the Palestinian poetic experience.[26] According to Jabra, Mahmud is grand because he enacts the Palestinian struggle in two ways: writing and fighting. Jabra's reading of Mahmud advances the claim that the struggle is the key activity that organises all other social and cultural relations and structures within Palestinian society.

Mahmud's dissatisfaction with an exclusively poetic role in the liberation permeates his love poetry. *'Jaffat 'ala Shafatayya al-Amani'* ('The Hopes Dried on my Lips'), is a *ghazal* (love) poem[27] that begins with love's metaphoric discourse. Mahmud transgresses the boundaries of the *ghazal* genre where love exists in an ahistorical vacuum and the passions of the heart and the beauties of the beloved do not refer to the historical or political moment of the poet. By introducing politics into this realm, he was the first to conflate the beloved with the land. This would become a defining metaphor in Palestinian poetry.

From the opening lines, the poet begs his lover to quench his sobriety. As he drinks the absinthe of love from her palms, he ascends to ecstasy in order to complain: 'I am from there, from heaven / who on this world had flung me?' He suddenly falls out of love's delights into the miseries of Palestine, where he is confronted with the impossibility of poetic love under colonial hegemony. He points his finger to accuse 'He who desecrated the Holy Quds / and deflowered it with a horse'. Snatched from the luxuries of love and the inner world of individual satisfaction, the poet realises that love will not bring him salvation. Juxtaposing love and political desire, Mahmud submits to the urgency of desire: 'Give me a drink from the blue dome / for your drink will not quench me.' The blue dome evokes the Dome of the Rock or the dome of heaven, the martyr's abode. Mahmud draws a climactic tension between the metaphors of love and of political desire. In this transgression of the classical poetic genres of classical literature,[28] love gives way to a new sense of individual responsibility, where the risk of death on the battlefront becomes the double of the poet/lover.

Death reaches its aesthetic climax in '*al-Shahid*' ('The Martyr'), the poem that celebrates the poet's death. Mahmud opens the poem as follows:

> On my palm I shall carry my soul
> and bring it to the abyss of death
> for either a life that pleases the friend
> or a death that provokes the foe.

These lines configure death as the organising paradigm of the poem. Here the poet takes leave to travel towards death, emphasising his absence.

Mahmud's irreplaceability as a poet permeates the entire poem. This irreplaceable 'I' opens the poem by bidding the reader farewell on the way to war. Thus establishing his absence in the opening verse, the poet's voice reaches us as an echo, in the wake of a journey, beseeching us from the depth of suffering: 'And what is life / I do not live if I cannot be.' He commands the attention of his people: '[I]f I should speak, the world would listen / and my poetry will resound in the distance.' The poet is the fighter who generously gives his life, but he is also the irreplaceable voice whose journey into death reaches its climax and final destination, the land. The movement of the imagery records the fragmentation of the body as the earth receives her martyr: 'A body wrangled on the hills / tussled by birds of death.' The movement is compelling and arrests the mind of the reader/reciter; this life into death is not for nothing; it is not suicide, but an intense act of hope born of desperation. The poet dreams of dissolving in his nation's soil, where the lyric of land will break open the consciousness of his people twice: once in poetry, then once again when this image that he so eloquently portrays becomes tied to al-Shajara, a small village at the edge of Jerusalem, where Mahmud was martyred in July 1948.

The apprehension of death that permeates the poem shapes the land. Mahmud intends more than the martyr symbol; he elevates poetry itself to a national symbol. The apprehension of death leads the poet to the possibility of martyrdom on his journey towards the land. This connection to land, penned in blood, ushers the poet back to poetry.

In Ibrahim Tuqan's masterpiece 'al-Thulatha' al-Hamra' ('Red Tuesday'), the poet asserts himself as a witness who can powerfully challenge the judicial tyranny of British rule. As the earliest martyr eulogy in Palestinian literature, this poem commemorates the execution of three mujahidin by the British authorities following the al-Braq events in 1929.[29] Written in the richly lyrical structure of an Andalusian *muwashshah*,[30] the poet's choice of rhyme evokes past Arab glories (and defeats), specifically the grandeur of the Arab presence in Andalusia and the remarkable nostalgia this loss inflicts on the Arab soul. The structure implicitly serves as a reminder and justification for Palestinian jihad. Written as a theatrical narrative whose protagonists are days and chunks of time personified to express their horror at the execution, this poem functions as an act of commemoration that is directly tied up with the construction of a national imagination.

In this poem, the eulogy turns into an opportunity to insist on the military option, on jihad, as the only possible language to use with the British. As witness, Tuqan overturns the British sentence on those men by pronouncing them martyrs. Opening the poem through a conversation with time itself, Tuqan begins:

> Your ill-fated star was scorned
> and cups swayed with naked rope.

> Prayer wailed and bells wept
> The night is turbid, the day is frowning.
> Storms gathered and revolted, and emotions
> And Death sometimes drifting, sometimes snatching.[31]

Tuqan relinquishes his narrative voice to the personification of Time, who proceeds to tell the story and replies to the poet's mournful accusations. The day answers with a question: 'Have the mortals seen the likes of this day?' Another day responds to say:

> 'Yes, I am the narrator
> to the courts of Inquisition,[32] those tyrants.
> I saw strange things
> but you harbor disaster and catastrophe.

Through personifying Time, Tuqan derives the legitimacy of his voice from the annals of history rather than the discourse of power. Al-Khalil, the founder of classical Arabic prosody, describes poets as 'masters of speech, conjugating it as they will',[33] and it is as such that Tuqan fulfils his role. As master of speech, Tuqan holds history responsible for the tragedy befalling the Palestinians. Tuqan exemplifies Edward Said's general observations about Palestinian literature:

> the struggle to achieve form expresses the writer's efforts to construct a coherent scene, a narrative that might overcome the almost metaphysical impossibility of representing the present . . . the present tense is subject to echoes of the past, verbs of sight give way to verbs of sound or smell, and one sense interweaves with another – in an effort to defend against the harsh present and to protect some particularly cherished fragment of the past.[34]

This observation also describes Tuqan's personification of Time. Casting the role of Time metaphorically wreaks havoc with the cognitive structure in order to tell his people that history is a human enterprise that is shaped by their commitment.

Tuqan proceeds to mythologise the three men to be executed, by singling out the martyr over all the other characteristics of the individual self. His construction of the hero fits with Salma Khadra Jayyusi's observation that in Arabic literature, heroes 'emphasize either directly or

obliquely the dignity and equality of all men, and their level of responsibility to forge their own destiny'.[35] This idea becomes especially clear
in the motif of anonymity imbuing the martyrdom poem. Even as he
names his martyrs (Muhammad Jamjum, Atta Zayr and Fu'ad Hijazi),
Tuqan effaces their personal traces and foregrounds them as symbols of
sacrifice that will restore Palestine to its people. The theatrical casting
of Time into the dramatis personae juxtaposes the impoverishment of
the self that renders the mujahidin as martyrs; they are at once anonymous yet larger than life. For the poet and his audience, martyrdom is
potent because of the corporal effacement that is replaced by a heroic
narrative of struggle. As the body fades away and the referent is left to
haunt, the symbol materialises from the act of naming, from the poetic
depiction of the absence of the body into the meaningfulness of the
symbol.

When the poet gives his blood to the earth, the nation becomes a
poem and the martyr its writer. Mahmud's dramatic performances and
Tuqan's dramatic poems both attest to an evolving notion of identity
that sheds religious sectarianism in favour of a more inclusive, if Is-
lamically inspired, national identity. A secular grounding of Palestine
in the historical struggle for the land had a marked impact on the way
religion evolved to service the cause. The Qur'an was transformed from
the supreme text into a source of poetic inspiration on a par with other
sources of literary inspiration. The Bible was not yet present, but would
become a mainstay of Palestinian poetry after the *Nakba*. With the war
for independence claiming so many lives, concepts derived from religious tradition like martyrdom and jihad were impoverished in order to
carry a more secular meaning. Furthermore, these concepts exceeded
religious as well as secular formulations to define the relationship of
poetry to Palestinian society. Poetry's closeness to the struggle allowed
the poet to produce a Palestinian idiom within early Arab poetic modernity. Sakakini writes: '[W]ar is a lot easier than revolt a thousand times;
war is conducted by soldiers, whereas revolts are comprised of all people, young and old, men, women and children are its soldiers, and
swords, and daggers, and stones and glass, even shoes.'[36] It is under
these conditions that Palestinians formed their national identity and
their literature.

Notes

1. I would like to thank The Deutsche Forschungsgemeinschaft for their generous funding of this research and Friederike Pannewick for her friendship and support.
2. Talal Asad, *Formations of the Secular: Christianity, Islam, Modernity* (Stanford, 2003), p. 54.
3. George Antonius, *The Arab Awakening* (Philadelphia, 1939), p. 37.
4. Albert Hourani, *Arabic Thought in the Liberal Age: 1798–1939* (Cambridge, 1983), pp. 95–6.
5. Tarif Khalidi, 'Palestinian historiography: 1900–1948', *Journal of Palestine Studies*, 10/3 (1981): 59–76 (62).
6. For more on the history of the period, refer to Rashid Khalidi's analysis of the leadership in *The Iron Cage* (Boston, 2006). Also refer to a critique of the Palestinian resistance by Ghassan Kanafani, 'Thawrat 1936–1939 fi Filastin: khalfiyyat wa-tafasil wa-tahlil', *Shu'un Filastiniyya* 6 (January 1972): 45–67. For a general history of the period, see 'Abd al-Wahhab Kayyali, *Tarikh Filastin al-Hadith* (Beirut, 1999) and Tom Segev, *One Palestine, Complete: Jews and Arabs under the British Mandate* (London, 2001). For the Zionist story, see James P. Jankowski, 'The Palestinian Arab Revolt of 1936–1939', *The Muslim World* 63/3 (July 1973): 220–33.
7. Five per cent of the male population would have amounted to around 17,000 Palestinian men killed in the period.
8. Official numbers are different, however. According to Hilde Henriksen Waage's *Konflikt og Stormaktspolitikk i Midtøsten*, where she uses an average figure, the numbers between April 1936 and August 1939 are closer to 3,000 Palestinians, 2,000 Jews and 600 British citizens. She contends that more Palestinians were killed through Palestinian infighting than through clashes with the British or the Jews. According to Waage, historians cannot agree on the figures. See Hilde Henriksen Waage, *Konflikt og Stormaktspolitikk i Midtøsten* (Oslo, 2013), footnote to p. 80.
9. The best example of this trend is Ihsan Abbas, 'Al-shi'r mundhu bidayat al-intidab hatta sanat 1967', in *al-Mawsu'a al-Filastiniyya* (Beirut, 1990), Vol. 4: 19–25.
10. Elias Khoury, *Al-Dhakira al-Mafquda* (Beirut, 1990), p. 244.
11. Khalid Karaki, *Hamasat al-Shuhada'* (Beirut, 1998), p. 40.
12. Khoury, *Al-Dhakira*, p. 235. See a very similar argument dealing with post-1948 poetry in Friederike Pannewick, 'The martyred poet on the cross in Arabic poetry: Sacrifice, victimization or the other side of heroism?',

in Friederike Pannewick (ed.), *Martyrdom in Literature: Visions of Death and Meaningful Suffering in Europe and the Middle East from Antiquity to Modernity* (Wiesbaden, 2004): 105–21.

13. See a survey of Palestinian poetry in Khalid A. Sulaiman, *Palestine and Modern Arab Poetry* (London, 1984) and 'Abd al-Rahman Yaghi, *Hayat al-Adab al-Filastini al-Hadith* (Beirut, 1968).

14. Khalidi, *The Iron Cage*, p. 32.

15. The presence of indigenous Palestinian Jews, a group that made up around 2 per cent of the population at the beginning of the century, was not acknowledged in the poetry or in other textual material that I have come across from this period. In official historical records this group is usually lumped under the label 'Jews' in contradistinction to Arabs. Waage quotes the 1918 population survey that reported the following groups: 688,957 Arabs and 58,728 Jews. The presence of indigenous Jews is not considered a category in this survey. Waage, *Konflikt*, p. 72.

16. Sa'di Abu Shawir, *Tatawwur al-Ittijah al-Watani fi al-Shi'r al-Filastini al-Mu'asir* (Beirut, 2003), p. 54.

17. Khalid A. Sulaiman, *Palestine and Modern Arab Poetry* (London, 1984), p. 55.

18. Abu Shawir, *Tatawwur al-Ittijah al-Watani*, p. 128.

19. Khalil Sakakini, Letter dated 25 January 1936, *Yawmiyyat Khalil Sakakini*, ed. Akram Musallam (Ramallah, 2006), p. 204.

20. Sakakini, Letter dated 25 April 1936, *Yawmiyyat Khalil Sakakini*, p. 240.

21. Sakakini, Letter dated 2 May 1936, *Yawmiyyat Khalil Sakakini*, pp. 242–3.

22. 'Al-Qiyada al-'Ulya li-l-Jihad al-Muqaddas li-Inqadh Filastin.' As Waage shows, the 1936–9 years were marked by an escalating fragmentation of political parties in Palestine where rivalry and tribal allegiances dominated the scene. Waage, *Konflikt*, p. 80.

23. Reproduced in Sakakini, *Yawmiyyat Khalil Sakakini*, p. 245.

24. 'Abd al-Rahim Mahmud, *Diwan 'Abd al-Rahim Mahmud*, ed. Kamal al-Sawafiri (Beirut, 2005), pp. 140–3.

25. This structure is called after Khalil ibn Ahmad (718–86), a lexicographer, grammarian and philologist from Basra. He set the rules of prosody and poetic metre for the Arabic *qasida*, or poem.

26. Jabra Ibrahim Jabra, *Al-Rihla al-Thamina* (Beirut, 1979), p. 45.

27. *Ghazal* poetry is one of the official genres of classical Arabic poetry dating back to the sixth century. It is a poem dealing with themes of love.

28. Classical Arabic poetry maintained a generic separation between *ghazal*, or love poetry, and other forms of poetry. Traditionally, *ghazal* never articulated political sentiment and was solely reserved for the glorification of love themes.

29. The al-Braq uprising was known to the Israelis as the Wailing Wall Incident, 1929. The Jews around Jerusalem demonstrated and called for the declaration of the city as Jewish. The Arabs were provoked and attacked them with stones and rifles. The British police were slow to intervene and eventually sentenced 1,000 Arabs to jail (and the three mujahidin to be hanged) while only one Jew received a sentence. See 'Abd al-Wahhab Kayyali, *Tarikh Filastin al-Hadith* (Beirut, 1999) for a full report on this incident.

30. *Muwashshah* is a strophic structure that originated in Andalusia. It revised the *khalili* metre by simplifying the classical prosodies in a way that made it especially amenable to song.

31. Ibrahim Tuqan, *Al-A'mal al-Shi'riyya al-Kamila*, ed. Zaki al-Mahasini (Beirut, 2005), pp. 274–85.

32. The 'court of Inquisition' is another link that Tuqan forges between the British treatment of the Palestinians and the Spanish Reconquista wars in Andalusia.

33. Quoted in Elias Khoury, 'In defense of metaphor', in Kamal Boullata (ed.), *Belonging and Globalization: Critical Essays in Contemporary Culture* (London, 2008): 75–84 (76).

34. Edward Said and Jean Mohr, *After the Last Sky* (New York, 1999), p. 38.

35. Salma Khadra Jayyusi, 'Two types of hero in contemporary Arabic literature', *Mundus Artium* 10/1 (1977): 35–49.

36. Sakakini, Letter dated 21 April 1936, *Yawmiyyat Khalil Sakakini*, p. 238.

Bibliography

Abbas, Ihsan, 'Al-shi'r mundhu bidayat al-intidab hatta sanat 1967', *al-Mawsu'a al-Filastiniyya* (Beirut, 1990), Vol. 4: 19–25.

Abu Shawir, Sa'di, *Tatawwur al-Ittijah al-Watani fi al-Shi'r al-Filastini al-Mu'asir* (Beirut, 2003).

Antonius, George, *The Arab Awakening* (Philadelphia, 1939).

Asad, Talal, *Formations of the Secular: Christianity, Islam, Modernity* (Stanford, 2003).

Hourani, Albert, *Arabic Thought in the Liberal Age: 1798–1939* (Cambridge, 1983).

Jabra, Ibrahim Jabra, *Al-Rihla al-Thamina* (Beirut, 1979).

Jankowski, James P., 'The Palestinian Arab Revolt of 1936–1939', *The Muslim World* 63/3 (July 1973): 220–33.

Jayyusi, Salma Khadra, 'Two types of hero in contemporary Arabic literature', *Mundus Artium* 10/1 (1977): 35–49.

Kanafani, Ghassan, 'Thawrat 1936–9 fi Filastin: khalfiyyat wa-tafasil wa-tahlil', *Shu'un Filastiniyya* 6 (January 1972): 45–67.

Karaki, Khalid, *Hamasat al-Shuhada': Ru'yat al-Shahada wa-l-Shahid fi-l-Shi'r al-'Arabi* (Beirut, 1998).

Kayyali, 'Abd al-Wahhab, *Tarikh Filastin al-Hadith* (Beirut, 1999).

Khalidi, Rashid, *Palestinian Identity: The Construction of Modern National Consciousness* (New York, 1997).

——, *The Iron Cage: The Story of the Palestinian Struggle for Statehood* (Boston, 2006).

Khalidi, Tarif, 'Palestinian historiography: 1900–1948', *Journal of Palestine Studies* 10/3 (1981): 59–76. (http://www.jstor.org/discover/10.2307/2536460? uid=3738744&uid=2&uid=4&sid=21102086445357, last accessed 3 April 2013).

Khoury, Elias, *Al-Dhakira al-Mafquda* (Beirut, 1990).

——, 'In defense of metaphor', in Kamal Boullata (ed.), *Belonging and Globalization: Critical Essays in Contemporary Culture* (London, 2008): 75–84.

Mahmud, 'Abd al-Rahim, *Diwan 'Abd al-Rahim Mahmud*, ed. Kamal al-Sawafiri (Beirut, 1987).

Pannewick, Friederike, 'The martyred poet on the cross in Arabic poetry: Sacrifice, victimization or the other side of heroism?', in F. Pannewick (ed.), *Martyrdom in Literature: Visions of Death and Meaningful Suffering in Europe and the Middle East from Antiquity to Modernity* (Wiesbaden, 2004): 105–21.

Said, Edward and Mohr, Jean, *After the Last Sky: Palestinian Lives* (New York, 1999).

Sakakini, Khalil, *Yawmiyyat Khalil Sakakini: Rasa'il Khalil Sakakini ila Sary fi Amrika, 1935–1937*, ed. Akram Mussalam (Ramallah, 2006).

Segev, Tom, *One Palestine, Complete: Jews and Arabs under the British Mandate* (London, 2001).

Sulaiman, Khalid A., *Palestine and Modern Arab Poetry* (London, 1984).

Tuqan, Ibrahim, *Al-A'mal al-Shi'riyya al-Kamila*, ed. Zaki al-Mahasini (Beirut, 2005).

Waage, Hilde Henriksen, *Konflikt og Stormaktspolitikk i Midtøsten* (Oslo, 2013).

Yaghi, 'Abd al-Rahman, *Hayat al-Adab al-Filastini al-Hadith* (Beirut, 1968).

16

Hollywood and Jihad

Thomas Riegler

This chapter explores the cultural representation of radical Islamist terrorism, subsumed under the label of 'jihadism', as an example of how American popular culture can organise and charge the perception of a particular issue. A review of Hollywood movies and American television series demonstrates that their portrayal of radical Islamist terrorism is essentialised and reduced to alleged characteristics like fanaticism, cruelty and totalitarian enmity towards 'Western freedoms'. In the process, depth and context are sacrificed to a simple dichotomy of good versus evil. Thus, the 'jihadist', as seen in cinema and on television since the 1980s, has morphed into the predominant 'enemy other' and provides a fitting antagonist for the USA in the post-Cold War era. While there have been some more nuanced explorations, the overwhelming majority of the films and television shows discussed here provide no insight into the meaning and complexities of jihad, but tend to reconstruct it as an unfathomable and alien spectre. In comparison, European perspectives tend to present more multilayered accounts of the jihadist theme, especially in addressing political and social 'root causes' of terrorist violence. As a result, stereotypes are subverted instead of being reinforced.

Hollywood and Radical Islamist Terrorism

Movies relating to political violence with an Arab or Islamic background began to emerge during the 1970s, when plane hijackings orchestrated by secular Palestinian groups made headlines (1976's *Victory at Entebbe*, 1977's *Black Sunday*). Since terrorism had not yet struck the US homeland, the entertainment industry mainly looked abroad for inspiration, and major events were dramatised for the screen. This more or less distanced perspective on terrorism changed abruptly once the USA was directly confronted with it: the hostage-taking of American diplomats in Tehran (1979) and the humiliating failure of the attempt to rescue them left a deep impression. Afterwards, devastating suicide bombings targeted the US Marines and the CIA presence in Lebanon (1982–4). Between 1985 and 1988, several US flights were either hijacked or bombed, with great loss of life. Responsible for this wave of terror were several Middle Eastern groups, among them Shi'ite religious extremists, who were organised, equipped and paid for by 'rogue states' like Libya, Syria and Iran. These events and the perceived weakness of the USA in the face of terror had far-reaching consequences for how the American public perceived and understood the Middle East, and the spectre of terrorist violence originating from that context.[1] During the 1980s, a set of movies – *The Delta Force* (1986), *Iron Eagle* (1986), *Death before Dishonor* (1987) – addressed the issue of rogue states aligned with terrorists and featured violent payback as well as armed rescue scenarios. Paradoxically, in retrospect, the emerging theatre of jihad got a remarkably different treatment from Hollywood: both the James Bond movie *The Living Daylights* (1987) and *Rambo III* (1988) represented the Afghan mujahidin as noble 'freedom fighters' in their struggle against the Red Army. At that time, jihad was a strategic asset in the struggle between East and West and had not yet taken aim at the 'far enemy'.

With the end of the Cold War, state-sponsored terrorists lost their symbolic value as villains. Instead, 1990s cinema offered the 'new threats' of the era: a crumbling world beset by failing state power, the emergence of asymmetric threats and new players in the form of transnational networks. The movies captured the phenomenon of decentralised local initiatives replacing the state-sponsored groups of the 1970s and 1980s quite accurately. Among the 'new' villains like Russian or Serb nationalists, narco-gangsters or African warlords, the jihadist featured prominently for the first time. This was mainly a consequence of the 1993 bombing of the World Trade Center. That first act of radical Islamist terrorism on US soil was a watershed event: no matter how destructive the terrorism of the 1980s had been, it was linked to the power struggle in Lebanon and limited to international flights and US installations abroad. The 'holy warriors' who tried to topple the Twin Towers with a car bomb were a different lot: lacking a state sponsor and a predictable strategic agenda, this act of terror was all about sending a message and engaging the USA in a war of ideas. Hollywood reacted swiftly and introduced the jihadist-terrorist in films like *Navy Seals* (1990), *True Lies* (1994), *Executive Decision* (1996), *Long Kiss Goodnight* (1996), *The Siege* (1999) and *Rules of Engagement* (2000).[2]

In the immediate period after the terrorist attacks of 11 September 2001, Hollywood shunned terrorism and focused instead on escapism, sci-fi and family entertainment. It took until 2005 for the subject to be picked up once again by mainstream cinema. The puppet comedy *Team America: World Police* (2005) satirised Hollywood's previous essentialism with regard to the Middle East. For example, the terrorists, all bin Laden lookalikes, keep uttering mangled gibberish like 'derka derka, Mohammad Jihad'.[3] A more earnest exploration was the indie production *The War Within* (2005), which focused on Hasan (Ayad Akhtar), a Pakistani engineer studying in Paris, who is kidnapped in broad daylight and brought to a secret prison in his home country to be brutally tortured. The violent experience transforms Hasan into a radical, who seeks revenge. He connects with a terrorist cell that is in the middle of planning an attack in New York. But Hasan's commitment is put under severe pressure from contradictions and conflicting emotions: the war in which he finds himself embroiled is fought 'within', inside his own mind.[4] A similar search for answers motivated *Syriana* (2005), a film that explores the political, economic, legal and social effects of the oil business. It is this corrupt system that produces terrorism in the form of blowback.[5]

The events of 9/11 were finally tackled directly in *United 93* (2006), in which Paul Greengrass retold the story of the one hijacked flight that did not reach its intended target. Instead, it crashed into a field in Pennsylvania, supposedly because the passengers revolted against the hijackers. The movie offers only a distanced portrait of the hijackers – although the very first scene, a prayer ritual during the morning hours of 11 September, depicts them as devout Muslims on a mission. But since *United 93* is all about the sacrifice of the passengers, the motivation and personal background of the terrorists remains totally obscure to the viewer. *Charlie Wilson's War* (2007) portrays how US efforts in Afghanistan during the 1980s led to the destabilisation of the country, but only hints at the far-reaching consequences of this process.[6]

As time established a growing distance from 9/11, film-makers focused on the progress of the global War on Terror and its consequences, both domestic and international. *Body of Lies* (2008) portrayed the endeavour as a morally ambivalent struggle in the shadows. CIA agent Roger Ferris (Leonardo DiCaprio) sets up a fictitious terror group to flush out a jealous al-Qa'ida mastermind, the Syrian-born, American-educated al-Sameen (Alon Aboutboul).[7] Gavin Hood's film *Rendition* (2007) took a contrary perspective by depicting an Arab as the victim of unlawful US counter-terrorism. Based on a true story, it involves Anwar al-Ibrahimi (Omar Metwally), an Egyptian natural scientist, who is married to an American woman and is caught in the trap of an overly vigilant security apparatus.[8] *The Kingdom* (2007) is one of the few examples where the action culminates in the successful accomplishment of a mission, in this case a counter-terrorism operation which is the result of cooperation between Western and Middle Eastern police forces. A team of FBI investigators works closely with Saudi police colonel al-Ghazi (Ashraf Barhom) to hunt down Abu Hamza, a mid-level al-Qa'ida operative, who is responsible for a bombing attack on an American compound in Riyadh.[9]

Iron Man (2008) marked the entry of the radical Islamist terrorist into the superhero genre: the 'Ten Rings', a group led by Raza (Faran Tahir), kidnaps arms dealer Tony Stark (Robert Downey Jr.) during his promotional tour in Afghanistan. To break out of captivity, Stark designs an armoured suit and vengefully returns later as 'Iron Man' to blast the terrorists from afar.[10] The movie is further proof that the jihadist is one of today's prime enemies, even in the sphere of science fiction. But due to some disappointing box office returns, especially from movies focusing on the Iraq war – *Land of the Brave* (2006), *In the Valley of Elah* (2007), *Badland* (2007), *Grace is Gone* (2007) – and a war-weary American public, the cinematic adaptation of terrorism-related themes decreased in the 2008–10 period. For example, *Unthinkable* (2010), which featured a scientist converted to Islam threatening the USA with nuclear destruction, was released directly to DVD. But shortly before the tenth anniversary of 9/11, some key policy decisions and events set both the US counter-terrorism approach and its cultural representation in a new framework: the killing of Osama bin Laden (2011) constituted a highly symbolic victory for the USA. Within a year, the US strike was undergoing dramatisation in one TV adaptation (*Seal Team Six: The Raid on Osama Bin Laden*, 2012) and two movies: *Zero Dark Thirty* (2012) and *Code Name: Geronimo* (2013). Also in 2011, the US withdrew its combat troops from Iraq and scheduled a retreat from Afghanistan for 2014, effectively concluding the global War on Terror as outlined by George W. Bush. The outlook on radical Islamic terrorism and 9/11 is therefore set to evolve away from social and political commentary as the subject is gradually relegated to history.

Jihadists on Television: 24 and *Sleeper Cell*

While Hollywood was initially reluctant to feature jihadists after 9/11, American television series like *24*, *The West Wing*, *Sleeper Cell*, *The Unit* and *E-Ring* dramatised terrorism scenarios shortly after the terrorist attacks. Since typical television scenarios primarily aim at domestic audiences, they are at less risk than Hollywood of alienating foreign market segments by casting enemies. Furthermore, the television series format provides writers and producers with the opportunity to explore events more profoundly than in feature films.[11] Yet this does not automatically mean a different outlook on jihad and radical Islamist terrorism. On the contrary, these issues are generally treated as dramatic story elements and their perpetrators are little more than cannon fodder for US agents with the occasional mastermind.

To underline this point, the following section focuses on two examples – *24* and *Sleeper Cell* – that deal substantially with the subject of radical Islamist terrorism. In *24* (nine seasons, 2001–14), the show's hero, Jack Bauer (Kiefer Sutherland), agent of the fictional Counter-terrorism Unit (CTU), has to fight against all kinds of nightmarish threats. Jihadists appear in Season 2 (2002–3): a shadowy group called 'Second Wave', led by Syed Ali (Francesco Quinn), plans to detonate an atomic bomb in Los Angeles. In Season 4 (2005), terrorist mastermind Habib Marwan (Arnold Vosloo), leader of the Turkish group 'Crimson Jihad', sets off a wave of terror: a commuter train explodes, the daughter of the Secretary of Defence is kidnapped and security breaches occur at several nuclear plants.[12] In Season 6 (2007), suicide bombers blow themselves up in subway trains, buses and public places. The terrorists even succeed in detonating a Soviet nuclear suitcase bomb. The following explosion destroys Valencia, a suburb of Los Angeles, and kills more than 12,000 people. To avert further attacks, Bauer teams up with an unlikely associate, the former terrorist al-Assad (Alexander Siddig) who now wants to pursue his goals through political means. When a colleague questions Bauer's decision to form this alliance because of al-Assad's past, the answer is pragmatic: 'The playing field has changed.'[13]

The jihadists in 24 may be formidable enemies, but the threat is subsidiary since all of these groups are revealed as mere puppets of powerful interests. 'Second Wave', for example, is being manipulated by a network of oilmen, who want to draw the USA into a Middle Eastern war.[14] Similarly, terrorist leader Abu Fayed from Season 6 is only an instrument used by Dmitri Gredenko (Rade Serbedzija), a former Soviet general, who frames the terrorists in order to provoke yet another disastrous Middle Eastern war that would allow Russia to become the dominant power. Effectively, 24 is full of treacherous characters in key government positions, inside the White House, CTU and even Jack Bauer's own family. This strong fictitious element makes 24 a perfect medium through which to explore safely one's own security nightmares – since the politics, targets, methods and motivations of the villains are so far-fetched.

While 24 represents a classic conservative fantasy, the Showtime series *Sleeper Cell* (two seasons, 2005–6) offers a more challenging portrayal, both of the inner workings of law enforcement agencies and radical Islamist terrorists. Season 1 (2005) depicts a jihadist sleeper cell in Los Angeles in the process of plotting an attack with biological agents. What its members do not realise is that their group has already been infiltrated: the mole, the African-American FBI undercover agent Darwyn al-Sayeed (Michael Ealy), is himself a devout Muslim. Equipped with a criminal cover story he was introduced to Faris al-Farik (Oded Fehr), the charismatic terrorist mastermind and leader of the cell who is a top operative of 'the base', as al-Qa'ida is called in the series.[15] Farik's subalterns, over whom he exercises absolute authority and the power of life and death, could not be a more disparate group: Illija (Henri Lubatti) is a Bosnian Muslim whose family was executed by Serb militiamen. Christian (Alex Nesic), a French convert and a former skinhead, now works as a tourist guide in Hollywood, while blue-eyed Tommy (Blake Shields) is the alienated son of a liberal professor at Berkeley. All in all, the cell is mostly composed of bloody amateurs, who panic easily and compromise their security by calling loved ones and relatives.[16]

In Season 2 ('American Terror', 2006), Darwyn embeds himself in a cell that was formed to avenge the break-up of the initial one. It is also composed of unusual recruits: an Iraqi-born engineer Salim (Omid Abtahi), a converted Latino gang member Benny (Kevin Alejandro) and Dutch convert Mina (Thekla Reuten), who is referred to as 'Osama Bin Dutch Chick'. Their radicalism is the result of personal grievances: Salim is driven by self-hatred because of his homosexuality. Mina, a former prostitute, seeks security behind the veil and wants to avenge her husband, who died a martyr's death in Iraq.[17] The situation soon gets out of hand: Salim improvises a dirty bomb and plans to set it off at the Hollywood Bowl, but is killed before he can do so. In Las Vegas, Mina carries out a suicide bombing at a gathering of veterans. At the same time Farik, who was captured at the end of Season 1 and whose interrogation was 'outsourced' to Saudi Arabia, escapes from prison. He hides with al-Qa'ida in Yemen, where Darwyn manages to track him down. The agent then coordinates a missile attack on the camp, but Farik again manages to slip away. *Sleeper Cell* has an open ending since it was cancelled in January 2007. The show may be more nuanced than *24*, yet it shares the same fixation on paranoia and tends to distort al-Qa'ida into a uniquely powerful terrorist enterprise already lurking in American suburbia.

Narratives of Jihad in American Television and Film

Having reviewed the cultural representation, five general conclusions may be drawn. First and most fundamentally, American popular culture envisions jihad and radical Islamism as a new totalitarian danger, superceding the previous threat of Communism. While typical post-Cold War villains tended to lack ideological depth, the emergence of the jihadist in the early 1990s again provided an enemy who kills and maims in the name of ideas set in radical opposition to core American values. American individualism, economic freedom and equality are set against this dogmatic and allegedly pre-modern and millenarian worldview.[18]

Second, there is almost no attempt at exploring jihad and its meaning beyond essentialising it as radical antagonism. There are, of course, exceptions to this rule, such as the television drama *Sleeper Cell*: the episode 'Scholar' (1.4) features a former convicted terrorist, who now successfully convinces imprisoned radicals of the 'true meaning' of jihad by teaching them to reject the violent path in favour of the 'jihad of the word'. The scholar almost succeeds in convincing cell member Christian that he follows a misinterpretation of Islam, crafted by political ideologues to manipulate their camp. When Christian replies that the 'greatest jihad' is 'to fight the unbelievers in battle', he is advised: 'The greatest jihad is to battle your own soul, to fight the evil in yourself.' Nonetheless, Christian obeys his orders and eventually murders the scholar, who has been identified as a threat by the terrorists.

Third, compared with other typical villains, the jihadist differs in his complete 'otherness', as Roland Bleiker has pointed out: 'The Middle East – or, rather, the Arab component of it – is the stereotypical image of the terrorist other, the one whose identity, whose religious affinities and practices are so strange that they cannot be seen as anything other than a threat to the existing societal order.'[19] If terrorists from Western backgrounds are shown, their purely criminal stance is immediately recognisable. The jihadist, on the other hand, comes across as radically different: fanatical, abusive towards women and more violent, because he regards all non-believers as enemies and is prepared to use indiscriminate terror and death to achieve his ends.[20] As screenwriter Steve De Souza told the BBC, Middle Eastern terrorists make perfect villains because they needed no explanatory context – the public immediately recognises them as a threat: 'They've got a turban, we don't have to know what's going on under the turban, just proceed with the story.'[21]

Fourth, both in movies and television shows, jihadists repeatedly lay down their agenda. But this communication takes on the form of 'loony' outbursts by fanatical and wild-eyed madmen. In *True Lies* (1994), a sweaty Abu Aziz – the villain – rants about the inhumanity of the US war machine that kills non-combatants in Arab countries. In retaliation, he threatens the US public with atomic bombs exploding in 'one major US city each week' until his demands are met. This stance immediately blurs and undercuts any brief insight into the motivation and legitimate grievances of the terrorists by emphasising the apparent irrationality and drive for self-aggrandisement of the character.[22] *Executive Decision* (1996), another telling example, features Arabs hijacking a Boeing 747 with the intention of blowing up the plane over Washington DC. 'We are the true Soldiers of Islam. Our destiny is to deliver the vengeance of Allah into the belly of the infidel,' brags Nagi Hassan (David Suchet), who describes himself as the 'sword of Allah'.[23] In his dogmatism and inhumanity, Hassan's identity is presented as fixed and closed off to outside influences. The same diagnosis can be applied to other terrorist masterminds. Thus, as politically motivated as some of their claims may be, they are rendered meaningless and delegitimised in the process.[24]

Fifth, while most of the films discussed here identify terrorists as devout Muslims, Hollywood appears to be taking care not to equate Islam with terrorism or to suggest that all Muslims are terrorists. Before 2001, portrayals of the practice of religion or notions of religious conviction as a motivation for terrorism are almost non-existent. *Death Before Dishonor* (1986) is one of the few examples where the conflict is presented in a religious context: a captured Marine hostage kisses his crucifix before dying, which evokes the image of the true Christian soldier fighting against terrorist jihad.[25] Elements of jihadist rhetoric can be found in *True Lies* and *Executive Decision*, but it was *The Siege* (1998) that showed for the first time a suicide bomber ritually purifying himself before 'martyrdom', before zooming in on a suicide bombing.[26] Since 9/11 such close explorations of the 'enemy other' have largely been abandoned. In fact, there seems to be less interest in the terrorists than before: as a result, 'an air of omission, even denial' hangs over Hollywood's contemporary portrayals of terrorists and terrorism.[27] In comparison, European productions like *The Hamburg Cell* (2004) or *Four Lions* (2010) address the subject of radical Islamist terrorism in a direct way. In doing so, these films provide a counter-narrative to prevailing views, because they reveal the enemy 'other' as much more human, Westernised and less professional than one might expect from viewing the American output. This sensitivity has been shaped on the one hand by the presence of large Islamic communities and the desire to convey accurate and nuanced accounts of political, social and security issues; and, on the other hand, by the fact that European targets have frequently been hit by jihadists since 2001, with the perpetrators often turning out to be second-generation immigrants.

Conclusion

In summary, radical Islamist terrorism is depicted in American television and film as essentially detached from reality and devoid of meaning. The threat it poses is fundamental and continues the older theme of totalitarian enmity to the American dream, which must be resisted relentlessly. In dealing with radical Islamist terrorism, films and television shows assemble an imaginary space and bring some of the hegemonic constants of the public discourse to life: a fantastical Middle East that seems naturally inhabited by terrorists preying on the West; sleeper cells already in place on US soil and waiting to strike with weapons of mass destruction; an enemy 'other', who kills and maims the innocent in the name of a totalitarian ideology and with whom no compromise is possible, and so forth. Hollywood's imperative is, of course, to entertain rather than to inform or educate. But while it is easy to shrug off its products as mere distraction, the role played by mass cinema's and television's easily transmitted and effective visions in shaping perceptions on a highly complex topic like jihad should not be underestimated.

Notes

1. Melani McAlister, 'Iran, Islam, and the terrorist threat, 1979–1989', in J. David Slocum (ed.), *Terrorism, Media, Liberation* (New Jersey, 2005): 137–70 (159).

2. Stephen Prince, *Firestorm: American Film in the Age of Terrorism* (New York, 2009), pp. 50–1.

3. Lina Khatib, *Filming the Modern Middle East: Politics in the Cinemas of Hollywood and the Arab World* (London, 2006), p. 180.

4. Ned Martel, 'The path from injustice to jihad', *The New York Times*, 30 September 2005.

5. Douglas Kellner, *Cinema Wars: Hollywood Film and Politics in the Bush-Cheney Era* (Oxford, 2010), p. 169.

6. Tom Pollard, *Hollywood 9/11: Superheroes, Supervillains, and Super Disasters* (Boulder, 2011), p. 66.

7. Oliver Boyd-Barrett, David Herrera and James Baumann, *Hollywood and the CIA: Cinema, Defense and Subversion* (London, 2011), p. 150.

8. A. O. Scott, 'When a single story has a thousand sides', *The New York Times*, 19 October 2007.

9. Ibid.

10. Dana Stevens, 'Iron Man', *Slate*, 1 May 2008.

11. Stephen Stockwell, 'Messages from the apocalypse: Security issues in American TV series', *Continuum: Journal of Media & Cultural Studies*, 25/2 (April 2011): 189–99.

12. *Fox.com*, '24: Episode guide' (n.d.) (www.fox.com/24/episodes/, last accessed 13 November 2006).

13. James Poniewozik, 'The evolution of Jack Bauer', *Time*, 14 January 2007.

14. Kolja Mensing, 'Ein amerikanischer Alptraum', *Taz*, 8 March 2004.

15. Alessandra Standley, 'Among terrorists a hero is lurking', *The New York Times*, 2 December 2005.

16. Lynn Smith, 'Showtime's *Sleeper Cell* brings terrorism home', *The Boston Globe*, 31 July 2005.

17. Troy Patterson, 'Uncovering the plot', *Slate*, 15 December 2006.

18. Sally Totman, *How Hollywood Projects Foreign Policy* (New York, 2009), p. 160.

19. Roland Bleiker, 'The "end of modernity"?', in Greg Fry, and Jacinta O'Hagan (eds.), *Contending Images of World Politics* (London, 2000): 227–44 (237).

20. Khatib, *Filming the Modern Middle East*, pp. 181–2.

21. *BBC Panorama*, 'September 11: A warning from Hollywood', 24 March 2002 (http://news.bbc.co.uk/hi/english/static/audio_video/programmes/panorama/transcripts/transcript_24_03_02.txt, last accessed 7 July 2009).

22. Helena Vanhala, *The Depiction of Terrorists in Blockbuster Hollywood Films, 1980–2001: An Analytical Study* (Jefferson, 2011), p. 238.

23. Prince, *Firestorm*, pp. 53–5.

24. Khatib, *Filming the Modern Middle East*, p. 181.

25. Robert Cettl, *Terrorism in American Cinema: An Analytical Filmography, 1960–2008* (Jefferson, 2009), pp. 94–6.

26. Ibid., p. 236.

27. Ross Douhat, 'The return of the paranoid style', *The Atlantic*, April 2008.

Bibliography

BBC Panorama, 'September 11: A warning from Hollywood', 24 March 2002 (http://news.bbc.co.uk/hi/english/static/audio_video/programmes/panorama/transcripts/transcript_24_03_02.txt, last accessed 7 July 2009).

Bleiker, Roland, 'The "end of modernity"?', in Greg Fry, and Jacinta O'Hagan (eds.), *Contending Images of World Politics* (London, 2000): 227–44.

Boyd-Barrett, Oliver, Herrera, David and Baumann, James, *Hollywood and the CIA: Cinema, Defense and Subversion* (London, 2011).

Cettl, Robert, *Terrorism in American Cinema. An Analytical Filmography, 1960–2008* (Jefferson, 2009).

Douhat, Ross, 'The return of the paranoid style', *The Atlantic*, April 2008.

Fox.com, '24: Episode guide' (n.d.) (www.fox.com/24/episodes/, last accessed 13 November 2006).

Fry, Greg and O'Hagan, Jacinta (eds.), *Contending Images of World Politics* (London, 2000).

Kellner, Douglas, *Cinema Wars: Hollywood Film and Politics in the Bush-Cheney Era* (Oxford, 2010).

Khatib, Lina, *Filming the Modern Middle East: Politics in the Cinemas of Hollywood and the Arab World* (London, 2006).

Martel, Ned, 'The path from injustice to jihad', *The New York Times*, 30 September 2005.

McAlister, Melani, 'Iran, Islam, and the terrorist threat, 1979–1989', in J. David Slocum (ed.), *Terrorism, Media, Liberation* (New Jersey, 2005): 137–70.

Mensing, Kolja, 'Ein amerikanischer Alptraum', *Taz*, 8 March 2004.

Patterson, Troy, 'Uncovering the plot', *Slate*, 15 December 2006.

Pollard, Tom, *Hollywood 9/11: Superheroes, Supervillains, and Super Disasters* (Boulder, 2011).

Poniewozik, James, 'The evolution of Jack Bauer', *Time*, 14 January 2007.

Prince, Stephen, *Firestorm: American Film in the Age of Terrorism* (New York, 2009).

Scott, A. O., 'FBI agents solve the terrorist problem', *The New York Times*, 28 September 2007.

———, 'When a single story has a thousand sides', *The New York Times*, 19 October 2007.

Slocum, David (ed.), *Terrorism, Media, Liberation* (New Jersey, 2005).

Smith, Lynn, 'Showtime's *Sleeper Cell* brings terrorism home', *The Boston Globe*, 31 July 2005.

Standley, Alessandra, 'Among terrorists a hero is lurking', *The New York Times*, 2 December 2005

Stevens, Dana, 'Iron Man', *Slate*, 1 May 2008.

Stockwell, Stephen, 'Messages from the apocalypse: Security issues in American TV series', *Continuum: Journal of Media & Cultural Studies*, 25/2 (April 2011): 189–99.

Totman, Sally, *How Hollywood Projects Foreign Policy* (New York, 2009).

Vanhala, Helena, The *Depiction of Terrorists in Blockbuster Hollywood Films, 1980–2001: An Analytical Study* (Jefferson, 2011).

17

'Jihadists of the Pen' in Victorian England

Eric Germain

Some 50 years ago, Norman Daniel published a book entitled *Islam and the West: The Making of an Image*.[1,2] This title would lend itself well to the present chapter as it will discuss how, in Europe, the academic debate about the true and unbiased meaning of jihad epitomises a much broader and deeper issue: that of the making of the image of Islam in the West.

In the British society of the late Victorian period, jihad ranked first among the elements highlighted by some individuals and groups to advocate the barbarian and backwards nature of Islam, anti-modern by essence, whose ultimate fate was to be overruled by Christianity. Jihad, alongside the issues of slavery and polygamy, was part of an oft-mentioned trinity of the most obvious proofs of the 'true nature of Muhammadanism'.[3] This essentialist vision displays an inbuilt stigma against Islam, 'attributing to the Koran and Muhammad the wars of aggression and compulsory proselytizing'.[4] It came not only from Christian missionary or political or military circles, but also received a great deal of support from leading scholars of the time like Sir William Muir (1819–1905), who have been described as 'evangelical orientalists'.[5]

G. W. Leitner: a Non-Muslim Scholar who Challenged Victorian Images of Islam

The response to the discourse on the 'deficiencies of Islam' came first from the Muslim elite of the British Empire. Some progressive Indian intellectuals of the stature of Sir Sayyid Ahmad Khan (1817–98) responded to the negative picture of their religion and challenged the European authoritative literature on jihad, reckoning that some of those 'misconceptions' were shared by Muslims themselves.[6]

A cornerstone of this intellectual response is the book of Cheragh Ali (1844–95), Khan's protégé, written in English, which has a great legacy on this very issue in Muslim literature. The full subtitle of this book, published in Calcutta in 1885, illustrates perfectly the intentions of its author: *Critical Exposition of the Popular 'Jihad.' Showing that all the Wars of Mohammad were Defensive and that aggressive War, or Compulsory Conversion, is not Allowed in the Koran*. This Muslim scholar is fully aware of the geopolitical dimension of this debate, and his book is deliberately written in English to target and challenge the view 'held by some of the European and American writers'.[7]

This, however, was the response 'from the East'. The response 'from the West' came mostly from a handful of European converts to Islam, such as the Liverpool solicitor Abdullah (formerly William) Quilliam (1856–1932).[8] This colourful personality published a weekly and a monthly magazine, *The Crescent* and *The Islamic World*, which were disseminated throughout the British Empire and beyond.[9] Quilliam's articles and public lectures were also published as pamphlets, such as *Fanatics & Fanaticism* (1890) or *The Religion of the Sword* (1891), addressing in a straightforward prose various stereotypes about the supposed inherent violence of Islam.

On the issue of jihad, the Muslim voice carried little weight in challenging the orientalist academic mainstream that supported the depiction of Islam as the 'religion of the sword', with jihad meaning a war of aggression waged against non-believers. In what remained an asymmetric battle over image, there were also a few academics who challenged the dominant vision of jihad and argued in favour of a conciliatory approach to Islam. Among the voices promoting Islam's civilising role were the Oxford professor Reginald Bosworth Smith (*Mohammed and Mohammedanism*,

1874), and before him Rev. Charles Forster (*Mahometanism Unveiled*, 1829) and Rev. John Frederick Denison Maurice (*The Religions of the World*, 1846).[10]

Barely any of those scholars who saw Islam as an ally of Christianity had many years of actual field experience in Muslim societies. One of the very first non-Muslim voices to have the authority of a 'colonial-proven' background was the Hungarian-born Gottlieb Wilhelm Leitner (1840–99).[11] This gifted linguist, educationalist, historian, explorer and art-collector – among several other pursuits – was born in 1840 to a cosmopolitan German Jewish family. In his childhood, he followed his parents to Malta and Constantinople where he learned Ottoman Turkish and some Arabic. At the age of 15, during the Crimean War, Leitner enrolled in the British army to serve as an interpreter. Demobilised, he went to study at King's College in London, where he was soon appointed a lecturer in Turkish, Arabic and Modern Greek. He joined the Indian Service in 1864 and served until 1886, becoming the first principal of the newly established Government College in Lahore, later to become the University of Punjab.

As an educationalist, Leitner favoured the introduction of Western knowledge to Indian pupils in their own language. In that spirit, Leitner even founded vernacular and English newspapers to promote his ideal of the renaissance of local cultures focusing on the study of Sanskrit and Arabic. He soon gained sympathy among the Punjabi gentry, especially among Muslims. He had a sincere interest and sympathy for Islam, although he did not condone Europeans converting to Islam,[12] being himself a Church of England neophyte. Upon his return to England, he founded in 1884 an Institute for Oriental Studies – affiliated to the University of Punjab and modelled on the Paris School of Oriental Languages – and for this purpose he bought a large estate in Woking (Surrey).

Leitner's Three Categories: 'Great Jihad', 'Small Jihad' and 'Crescentade'

Leitner's article entitled 'Jihad – Misconceptions about Islamic teaching' appeared in the *Asiatic Quarterly Review* edition of October 1886.[13] The article begins with the following assertion: 'The subject of *jihad* is so thoroughly misunderstood both by European scholars and by the bulk of Muhammadans themselves that it will be well to point out what really constitutes *jihad*.' He continues with the assertion that 'in order to do so, it is necessary to analyse the word and to show when and how it was first used';[14] that is to say, he advocates the analysis of jihad in the Qur'anic text and its historical context.

This preliminary observation on the wide misconception of the word jihad is similar to the argument adopted in the book *Critical Exposition of the Popular 'Jihád'* published in Calcutta the year before by Cheragh Ali. Its first appendix, under the title 'Jihad does not mean war or crusade', begins with the following sentence (emphasis in the original):

> The popular word *Jihad* or *Jihd*, occurring in several passages of the Koran, and generally construed by Christians and Moslems alike as meaning hostility or the waging of war against infidels, does not classically or literally signify war, warfare, hostility or fighting, and it is never used in such sense in the Koran.[15]

But if Cheragh Ali confines himself to a lexicological field and speaks only for the Qur'an and the ethics of war of the Prophet Muhammad, Leitner goes much further in discussing jihad's eminently political dimension. Indeed, Leitner explains at length that the Qur'anic meaning of jihad is 'utmost exertion' and discusses this philologically, concluding that the several ordinary meanings given by Arabic lexicographers clearly include jihad as a war with an enemy. He writes:

> It was only natural that when reference was made to a '*jihad* in the path of God' the word should have come to mean a fight in the cause of religion, and that, finally, when the words 'in the path of God' were dropped in ordinary conversation, or writing, it should assume the meaning of a 'religious war', which it has kept to the present day.[16]

Explaining Muhammad's perception of holy war, he notes that in his time 'the war with the aggressors on the Muhammadan faith' was called the 'small jihad', the 'great jihad' being the 'war with sin'.[17] Leitner insists on the fact that the lesser jihad is holy war but has nothing to do with a war against infidels with the aim of proselytising. Quoting exhortations to non-violence in the Qur'an and in Muhammad's life and sayings, Leitner emphasises that this lesser jihad should not be confused with what he called 'Crescentade', meaning the Islamic counterpart of the Christian 'Crusade'. He asserts that this 'Crescentade' is as distant from the teachings of the Qur'an as the Crusade was from the teachings of the Bible.

Historicising and Contextualising Jihad in 1880s World Affairs

Leitner was addressing an audience that had a vivid memory of the findings of the sensational 'Wahhabi Trials' that followed the 1857 'Indian Mutiny' and that was likely to have read of General Gordon's recent beheading in Khartoum. He refutes the thesis of 'global jihadism' as a synonym of 'global Wahhabism'. The idea of an international jihadist conspiracy originating from the Arabian peninsula gained popularity as more Western scholars depicted Mecca as a conspicuous and dangerous cosmopolitan hub (the famous Dutch orientalist Christiaan Snouck Hurgronje visited Mecca in 1885). Leitner opposed this vision and, speaking about Mahdist rule in Sudan (that lasted until 1889); he claims:

> (The Khartoum affair) has not, and cannot have, the faintest influence on the attitude of Muhammadans under Christian rule [Muslim Indians], whatever their condition or treatment [. . .] From a religious point of view, I shall go further and prove that the most suspected class in the Muhammadan community, the so-called Wahabi [sic.], is the one that, under all circumstances, is the foremost in deprecating resistance to constituted authority, however obtained and by whomsoever exercised.[18]

He distinguished between the emotional 'Crescentade' of dervish fanatics in Sudan and the rational 'defensive jihad' as understood by Wahhabis in India (who would not contemplate rebelling against the British Queen acting as the protector of her Muslim subjects). Leitner thus opposes most of his contemporaries, who equated jihad with Wahhabism's transnational influence following various events: the activities of Ahmad Barelwi (1786–1831) and Muhammad Ismail (1779–1831) in northern India in the 1820s,[19] the 'Indian Mutiny' of 1857 and the assassination of Lord Mayo, the Viceroy of India, in February 1872. Despite – or maybe because of – his iconoclastic stance, Leitner's scholarly discourse found an attentive ear within some Whitehall circles (opened to him by his acquaintance with Sir Alfred Comyn Lyall and Sir Lepel Griffin). As Leitner himself predicted about his article on jihad, 'this inquiry will not only be of academical interest, but will also perhaps be of some political importance, because it is immediately connected with the question of the *Khalifa* and of the *Imam*, as understood by the two great sects, the *Sunni* and the *Shi'ahs*'.[20] In fact, Leitner's article was specifically written in reaction to a recent article published by the London evening newspaper, *The Globe and Traveller*. The *Globe* article commented on an appeal in a Tehran newspaper to form an Islamic Confederation with the purpose of launching a 'joint jihad' in the case of one member of the confederation being attacked by a non-Muslim power. The British paper claimed that such a confederation would put all 'non-Muhammadan' governments under the threat of their own Muslim subjects, 'who are assumed to be under a tacit treaty of allegiance with [the confederation]'.[21] In giving what he presents as being the correct religious interpretation of jihad, Leitner explains how the true intentions of Persia have been misinterpreted.

He presents the proposed 'Islamic Confederation' as designed to cement a feeling of brotherhood between Sunni and Shi'ite Muslims, which would have a positive impact in India. He continues by suggesting that such an alliance of Muslim states – which at that time would have a noticeable Central Asian identity – should be placed under the aegis of Great Britain rather than Russia. In this pragmatic vision of the Great Game, jihad was normalised as an ethical and cultural bond, providing a firmer structure to the natural relationship of neighbouring states in the region. He advocates that such a regional Islamic Confederation, capitalising on the effective deterrence of jihad, could oppose Russian expansion in Central and South Asia and therefore assert the stability of the British Empire in India.

The Political and Mercantile Dimensions Underlying Leitner's Article

The author of this audacious analysis of the Shah's benevolent disposition towards the British Crown may have not been entirely convinced by his own advocacy. Such claims were not only received positively by the Persian government, but among some high civil servants such as Sir Lepel Griffin (1838–1908), the Agent to the Governor General for Central India. The latter had responsibility for a number of princely states, including Bhopal, and had financed most of Leitner's initiatives in Punjab as well as in England, being one of the main sponsors of his Oriental Institute in Woking.[22]

This justification of Persia's mild 'defensive jihad' came at a time when Griffin, the owner of the *Asiatic Quarterly Review* in which Leitner's article was published, was seeking the goodwill of Tehran's regime and India's Muslim rulers. Its publication date (1886) was also the year when Leitner retired from the Indian Civil Service and Griffin temporarily left his position of Agent to the Governor General for Central India, to be appointed Royal Commissioner of the Indian and Colonial Exhibition in London, preparing a second career for himself. Retiring from the Indian Civil Service in 1889, Griffin clearly expressed his interest in business and politics, becoming Chairman of the Imperial Bank of Persia and, from 1894, Chairman of the East India Association.

Leitner's defence of Islam and friendly disposition towards Muslim rulers from Persia to India assisted him in finding funding for his Oriental Institute,[23] but also helped to open doors in London's political and financial circles. This more practical dimension entwined with Leitner's scholarly views may be observed in other publications such as his articles praising Griffin's role in securing the Amir of Afghanistan's positive disposition towards the British Crown.[24] In today's diplomatic language, one could say that Leitner was able to articulate some of the tools of 'soft power' in furthering British imperial domination. Nevertheless, the 1886 article on jihad remains a pioneering work and the contextual aspects mentioned above do not detract from Leitner's intellectual impact.

The Impact of Leitner's Article on Jihad

The article was translated into Arabic by Leitner himself and appeared in 1890 in his quarterly magazine in Arabic, *Al-'Aqa'id* ('*Islamic Beliefs*'), published in Woking and Hyderabad.[25] A comparison of the various translations, in Arabic and probably also in Urdu and other Indian vernacular languages, still remains to be done. The article in English has attained a posterity of its own, essentially connected with the activities of the Woking Muslim Mission and Literary Trust in the twentieth century following a tradition of a 'jihad of the tongue' or a 'jihad of the pen'.[26]

Leitner's Oriental Institute did not survive its founder's death in 1899, but the Mogul-style mosque built on the Woking estate with the generous help of the rulers of Bhopal and Hyderabad was occasionally used by local Muslims. In 1913, the Woking Mosque and its premises were given to Khwaja Kamaluddin (1870–1932), who founded the Woking Mission financed by the Lahore branch of the Ahmadiyya,[27] a missionary movement holding very radical views on jihad.[28] As the first fully fledged mosque on British soil, it was – until the end of the Second World War – the beacon of Islam in Britain and visited by many Muslim world leaders.[29] Operating on a non-sectarian basis,[30] the Woking Muslim Mission and Literary Trust played a significant role in rooting Islam in England.[31]

As the founder of the Woking Mosque and, more importantly, as a Muslim convert who held progressive views similar to those promoted by the Ahmadiyya movement, the very first global Muslim missionary network, Leitner's articles were reprinted in the Woking Mission's *Islamic Review*, which was popular with the English-speaking Muslim social elite in Europe, the USA and throughout the British Empire.[32] In some of the countries where the *Islamic Review* was circulated, articles took on a life of their own, being reprinted and quoted in local Muslim newspapers. This was the case with Leitner's article on jihad, which made a strong impact in the remote lands of southern Africa and South East Asia.[33]

Leitner's intellectual legacy was clearly evident in the numerous booklets and leaflets published by the Woking Mission and Literary Trust. This literature continued the process of the 'euphemisation of jihad' when dealing with the highly controversial subject of Islamic warfare; the concept of jihad was narrowed, made more palatable, then finally erased. Thus, while the discussion on jihad constituted only one out of the five chapters of Marmaduke Pickthall's 1919 book *War & Religion*, the word 'jihad' is completely omitted in the booklet *Ethics of War* published a few years later by Khwaja Kamaluddin.[34] The leader of the Woking Mission seems to have concluded that, if the genuine meaning of 'lesser Jihad' was '(Islamic) Ethics of War', the most effective way of avoiding confusion when addressing a Western audience was simply to shun the term jihad entirely.

Conclusion: Leitner's Relevance Today

In 2002, a compilation of Leitner's articles was published in Lahore, in memory of the founder of the University of Punjab.[35] But the views on Islam of this nineteenth-century Victorian Christian have found today a much more globalised audience through the internet. In the Wikipedia article dealing with 'Islam and violence', the chapter 'Islamic sources' refers to Leitner's 1886 article on jihad, presented alongside articles from twentieth century 'jihadists of the pen' (English-speaking Muslim scholars linked to the Woking Mission).[36]

In a post-Edward Said twenty-first century academic world, the work and legacy of Leitner cannot be limited to a nineteenth-century 'counter model' constrained to some mainstream, prejudiced 'evangelical oriental-ism' represented by the likes of William Muir. What may be considered today a well-balanced and academically sound vision of jihad was never-theless highly political (and perfectly consistent with colonial strategies), as the subject itself – jihad and perceptions of it – has more to do with politics than with religion. Leitner's 1886 article was purposely written not only to influence the Whitehall policymakers' understanding of ji-had, but also to convince contemporary Muslim rulers (especially those in Persia) of the strength of an unbiased discourse on Islam among London's political elite and to convince them of the good intentions of British foreign policy. Today, Leitner deserves much more than an eru-dite footnote. His philologist's taste for semantic precision remains of central importance to contemporary debates on jihad.

Some Western leaders have recognised the need for semantic pre-cision when dealing with religion in their public speeches. One of the issues is the need to differentiate the word 'Islam' as referring to the 're-ligion of Islam' from its use to characterise the cultural and civilisational dimension of an 'Islamdom' or 'Muslim world' in contradistinction to 'Christendom' or the 'Western world'. This initial binary division would then allow differentiation between a 'Muslim world' – which some would like to see as an essential civilisational entity – and 'Muslims around the world'. De-essentialising the idea of a 'Muslim world' was central to

President Obama's Cairo speech of June 2009, when he made careful use of the expressions 'Muslims around the world' and 'Muslim-majority countries' instead of 'Muslim world'.[37] Such phrasing not only reflects the reality of the *umma* (Islamic community), but allows Barack Obama to contest, on a linguistic level, the perception prevalent in some circles that American Muslims are doubtful citizens or even fifth columnists with an allegiance to one 'Islamdom' – seen as essentially violent and jihadist.

In 1886, Leitner not only stated that 'the subject of *jihad* is [...] thoroughly misunderstood both by European scholars and by the bulk of Muhammadans themselves', but also that it was of 'some political importance, because it is immediately connected with the question of the *Khalifa* and of the *Imam*'.[38] The most interesting dimension of his argument was not that it drew a line between the 'great jihad' or war with sin and 'small jihad' or military warfare, but rather the light it shed on the dual understanding of this 'small jihad' which can apply both to ethical norms of warfare as well as to the notion of 'holy war' or 'Crescentade'.

Leitner may not have coined the neologism of 'Crescentade'/ 'crescentader(s)' – which was commonly used during the thrilling 'Wahhabi Trials' of the 1860s and 1870s[39] – but he was the first person to use the term with the clear purpose of divesting the word 'jihad' of its harmful connotation of holy war. The need to rethink jihad in order to bring greater clarity to a heated public debate endures, and is as pressing – if not more so – than in Leitner's time. Analysing mujahidin discourse on jihad, one can recognise that this political ideology ('Crescentade') might contain some degree of religiously based ethical norms of warfare ('jihad'),[40] but, as Leitner rightly recognised and attempted to establish, the two need to be duly detached from one another.

Notes

1. The views expressed in this chapter are solely those of the author in his private capacity.
2. Norman Daniel, *Islam and the West: The Making of an Image* (Edinburgh, 1960).
3. *Remarks on the nature of Muhammadanism* was a booklet written by Rev. C. G. Pfander and published in Calcutta in 1840. Carl Gottlieb Pfander (1803–65) was a famous Christian missionary in northern India.

4. Cheragh Ali, *Critical Exposition of the Popular 'Jihâd'* (Calcutta, 1885), p. 138, illustrates this with a quotation from William Muir, *Life of Mahomet* (London, 1861), Vol. 4, pp. 251–2.

5. Avril Ann Powell, *Muslims and Missionaries in Pre-Mutiny India* (London, 1993), p. 144. In the mid-1880s, William Muir (1819–1905) was at the pinnacle of his academic career, being successively elected president of the Royal Asiatic Society and principal of Edinburgh University.

6. See, for example, his *Review on Dr. Hunter's 'Indian Musalmans; are they bound in conscience to rebel against the Queen?'* (Benares, 1872).

7. Ali, *Critical Exposition*, p. xxviii.

8. The long-awaited biography of Abdullah Quilliam has been written by Ron Geaves, *Islam in Victorian Britain: The Life and Times of Abdullah Quilliam* (Markfield, 2010).

9. See, for instance, Abdullah Quillam, 'The Crusades and their effect upon European civilisation', in *The Islamic World* (August 1894): 114–9. The international impact of Quilliam's press is discussed in Eric Germain, 'Southern hemisphere diasporic communities in the building of an international Muslim public opinion at the turn of the twentieth century', in *Comparative Studies of South Asia, Africa and the Middle East* 27/1 (2007): 126–38.

10. In his article 'Victorian images of Islam', Clinton Bennett identifies two schools of scholarship toward Islam 'mutually aware and mutually critical of each other'; *International Bulletin of Missionary Research*, 25/5 (July 1991): 115–19. William Muir (1819–1905) would represent those who had a 'confrontational' attitude towards Islam, as opposed to a 'conciliatory' school of thought personified by Professor Reginald Bosworth Smith (1839–1908), and before him Rev. F. D. Maurice (1805–1872) and Rev. Charles Forster (c.1787–1871), the author of *A Vindication of the Theory of Mahometanism Unveiled* (London, 1830).

11. Ahmad Nasir, 'Dr. Gottlieb Wilhelm Leitner', www.muslim.org (n.d.) (http://www.muslim.org/woking/dr_leitner.htm, last accessed 29 December 2013); see also 'Mezzofanti outdone by Leitner' (a notice reprinted from *The Westminster Gazette*), *New York Times*, 18 March 1994 and 'G. W. Leitner dead: An orientalist and linguist of great attainments', *New York Times*, 25 March 1899.

12. In his correspondence with William 'Abdullah' Quilliam, Leitner objected to the use of the mosque he built on his Woking estate to promote 'generally unhappy marriages between Mohammedans and Englishwomen'; Geaves, *Islam in Victorian Britain*, p. 263.

13. G. W. Leitner, 'Jihad – misconceptions about Islamic teaching', *The Asiatic Quarterly Review* 2/4 (October 1886): 338–53.

14. Leitner, 'Jihad', p. 338.

15. Ali, *Critical Exposition*, pp. 163–4.

16. Leitner, 'Jihad', p. 346.

17. Ibid., p. 348.

18. Ibid., p. 340.

19. Marc Gaborieau, *Le Mahdi Incompris – Sayyid Ahmad Barelwî (1786–1831) et le Millénarisme en Inde* (Paris, 2010).

20. Leitner, 'Jihad', p. 340.

21. Cited in Leitner, 'Jihad', p. 341.

22. On Sir Lepel Griffin see Barbara D. Metcalf, 'Colonial Bhopal', presidential address, 125th Annual Meeting of the American Historical Association, Boston, 2011 (http://www.historians.org/info/aha_history/metcalf.cfm, last accessed 1 March 2012).

23. Leitner's article 'In defence of Muhammadanism', first published in *The Globe and Traveller* on 16 February 1894, received great acclaim from the Persian ambassador in London. It was reprinted together with the letter of the Persian ambassador in *The Asiatic Quarterly Review*, 7/13–14 (January–April 1894): 456–8.

24. Griffin had been the Chief Political Officer of Great Britain in Kabul at the end of the Second Afghan War in 1880. In 1894, Leitner wrote an article to contest the popular perception of Sir Mortimer Durand's role 'in strengthening the friendship between the Amir of Afghanistan (Abdul Rahman) and Great Britain', attributing this friendship to the actions of Sir Donald Stewart and Sir Lepel Griffin; G. W. Leitner, 'The Amir of Afghanistan and Great Britain', *The Asiatic Quarterly Review* 7/13–14 (January–April 1894): 283–94.

25. G. W. Leitner, 'Jihad', *Al-'Aqa'id*, Oriental Institute: Woking, Hyderabad, Deccan, 2/2 (30 April 1890): 41–53.

26. The archives of the Shah Jehan Mosque (Woking) were given to the Surrey History Centre in August 2008. See Shah Jehan Mosque Archives (Woking), 'Woking Muslim Mission and Literary Trust correspondence and publications, 1920–1985', Ref. 8382.

27. Ahmadiyya is a reformist and pioneering global Muslim missionary movement founded in Punjab by Mirza Ghulam Ahmad (1836–1908). In 1914, his followers split into two groups (the Lahore and Qadian branches) owing to a disagreement about the prophetic nature of Mirza Ghulam Ahmad. The controversial claims of the founder of the movement led many Sunni religious authorities to declare Ahmadiyya members non-Muslims (nevertheless, the institution of al-Azhar and some Indonesian ulama distinguished so-called 'Qadianis' from more orthodox 'Lahoris').

28. In his booklet in Urdu, *The British Government and Jihad* (1900), Mirza Ghulam Ahmad distinguished (similar to Leitner's distinction between 'emotional' Sudanese Mahdists and 'rational' Indian Wahhabis) the 'highly emotional sermons (on jihad) made by contemporary Muslim leaders called *maulvis*' from his own claim that 'this is not the age for a jihad (with the sword)' and that 'it is the duty of every Muslim to abstain from jihad (with the sword)'. Mirza Ghulam Ahmad, *The British Government and Jihad* (Tilford, 2006; 1st ed. in Urdu, 1900).

29. Among the Muslim activists and dignitaries who came to Woking were Muhammad Ali Jinnah, Adil Arslan (brother of Shakib Arslan), Muhammad Iqbal, Muhammad Ali Jauhar, Ayub Khan, Tunku Abdur Rahman, the Begum of Bhopal and princes from the Afghan, Persian and Hijazi royal families (including the future King Faisal).

30. Woking imams consciously rotated those who led the congregations in order to represent a diversity of Muslim nations and followers of different schools. See Humayun Ansari, 'Muslim engagement with British society in the 20th century: the Woking Mosque', *PlainIslam* (http://www.plainislam.com/in-depth/muslim-engagement-with-british-society-in-the-20th-century-the-woking-mosque.aspx, last accessed 29 December 2013).

31. Eric Germain, 'The first Muslim mission on a European scale: Ahmadi-Lahori networks in the inter-war period', in N. Clayer and E. Germain (eds.), *Islam in Inter-War Europe* (Hurst, 2008): 89–118.

32. Germain, 'Southern hemisphere diasporic communities', pp. 126–38.

33. 'Dr. Leitner on jihad', *Muslim Messenger* (June 1936): 24.

34. Marmaduke Pickthall was famous for his 1930s English translation of the Qur'an; Khwaja Kamaluddin, the imam of the Woking Mosque, wrote a booklet entitled *Ethics of War* a few years later.

35. M. Ikram Chaghatai, *Writings of Dr. Leitner* (Lahore, 2002).

36. Wikipedia.org, 'Islam and violence', n.d. (http://en.wikipedia.org/wiki/Islam_and_violence, last accessed 1 March 2012).

37. Barack Obama, 'A new beginning', Cairo University, 4 June 2009 (full text available at www.huffingtonpost.com/2009/06/04, last accessed 1 March 2012).

38. Leitner, 'Jihad', p. 340.

39. See for instance the numerous occurrences in W. Hunter, *The Indian Musalmans: Are they bound in conscience to rebel against the Queen?* (London, 1871).

40. Muhammad Munir, 'The Layha for the Mujahideen: an analysis of the code of conduct for the Taliban fighters under Islamic law', *International Review of the Red Cross* 93/881 (March 2011): 81–120.

Bibliography

Ahmad, Mirza Ghulam, *The British Government and Jihad* (Tilford, 2006; 1st ed. in Urdu, 1900).

Ahmad, Nasir, 'Dr. Gottlieb Wilhelm Leitner', www.muslim.org (n.d.) (http://www.muslim.org/woking/dr_leitner.htm, last accessed 29 December 2013).

Ali, Cheragh, *Critical Exposition of the Popular 'Jihád'* (Calcutta, 1885).

Ansari, Humayun, 'Muslim engagement with British society in the 20th century: the Woking Mosque', *PlainIslam* (http://www.plainislam.com/in-depth/muslim-engagement-with-british-society-in-the-20th-century-the-woking-mosque.aspx, last accessed 29 December 2013).

Bennet, Clinton, 'Victorian images of Islam', *International Bulletin of Missionary Research* 15/5 (July 1991): 115–19.

Chaghatai, M. Ikram, *Writings of Dr. Leitner* (Lahore, 2002).

Daniel Norman, *Islam and the West: The Making of an Image* (Edinburgh, 1960).

Gaborieau, Marc, *Le Mahdi Incompris – Sayyid Ahmad Barelwî (1786–1831) et le Millénarisme en Inde* (Paris, 2010).

Geaves, Ron, *Islam in Victorian Britain: The Life and Times of Abdullah Quilliam* (Markfield, 2010).

Germain, Eric, 'Southern hemisphere diasporic communities in the building of an international Muslim public opinion at the turn of the twentieth century', *Comparative Studies of South Asia, Africa and the Middle East* 27/1 (2007): 126–38.

———, 'The first Muslim mission on a European scale: Ahmadi-Lahori networks in the inter-war period', in N. Clayer and E. Germain (eds.), *Islam in Inter-War Europe* (London, 2008): 89–118.

Hunter, W., *The Indian Musalmans: Are they bound in conscience to rebel against the Queen?* (London, 1871).

Kamaluddin, Khwaja, *Ethics of War* (Woking, n.d.) (http://aaiil.org/text/books/kk/ethicswar/ethicswarpdf.shtml, last accessed 29 December 2013).

Khan, Ahmad, *Review of 'Dr. Hunter's Indian Musalmans; are they bound in conscience to rebel against the Queen?'* (Benares, 1872).

Leitner, G. W., 'The Amir of Afghanistan and Great Britain', *The Asiatic Quarterly Review* 7/13–14 (January–April 1894): 283–94.

———, 'In defence of Muhammadanism', *The Asiatic Quarterly Review*, 7/13–14 (January–April 1894): 456–8.

———, 'Jihad – misconceptions about Islamic teaching', *The Asiatic Quarterly Review* 2/4 (October 1886): 338–53.

————, 'Jihad', *Al-'Aqa'id*, Oriental Institute: Woking, Hyderabad, Deccan, 2/2 (30 April 1890): 41–53.

Metcalf, Barbara D., 'Colonial Bhopal', presidential address, 125th Annual Meeting of the American Historical Association, Boston, 2011 (http://ahr .oxfordjournals.org/content/116/1/1.full.pdf, last accessed 3 February 2014).

Munir, Muhammad, 'The Layha for the Mujahideen: an analysis of the code of conduct for the Taliban fighters under Islamic law', *International Review of the Red Cross* 93/881 (March 2011): 81–120.

Muir, William, *Life of Mahomet* (London, 1861).

Muslim Messenger, 'Dr. Leitner on Jihad', June 1936.

New York Times, 'G. W. Leitner dead: An orientalist and linguist of great attainments', 25 March 1899.

New York Times, 'Mezzofanti outdone by Leitner', 18 March 1894.

Obama, Barack, 'A new beginning', Cairo University, 4 June 2009 (full text available at www.huffingtonpost.com/2009/06/04, last accessed 1 March 2012).

Pickthall, Marmaduke, *War and Religion* (Woking, c.1919).

Powell, Avril Ann, *Muslims and Missionaries in Pre-Mutiny India* (London, 1993).

Quilliam, Abdullah, 'The Crusades and their effect upon European civilisation', *The Islamic World* (August 1894): 114–9.

Shah Jehan Mosque Archives (Woking), 'Woking Muslim Mission and Literary Trust correspondence and publications, 1920–1985', Ref. 8382.

Wikipedia.org, 'Islam and violence', n.d. (http://en.wikipedia.org/wiki/Islam_ and_violence, last accessed 1 March 2012).

18

The Appeal of Yusuf al-Qaradawi's Interpretation of Jihad

Sherman Jackson

My introduction to Sheikh Yusuf al-Qaradawi's latest opus, *Fiqh al-Jihad* (*The Jurisprudence of Jihad*), was quite serendipitous. Soon after arriving in Cairo in the summer of 2009, I proceeded, as had become my habit, to cruise the bookstores. I was particularly interested in anything that could shed light on the substance of or general response to Egypt's notorious Islamic Group (al-Gama'a al-Islamiyya)'s so-called 'Initiative to Stop the Violence' (*Mubadarat Waqf al-'Unf*) on which I had recently published an article and was continuing my research. As I strolled in and out of a handsome little row of bookshops on Gumhuriyya Sreet, I stumbled into conversation with the proprietor of the Wahba Bookshop about the Gama'a Islamiyya's stream of revisionist writings in which its leaders renounced political violence and declared themselves to have been wrong in carrying out their bloody campaign against the Egyptian state. Coincidentally, this was around the time of President Obama's historic address at Cairo University in June 2009. Having discovered – or I should say finally accepted – that I was an American, the bookshop proprietor's conversation with me seemed to sputter along in a liminal space between a painful past and the uncertain future of the relationship between Islam and the West. In the end, however, my friend assured me that he would soon bring forth the book that would settle the matter once and for all, putting an end to all the rumors, false representations, misunderstandings and misappropriations of jihad, in the East and in the West. Like any good marketer, however, he insisted on adding to the suspense by withholding the title of this magisterial work of which he so enthusiastically spoke.

It would not be for another week or two that I would make the connection. Out of the blue, several reviews and editorials seemed to burst onto the pages of Egyptian newspapers, mainstream and 'opposition', in which supporters and occasionally a mild critic analysed the broad outlines and speculated on the likely impact of a new book by Sheikh Yusuf al-Qaradawi entitled *Fiqh al-Jihad*. It was clear from the tone and length of these features (some were actually serialised) that this work was debuting on the tail end of a long stream of powerful anticipation. Upon learning that the book's publisher was none other than the Wahba Bookshop, I returned to my friend on Gumhuriyya Street to find stacks of the work freshly piled on the floor, literally just removed from their crates. I bought my copy, as it were, 'hot off the press'.

I had learned from the reviews and editorials that this was a very serious undertaking by al-Qaradawi. In contradistinction to the many smaller works he had penned, this was the result of more than seven years of research and rumination. In fact, in terms of depth and comprehensiveness, al-Qaradawi himself compared *Fiqh al-Jihad* to his earlier major work, the two-volume *Fiqh al-Zakat* (*The Jurisprudence of Obligatory Alms*). Whether or not *Fiqh al-Jihad* would live up to the expectations it had generated, not to mention the endorsement of my friend at the Wahba Bookshop, al-Qaradawi's aims in writing this book certainly seemed to be both ambitious and serious.

Fiqh al-Jihad falls into two hefty volumes of more than 1,200 pages of actual text. At bottom, its basic argument is that Islam is a religion of peace, not in the sense of being pacifist or rejecting violence on principle but in the sense of preferring peaceful coexistence over armed conflict with non-Muslims who pose no physical or otherwise mortal threat to Islam or Muslims. As for jihad, as the Muslims' religiously sanctioned institution of organised violence, al-Qaradawi is explicit in insisting that its *raison d'être* is the defence of the religion against aggression, not the spread of Islam by force nor the bringing of all non-Muslims to heel before some global, Muslim, imperial power. All of this is set against a backdrop of any number of starkly contrasting pre-modern and modern positions. Al-Qaradawi sets out thus to vindicate his view in light of these pre-modern and modern counter-theses and to extract enough authority from the Muslim scholarly tradition to raise his perspective to the status of the 'going opinion' (*mashhur*) of modern Islam, with the capacity to marginalise, if not subvert, the views of those who disagree with him.[1]

In his introduction, al-Qaradawi situates himself among three main positions on jihad espoused by modern Muslims. At one extreme are those who would jettison the concept of jihad-as-armed-struggle altogether and limit its meaning and function to the purely spiritual realm, where it would be directed solely, even if assiduously, against the inner adversary. Among the proponents of this view he includes certain groups of Sufis, along with Westernised secularists and various agents and supporters of imperial powers.[2] At the other extreme are those who understand jihad to bind Muslims to declare war on the entire non-Muslim world, with no distinction between those who attack or express hostile intentions towards Islam or Muslims and those who do not. This group, in seeming agreement with Western scholars such as Patricia Crone, essentially understands the god of Islam to be an imperial god, Islam itself to be an imperial religion and Muslims to be religiously obligated to pursue a policy of 'divinely enjoined imperialism'.[3] In this light, international organisations, such as the United Nations, and international treaties, such as the Geneva Conventions, are not only meaningless but inimical to the very mission of Islam, which, according to this view, is to subdue all non-Muslims and then, if they refuse to embrace the Faith, execute, ransom or enslave them, as they – that is, Muslims, and only Muslims – see fit.[4]

Straddling these two groups, however, are 'those of moderation and temperance' (*fi'at al-tawassut wa-l-i'tidal*). They see jihad neither as some kind of venereal disease to be quickly disposed of or apologised away nor as a blind declaration of war against the entire non-Muslim world. Rather, jihad is reserved solely for those who attack or express hostile intentions towards Muslims. As for those who are willing to live in peace with Muslims, there is no religious justification, let alone obligation, to fight them.[5] This is the group in which al-Qaradawi places himself. And to preempt those who would castigate the proponents of this view as 'apologists' or 'defenceniks', he boldly and explicitly announces that he is proud to be among those who see jihad as primarily an institution for the defence of the physical integrity of the Muslim community.[6] Indeed, according to him, he is joined in this regard by some very eminent company, including Muhammad 'Abduh, Rashid Rida, Mahmud Shaltut, Muhammad al-Ghazali, Hasan al-Banna, Muhammad Abu Zahra, Sayyid Sabiq, 'Abd Allah ibn Zayd al-Mahmud and others among the moderns, and Ibn Salah, Ibn Rushd the Grandson, Ibn Taymiyyah, Ibn Qayyim al-Jawziyya and others among the pre-moderns.

Ultimately, al-Qaradawi parlays all of this into an attempt to displace (or at least drastically reduce the authority and currency of) the view and attitude of those he characterises as 'the hawks' (al-hujumiyyun). Indeed, rather than abandon or declare his independence from the juristic tradition, he is explicit in rejecting the view of those who deem it appropriate or necessary to abandon jurisprudence (fiqh) altogether and 'start all over via a return to the sources alone'.[7] As he proceeds with this approach, the views of certain scholars out of Saudi Arabia seem to come in for special treatment, followed – albeit with a bit more indulgence – by those of the likes of Sayyid Qutb, Abu al-A'la Mawdudi and the founder of Hizb al-Tahrir, Taqi al-Din al-Nabahani. From the beginning, however, al-Qaradawi makes it clear that he will give absolute primacy to the Qur'an, followed by the Sunna of the Prophet. And while he will pay homage to the classical tradition of exegesis (tafsir), law (fiqh), legal theory (usul al-fiqh) and the like, he will neither assent to them blindly nor shy away from cross-examining or even criticising those aspects of these traditions that warrant it. Indeed, part of the problem, as he sees it, is that classical opinions are often passed on uncritically, in which capacity they go on to gain popularity to the point of being deemed the only legitimate position on a given matter. Upon closer examination, however, one finds not only that these are not the only opinions espoused by classical scholars but that they are not necessarily the strongest or even most plausible ones.[8] In this spirit, al-Qaradawi declares that he will not limit himself to the four Sunni schools but will draw freely from the Zaydi, Ja'fari, Zahiri and even Ibadi traditions.[9] And here he will not hesitate to correct any number of sophistries and misunderstandings that may have casually or uncritically gained acceptance and reigned unquestioned among Sunni *fuqaha'* (jurists).[10] All of this is reflective of what he boldly presents as his understanding of the due diligence to be applied to the enterprise of (modern) *fiqh*:

> True *fiqh* is not simply transmitting the contents of books. For books reflect their respective times and places. True *fiqh* obtains when the jurist engages in *ijtihad* for his own time and place, just as the ancients engaged in *ijtihad* for their time and place. Not everything that is appropriate for one time is necessarily appropriate for another. And not everything that is appropriate to one place is necessarily appropriate to another, especially given that the changes that have obtained in these our modern times are so very substantial.[11]

As we proceed to a more substantive examination of al-Qaradawi's effort, it is important to bear in mind that the issue for him is not whether jihad in the form of organised violence is a valid institution of Islamic law but whether the fundamental dictates of jihad make it obligatory or even permissible to target non-Muslims who conduct themselves peacefully towards Muslims. While al-Qaradawi's position is that this is emphatically not the case, he acknowledges that there are pre-modern and modern scholars who oppose this view. As a preliminary to his critique of his adversaries, he enumerates the following as the primary proofs, or *adilla*, upon which they generally rely:

1) A number of Qur'anic verses, such as: 'Fight them until there is no *fitna* and religion is solely for God' (Q. 2:193).
2) A number of Prophetic hadiths, such as: 'I have been commanded to fight the people until they say, "There is no god but God . . . "'
3) The precedent of the Prophet's numerous military campaigns against non-Muslims.
4) The precedent of the Rightly Guided Caliphs' military campaigns against non-Muslims.
5) An alleged unanimous consensus (*ijma'*) to the effect that the Muslim community is religiously bound to invade non-Muslim territory at least once a year.
6) The principle that the efficient cause for fighting against non-Muslims is their non-Islam (*kufr*) alone (not their aggression).

7) The view that it is necessary to bring non-Muslims under Muslim control in order to enable them to see the efficacy of Islam as a lived reality.

8) The so-called abrogation or 'sword verse' (*ayat al-sayf*).[12]

Al-Qaradawi takes up each of these proofs seriatim. Regarding some, he simply disputes their status as actual proof, such as with the claim of unanimous consensus or the view that non-Islam is an efficient cause to attack non-Muslims, a position, he notes, that was only upheld as the going opinion in the Shafi'i school.[13] As for the other would-be proofs, he points up what he argues to be plainly superior alternative constructions to be put on the verses and Prophetic statements and actions adduced, especially when these are placed in tandem with other explicit verses from the Qur'an and the overall thrust and spirit of the Holy Writ.[14] In all of this, he draws support from both pre-modern and modern authorities, in an apparent effort to signal that his is not a completely *de novo* rendering, a move that becomes especially conspicuous when he confronts the historical precedent of the Prophet's military campaigns.[15] In the end, however, there remains one nagging nemesis that seems to pop up time and again, like a would-be forgotten cache of buried landmines, threatening to blast the life out of al-Qaradawi's project. This is the so-called sword verse, whose ultimate effect is to deny access to all those Qur'anic verses that suggest, with varying degrees of explicitness, that Islam's primary medium of exchange is argument, example, persuasion and mutual cooperation and that violence is reserved strictly for those who threaten the physical integrity of the Muslim community.

What is this so-called sword verse? As we shall see, this question itself has become a point of contention. Among pre-modern jurists who promulgated the concept, however, the general consensus was that it was the fifth verse of chapter nine, *Surat al-Tawba*, itself believed to be among the last chapters of the Qur'an to be revealed. That verse reads: 'So when the Forbidden Months have expired, slay the polytheists wherever you find them. Seize them, besiege them and lie in wait for them in every ambush. But if they repent, establish prayer and pay the poor-due, then clear their way. Verily God is forgiving, merciful' (Q. 9:5). Now, the argument promulgated among the ancients and passed down to modern Muslims was that this verse had abrogated all those verses in the Qur'an that suggest the possibility of a more civil or tolerant relationship with non-Muslims. This both bewildered and disappointed al-Qaradawi, who depicts the wanton deployment and influence of this verse as well-nigh sacrilegious.[16] In the end, however, there was, alas, little point in denying the fact that the tradition had indeed imputed this far-reaching power and authority to this lone verse:

> If you adduce God's statement, 'There is no compulsion in religion; the distinction between guidance and misguidance has become manifest' [2:257], they will say, 'This has been abrogated by the sword verse.' If you adduce God's statement, 'Call to the way of your Lord with wisdom and beautiful exhortation [16:125],' they will say, 'This has been abrogated by the sword verse.' If you adduce God's statement, 'And if they incline towards peace, you incline thereto and place your trust in God' [8:61], they will say, 'This has been abrogated by the sword verse.' If you adduce God's statement, 'If they withdraw from you such that they are preempted from attacking you, extending to you in effect an offer of peace, God has not granted you any way against them' [4:90], they will say, 'This has been abrogated by the sword verse.' If you adduce God's statement, 'God does not forbid you to treat with goodness and justice those who do not fight you based on your religion and who do not drive you out of your homes' [60:8], they will say, 'This has been abrogated by the sword verse.'[17]

On and on the sword verse proceeds, in al-Qaradawi's depiction, to 'decapitate verse after verse, leaving them as limp, spiritless, lifeless corpses'.[18] Indeed, at the hands of this 'revelatory executioner' some 114 verses are said to have met their fate. This, incidentally, is a conservative estimate. Some authorities placed the number of abrogated verses as high as 140, while others topped it off at a full 200 verses! The end result would be that the Qur'an could never be appealed to as the source for a doctrine of peaceful coexistence and non-aggression, not to mention cooperation, between Muslims and non-Muslims.

It is this very specific and concrete deployment of the sword verse that compels al-Qaradawi to take up the issue of abrogation. For it is on the basis of this interpretive instrument that the sword verse is granted its far-reaching powers of nullification. To be sure, the topic of abrogation is hardly new. Western scholars from John Wansborough, John Burton and David Powers to Joseph Lowry and Christopher Melchert have produced studies on it. This is not to mention the rich pedigree in the Islamic legal tradition going all the way back to the writings of al-Shafi'i, who died at the beginning of the ninth century CE. Compared to the detail and comprehensiveness of these classical Islamic and modern Western treatments, al-Qaradawi's analysis appears, at least at first blush, disappointingly superficial.[19] Rather than attribute this, however, to any lack of scholarly acumen or an unwillingness to confront potentially embarrassing controversies (for example, the relationship between abrogation and the integrity of the Qur'anic text), it might be more prudent to recognise that in this particular work al-Qaradawi is addressing a very specific audience with a palpably concrete goal in mind. His is not a purely academic exercise but an explicitly practical one. His concern rests primarily with the actual state of contemporary Muslim thought and only secondarily with the various historical precedents and accretions that have come to inform it. In this light, he must steer clear of confusing his audience or alienating them from their religious tradition, for example by intimating too close an identification with 'Orientalist' obsessions and critiques. At the same time, he must be careful about displaying inadequate mastery of or loyalty to tradition, since part of his ultimate strategy will be to place the authority of this tradition behind his rendering of jihad and its relationship to abrogation and the sword verse, as opposed to trying to establish himself as some sort of new, independent interpretive authority.

Ultimately, al-Qaradawi's argument is that abrogation (in the sense of *naskh*, or a later verse rescinding an earlier verse and/or the legal ruling laid down by the latter) could only be sustained on the basis of absolutely apodictic proof (*dalil qat'i* or *burhan qat'i*). Once the proofs of those who advocate abrogation are actually examined, however, they will all be found to fall short of this basic criterion. In this way, al-Qaradawi is able to subvert, or at least severely limit, the actual application and impact of abrogation, without categorically denying its theoretical validity.[20] In other words, rather than oppose the classical jurists in their theoretical subscription to the abrogation, al-Qaradawi simply argues that a more faithful adherence to their very criteria for its application will justify, if not compel, a patently negative attitude towards the sweeping, uninhibited claims about how much work it actually does. To this end, he states: 'If we apply the rules, strictures and preconditions laid down by the scholars of the principles of religion (*usul al-din*), the scholars of legal theory (*usul al-fiqh*), the scholars of the principles of exegesis (*usul al-tafsir*) and the scholars of the principles of hadith (*usul al-hadith*), we will hardly find – nay, we will not find! – a single verse from the Qur'an whose abrogation is established with certainty.'[21]

Al-Qaradawi enumerates three basic proofs relied upon by those whom he characterises as 'abrogation-happy' in their attempt to bolster and shield the concept from critique. First, there is a series of verses from *Surat al-Baqara* and *Surat al-Nahl*. Those of *Surat al-Baqara* (Q. 2:106–8) read:

> 'We do not abrogate nor cause a verse to be forgotten without bringing forth one that is better than it or like it. Do you not know that God has power over all things? Do you not know that God owns the dominion of the heavens and the earth and that you have besides Him neither friend nor helper? Or do you wish to inundate your messenger with questions, as Moses was inundated before you?'

As for verse 101, *Surat al-Nahl*, it reads: 'And when we exchange one verse for another – and God knows best what He reveals – they say, "You are simply a forger. Nay, most of them know not."'[22] The second major proof adduced by the advocates of abrogation is the fact that tradition itself so widely recognises it: all of the books of exegesis cite it; it is a standard feature in virtually all the books of legal theory; and even a number of prominent jurists wrote monographs devoted specifically to the topic, men such as Abu 'Ubayd, Abu Ja'far al-Nahhas, Abu Bakr ibn al-'Arabi and others.[23] The final proof is those instances of the actual occurrence of abrogation in Islamic law, based on the presumed irreconcilability between certain verses in the Qur'an (for example, the verse in *Surat al-Baqara* that places the waiting period for widows at four months and ten days, and then the verse in *Surat al-Nisa'* that grants all widows the benefit of housing – that is, a waiting period – that extends up to a full year).[24]

Al-Qaradawi cross-examines these proofs in significant detail in order to show that they are simply not apodictic. Regarding the verses in *Surat al-Baqara* and *Surat al-Nahl*, he enlists the view of those who interpret them to refer not to any substitution of one Qur'anic verse for another verse or ruling but to Islam's abrogation or rescission of the legal order implied by previous dispensations, that is, Judaism and Christianity.[25] Similarly, he argues that there is nothing in the Sunna that explicitly identifies abrogation as an operative principle. As for unanimous consensus (*ijma'*), al-Qaradawi flatly insists that there simply is no such consensus, neither on the theoretical possibility of abrogation nor on its actual occurrence in the Qur'an.[26] In fact, he notes that there is hardly a verse in the Qur'an regarding which scholars have made a claim of abrogation but that other scholars are found who flatly oppose this claim.[27] True to his earlier proclamation, he does not limit himself here to luminaries of Sunni orthodoxy. Indeed, among those he cites as proof in this regard is Abu Muslim al-Isfahani, whom he explicitly and unceremoniously identifies as a Mu'tazilite![28]

As for the notion of reverting to abrogation in the face of apparently irreconcilable verses, al-Qaradawi reiterates the principle upheld by the generality of classical scholars to the effect that the contradiction in question must be not apparent but actual and absolute. In other words, the presumably contradictory language of both verses must be univocal to the point of not accommodating any alternative interpretations. Nor can it be possible to reconcile them through other recognised processes, such as restricting their scope (*takhsis al-amm*), qualifying their referents (*taqyid al-mutlaq*) or drawing simple exceptions (*istithna'*).[29] Here, in fact, al-Qaradawi complains that one of the reasons that so many claims of abrogation are made is that later scholars overlooked the fact that earlier scholars often used the term '*naskh*' to refer not to the displacement of one verse or ruling by another but to such procedures as restricting scope, qualifying referents, drawing simple exceptions and other such synthetic modifications.[30] In other words, closely examined, the classical tradition will reveal itself to have been far more parsimonious than appears at first blush in terms of what it was willing to consign to the knife of abrogation.

Beyond this, al-Qaradawi introduces three additional arguments in his effort to loosen the grip of abrogation and with it the would-be effect of the sword verse. The first of these relates to the actual identification of the sword verse itself. Here he reports that there was not one but at least four verses that had been accorded this proud preeminence. These all appear in the ninth chapter of the Qur'an, *Surat al-Tawba*, and included verses 5, 29, 36 and 41.[31] Of course, the cumulative insinuation of this argument is that this level of controversy over the very identity of the sword verse should raise suspicion about the reliability of arguments that grant it the power to set aside literally dozens if not hundreds of verses of divine revelation!

The second argument relates to the actual means by which one can know that one verse has abrogated another. Beyond the general tendency to rely on chronology alone, al-Qaradawi insists that, since abrogation entails the rescission of a rule that was instituted or at least confirmed by the Prophet, there must be a reliable transmission from the Prophet himself to the effect that such abrogation has actually taken place. Quoting Jalal al-Din al-Suyuti's *al-Itqan fi 'Ulum al-Qur'an*, he insists that one cannot merely rely on casual statements by exegetes or even the *mujtahids*, in the absence of sound narrations from the Prophet to back their claims. Indeed, he insists, even when Companions affirm an instance of abrogation, it must be determined that they were not simply speaking on the basis of their own interpretive discretion but were actually relaying an explicit teaching of the Prophet. On this criterion, al-Qaradawi concludes, 'I do not know of a single explicit narration on the authority of the Prophet wherein it is stated that such and such verse has abrogated such and such verse. And whoever knows of such a narration, let him direct me to it.'[32]

Finally, al-Qaradawi comes full circle in what might be taken as a gesture of conciliation of sorts. He cites the fourteenth-century jurist Badr al-Din al-Zarkashi – a Shafi'i! – whose interpretation of *naskh* as the would-be effect of the sword-verse might be described as 'organic'. According to al-Zarkashi (d.1392), *naskh*, as it pertains specifically to the sword verse,[33] is not a full rescission of a verse or ruling but merely the fixing of its application such that the latter follows the presence or absence of its *raison d'être* (*sabab*). To arrive at this conclusion, al-Zarkashi takes the word '*nunsi*' in the verse 'We do not abrogate or cause a verse to be forgotten...' to be not from the root *na-si-ya* (to forget) but from the verb *na-sa-'a*, with a final *hamza*, which renders the meaning of the verse 'We do not abrogate or cause a verse to be postponed...' On this rendering, the actual cause and duration of postponement is determined not by God through revelatory intervention but by the concrete circumstances facing Muslims on the ground.[34] In other words, the sword verse might be said to justify the *postponement* of the application of the verses it is said to abrogate, but it should *not* be said to have rescinded or decommissioned these verses, such that their application is permanently nullified. For, according to al-Zarkashi, under the right circumstances, all of these would-be abrogated verses could come back into full effect and remain fully operational as long as circumstances dictated.

Given the reality of what I have described elsewhere as the overall 'state of war' that characterised the pre-modern world, where, in the absence of a United Nations or a globally recognised notion of territorial sovereignty, communities invariably existed in an offensive or defensive state of military mobilisation,[35] al-Zarkashi almost certainly understood that Muslims could and should maintain peace with non-Muslims as long as circumstances prevented them from prosecuting jihad. Al-Qaradawi seems to recognise both that this was al-Zarkashi's understanding and that Muslims no longer occupy the kind of world that shaped al-Zarkashi's geopolitical presumptions. Thus, while al-Zarkashi's textual interpretation allows al-Qaradawi to pay homage to a classical understanding of the abrogation/sword verse nexus, al-Zarkashi's tying the ultimate impact of this interpretation to factual assessments on the ground empowers al-Qaradawi to envision an outcome of his own, based on commonly accepted factual differences between his and al-Zarkashi's time, in addition to a number of practical considerations that could not have occurred to his medieval predecessor. 'Postponement', in other words, might be a plausible rendering of *nunsi*. But, al-Qaradawi insists,

> for this postponement [insa'] to be interpreted to mean that we will refrain
> from attacking others as long as we are in a state of weakness, but in a state
> of strength we will attack the entire world – those who attack us as well as
> those who refrain from attacking us but extend their hand in peace to us, as
> 'the hawks' and 'advocates of war against the world' say – this is precisely
> what we reject, as it contradicts so many other verses in the Qur'an: *Surat
> al-Baqara, Surat al-Nisa', Surat al-Anfal, Surat al-Mumtahina*, nay, *Surat
> al-Tawbah* itself, including some of the verses identified as the sword
> verse.[36]

For al-Zarkashi, 'postponement' implied that the obligation to wage jihad could be temporarily relaxed if Muslims were incapable of prosecuting it. Al-Qaradawi, on the other hand, takes the Qur'anic verses he cites to imply that jihad can be permanently retired, even where Muslims are fully capable of executing it, assuming, that is, a reliable pattern of non-aggression on the part of non-Muslims. In other words, not only does al-Qaradawi privilege and interpret contemporary reality in a manner that brings al-Zarkashi's scriptural interpretation to a different practical conclusion, he interprets the Qur'an itself as basing its injunction to wage jihad on the presence or absence of non-Muslim aggression, and not, as al-Zarkashi implied, on Muslim capacity or incapacity to execute armed campaigns.

This brings us to an underlying tension pervading al-Qaradawi's approach overall, namely, the oscillation between scripture (including juristic renderings thereof) and socio-political reality as the basis of juristic deliberations. Beyond the matter of extracting transcendent meaning from scripture (and juristic precedent), al-Qaradawi wants to alert us to the fact that *fiqh* – pre-modern or modern – is the repository of a *practical* meaning that is informed by the concrete socio-political circumstances to which the transhistorical understandings of Qur'an, Sunna and juridical tradition are applied. This is important, inasmuch as whenever it is overlooked, subsequent (for which read 'modern') generations can end up shackled to bygone histories (or historical perspectives) in the name of particular texts, labouring under the assumption that all juristic meaning is dictated by scripture and that the only way to challenge or revise a particular scripture-based rule is to challenge or seek to revise the text(s) on which it is based. Of course, the great strength of this insight lies in its ability, assuming due diligence, to insulate scripture from unwarranted tampering or manipulation, even as it instructs and empowers subsequent generations to grant their reality – as well as *their* assessments thereof – the same consideration their predecessors granted theirs. And yet, for all of this utility, a number of unsettled difficulties remain.

To begin with, the idea that scripture should be processed on the basis of a socio-political reality (read, modernity) that is largely experienced by Muslims as having been imposed from without, as opposed to a pre-modern reality to which Muslims relate more as possessors of determinative agency than as objects of some other's will, can be a very difficult sell.[37] At the same time, even assuming the successful piercing of this psychological barrier, socio-political reality rarely yields univocal assessments and is thus rarely productive of unanimous consensus. This is further complicated by the fact that the factual assessment of socio-political reality admits a much larger pool of 'authoritative interpreters' and thus conclusions that can neither be easily dismissed nor reined in through traditionally recognised means of regulating interpretive author-ity.[38] Thus, while al-Qaradawi appeals to contemporary reality to steer al-Zarkashi's (and the rest of the classical tradition's) theoretical artic-ulations to a different practical conclusion, he is aware that this same contemporary reality could be invoked with radically different implica-tions by advocates who might claim just as much authority to undertake these factual assessments as he can. Seeking to preempt some of these, he asks rhetorically:

> Is it logical for us to say to people in the East and the West: We are not obligated to fight you now, because we are militarily weak and lack the arms you possess. But as soon as we acquire what you have – or come close to it – we will fight you all?[39]

In response, al-Qaradawi notes that this would completely undermine Muslim credibility and mobilise the entire world against Islam, as the entire world concludes that Muslim ethics are unstable and unreliable and that the global community

> cannot trust Muslim commitments to their treaties and agreements, be-cause they will only honor these as long as they are weak; but when they gain strength, the ruling will change and their religion will permit them to deal with others in a manner that had been theretofore forbidden.[40]

Two problems push through to the surface here. First, while it is clear why al-Qaradawi's specific training in law and the juristic tradition should confer a religious authority upon his interpretations of the sources that does not accrue to the views of those not so trained, the question of why his *factual* assessments should hold forth against those of Muslims of equal or perhaps even superior training in modern history, international relations, political science or other relevant disciplines remains outstand-ing. Second, the question of how much *fiqh* is or should be informed by scripture and how much by socio-political reality is one for which a fixed and permanently definitive answer remains allusive. This is why it is not always clear whether 'reform' is a matter of re-interpreting scripture (*ijtihad*) or simply raising one historical context (or one's assessment thereof) over another as the ground on which scriptural understandings are to acquire concrete, practical application (*takhrij*). In the end, these questions remain fundamental challenges not only for al-Qaradawi but for modern *fiqh* in general. And it seems that in the absence of some fairly broadly shared answers, Muslims will continue to experience a certain frustrating disharmony and discomfiting liminality in their communal attempts to negotiate the substance of Islamic law.[41]

In the meantime, al-Qaradawi clearly intends to make the best of the situation, moving freely between scriptural interpretation and the factual assessment of socio-political reality. Given, as Middle Eastern historians such as Fred Donner have argued, that the pre-modern world was one in which religious communities were either on offence or defence and that to be on defence meant to be under attack, it would have been grotesque for jihad to emerge in pre-modern Islam as a purely defensive mechanism.[42] Yet this is clearly no longer the world we inhabit, and the question is how much these changed circumstances should inform modern Muslims' understanding of their scripture-based religious obligations and commitments. For some, these changes will exert no legitimate effect at all on the presumably transcendent meanings handed down from an authoritative Muslim past. For others, the new historical context alone will prove fully dispositive. Between these two poles, however, will be those who seek to hold scripture (including established juridical renderings thereof) and socio-political reality in a balanced, dynamic, creative, dialectical tension, even as they recognise that the question of which is to be privileged, when, how and for how long admits of no permanently definitive answer, the most to be hoped for being the successful and principled management of this tension in ways that promote and protect the commonweal.

Sheikh Yusuf al-Qaradawi belongs to this last group. Were the matter for him purely one of re-interpreting scripture, he might have limited himself to an attempt to vindicate those Qur'anic verses that encourage peaceful coexistence between Muslims and non-Muslims. This would have included questioning the abrogating authority of the sword verse, but, in and of itself, socio-political context would have added little to his argument. On the other hand, had he seen the matter as simply one of elevating modern over pre-modern history, much of his discussion of the sword verse might have proved superfluous, as context rather than scripture per se would have been the focal point determining the ultimate outcome.

In the final analysis, however, while al-Qaradawi is clearly alive to both these dimensions of the juristic enterprise, he seems far more committed to raising modern reality to what he deems to be its rightful status and place as the object of modern juridical/juristic deliberations. He recognises that the world is no longer in an overall 'state of war', wherein non-Muslims can be presumed to be simply lying in wait for the opportunity to pounce on Muslims, and thus the main, if not only, considerations informing a decision whether or not to attack them is simply material cost and likelihood of success. Nor, given the many advances in modern technology, can it be assumed that those principles and powers that oppose Islam in general can physically prevent Muslims from spreading their religious message, as they might have been able to do in the past. On this understanding, al-Qaradawi affirms that jihad is a defensive mechanism directed only against those 'who attack the persons, property, lands or religion of the Muslims, in an attempt to undermine the latter or block the path to it, or to those who oppress the weak among the Muslims or their allies'.[43]

And yet al-Qaradawi plainly recognises that this position must be vindicated in the context of a broader Muslim experience that has been shaped by and given rise to a whole composite of prejudices, obsessions, fears, sensibilities and anticipations. Indeed, if nothing else it seems reasonable to assume that part of the whole value and function of the sword verse was to inoculate pre-modern Muslims against any anesthetising tendencies that might lull them into relaxing their geopolitical guard, tendencies that many, such as 'the hawks', might point to in explaining the entire colonial experience. While al-Qaradawi is sensitive to these considerations, he is simply not convinced that non-Muslims in general are out to destroy Islam or that the modern context as a whole affords them the ability to preempt Muslim efforts to call others to the Faith (da'wa). As for the fears and obsessions engendered by the modern Muslim experience, al-Qaradawi effectively turns to the transcendent values and injunctions of scripture to tame and hold these in check. In this light, not only does an 'abrogation-happy' rendering of the sword verse impose palpable distortions upon the Qur'anic message, it carries practical liabilities and aggravates unarticulated prejudices that contemporary Muslims can ill afford to ignore or accommodate.

Ultimately, however, rather than end up in effective agreement with those who would jettison jihad altogether, al-Qaradawi's assessment of modern reality brings him to a new and different understanding of the role and substance of jihad. To his mind, in this age of satellite television, air travel, radio, print media and the internet, violence is simply no longer the greatest threat posed by those who harbour ill will towards Islam. And just as violence is no longer the greatest threat, no longer is it an appropriate, or in many instances even an effective, response. Thus, according to al-Qaradawi, rather than committing themselves to declaring military war against the world, what Muslims, including 'the hawks', need today is

> a massive army of preachers, teachers, journalists and those who are competent in training people in how to address today's public in the language of the age and the style of the times, through voice, image, spoken word, physical gesture, books, pamphlets, magazines, newspapers, dialogue, documentaries, drama, and motion pictures . . . [44]

While Muslims, according to al-Qaradawi, have thus far failed to develop as little as one-tenth of what is needed in this regard, it is this, he concludes, and not militarised confrontation, that constitutes 'the jihad of our times'.[45] In the end, however, one is left to contemplate the subtle irony of the conclusion that, even if the sword verse were left to run its course and abrogate all of the peace-inspiring verses of the Qur'an, the jihad that would remain most operative, at least in al-Qaradawi's view, would be palpably different from the one that continues to dominate modern discourses on Islam, in the East as well as in the West.

Notes

1. On the concept of the *mashhur*, see Sherman Jackson, *Islamic Law and the State: The Constitutional Jurisprudence of Shihab al-Din al-Qarafi* (Leiden, 1996), pp. 83–4, 86–9. Meanwhile, it should be noted in this context that,

while elevating his opinion to the point of gaining wide acceptance is clearly al-Qaradawi's practical objective, he is careful to steer clear of ideological extremism and schism, a tendency he points to disapprovingly even in other thinkers whose efforts he otherwise respects, such as Sayyid Qutb and Abu al-A'la Mawdudi, who in their zeal to promote or defend their point of view might go so far as casting those who oppose them as enemies of Islam. See, for example, Yusuf al-Qaradawi, *Fiqh al-Jihad* (Cairo, 2009), 1:19.

2. Al-Qaradawi, *Fiqh al-Jihad*, 1:13–14.

3. See Patricia Crone, *God's Rule, Government and Islam: Six Centuries of Medieval Islamic Political Thought* (New York, 2004), p. 366, but see also the discussion on pp. 364–75.

4. Al-Qaradawi, *Fiqh al-Jihad*, 1:14–15. Al-Qaradawi notes that this group also rejects such international consensuses as that covering the abolition of slavery!

5. Ibid., 1:15–16.

6. Ibid., 1:256.

7. Ibid., 1:25.

8. Ibid., 1:18.

9. Ibid., 1:23. One might note that al-Qaradawi sees no need to vindicate the practice of *talfiq* or legal eclecticism, which some have characterised as 'juristic opportunism', nor to address how his position relates to classical discussions of *ijma' dimni*, or 'implicit unanimous consensus', according to which a good number of jurists insist that where the community of jurists settles on two or three opinions it becomes a violation of *ijma'* to go beyond these to others. For a brief depiction of *ijma' dimni*, see 'Iyad bin Nami al-Sulami, *Usul al-Fiqh alladhi la Yasa'u al-Faqih Jahluh* (Riyadh, 2008), pp. 132–4; Shihab al-Din al-Qarafi, *Sharh Tanqih al-Fusul fi Ikhtisar al-Mahsul fi al-Usul*, ed. T. 'A. Sa'd (Cairo, 1973), p. 326.

10. Al-Qaradawi, *Fiqh al-Jihad*, 1:24.

11. Ibid., 1:25.

12. Ibid., 1:257. This list does not appear in this order. The sword verse actually appears as no. 2.

13. Indeed, regarding the latter, he points out that Abu Hanifa, Malik and Ibn Hanbal all opposed this view and held that non-Muslim hostility had to be added to their unbelief (*kufr*). See al-Qaradawi, *Fiqh al-Jihad*, 1:273–8.

14. For example, regarding the hadith 'I have been commanded to fight the people until they say, "There is no god but God.... "', al-Qaradawi notes that there has never been a consensus among the *fuqaha'* that 'the people'

(*al-nas*) here means 'mankind' or 'all the people of the world'. In fact, he insists, 'no scholar of this Community has ever held this view, not a jurist, not an exegete, not a hadith expert' (*Fiqh al-Jihad*, 1:327). He notes that the definite article in Arabic can be used to denote a general or specific category and that the general consensus is that it is used in this hadith to refer specifically to the pagan Arabians who refused peaceful coexistence with the Prophet. Beyond this, he cites, *inter alia*, the view of Ibn Taymiyyah to the effect that the hadith merely binds the Prophet to a specific goal – that is, to bring them to Islam – in fighting those he ends up fighting, as opposed to merely despoiling them of their wealth or lording over them politically or obligating him to fight all the people. Indeed, Ibn Taymiyyah insists: 'This would violate scripture and unanimous consensus. For he never did this. Rather, his way was to refrain from fighting those who conducted themselves peacefully towards him.' See *Fiqh al-Jihad*, 1:327–37, esp. 1:327 and 1:335 for the quoted segments, respectively.

15. Ibid., 1:339–64.
16. Ibid., 1:270–71.
17. Ibid., 1:268.
18. Ibid., 1:268.
19. Major questions are left untreated, such as the question of whether the Qur'an can be abrogated by the Sunna or the Sunna by the Qur'an, or the question of verses that have been allegedly abrogated while the rulings they imparted remained valid (e.g. the verse '*al-shaykh wa-l-shaykha*' as the alleged basis for rendering adultery a capital offence). Nor does al-Qaradawi deal with glaring examples of apparent abrogation, such as between the allowance of bequests to 'parents and other blood-relatives' and the imposition of set shares of inheritance.
20. Actually, he appears to be a bit coy about this. While he is clearly hostile towards abrogation and openly states that there is no apodictic proof from the Qur'an or Sunna to support the doctrine, his overall tone remains respectful of the explicit views of those classical scholars who endorse it.
21. Al-Qaradawi, *Fiqh al-Jihad*, 1:281–2.
22. Ibid., 1:271–2.
23. Ibid., 1:272.
24. Ibid., 1:274.
25. Ibid., 1:274–7.
26. Ibid., 1:278.
27. Ibid., 1:280.
28. Ibid., 1:278–9, and n.1 at 1:278–9.

29. For example, one would not need to argue that any verse abrogated God's statement that God is the creator of every 'thing' on the understanding that He Himself, as a thing, would thus have to be created. For reason allows us to exempt Him from the meaning of 'every' here, just as it does in the case of the dominion of the Queen of Sheba, who, according to the Qur'an, was given 'every' thing, which would clearly not include the kingdom of Solomon. See Q. 27:23.

30. Al-Qaradawi, *Fiqh al-Jihad*, 1:272–3; 1:284.

31. Q. 9:5 reads: 'So when the Forbidden Months have expired, slay the polytheists wherever you find them. Seize them, besiege them and lie in wait for them in every ambush. But if they repent, establish prayer and pay the poor-due, then clear their way. Verily God is forgiving, merciful.'

    Q. 9:29 reads: 'Fight those who do not believe in God and the Last Day and who do not forbid what God and His Messenger have forbidden nor follow the religion of truth from among those who have been given the Book, until they pay the *jizya* [tax on non-Muslims] and are in a state of subjection.'

    Q. 9:36 reads: '. . . and fight the polytheists altogether as they fight you altogether. And know that God is with the God-conscious.'

    Q. 9:41 reads: 'Go forth, light or heavy, and fight in the path of God with your money and your persons. That is best for you, if you but knew.'

32. Al-Qaradawi, *Fiqh al-Jihad*, 1:283.

33. Al-Zarkashi actually acknowledges that abrogation takes place in the Qur'an, but this, he insists is 'rare' (*qalil*). He specifically rejects the far-reaching power of abrogation attributed to the sword verse, insisting that most of the verses that relax the burden to fight, which the exegetes hold to have been abrogated by the sword verse, are verses whose effect has been postponed not abrogated. See Badr al-Din Muhammad ibn 'Abd Allah al-Zarkashi, *Al-Burhan fi 'Ulum al-Qur'an*, 4 vols. (Cairo, 1984), 2:35–44, esp. 2:42 and 2:43.

34. Al-Qaradawi, *Fiqh al-Jihad*, 1:310–13. Al-Qaradawi takes this from al-Zarkashi's *al-Burhan fi 'Ulum al-Qur'an*.

35. See Sherman Jackson, 'Jihad in the modern world', *The Journal of Islamic Law and Culture* 27/1 (2002): 1–26.

36. Al-Qaradawi, *Fiqh al-Jihad*, 1:313.

37. One might note the deeply negative attitudes al-Qaradawi cites of some Muslims who reject such modern institutions as the United Nations, the Geneva Conventions or modern treaties outlawing slavery and compare this

with their presumptive attitude towards the various treaties and compromises contracted by pre-modern Muslims.

38. Indeed, depending on what the facts in question are, 'lay' interpreters – that is, trained professionals in particular fields – may be more qualified and thus authoritative than their counterparts among the *fuqaha'*. For more on this point, see Sherman Jackson, 'Shari'ah, democracy and the modern nation-state: Some reflections on Islam, popular rule and pluralism', *Fordham International Law Journal* 27/1 (2004): 88–107, especially pp. 93–101.

39. Al-Qaradawi, *Fiqh al-Jihad*, 1:313.

40. Ibid., 1:313.

41. I am referring here not to the problem of pluralism (which I do not consider a problem in and of itself) but to the absence of a common language, shared principles and clear jurisdictional boundaries.

42. See F. M. Donner, 'The sources of Islamic conceptions of war', in J. Kelsay and J. T. Johnson (eds.), *Just War and Jihad: Historical and Theoretical Perspectives on War and Peace in Western and Islamic Traditions* (New York, 1991): 31–70.

43. Al-Qaradawi, *Fiqh al-Jihad*, 1:256.

44. Ibid., 1:403.

45. Ibid., 1:16.

Bibliography

Crone, Patricia, *God's Rule, Government and Islam: Six Centuries of Medieval Islamic Political Thought* (New York, 2004).

Donner, F. M., 'The sources of Islamic conceptions of war', in J. Kelsay and J. T. Johnson (eds.), *Just War and Jihad: Historical and Theoretical Perspectives on War and Peace in Western and Islamic Traditions* (New York, 1991): 31–70.

Jackson, Sherman, *Islamic Law and the State: The Constitutional Jurisprudence of Shihab al-Din al-Qarafi* (Leiden, 1996).

———, 'Jihad in the modern world', *The Journal of Islamic Law and Culture* 27/1 (2002): 1–26.

———, 'Shari'ah, democracy and the modern nation-state: Some reflections on Islam, popular rule and pluralism', *Fordham International Law Journal* 27/1 (2004): 88–107.

al-Qaradawi, Yusuf, *Fiqh al-Jihad* (Cairo, 2009).

al-Qarafi, Shihab al-Din, *Sharh Tanqih al-Fusul fi Ikhtisar al-Mahsul fi al-Usul*, ed. T. 'A. Sa'd (Cairo, 1973).

al-Sulami, 'Iyad ibn Nami, *Usul al-Fiqh alladhi la Yasa'u al-Faqih Jahluh* (Riyadh, 2008).

al-Zarkashi, Badr al-Din Muhammad ibn 'Abd Allah, *Al-Burhan fi 'Ulum al-Qur'an*, 4 vols. (Cairo, 1984).

19

What is New about Yusuf al-Qaradawi's Jihad?

Sheikh Rachid al-Ghannouchi

In the name of Allah, the Most Merciful,
the Most Beneficent

Jihad is the most critical concept in contemporary Islamic thought. Jihad is the 'summit of Islam and its pinnacle' according to a hadith, and is the subject of widely divergent views and stances from both within and outside Islam. These views have serious consequences for international relations, given Islam's growing role internationally. They also effect relations among Muslims themselves – with one another, with their governments and with non-Muslims – in view of the awakening in both faith and practice that is being witnessed across the Muslim world. This has led to a greater connection between Islam as a religion (creed, rituals and morals) and as an ideology that is highly influential on the thought and behaviour of Muslims, socially and politically, or what is known as 'political Islam', in which jihad occupies a central position.

This chapter attempts to present the views of Sheikh Yusuf al-Qaradawi on this crucial concept. Al-Qaradawi occupies an important position in contemporary Islam, to which his various roles testify. At the intellectual level, his writings have exceeded 150 published works covering all aspects of Islamic thought. In addition to his membership of the major intellectual and juristic councils, he was elected President of the International Union of Muslim Scholars, as well as being the Chairman of the European Council for Fatwa and Research and a number of charities, and a member of various academic boards for Islamic Studies, including the Oxford Centre for Islamic Studies. As for 'political Islam', he grew up inside one of its groups, the Muslim Brotherhood, and rose to occupy a leading position within it. He is also a rising star in the world of modern media, through his patronage of the most important Muslim website, IslamOnline, and through his famous weekly television programme on al-Jazeera Arabic, *Islamic Law and Life*, which is followed by over 60 million viewers per week.

Al-Qaradawi has developed a theoretical principle in contemporary Islam, from which all his views and stances emanate and the broader application of which he tirelessly calls for, to broaden Islam's appeal and marginalise its opponents. This is the principle of Islamic *wasatiyya* or moderation. This was inspired by the verse in Chapter 2 of the Qur'an: '[A]nd thus we made you into a middle (*wasat*) nation.' He presents Islam as the middle ground between rigid opposing and conflicting positions, the middle ground that brings everything together, a middle position between materialism and spiritualism, between individualism and collectivism and between idealism and realism. This principle of the middle ground is the starting point of all his exercises in *ijtihad* (reasoned interpretation) on all aspects of Islamic thought, including on the question of jihad, as revealed in his latest book, *The Fiqh of Jihad: A Comparative Study of its Rulings and Philosophy in Light of the Qur'an and Sunna*. Al-Qaradawi described this momentous two-volume study as having taken several years of continuous work and occupied his thought for decades. In it he elaborates his theory on jihad from the *wasati* perspective, which he hopes will help to form a consensus. The book springs from the conviction that: '[I]t is dangerous and wrong to misunderstand jihad, to shed inviolate blood in its name, to violate property and lives and to taint Muslims and Islam with violence and terrorism, when Islam is completely innocent of such an accusation. However, our problem in such grave matters is that the truth gets lost between the two extremes of exaggeration and laxity.'[1]

My exposition of this momentous work will focus on clarifying the general view of jihad in Islam, according to Sheikh Qaradawi, based on the Qur'an and the Sunna and their interaction with the *tafsir* (interpretation) and *fiqh* (jurisprudence) traditions of the historical contexts in which the concept of jihad emerged. Jihad is also viewed through the current state of the *umma* (Islamic community) as it engages in major conflicts with the forces of despotism or with external forces, under the current balance of power, in a modern culture that glorifies the value of freedom and under international law that recognises state sovereignty and limits legitimate war to self-defence. Al-Qaradawi's view of jihad was formed in these contexts. We do not wish to explore the details of his view, but rather the general picture – what is novel in it, particularly with regard to major questions such as jihad's relation to freedom and to relations among Muslims and between Muslims and others, and whether it occurs inside or outside Muslim societies. So, what are the foundations of this methodology? What is jihad? What are its forms? What are its goals? Is it defensive or offensive? Is it between the Abode of Islam (*Dar al-Islam*) and the Abode of Unbelief (*Dar al-Kufr*)? What are the rulings regarding captives in Islam? Should jihad exist within the *umma*? How high a priority is jihad among the *umma*'s current causes?

Issues of Methodology

In his introduction, al-Qaradawi defines the foundations for his study thus:

a. He relies on the Qur'an as the ultimate authentic text which serves as the criterion for other sources including the Prophetic Sunna. It is to be understood using the logic of its original language, Arabic, without forcing meaning onto the text, and on the basis that all its verses were revealed to be applied. Al-Qaradawi questions at length those who claim that there is a verse in the Qur'an, which they call *Ayat al-Sayf* (the sword verse) although they differ over the identification of that verse, which has allegedly abrogated at least 140 verses. Qaradawi almost entirely invalidates the principle of abrogation in the Qur'an, thereby depriving extremists of a sharp weapon with which they had disabled hundreds of verses promoting kindness, forgiveness and dealings with non-Muslims using wisdom and eloquent preaching, and distinguishing between a hostile unjust minority amongst non-Muslims against whom defensive jihad can be used, and the peaceful majority of non-Muslims who should be shown justice and kindness.

b. He relies on authentic Sunna which do not contradict stronger evidence, such as the Qur'an. Thus such sayings as 'I was sent with the sword', among others, are judged to be weak by using the tools of the science of hadith. He also interprets an authentic hadith which commands fighting against people until they say 'there is no god but Allah' by interpreting the generic word 'people' as denoting a specific group: hostile Arab polytheists.

c. He derives benefit from the rich heritage of *fiqh*, without bias towards a particular school or restricting himself to the well-known schools. He bases his approach on the methods of comparative law, analysis and critique to select the most suitable opinion. He distinguishes between *fiqh* and shariah, the latter being of divine origin, and the former the product of intellectual effort to deduce the rulings of shariah. True *fiqh* is not copied from books, but rather represents the jurist's own *ijtihad* (intellectual reasoning) to produce something suitable for his specific time and place, particularly as major changes have taken place in our time.

d. He uses a comparative methodology between Islam and other religions and legal systems.

e. He relates *fiqh* to current reality. When speaking about jihad, the Muslim jurist must recognise fixed principles, such as the law of *tadafu'* (mutual checking), the obligation to prepare all possible sources of power to ward off enemies and fight against those who initiate fighting against the Muslims, the prohibition of transgression and so on. There are, however, other matters that have emerged (which are considered *mutaghayyirat*, or changing factors), such as the condemnation of war, seeking peace and the emergence of international law, human rights conventions, the United Nations and the sovereignty of states. In this respect, the author affirms: '[W]e can live, under Islam, in a world that promotes peace and security not fear; tolerance not fundamentalism; love not hatred. We can live with the United Nations, international law, human rights conventions and environmentalist groups. In truth, our main problem is with our rigid brothers who have closed all doors and insist on a single viewpoint as they live in the past and not the present, in books rather than reality.'

f. He adopts the methodology of *wasatiyya* (moderation) in *da'wa* (preaching), teaching, *ifta'* (issuing legal edicts), research, reform and revival. Among the principles of this methodology in *fiqh* is the need to revive religion from within through new interpretive reasoning for our time, just as previous scholars did for their times; understanding secondary texts in the light of primary objectives, being firm when it comes to fundamentals and flexible in *furu'* (secondary matters), seeking wisdom whatever its source and finding a balance between contemporary change and fundamental shariah principles.

g. In *Fiqh al-Jihad*, al-Qaradawi is careful not to present himself as the sole proponent of the above views amongst jurists. Instead he is keen to refer to supporting views among former and contemporary scholars, even if such views have been neglected or ignored, blowing off the collected dust and shedding light on them, presenting them in a more attractive light and giving them new life. He is also careful to support his views with relevant values and expertise from modern culture, benefiting from both his profound knowledge of the sources of Islamic culture and his familiarity with modern culture. Thus he constructs a new, coherent and well-rooted yet contemporary view of Islamic jihad, and it is a view which shares much with contemporary culture with regard to war and peace. What is new in this view is not the details, for the component parts are scattered and buried deep inside books, but rather the whole picture. The resulting picture makes this work a meeting point and a point of consensus, wherein all – or most – parties can find something familiar that facilitates their acceptance of that which is unfamiliar. This ability to build consensus is a traditional characteristic of the great scholars. Thus al-Qaradawi is not exaggerating when he outlines the dire need for such a study among jurists, lawyers, Islamists, historians, orientalists, diplomats, politicians, military men and the educated masses.

The Essence and Forms of Jihad

No Islamic concept has been the target of such a continuous flow of attacks against Islam and Muslims as jihad. It suffers from the two extremes of exaggeration and laxity. Laxity is promoted by those who want to abolish jihad from the life of the *umma* and spread a spirit of submission and surrender under the guise of calls for tolerance and peace. Al-Qaradawi describes these proponents as agents of colonialism whose hostility to jihad has led to the creation of groups that have fabricated an Islam without jihad, such as Baha'is and Qadianis. At the other extreme are those who exaggerate the concept of jihad into a raging war against the whole world, taking war to be the natural stance toward non-Muslims.

The author tackles this extremism on both sides through linguistic analysis of the word jihad – which essentially means exerting oneself and making an effort – and through examining its usage in the Qur'an and Sunna, and by Muslim jurists. He concludes that there is a clear distinction between jihad and fighting (*qital*), as the command to engage in jihad was revealed in Mecca, where there was no fighting but rather jihad of preaching (*da'wa*) through the Qur'an: 'And strive against them with the utmost endeavour with it [the Qur'an]' (pp. 50–2). Jihad is also used in the Qur'an and Sunna with various meanings, including exerting oneself to resist the enemy, the devil, one's desires and so forth. Thus the word, 'jihad', is much wider in meaning than just fighting. As al-Qaradawi quotes from Ibn Taymiyyah, jihad 'can be with the heart, by calling to Islam, by countering invalid arguments, by advising or facilitating what is beneficial to Muslims, or by one's body, that is fighting'.

The author further seeks support from a fourteenth-century scholar, the eminent Ibn al-Qayyim, who was a student of Ibn Taymiyyah, to clarify the vast scope of jihad, which makes every Muslim a *mujahid* but not necessarily a *muqatil* (fighter). Ibn al-Qayyim concluded from his study of the process of Islamic preaching that there are 13 levels of jihad. The first is jihad of the self (*al-nafs*) which comprises four levels – exerting oneself to learn guidance, to act upon it, to call for it and to persevere in it. The second is jihad against Satan, which includes two levels – struggling against doubt in one's faith instigated by Satan and resisting the desires and corruption to which Satan calls. The third is jihad against unbelievers and hypocrites, the oppressors and the corrupt, that comprises three means – with one's hand if possible, then with one's tongue, then with one's heart. Al-Qaradawi differs from al-Qayyim with regard to the notion of jihad against oppression and corruption taking precedence over jihad against unbelief and external transgression, stressing that peaceful confrontation is to be adopted against oppressors, 'profiting from the reasonable forms which others have developed in confronting unjust rulers, such as elected parliaments, parties, and the separation of powers' (p. 198).

Al-Qaradawi also emphasises the importance of intellectual and cultural jihad

> through the establishment of specialist Islamic academies catering for youth who are academically and morally exceptional in order to prepare them academically and intellectually with a methodology that unites our heritage and modern culture . . . We do not call for isolation from the rest of the world, but rather for cultural and civilizational interaction. We choose what to take or leave based on our own philosophy and criteria, just as they [the rest of the world] borrowed concepts and inventions from us in the past which they then developed and used to build their civilisation. What we take will be imbued with our own spirit, character and moral heritage such that it becomes a part of our intellectual and moral system, losing its original character. (pp. 190–2)

Al-Qaradawi concludes that there are two types of jihad, civil and military. Military jihad means fighting against enemies who attack Muslims, necessitating preparation for this eventuality, which is a matter for states. Spiritual civil jihad

> encompasses the academic, scientific, cultural, social, economic, educational, health, medical, environmental and civilizational fields. The objective of this civil jihad is to exert oneself for the sake of Allah to educate the ignorant, employ the unemployed, train workers, feed the hungry, clothe the naked, house the homeless, treat the ill, achieve self-sufficiency for the needy, build schools for pupils, universities for students, mosques for worshippers and clubs for sports lovers to practise their hobbies (p. 215).

Objectives of Jihad

Islam is a call for peace. It abhors war, but cannot prevent it; hence, it prepares for but does not wage war unless it is forced to do so, which is due to Islam's realistic nature and its recognition of *sunnat al-tadafu'*, the law of mutual deterrence. However, Islam has sought to limit war's consequences by surrounding it with rules and ethics. Islam is not alone among religions in recognising the notion of a war of necessity. Followers of Christianity, for example, have been among the most frequent participants in conflicts and wars, both against other Christians and against others. Luke's Gospel reads: 'I have come to bring fire on the earth . . . Do you think I came to bring peace on earth?' (Luke 12:49–51). The Old Testament contains numerous calls to genocide against seven nations that inhabited Palestine and had to be completely eradicated; calls for population 'transfer' and the massacres committed by Zionist groups in the modern world are mere miniatures of the virulence of these divine demands.

Jihad in Islam has specific objectives which al-Qaradawi summarises as repelling transgression, preventing discord (*fitna*) by guaranteeing freedom of faith for Muslims and others, saving the oppressed, punishing those who break treaties and enforcing internal peace within the Islamic community. Thus, expansion and appropriation are not among the objectives of jihad, nor is the eradication of unbelief from this world, for that is against Allah's law of difference and mutual deterrence. Nor do the objectives of jihad include imposing Islam on those who do not believe in it, for that contravenes Allah's law of diversity and pluralism (p. 423).

Military Jihad: between Defensive and Offensive Jihad

Following the tradition of classical and contemporary jurists, al-Qaradawi questions the nature of jihad and its status in Islam. Is it religious in nature, meaning that Muslims are obliged to fight unbelievers until they embrace Islam or submit to its authority? This is known as offensive jihad (*jihad al-talab*). Or is it political in nature, necessitated by the need to defend Islamic lands against transgressors and to defend Muslims against those who curtail their freedom of faith, and to defend the oppressed generally? This is termed defensive jihad (*jihad al-daf'*). If it is necessary, then Muslims must engage in it with pure intentions, for the sake of Allah and following strict ethical guidelines which cannot be ignored.

In both the classical and modern eras, jurists have been divided between two groups, which al-Qaradawi calls the aggressors (*hujumiyyun*) and defenders (*difa'iyyun*), proclaiming his proud adherence to the second group. The aggressors consider it an obligation upon the Muslim community to attack the lands of unbelievers at least once a year in order to 'call for Islam' and expand its territories. They hold the state of unbelief in and of itself as a valid reason to initiate war and legitimate killing, to the extent that Muslims would be sinful if they do not engage in aggression, even if those unbelievers are not attacking or harming Muslims. A large number of jurists support this view, with the most prominent among classical scholars being Imam al-Shafi'i and, among contemporary thinkers, Sayyid Qutb and Abu al-A'la Mawdudi. They support this view with evidence from the Qur'an, Sunna and historical practice. The Qur'anic texts identified to call for fighting against all polytheists are from *Surat al-Tawba*: '[A]nd fight the polytheists all together as they fight you all together' (Q. 9:36), 'Kill the idolaters wherever you find them' (Q. 9:5), and '[f]ight those who believe not in Allah nor the Last Day ... until they pay the tribute tax with willing submission' (Q. 9:29). They differ as to which of these verses is the 'sword verse' (*ayat al-sayf*) which, according to them, abrogated all contradicting verses. These allegedly abrogated verses – some believe over 200 in number – call for mercy, forgiveness and freedom of belief, considering the judgement of a person's faith to be a matter for Allah alone. These aggressors also sought support from hadith such as: 'I have been commanded to fight people until they say "there is no god but Allah"', narrated by al-Bukhari (*Salih al-Bukhari*, II:2:24). They also consider the early Islamic conquests to be evidence that war, rather than peace, is the natural state of Muslims' dealings with other faiths.

Al-Qaradawi's disagreement with the above group does not prevent him from looking for excuses for its scholars, particularly the classical scholars. He attributes their views to the relations based on power and war that existed between states at the time and to the existential threat to which Islam had been subjected since its birth on the Arabian Peninsula. In line with classical and contemporary scholars, al-Qaradawi stresses the consensus that jihad becomes obligatory for every Muslim if a Muslim land is attacked or Muslims suffer *fitna* (and are prevented from freedom of faith). He believes that every Muslim must practise some form of jihad, be it striving against one's desires, against evil and corruption or striving to promote good and support religion to the best of his ability. However, al-Qaradawi concludes the following through his study and analysis of the various texts related to jihad and the views of classical and contemporary scholars:

1. Qur'anic verses, particularly those of *Surat al-Tawba* that command fighting against all polytheists, are to be understood as a reaction and an equitable retribution; the verse says 'as they fight you all together', implying that those addressed by the Prophet are under concerted attack by unbelievers. The verses should not be understood as a general command or a basis for dealing with all non-Muslims. Rather, they concern a specific group of Arab polytheists that declared war on Islam after its emergence, chased it away, followed it to its new home, broke treaties and mobilised all their forces to eradicate it. Hence the verse: 'Will you not fight people who violated their oaths, plotted to expel the Messenger and started the aggression by being the first to assault you?' (Q. 9:13). Here and in other chapters, there are limits and conditions restricting the apparently general command above, such as: 'And if they incline to peace, then incline to it' (Q. 8:61). There is no need to set one verse of the Qur'an against another; rather one should look at all relevant verses and hadiths, all of which confirm the rule that Islam seeks peace with those who are peaceful towards it, and fights those who fight it.

2. Military jihad is not an individual obligation for every Muslim at the same level as the core obligations of the testimony of faith, prayer, fasting, almsgiving (*zakat*) and pilgrimage (*hajj*). Despite its importance in Islam, it was not included among the inherent characteristics of those who heed Allah in *Surat al-Baqara*, nor in the characteristics of the believers as described in *Surat al-Anfal* or *Surat al-Mu'minun*, nor in the characteristics of those with true understanding as described in *Surat al-Ra'd*, nor in the characteristics of the servants of the Most Merciful as described in *Surat al-Furqan*, nor in the characteristics of the pious in *Surat al-Dhariyat*, nor of the righteous ones described in *Surat al-Insan*. Thus, the practice of military jihad only becomes an obligation when certain conditions arise, such as an attack on Muslims, their land or their religion. Preparing for such an incident, on the other hand, is an obligation, according to one's ability, in order to deter enemies and maintain peace.

3. There is no obligation for Muslims to invade the lands of non-Muslims, if they are safe from them. To fulfil the collective duty, it is sufficient for them to have a powerful army in possession of the latest weapons and trained soldiers guarding their borders and deterring enemies so that the latter do not think of attacking Muslims (p. 91). It is worth noting that al-Qaradawi prefers using the term non-Muslims to *kufr* (infidels) or unbelievers, for that echoes the Qur'an, which uses the expressions 'O people of the Book', 'O people', 'O Man', 'O Children of Israel', 'my people' and 'O Children of Adam'. It never addressed non-Muslims as unbelievers, except in a few exceptional cases relating to negotiations about creed.

4. Islam recognises freedom of belief and individual responsibility before Allah for one's belief. On that basis, societies in the lands of Islam, on the whole, did not experience religious wars. Under Islam, various monotheistic and pagan religions coexisted and continue to coexist, through the system of a protection agreement (*dhimma*) which granted citizenship to non-Muslims regardless of religion. All that was required of non-Muslims to enjoy the rights of protection by the Muslim state alongside Muslims was to pay the *jizya* (a tax on non-Muslims) if they had sufficient means to do so, which can be seen as equivalent to the military service tax in some modern systems. According to al-Qaradawi, unifying the tax rate and universalising military service render a system such as *dhimma*, which has been misunderstood and misused, unnecessary.

5. Historical conditions, rather than Islamic texts, led many jurists to believe that offensive jihad was obligatory. The Islamic community was constantly threatened by its powerful neighbours, the Persians and Romans (p. 82). There were no international laws, as there are today, based on mutual recognition of state sovereignty and prohibition of hostility (although various powers today may contravene them).

6. The natural state of affairs between Muslim and non-Muslims is peace, cooperation and goodwill. Islam abhors war and only engages in it unwillingly and when it is necessary, as is indicated by the Qur'anic verse: 'Fighting is proscribed for you, though it is hateful to you' (Q. 2:216). Peace is the essential characteristic of Islam. The word 'peace' is used in the Muslim greeting ('Peace be upon you')

and in greeting arrivals in Paradise, and it is one of the epithets of Allah. The most hated term in Allah's view is 'war' (*harb*), which is an ancient Arab term, since Arabs were warriors. However, when the Prophet (peace be upon him) was told by his son-in-law that his daughter Fatima had given birth to a boy and that he had called him Harb, he commanded him to rename him Hasan, meaning 'good'.

7. Islam welcomes international conventions that prohibit transgression and promote peace between nations, and welcomes international bodies that protect international law, such as the United Nations and UNESCO. However, the West still maintains its belief in the principle of power in its relation with other states and nations. An example of this is the exclusive enjoyment by major Western states of the right to veto in such bodies. This shows a flagrant disregard for the principle of equality, thus guaranteeing the protection of their interests and the avoidance of any condemnation of their violations. Thus the USA and UK invaded Iraq without any legitimacy and with full impunity from any condemnation. Similarly, they continue to protect various forms of Zionist hostility against Palestine and its people.

8. International recognition of human rights, including freedom of belief and preaching, as well as the freedom to establish institutions and protect minorities, renders one of the principal justifications for offensive jihad redundant. It is not acceptable to enable the call to Islam by invading and dismantling oppressive regimes that prevent people from thinking freely or choosing beliefs that are different from those of their rulers, such as the Pharaoh who reprimanded the Children of Israel for believing without his permission, questioning, 'You believe in him before I give you leave?' (Q. 20:71). Today, by contrast, mosques and Muslim minorities are found everywhere to an extent unprecedented in any previous era of Islamic history. This increases our need for 'huge armies of competent preachers, teachers, media experts, all suitably trained and able to address the world in its different languages, using modern methods, of which, unfortunately, we possess less than a thousandth of what is required' (p. 16). Al-Qaradawi laments that one may find many who are ready to die for the sake of Allah, but very few who are willing to live for His sake.

9. The sources of Islam reveal that, according to Islam, the world is divided into three abodes: the Abode of Islam (*Dar al-Islam*), where the law of Islam reigns, its rituals are publicly practised and its adherents and preachers are secure; the Abode of Truce (*Dar al-'Ahd*), comprising those non-Muslim and Muslims states between which there is mutual recognition and prohibition of hostility; and finally the Abode of War (*Dar al-Harb*). In view of Muslims being part of the system of the United Nations, al-Qaradawi regards them as being in a state of truce with other states, except with the Zionist state owing to its usurpation of the land of Palestine and its dispossession of the Palestinian people, an occurrence that unfortunately took place with the support of major states. Thus al-Qaradawi considers the greatest problem in our relation with the West to be its constant and unlimited support for Israel and its continuous aggression against Palestine and its people.

10. Al-Qaradawi distinguishes between jihad and terrorism (*irhab*), or between legitimate terrorism (ensuring one is feared by the enemy to deter it from aggression) and illegitimate terrorism (terrorising innocent people using the name of Islam). Declaring war on the whole world and terrorising innocent people, both Muslims and non-Muslims, for alleged political goals inside or outside Muslim lands flagrantly contravenes the principles and ethics of jihad in Islam. Hence, al-Qaradawi condemns violent acts committed by extremist groups in Muslim and non-Muslim countries against innocent people, whether tourists or others. He further strips of any legitimacy the indiscriminate killing and shedding of innocent lives committed by these groups.

11. Al-Qaradawi is extremely careful to distinguish between extremist groups that declare war on the whole world, killing indiscriminately, tainting the image of Islam and providing its enemies with fatal weapons to use against it on the one hand, and those groups that are resisting occupation on the other. As much as he condemns and delegitimises the former, he defends the latter, and calls on the Islamic community to support them, particularly in Palestine, as long as their operations are against military targets. He does not hesitate to justify martyrdom operations, considering them to be the

only weapon left for those with no other options who are deprived of military force equivalent to those of the enemy to defend his home and his land. Allah's justice does not allow the weak to be completely deprived of any weapon, hence the latter's use of his own body as a deterrent weapon. Nevertheless, the ethics of jihad must always be respected and only combatants can be targeted.

12. Al-Qaradawi stresses that the first jihad to be obligatory for the Islamic community in this age is the liberation from colonialism, particularly in Palestine. However, he stresses and warns against the fallacy that the conflict between us and Zionists is due to the fact that they are Semites, for we are also Semites and both of us come from the progeny of Abraham. Nor is it a religious conflict, for Muslims regard Jews as People of the Book, whose food is lawful, with whom marriage is lawful and who have lived among Muslims in safety and sought refuge in our lands when Spain and other European countries expelled them, finding refuge nowhere but among Muslims. In reality, the conflict between us and Zionists started for one single reason: they appropriated the land of Palestine, dispossessed its people and imposed their presence with violence. The conflict will continue as long as its causes remain. No one can give up any Muslim land, but it is possible to have a truce with Israel for an agreed period of time. As for the principle of 'Land for Peace', it is indeed a bizarre principle imposed by the logic of the enemy's brute force, for the land is our land, not the enemy's such that it can bargain with it in return for peace (p. 1090).

13. Al-Qaradawi, and his mentor Sheikh Muhammad al-Ghazali, played a leading role in confronting extremist groups and preventing them from hijacking Islam and diverting it from its mainstream toward the margins, through stripping their actions of any legitimacy based on jihad, both inside and outside Muslim lands. Al-Qaradawi also praised the significant revisions made by the most important of these groups, which found great support in his writings (even after having attacked and rejected his views) to encourage implementation of their revisions, which he described as brave and enlightened (p. 1168).

Ethics of Jihad

Al-Qaradawi writes that war in Islam is ethical, just like politics, economics, science and work, none of which are divorced from ethics; and
that this contrasts with war in Western civilisation, which is not necessarily bound by ethics. For Muslims, war is governed by a moral code,
because morality is not simply a choice but rather a fundamental part of
religion, and the code includes the following. Islam prohibits the use of
unethical methods, such as sex or intoxicants, to infiltrate the enemy and
obtain secrets. Islam prohibits transgression, for the Qur'an commands:
'Fight in the path of Allah against those who fight against you, but do
not transgress. Lo! Allah loveth not aggressors' (Q. 2:190). Qaradawi interprets 'transgression' to mean killing non-combatants, such as women,
children, the elderly, the ill, farmers and others not engaged in fighting (p. 728). Mutilation of the enemy is also prohibited. Islam requires
the fulfilment of agreements and prohibits treachery and betrayal. Islam
prohibits the cutting down of trees and demolition of buildings. Islam
prohibits the use of weapons of mass destruction, such as chemical,
biological or nuclear weapons, which kill thousands or millions at once
without discriminating between the guilty and innocent. Islam prohibits
the use of such weapons because Islam prohibits the killing of non-
combatants, for the Prophet (peace be upon him) strongly condemned
the killing of one woman in one battle. However, that does not prevent the Islamic community from seeking to acquire such weapons for
the purpose of deterrence, since others possess them and can threaten
Muslim nations with them. This is particularly so as the Zionist enemy that has usurped land belonging to Muslims is in possession of such
weapons and its scripture legitimises the obliteration of all its neighbours.
What is astonishing is that the USA and other great nations prohibit other
nations from possessing these weapons while they themselves possess
them. They prevent Arab and Muslim states from acquiring them, while
Israel possesses over 200 nuclear warheads. The mutual deterrence between the Western and Eastern blocs, and similarly between India and
Pakistan, has contributed to the maintenance of world peace. Such
weapons cannot be used, except in the most exceptional circumstances,
when a nation is subject to an existential threat (p. 592). Islam enjoins
its mujahidin to treat captives kindly. After a detailed discussion of all

texts and all juristic opinions concerning prisoners of war, particularly on the question of whether they can be killed, al-Qaradawi concludes that the final ruling is that revealed in *Surat Muhammad*, 'either set them free as a favour or let them ransom (themselves)' (Q. 47:4), possibly with the exception of war criminals. On the whole, al-Qaradawi approves the articles of the Geneva Convention regarding the treatment of captives.

Conclusion

Al-Qaradawi's study on the jurisprudence of jihad may be regarded as an authentic example of Islamic interpretative reasoning (*ijtihad*), upholding the principle of jihad as an eternal Islamic mechanism of defence in its wider meaning, although it has suffered a great number of misrepresentations that have tainted the image of Islam. Al-Qaradawi recuperates the effectiveness and moderation of this mechanism, taking it out of the hands of extremists. His courage in standing up to the campaigns waged against the concept of Islam has been just as great as his courage in rejecting the arguments of extremist groups who declare war against the entire world. He does not shy away from criticising the large number of jurists who uphold the principle of offensive war, nor is he ashamed to proclaim his adherence to the group believing in jihad as defensive only. He continues to counter the arguments of the former group, without fear or hesitation, without resorting to injustice or misrepresenting the views of those with whom he disagrees, but rather seeking excuses for them. He has continued to do so, until he almost destroyed what is known as offensive jihad (*jihad al-talab*), establishing instead defensive jihad in its wider meaning of jihad with no trace of terrorism. He clearly distinguishes terrorism from legitimate resistance of occupation, which he considers a jihad with ethics that accord with international conventions and the principles, values and laws prohibiting aggression, occupation, the use of weapons of mass destruction and the torture of captives. Defensive jihad welcomes an open world in which ideas and people move freely, dealing with matters through proofs and arguments rather than violence and power, until the most valid view triumphs. Through such a presentation of jihad, al-Qaradawi has opened a vast space for dialogue, tolerance, agreement and coexistence between Islam and other religions, human values and international accords. Thus he enables a response to the eternal Qur'anic call: 'O mankind! Lo! We have created you male and female, and have made you nations and tribes that ye may know one another. Lo! the noblest of you, in the sight of Allah, is the best in conduct' (Q. 49:13).

Note

1. Unless otherwise indicated in the text, all quotations are taken from Yusuf al-Qaradawi, *Fiqh al-Jihad* (Cairo, 2009). It has not been possible to provide precise references in every case, owing to the difficulties of communicating with the author following the Tunisian revolution.

Index

351